Understanding
Developmental Language Disorders

Understanding Developmental Language Disorders

From Theory to Practice

edited by

**Courtenay Frazier Norbury, J. Bruce Tomblin,
and Dorothy V. M. Bishop**

Psychology Press
Taylor & Francis Group
HOVE AND NEW YORK

First published 2008 by Psychology Press
27 Church Road, Hove, East Sussex BN3 2FA

Simultaneously published in the USA and Canada
by Psychology Press
270 Madison Avenue, New York, NY 10016

Psychology Press is an imprint of the Taylor & Francis Group, an Informa business

Copyright © 2008 Psychology Press

Typeset in Times by Communication Crafts, East Grinstead, West Sussex

Printed and bound in Great Britain by
Bell & Bain Ltd, Glasgow

Cover design by Hybert Design

This publication has been produced with paper manufactured to strict
environmental standards and with pulp derived from sustainable
forests.

British Library Cataloguing in Publication Data
A catalogue record for this book is available from the British Library

Library of Congress Cataloging in Publication Data

Understanding developmental language disorders in children / [edited by] Courtenay
Frazier Norbury, J. Bruce Tomblin, and Dorothy V. M. Bishop.
     p. ; cm.
   Includes bibliographical references and index.
   ISBN 978–1–84169–666–9 (hb)—ISBN 978–1–84169–667–6 (pb) 1. Language disorders
in children. I. Norbury, Courtenay. II. Tomblin, J. Bruce. III. Bishop, D. V. M. (Dorothy
V. M.)
   [DNLM: 1. Language Development Disorders—diagnosis. 2. Language Development
Disorders—therapy. 3. Child. 4. Language Therapy.   WL 340.2 U55 2008]
   RJ496.L35U53 2008
   618.92′855—dc22
                                                                                    2008004337

ISBN: 978–1–84169–666–9 (Hbk)
ISBN: 978–1–84169–667–6 (Pbk)

Contents

List of contributors

Catherine Adams
School of Psychological Science
Human Communication and Deafness
The University of Manchester
Manchester M13 9PL, UK

Gillian Baird
Consultant Pediatrician
Guy's & St. Thomas' NHS Trust
Newcomen Centre, Guy's Hospital
St Thomas Street
London SE1 9RT, UK

Dorothy V. M. Bishop
Department of Experimental Psychology
University of Oxford
South Parks Road
Oxford OX1 3UD, UK

Gina Conti-Ramsden
School of Psychological Science
Human Communication and Deafness
The University of Manchester
Manchester M13 9PL, UK

Frederic Dick
School of Psychology
Birkbeck College

University of London
Malet Street
London WC1E 7HX, UK
also Center for Research in Language
University of California–San Diego
La Jolla, CA 92092, USA

Julie E. Dockrell
Institute of Education
University of London
25 Woburn Square
London WC1H 0AA, UK

Susan Ebbels
Moor House School
Mill Lane
Hurst Green
Oxted, Surrey RH8 9AQ, UK

Charles Hulme
Department of Psychology
University of York
York YO10 5DD, UK

Geoff Lindsay
CEDAR
University of Warwick
Coventry, CV4 7AL, UK

Anthony P. Monaco
Wellcome Trust Centre for Human Genetics
University of Oxford
Roosevelt Drive
Oxford OX3 7BN, UK

Kate Nation
Department of Experimental Psychology
University of Oxford
South Parks Road
Oxford OX1 3UD, UK

Dianne F. Newbury
Wellcome Trust Centre for Human Genetics
University of Oxford
Roosevelt Drive
Oxford OX3 7BN, UK

Courtenay Frazier Norbury
Department of Psychology
Royal Holloway
University of London
Egham, Surrey TW20 0EX, UK

Fiona Richardson
Centre for Brain and Cognitive Development
School of Psychology
Birkbeck College
London WC1E 7HX, UK

Michael Rutter
PO 80, SGDP Centre
Institute of Psychiatry
De Crespigny Park, Denmark Hill
London SE5 8AF, UK

Maria Cristina Saccuman
Fondazione Centro San Raffaele
Milan, Italy

Margaret J. Snowling
Department of Psychology
University of York
Heslington, York YO10 5DD, UK

J. Bruce Tomblin
Speech Pathology and Audiology Department
Room 3, Speech and Hearing Center
University of Iowa
Iowa City, IA 52242-1012, USA

Maggie Vance
Department of Human Communication Sciences
The University of Sheffield
31 Claremont Crescent
Sheffield S10 2TA, UK

Foreword

Language and communication are integral to our daily lives. Take a moment to think about the language you have used today, before you came to read this book. Who did you talk to? What did you talk about? How often did you listen to your child, your partner, a friend, a professional colleague, the news? What stories did you tell? What arguments did you have? Did you phone the bank, the electrician, the doctor? Or order your shopping on-line? How many text messages have you sent? How many television programs watched, emails answered, dinners arranged?

All of these activities require language and communication. For most of us, these tasks are effortless: our ability to engage with the world using language is something we have taken for granted for most of our lives. But what if we didn't have this ease with language? For a substantial minority of children—between 5 and 10% of the school-aged population—language can be confusing, and finding the right words can be a huge challenge. Instead of enriching life, language can be a source of frustration and unhappiness.

Four decades ago, in England, a pioneering speech and language therapist named Margaret Greene recognized the stresses and worries that families faced when a child failed to develop language, often for no apparent reason. In 1968, she founded Afasic, with the specific aim of providing information and support for families of children with developmental language disorders. Unusually for the time, Margaret Greene also realized the importance of bringing together families, clinicians, and researchers in order to share expertise and experiences of supporting children with language impairment.

Sadly, Margaret Greene died in 2007, at the age of 94. However, her legacy lives on, as Afasic celebrates its 40th anniversary in 2008. The 4th Afasic International Symposium, held in April 2007 at the University of Warwick, brought together families, clinicians, educators, politicians, and researchers from all over the world: a testament to Margaret's vision. The chapters in this book, which arose from the Symposium, represent the cutting edge in research and practice in the field of developmental language disorders and provide signposts to the exciting work ahead of us in the next 40 years. We outline the contents of this volume with reference to the key questions parents ask when their child is diagnosed with a developmental language disorder.

For many parents, when a communication difficulty is suspected, the first question to be answered is, "What exactly is wrong with my child's speech and language development, and why?" The first six chapters in this volume consider this question from differing perspectives.

A first step for families is to obtain a detailed assessment of the child, to ascertain the child's abilities and difficulties, and to rule out other medical conditions that may be contributing to the language deficit. Gillian Baird (chapter 1) details the process of differential diagnosis and outlines, for parents and clinicians, what investigations are necessary at various stages of the assessment process. For many families, a referral to a speech-language therapist will be enough to meet the child's needs; for others, a more detailed assessment by a multidisciplinary team is warranted. Baird's chapter outlines what to expect from these assessments.

Very often there are no obvious reasons for the language impairment, leaving parents to wonder why language is so difficult for their child to master. This is not an easy question to answer, and the reasons may very well be different for different children. Researchers spend most of their time investigating answers to this "why" question; if we have a better understanding of what causes language impairment, then we are in a better position to design treatments that target these causal mechanisms, rather than just the language behaviors. Researchers focus their investigations on three levels of explanation: genetic, neurobiological, and cognitive.

We have known for some time that language impairments often run in families, hinting that genetic factors may play a role in language impairment. Since Afasic was founded in 1968, there has been an explosion of research into the genetics of specific language impairment (SLI). The fruits of this research effort are summarized in the chapters by Dorothy Bishop (chapter 5) and by Dianne Newbury and Tony Monaco (chapter 6). Bishop's chapter explains "behavioral" genetics, or what we can learn from studying language processes in families and, more specifically, twins. Her work demonstrates how this line of research may help us to distinguish between more specific language impairments and other disorders, such as dyslexia and autism. Newbury and Monaco focus on "molecular" genetics, or how scientists find the genes that are implicated in disorder and then discover how those genes work to alter the course of development. Their work has shown

that there are likely to be many genes and environmental factors that together increase the risk for language disorder. However, it is important to realize that knowing that there are genetic factors implicated in language impairment does not mean that we are powerless to intervene. Genetic studies of developmental language disorder are only just beginning but will constitute an important area of future research.

Frederic Dick and colleagues (Dick, Richardson, & Saccuman, chapter 4) explore how language is processed in the brain. There is substantial evidence that genetic mechanisms alter the way the brain develops, making it less efficient for language learning. Over the last 40 years, significant advances in technology have allowed us to look at living brains in action. As demonstrated by Dick, we are increasing our understanding of how the brain develops throughout childhood and adolescence, what regions of the brain are active during different language tasks, and how different parts of the brain communicate with one another. Studies of brain structure and function in children with language impairment are rare at the moment but will increase in the future as we try to understand more about the neurological underpinnings of language impairment and how the brain may reorganize itself in response to environmental experiences such as intervention.

The cognitive level refers to psychological processes that mediate the link between brain and behavior. At the cognitive level, researchers are primarily interested in whether or not children with language impairment process information in a qualitatively different way from children with typical language development. One dominant theory of language impairment involves the role of memory in language development and disorder. Parents will be well aware of difficulties many children with language impairments have in remembering verbal messages! Maggie Vance (chapter 2) outlines different types of memory processes and how they might be involved language learning. She concludes her chapter by providing a number of very useful strategies that can be used at home and at school for supporting memory.

Of course, our understanding of causal mechanisms depends crucially on how we test the constructs we are interested in. This can be particularly challenging for children with language difficulties, as many traditional assessments rely on verbal input and verbal responses. For example, we often assess children's understanding by telling them a story and then asking them questions about it. Many children with language impairment will fail in this task, but why? Is it because they don't understand the words in the story or the sentences that make up the story? Did they understand the story when they heard it, but then forget it rapidly? Did they understand the story perfectly, but had trouble with the questions? Or did they understand both story and questions, but could not formulate an answer to those questions?

Kate Nation (chapter 3) describes a relatively new technique for trying to pinpoint *when* comprehension breaks down. This involves monitoring what children look at when they are listening to language. This is done by recording eye movements and is driven by the principle that language influences our attention: if we are out with friends and someone says, "I'm hungry," the friends will start to look out for cafés with tempting cakes! Most eye-tracking studies to date have been conducted with skilled adult language users. However, as Nation explains, these studies set a research agenda for understanding more about language processing in real time for children with language impairment.

A second question of great importance for parents is what will happen to their child in the longer term—where will they be educated, and what will happen when they leave school?

Although outcomes may be variable, the message from the next three chapters is that the outlook is certainly more positive than it was 40 years ago. We are only just at the point where we can report on older individuals with language impairment. Bruce Tomblin (chapter 7) and Gina Conti-Ramsden (chapter 8) report on their longitudinal studies—in the United States and the United Kingdom, respectively—of children diagnosed in primary school with developmental language disorder. These children were followed up over a 10-year period, to adolescence and the end of compulsory schooling. Both authors consider what we mean by good outcome and what aspects of development are most affected by early language impairment. Both report very similar findings, showing that while many children continue to have language needs, a significant minority can overcome their early difficulties. As we might expect, early language deficits have the greatest impact on academic achievement, particularly literacy. Somewhat surprisingly, though, outcomes for other aspects of development, such as friendships and self-esteem, are much more encouraging.

Julie Dockrell and Geoff Lindsay (chapter 9) present an educational perspective. More and more children with language disorders are being educated in mainstream schools: is this a good thing? Dockrell and Lindsay stress that it is not the placement itself, but the teaching and therapy support available at the placement that makes all the difference. Their work has highlighted important factors in good educational practice—things parents can look for when considering school placements.

Last, but certainly not least, parents will want to know what can be done about their child's language impairment. There is constant tension between the parents' desire for more therapy, clinicians and educators managing services with often limited resources, and researchers who are testing different interventions to find those that are most effective. This is no easy task. One cannot simply ask, "what works?" Instead, we need to consider which types of interventions are most effective for which children; who is best placed to deliver the intervention; how long we need to provide intervention; and whether is there an optimal time to intervene.

Margaret Snowling and Charles Hulme (chapter 11), Susan Ebbels (chapter 10), and Catherine Adams (chapter 12) each report intervention studies focused on different aspects of the language system. Snowling and Hulme report a large-scale trial that focused on developing early phonological (speech sound) and language (word meanings, grammar) learning in reception classes with the specific aim of circumventing later literacy difficulties. An important aspect of their study design was to provide training and ongoing support to classroom teaching assistants, so that they could deliver the intervention. This enabled more children to benefit from the intervention. They also consider the numbers of children who do not benefit immediately from intervention and reflect on how we determine when therapy ends—when the predetermined "therapy block" is over, when the term ends, or when children reach a certain level of competence? These are important debates that no doubt occur within clinical services on a regular basis.

Ebbels reports on the different types of interventions that have been used to facilitate the learning of grammatical rules. Specifically, she reports on the Shape Coding technique, which makes different parts of speech and the ways in which they can be combined explicit through the use of shapes and color. Crucially, she highlights the dearth of evidence for and availability of intervention for older, school-aged children but provides preliminary evidence that this technique is effective for pupils with language impairment in secondary school.

Adams investigates a comprehensive approach to assessing, targeting, and developing broader pragmatic language and social skills. She describes intervention as "hypothesis testing" and specifically links assessment results to treatment goals and activities. Again, her work targets the older age group—often left out of treatment studies but clearly in need of developing communication skills. She also shows that individually tailored treatment can have a positive effect on school-aged children.

All three chapters illustrate the fundamental components of a good intervention study and demonstrate how challenging it is to find such well-designed treatment studies in the literature. This reminds us that we must be cautious when we hear about "miracle cures" in the media. Instead, it is very likely that there will be no "quick fix" for language impairment: the most effective interventions will be those that are incorporated into the child's daily life, both at home and at school.

Michael Rutter (chapter 13) brings together the main themes raised in this book and looks ahead to the future. Specifically, he questions our diagnostic concepts and how these influence our understanding of causal factors. It is often the way in science that the more we learn, the less we feel we know: as soon as we answer one question, many more spring to mind. This can be frustrating for parents and researchers alike, but it is also what makes developmental language disorder such a rich and rewarding field in which to work.

We end this foreword by extending a warm thank you to the staff and trustees of Afasic, the Advisory Committee, and the Nuffield Foundation, the Gatsby Foundation, and SENAD for their generous funding, as well as the volunteers and all the delegates who made the Fourth International Symposium such a resounding success. We look forward to the next 40 years of Afasic and will continue to integrate theory and practice in a way that benefits us all. Finally, we dedicate this book to the children and families who are the bedrock of Afasic and who continue to teach us the most about developmental language disorders.

Courtenay Frazier Norbury, Research Fellow,
Royal Holloway, University of London

Linda Lascelles, Chief Executive Officer, Afasic

London
December 2007

A note on terminology

Anyone browsing through this book will become aware of the wide range of terminology that is used to refer to children who have difficulties with speech and language. The fact that the field has not settled on an agreed term for talking about these difficulties is a consequence of continuing uncertainties as to how best to conceptualize children's problems. The choice of terminology is sometimes rather arbitrary, with different authors using different terms to refer to the same conditions, but there can be subtle differences in meaning.

Different terms in current use

Historically, the preferred term to describe clinically significant language difficulties of unknown origin was "developmental dysphasia" or "developmental aphasia." These terms are still used in mainland Europe, but they have largely fallen into disuse in the United Kingdom and the United States. The move away from this terminology almost certainly arose because it placed children's developmental language problems in the framework of a medical model—the terms *aphasia* and *dysphasia* have their origins in adult neurology, where they refer to language difficulties acquired after focal brain damage. As is evident from chapter 1, medical investigations seldom uncover any specific cause of developmental language problems, unless there are other associated features. As noted in chapter 5, the etiology of developmental language problems is usually genetic rather than due to acquired brain damage. Furthermore, most would agree that the boundary between language impairment and normality is arbitrary, and so it is rather misleading to use a label that implies a "disease" category (see chapter 13). A range of labels came to replace developmental dysphasia, such as *specific developmental language disorder* or *specific language impairment* (SLI). SLI is probably the commonest term used over the past decade in the UK and US literature, with the term "impairment" being preferred, insofar as it can encompass poor skills that are at the limit of normal variation, whereas "disorder" implies some qualitative disruption of normal development (see chapter 7). Nevertheless, most of those in the field would agree that in practice the two terms have been used to refer to the same children. A further step away from medical notions of disorder is taken by those who prefer to talk in terms of language "difficulties," "problems," or "delay." The latter term is sometimes used more restrictively in talking of children who are late bloomers who subsequently catch up, but *language delay* can also be a more general synonym for SLI.

Discrepancy with nonverbal ability

Inherent in the concepts of developmental dysphasia and SLI is the idea that it is important to distinguish between children whose language difficulties are "specific"—that is, part of a more general impairment in cognitive development—and those who have selective difficulties in the context of otherwise normal development. As discussed in chapter 7, the requirement that language be discrepant with IQ is referred to as *cognitive referencing*. There are in fact two ways of interpreting cognitive referencing (Bishop, 2004). The strict interpretation, embodied in the International Classification of Diseases (ICD–10), is that there should be a discrepancy of at least one standard deviation (equivalent to 15 IQ points) between a standardized language measure and a measure of nonverbal ability. However, there is widespread dissatisfaction with such criteria, for three reasons: first, the cutoff that is used is arbitrary, and the apparent precision of language and IQ scores is misleading—for instance, on an IQ test, a child's score may vary by ±5 points or more from one testing occasion to another. Thus a child who meets a discrepancy criterion at one time may not do so at another, making it dangerous to use this as a basis for diagnosis of SLI (which can be a condition for access to services). Second, different test instruments can yield very different test scores, and so a child who has an impairment on one IQ or language test may score in the normal range on another. Third, there is no good evidence that children who meet such discrepancy criteria differ from those who do not. The distinction between SLI and nonspecific language impairment thus appears wanting both in terms of being workable in practice and in terms of its conceptual basis. Increasingly, studies tend nowadays to adopt a weaker form of cognitive referencing, focusing on children who have language impairments in the context of broadly normal nonverbal ability, without requiring that there be a discrepancy of a given magnitude between language and nonverbal scores. This was the approach adopted in the epidemiological study by Tomblin et al. (1997) that is discussed in chapter 7. Tomblin, however, queries whether even this weaker version of cognitive referencing is appropriate, noting that there

are few qualitative differences between children whose language impairments are accompanied by normal nonverbal IQ and those who have more even impairment of verbal and nonverbal skills. As attitudes to cognitive referencing have changed, so too has terminology, with many specialists preferring now to talk of language impairment (LI) rather than SLI. This implies that the important thing is that the child's language is poor for his or her age, without giving any significance to IQ level.

Speech, language, and communication difficulties

One can draw a conceptual distinction between speech—the process of articulating sounds—and language, the system whereby small numbers of elements (words and grammatical inflections) are combined in a rule-based manner to generate an infinite number of possible meanings. It is possible to have normal speech but impaired language, as when an 8-year-old child articulates all sounds clearly but speaks in immature sentences, making grammatical errors and keeping to a simple sentence structure, such as "yesterday me go to school." It is also possible for a child to have speech difficulties but normal language—for instance, a child might have difficulty in producing the sounds "s" and "sh" distinctively, so that "sheep" is produced as "seep," but have an entirely normal ability to speak in complex sentences and understand what others say. A complication is that there can be different underlying reasons for a child to produce speech sounds inaccurately: on the one hand, this can be a consequence of abnormal structure or function of the articulatory apparatus, but, on the other hand, it may reflect immaturity or abnormality of learning the speech system of one's native language. To illustrate how errors in speech production can arise for nonphysical reasons, consider the difficulty many people have in speaking a foreign language that uses a different set of speech sounds from their native language. My difficulty in producing French "*roux*" and "*rue*" distinctively has nothing to do with my articulatory apparatus—it is a failure to learn to perceive and produce a distinction that is not used in English. Most experts would agree that speech problems that have a physical basis should be treated separately from those that reflect a failure to learn, but the distinction is not always easy to make, and the terminology in this area is hugely complex and inconsistent from one specialist to another. Those with a linguistic background will often talk of phonological disorder/impairment/difficulty and regard this as a subtype of language disorder (i.e., the child has not learned the correct phonological distinctions for the language), whereas the terms *speech disorder*, *articulation disorder,* or, in more severe cases, *dysarthria* or *dyspraxia* are restricted to problems with a physical basis. However, *speech* or *articulation* disorder is commonly used more broadly to refer to difficulties in producing speech sounds accurately. In the United States, *speech sound disorder* has become popular as a general term for difficulties in producing speech sounds accurately without implying a specific etiology or mechanism.

Although speech and language impairments can be distinguished from each other, they occur together more commonly than one would expect by chance. A common picture is for a young child to present initially with immature speech and delayed language development, but as the child gets older, the speech problems may resolve themselves. The term *speech and language disorder* is commonly used but is inherently ambiguous, because it can either mean problems with both speech and language, or it can be used as a catch-all term to refer to speech and/or language difficulties. This latter usage is imprecise but allows one to group together children who are likely to be of interest to speech and language therapists, or whose pattern of difficulties may change with age.

Finally, we turn to *communication*, which encompasses speech and language but also incorporates nonlinguistic ways of conveying meaning, such as gesture and facial expression. The term *communication disorder* includes the kinds of speech and language disorders discussed above, but it may be used when we want to include a wider range of difficulties, including the kinds of nonverbal communication problems seen in autistic disorder, as well as the more circumscribed problems typically seen in SLI.

Developmental language disorder

We chose *developmental language disorder* for the title of this book after much debate. In doing so, we hoped to adopt a phrase that would largely encompass the variety of terms used by the authors of the chapters in this book. Our focus is primarily on those children who fail to acquire their native language at the typical rate, for no obvious reason. Thus, for the majority of children discussed in this book, language impairment is not associated with any other developmental disorder, sensory impairment, or cognitive delay. However, we avoid the term *specific* in recognition of the fact that many of the children who take part in research studies and who present at speech-language therapy clinics are likely to have subtle difficulties outside the language system, and the fact that the boundaries between *specific language impairment* and other developmental disorders that involve language are frequently difficult to distinguish.

REFERENCES

Bishop, D. V. M. (2004). Specific language impairment: Diagnostic dilemmas. In L. Verhoeven & H. Van Balkom (Eds.), *Classification of developmental language disorders* (pp. 309–326). Mahwah, NJ: Lawrence Erlbaum Associates.

Tomblin, J. B., Records, N. L., Buckwalter, P., Zhang, X., Smith, E., & O'Brien, M. (1997). Prevalence of specific language impairment in kindergarten children. *Journal of Speech and Hearing Research, 40*(6), 1245–1260.

Assessment and investigation of children with developmental language disorder

Gillian Baird

Speech and language problems are some of the most common developmental concerns resulting in referral to child health services in the preschool years, often in the first instance to speech and language therapy services. A speech and language problem in a young child is a symptom that needs a differential diagnosis, an investigation of causation where appropriate, and a management and treatment plan. Many children will see only the speech and language therapist and never need the services of the multiprofessional team; others will. This chapter addresses the approach to investigative assessment that is reasonable for the clinician to consider in a child with a speech and language impairment.

SPEECH AND LANGUAGE DEVELOPMENT

The typically developing child shows remarkably rapid acquisition of the skill of extracting meaning from language and communicating using speech. The precise process whereby children learn to understand language and then speak is not known, but a range of language and cognitive processes needs to be smoothly integrated. Infants are both socially motivated to attend to and highly sensitive to the stress patterns, rhythms, and spaces of speech (Jusczyk, 1997). Fine-tuning of auditory perception with increasing familiarity of the child's own language is evident between 6 and

9 months of age (Kuhl, 2004). The child brings both motivation and an ability to read other people's mental states to infer a speaker's intended referent and meaning—that is, to know what is being talked about and thus to what the sequence of sounds refers. This is characterized by joint attention, in which the child's gaze switches to an object or action the speaker is focusing on (Pruden, Hirsh-Pasek, & Golinkoff, 2006). Cues from speech sounds alert the child to changing word meaning and support the learning of grammar. By the age of 5 the typically developing child has not only mastered the fundamental structural aspects of language but has acquired a knowledge of pragmatics—the ability to determine how to use verbal and nonverbal communicative signals (i.e., gesture and facial expression) to understand and convey a wide variety of different messages according to context.

DECIDING WHO HAS A SIGNIFICANT SPEECH AND LANGUAGE PROBLEM

There is a wide normal variation in the acquisition of speech and language. Using the MacArthur Scale of Communicative Development Inventory, Fenson et al. (1994) reported that at 16 months of age, 80% of children understand between 78 and 303 words. Those in the top 10% produce 154 words, and those in the lowest 10% produce none.

In the preschool years, many children who are late to talk improve spontaneously (Paul, 1996); however, predicting which child is going to improve spontaneously is difficult. Any single measure, particularly in a very young child, may be a poor predictor of outcome. Silva, McGee, and Williams (1983) assessed the same children at 3, 5, and 7 years of age and reported that, while some children failed at each of three assessment points, others failed at only one or two.

A common way of measuring a child's abilities is to express a score as a centile (also known as percentile)—that is, in terms of the percentage of children of the same age who would obtain an equivalent or lower score. Thus the 50th centile is average, the 90th centile is well above average (only 10% do better than this), and the 10th centile is well below average (90% of children will score higher than this). Traditionally it is those children on the lowest centiles of speech and language acquisition who have been considered to have an impairment, although exactly which centile marks impairment (bottom 10th centile versus bottom 3rd centile) at any given age remains a matter of debate. An epidemiological study defined specific language impairment (SLI) as having two of five language composite scores below the 10th centile and estimated the preschool prevalence of language impairment (LI) as approximately 7% of children (Tomblin et al., 1997), although the authors noted that a more stringent criterion would yield a much lower rate. In the same sample, speech delay was found in 3.6%, with a comorbidity (i.e., co-occurrence of two disorders) between persisting speech and language impairment of nearly 2%. Of those children with persisting language impairment, 5–8% had speech delay, and 11–15% of those with a persisting speech delay had a language impairment (Shriberg, Tomblin, & McSweeny, 1999).

It should be noted that the specific test battery used will affect findings, and some difficulties may be more obvious than others. For instance, more recent studies have shown that serious language impairments are not always obvious in children who have good phonological ability (i.e., ability to analyze speech sounds) and appear, superficially, at least, to read well (Nation, Clarke, Marshall, & Durand, 2004; Spaulding, Plante, & Farinella, 2006). Persistent severe delay in receptive or expressive language skills is likely to have predictive significance; degree of parental concern may also be a very good guide to severity of problem.

CLASSIFYING SPEECH AND/OR LANGUAGE PROBLEMS

Speech and language problems may be classified in terms of the area of impairment:

- receptive language (understanding)
- expressive language
- speech (articulation)
- dysfluency
- other.

These are not mutually exclusive—indeed, it is common to find more than one aspect of communicative functioning to be impaired.

Speech and language problems can also be classified in terms of underlying causes—that is, etiology. Exhibit 1.1 lists factors that are associated with increased risk of speech or language impairment in children. Some problems are secondary to etiologies such as deafness, motor disorder, structural palatal problem, acquired brain disorder, and so forth. These causal factors are discussed in greater detail below. In other cases, the language disorder occurs in the context of a more complex syndrome, such as autistic disorder.

The disorder is regarded as primary where no obvious underlying etiology is detected and the language impairment is not part of another recognized syndrome. Primary problems are referred to as *specific LI* and are of two main types:

1. Affecting structural aspects of language: lexical knowledge, syntax, and phonology. This may be manifested as an auditory processing deficit, difficulties with word retrieval and output, and dyspraxic speech impairments. Receptive and/or expressive components may be variably affected.

2. Affecting mainly pragmatics and abstract understanding, also sometimes called "higher order functions." This may be manifested in social communication difficulties and problems comprehending and producing language beyond the here and now.

The term *specific language impairment* refers to the fact that the language impairment is disproportionate in relation to other aspects of

---

EXHIBIT 1.1: Factors associated with increased risk of speech or language impairment in children

Etiologies leading to secondary speech and language impairment
- hearing impairment
- genetic disorders (e.g., sex chromosome trisomies, 22q deletion)
- prenatal exposure to substances such as antiepileptic drugs, alcohol, narcotics
- acquired epileptic aphasia
- acquired disorders resulting from neurological damage (e.g., strokes)
- oromotor structural defects (e.g., cleft palate)
- motor dysfunction of central origin (e.g., cerebral palsy, cortical dysplasia, cerebellar hypoplasia) or of peripheral origin (neuromuscular disorders)
- impoverished environment socially and linguistically (has to be severely impoverished and/or in association with other factors)

Syndromes in which speech or language impairments are associated and often presenting symptoms
- autism spectrum disorder
- general learning difficulty (mental retardation)
- anxiety disorder associated with mutism

Factors associated with primary speech and language impairment
- male gender
- family history of speech and language problems
- specific learning disability affecting literacy acquisition

development, especially nonverbal ability. However, it does not entail that the child is free from other problems. It is common to find associated impairments in motor skills, cognitive function, attention, and reading in children who meet criteria for specific language impairment (Hill, 2001).

ROLE OF PRIMARY CARE PROFESSIONALS

Several professionals and disciplines need to be involved in the strategic planning of appropriate referral pathways for children with speech and language problems and in the clinical assessment.

Screening

Screening of speech and language problems as a population-based public health activity is not currently recommended in the United Kingdom or the United States. For screening to be feasible, it is necessary, first, to have screening tools that are sensitive and specific enough to detect children with problems and, second, to have an effective treatment in place for those who are identified. Neither requirement is currently met. Nelson, Nygren, Walker, and Panoscha (2006), in a review for the US taskforce, concluded that there was insufficient research to draw conclusions on whether to screen or enhance professional and parental surveillance, which tests to use, and which ages to test. Research on the effectiveness and outcome of early intervention is also limited.

The task of the primary care practitioner is to enable concern about a child's speech and language development on the part of a parent or professional to be dealt with promptly and to be clear about local referral pathways. As a first step, any child with suspected speech and language delay should be referred for hearing testing.

If the problem is confined to speech and language, the child should usually be managed by the speech and language therapist. A general developmental screening questionnaire—for example, the parent-completed Early Developmental Checklist

(Glascoe & Robertshaw, 2006), which inquires about a range of development areas—may be helpful in eliciting parental concerns systematically. If a more wide-ranging developmental delay is suspected, indicated by report of a problem in more than one area of development, or if there are concerns about social and communicative skills, the child should be referred to the Child Development Team (CDT) for a multiprofessional assessment.

Population screening for autism is not recommended in the United Kingdom (National Initiative for Autism Screening and Assessment, 2003), but awareness of the alerting signs of an autism spectrum disorder is recommended (see Exhibit 1.2) and should prompt referral to the CDT.

ROLE OF THE SPEECH AND LANGUAGE THERAPIST

Who is referred to speech-language therapists (SLTs) will be influenced by locality as well as other considerations. For instance, 8.4% of children had been referred to speech therapy by the age of 3 in the UK CHAT (Checklist for Autism) project (Baird et al., unpublished data from a general population cohort in South East England), yet Broomfield and Dodd (2004) estimated that in the United Kingdom, as many as 14.6% of children per birth year may be referred to speech and language therapy services in areas of social deprivation.

The first priorities of assessment are to:

1. establish the nature of parental or other professional concerns;
2. assess the type and impact of the speech/language problem;
3. assess the severity of the problem;
4. decide whether there are other developmental and/or emotional/behavioral problems;
5. decide
    a. who needs "watchful waiting and review"
    b. who needs active treatment

EXHIBIT 1.2: Symptoms suggestive of autistic spectrum disorder

- *Language delay:* no babble or pointing or other gesture by 12 months, no single words by 16 months, no nonechoed 2-word phrases by 24 months
- *Regression:* loss of skills at any time
- *Communication:* delays in speech and language development, lack of pointing, difficulty following a pointing finger, poor response to name, unusual use of language
- *Social interaction:* poor imitation, child does not show things to others, lack of interest in other children or odd approaches in older children, lack of or limited variety of imaginative play/pretence, "in his own world," odd relationship with adults (too friendly or ignores them)
- *Other behaviors:* oversensitivity to sound/touch, motor mannerisms, biting/hitting, aggression to peers and oppositional to adults, overliking for sameness, inability to cope with change, especially in unstructured settings, repetitive play with toys (e.g., lining up cars), overfocused and intense preoccupation with unusual features of environment

---

c. whether the problem is more complex because of other developmental/behavioral problems and needs further assessment, or

d. whether there is no significant problem.

Speech-language therapy assessment

A full description of all aspects of assessment is beyond the scope of this chapter, but it should include pre-, peri- and postnatal events and development, family history, environmental experience, broad aspects of communication both verbal and nonverbal, play and imagination, cognitive skills, attention and concentration, motor competence and emotional regulation and behavior, in addition to the speech and language. A friendly, informal atmosphere should be arranged where child and parent feel relaxed and where there are suitable toys for the age of the child.

Assessing speech and language

It is difficult even for the very experienced professional to guess a child's comprehension accurately. This should be formally assessed using standardized tests of speech and language. The clinician should be aware that the many tests available all measure slightly different functions, and one child can achieve different scores in individual tests (Howlin & Cross, 1994). The

Clinical Evaluation of Language Fundamentals (CELF; Semel, Wiig, & Secord, 2004) has now become the standard in-depth assessment used for children in child development centers and speech units. As a test of global language function in the preschool child, the Bus story for preschool children (Renfrew, 1991), in which the adult tells a story with pictures and the child retells it, is a very good guide to overall language competence and a good prognostic indicator of long-term language functioning (Bishop & Edmundson, 1987).

General assessment points

1. Hearing testing is mandatory for any child with a speech/language problem.

2. It is important to get information about a child from several sources and contexts—for example, it is important to ask parents about the child's communication and behavior at home, whereas preschool or school staff may be asked about social and communicative development, learning, and behavior in the more structured school setting. It may be helpful to arrange a school or nursery visit as part of the assessment.

3. Questionnaire screens for specific developmental problems such as autism and coordination problems are being evaluated. The

use of the Modified Checklist for Autism (M-CHAT; Barton, Robins, & Fein, 1999) in young preschool children, the Social Communication Questionnaire (Rutter, Bailey, & Lord, 2003) or the Children's Communication Checklist–2 (Bishop, 2003) in older children may identify children at high risk of language and social communication deficits, providing signposts to further assessment.

4. One should look for signs of general developmental delay; this may be especially evident when observing behaviors that should have disappeared, such as mouthing objects in a preschool child.

5. The assessment should include evaluation of the communicative environment and take note of any difficulties the parent and child may have in interacting socially together.

6. When testing expressive language, there may be a difference between the fluency the child shows when talking about his or her own ideas as opposed to when asked to do something more specific, such as naming a picture. This may indicate a problem generating novel ideas or language.

7. Receptive language is usually in advance of expressive in normal development, but the opposite pattern is sometimes seen in semantic-pragmatic disorders or autism spectrum problems.

8. Pragmatic problems may be much more apparent in open conversation and play than in formal tests.

9. Behavior problems should be assessed, remembering that the outcome is less good generally for speech and language impairments that are accompanied by more widespread behavior problems.

10. Techniques of nondirective play and occasional imitation of the child's actions or sounds is a useful technique, but in the assessment setting there should be two aims: (a) to see what the child can generate and initiate in terms of social communicative, play, and language behavior and (b) what

is possible with some "scaffolding" from the professional. For many children, the gap between elicited behavior and spontaneous behavior is very significant. Some children with language and communication problems are able to achieve skills in a structured situation with a helpful adult that they cannot sustain in "real life," especially with peers.

Which children should be referred to the CDT for multiprofessional assessment?

Type of problem with speech and language as a guide

Broomfield and Dodd (2004) provided details of all children aged 2–6 years referred to a regional speech-language therapy service over 15 months. Of these referrals, 14.9% failed to attend the first appointment, and 9.8% of those who were assessed had normal language function. Diagnoses made were: dysfluency (stuttering), 5.3%; voicing problems, 2%; receptive language impairment, 20.4%; expressive language impairment, 16.9%; speech impairment, 29.1%. Of the latter, 57.7% had phonological delay; 20.6% made consistent errors; 9.4% made inconsistent errors; and 12.5% had an articulation problem diagnosed as developmental dyspraxia.

Dysfluency in the absence of any other speech, language, or developmental concern may require no further medical investigation, whereas a voicing problem may require an opinion from an ear-nose-throat specialist.

Developmental speech impairments are common: Shriberg et al. (1999) estimated prevalence at 3.8%. Most abate, and those that are more persistent often respond positively to intervention (Law, Garrett, & Nye, 2004). Precise terminology varies, with some focusing on the linguistic nature of the problem (e.g., a phonological problem), and others focusing more on the motor aspects, using terms such as verbal dyspraxia or speech articulation problem. The severity of such difficulties is variable, as is involvement of oromotor immaturity shown in delayed chewing, dribbling, and so forth. This group of problems should be distinguished from those with structural abnormalities of articulators or motoric impairment. The term dysarthria is used for speech disorder resulting from neurological injury, characterized by poor articulation and slurred, slow, and difficult-to-produce speech. Speech problems are the most obvious to parents and hence frequently prompt referral. Most isolated speech difficulties have a good prognosis. However, speech disorders with marked oromotor problems have clear qualitative differences and a specific differential diagnosis requiring referral for further medical assessment (see below).

Where only expressive language is delayed, the problems are likely to resolve themselves spontaneously in the preschool period, with up to 60% abating without input between the ages of 2 and 3 years (Law, Boyle, Harris, Harkness, & Nye, 1998). These cases are usually managed appropriately by speech and language therapy services, and referral to tertiary services is not usually warranted unless the delay is very severe or there is no evidence of improvement.

Mutism should prompt enquiry about other manifestations of anxiety and should be referred (see below). Regression of language is discussed below and is also an indication for referral.

Comprehension deficits can be much more subtle, as many children are good at relying on contextual information to guide their understanding. Impaired nonverbal communication alerts the clinician to a broader problem. Mixed receptive/expressive disorders are less specific markers for particular etiologies, are least likely to resolve themselves spontaneously, and are most likely to be associated with other comorbidities; hence referral to tertiary services should seriously be considered.

Much debate continues in speech and language research as to whether or not the pattern of speech and language development in a disorder is an exaggeration of the normal developmental pattern or qualitatively different in a way that can guide diagnosis, prognosis, investigation, and treatment. The communicative features listed in Exhibit 1.2 indicate that communicative development is abnormal, rather than merely delayed, and should prompt referral for more detailed assessment.

ROLE OF THE PEDIATRICIAN/CHILD PSYCHIATRIST

The purpose of any medical assessment, including physical examination and laboratory or other tests, is to identify causative, associated, or exacerbating medical problems. There are several reasons for establishing the cause of a particular pattern of development. This may be because the situation can be immediately remedied; for example, a hearing loss may be ameliorated by prescribing hearing aids. On other occasions, establishing the etiology may give useful information about the course, prognosis, and likely response to particular therapeutic interventions; for example, structural causes of speech impairment may require surgery. There is also the need for families to know that there has been a thorough search for a causative mechanism as part of the process of adjustment to a developmental problem.

ROLE OF THE CHILD DEVELOPMENT TEAM

Children with severe persistent language impairments, specific speech impairments with oromotor dysfunction, acquired impairments, and any comorbidities (behavior, communication, social, motor, etc.) should all have the opportunity of a multiprofessional assessment, including medical, psychological, educational, occupational therapy, psychiatric, and specialist speech-language therapy expertise. In the United Kingdom, this will usually be via the CDT.

Although children may present with apparently isolated speech and language delays in the preschool years, follow-up studies have shown that many have impairments and dysfunction in other areas, including, but not restricted to, literacy impairment (Snowling, Bishop, & Stothard, 2000). Behavior problems and psychiatric disorders are also found more commonly in those with speech and language impairments (Beitchman et al., 2001; Stevenson & Richman, 1978). In a prospective study, Shevell, Majnemer, Webster, Platt, and Birnbaum (2005) found that almost half of a cohort of preschool children diagnosed with developmental language impairment at a mean age of 3.6 ± 0.7 years and reassessed at a mean age of 7.4 ± 0.7 years showed functional impairment in at least two domains of the Vineland Adaptive Behavior Scales. Severe persistent language impairment can result in lifetime impairment, with particular difficulties in social adaptation and employment (Clegg, Hollis, Mawhood, & Rutter, 2005).

In view of this association of speech and language impairments with other developmental and behavioral disorders that are so relevant to long-term outcome (see also Tomblin, chapter 7, and Conti-Ramsden, chapter 8, this volume), a systematic assessment should be made of all potential associations so that intervention can take these into account.

Subtle cognitive impairments and attention deficits should be systematically considered in assessment. Developmental coordination disorder is a particularly common comorbidity (Webster et al., 2006).

ETIOLOGICAL FACTORS IN SECONDARY SPEECH AND LANGUAGE DISORDERS

Hearing loss

Sensorineural hearing loss

The term *sensorineural hearing loss* refers to hearing loss due to damage to the peripheral auditory system—that is, cochlea or auditory nerve. Persistent hearing loss has a significant impact on speech and language development, dependent on the level of loss (Wake, Poulakis, Hughes, Carey-Sargeant, & Rickards, 2005). Universal hearing screening for all children has been available in the United Kingdom for many years from about 8 months of age but the current focus is on universal neonatal hearing screening. Results of early identification of hearing loss via neonatal screening,

followed by appropriate aids, show considerable benefits for speech and language development (Kennedy et al., 2006).

Some sensorineural hearing impairments are gradually progressive, and thus if there is any concern about a hearing loss, referral to an audiologist should be made. It should not be forgotten that there are also acquired causes of hearing loss—for example, deafness occurs in approximately 7% of children following recovery from bacterial meningitis (Koomen et al., 2003), and pneumococcal meningitis is particularly likely to cause hearing loss. Exhibit 1.3 presents a case study that emphasizes the need for careful hearing testing, even if the child appears responsive to sound on informal assessment.

Otitis media with effusion (OME) or glue ear

Otitis media refers to disease of the middle ear, where fluid can collect behind the eardrum, often after a cold. The role of such middle ear effusion in either the causation or the exacerbation of speech and language impairment has been the subject of a number of studies and reviews, with variable results. Otitis media with effusion is extremely common. In a meta-analysis Roberts, Rosenfeld, and Zeisel (2004) found that OME and associated hearing loss in preschool children had little or no association with children's speech and language development. But they noted that most studies did not adjust for factors such as socioeconomic status, and they concluded that for otherwise healthy children in language-rich environments the clinical relevance of OME is uncertain. Thus for most children OME will have a marginal effect, if any, on language; however, for some children OME may be important when combined with other risk factors.

It is important to distinguish cases where otitis media with effusion is associated with craniofacial or other neurological or sensorineural deficit, since these will be at far greater risk of impairment from additional hearing loss or are likely to have very persistent OME. Clinical practice guidelines recommend intervention specifically for this group (Rosenfeld et al., 2004).

EXHIBIT 1.3: Case study: hearing and language impairment

James was referred aged 6 because of concerns about language development. He had normal hearing when tested in his first 2 years and normal language development. He was admitted to hospital at the age of 3 years with a severe illness that affected his consciousness, although the cause was unclear. Large amounts of antibiotics were used, and a full recovery was apparently made. There were continuing concerns about hearing, but James frequently displayed normal responses to sounds, which delayed recognition of the hearing loss shown on the audiogram at 4 years. There is a sharp drop between 500 and 1,000 Hz, which will have a marked effect upon language learning while permitting some occasional but inconsistent responses to environmental sounds.

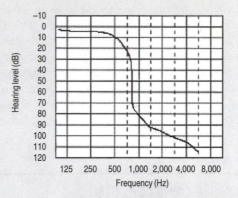

Audiogram depicting sharp drop in hearing level between 500 and 1,000 Hz

---

CHROMOSOME ANOMALIES

A chromosome is a single large package of tightly coiled DNA in a cell, which contains many genes and other regulatory elements. Humans usually have 23 pairs of chromosomes. Sometimes an extra chromosome is incorporated during gamete formation, so that there are three rather than two copies, and in other cases all or part of a chromosome may be deleted. An increase in chromosome abnormalities in children with SLI has been reported, particularly abnormalities of sex chromosomes (Mutton & Lea, 1980). Language impairment has been described in studies of children who have an extra sex chromosome (see Table 1.1).

TABLE 1.1

Sex chromosome abnormalities that may present with delayed speech

Karyotype	Gender	Syndrome	Physical traits
XXY, XXYY, XXXY	male	Klinefelter syndrome	Delayed speech, learning difficulties, sterility, small testicles, breast enlargement
XYY	male	XYY syndrome	Normal male traits, learning difficulties, delayed speech, larger body size
XXX	female	Trisomy X	Delayed speech, tall stature, learning disabilities, limited fertility

Note. Modified from Ratcliffe, 1999.

Another instance in which a chromosomal abnormality is associated with poor language is Down syndrome, where there is an additional copy of chromosome 21. Children with Down syndrome typically have a marked delay in expressive language and speech, associated with general learning difficulties. Their language profile has much in common with that seen in SLI, albeit in the context of low IQ (Laws & Bishop, 2004).

SINGLE-GENE DEFECTS

Certain single-gene defects are associated with particular patterns of strengths and weaknesses in language and speech acquisition; many, but not all, are usually associated to a greater or lesser degree with learning difficulties. Williams syndrome, in which there is a deletion of genetic material from chromosome 7, has attracted a lot of interest because of claims that affected children have normal language skills despite their low IQ. However, this is rather misleading: early language development is typically delayed, and, although some individuals with Williams syndrome may use fluent and complex language, they nevertheless have major limitations of comprehension (Bates, 2004; Brock, 2007). One syndrome in which expressive language is severely impaired is Angelman syndrome, in which a small region on chromosome 15 is deleted.

The combination of features of particular speech impairment plus or minus learning difficulties and palatal dysfunction should prompt investigation for the specific deletion of chromosome 22q causing velo-cardio facial syndrome. The core eight clinical features are: cardiac defects, non-visible/hypoplastic thymus or infection problems, hypocalcaemia, feeding difficulties, cleft palate/speech-language impairment, developmental delay/learning difficulties, characteristic dysmorphic features (i.e., structurally abnormal body parts), and other malformations and deformities. This disorder is often missed in the preschool years; in one large case series, the median age at diagnosis was 6.7 years (Óskarsdóttir, Persson, Eriksson, & Fasth, 2005). All presented with a combination of many of the core features. Of those diagnosed after 2 years of age, the majority presented with speech-language impairment, developmental delay or learning difficulties, and recurrent infections. A high proportion have no cardiac defect and hence a risk of diagnostic delay; however, characteristic mild dysmorphic features were noticed in all children. The main message is that this diagnosis needs to be considered by clinicians, even when there are no apparent cardiac complaints.

FOXP2 gene mutation

Members of one family with marked speech and language impairments with oromotor problems and some mild learning difficulties have been found to have a deletion affecting part of the *FOXP2* gene (Newbury & Monaco, chapter 6, this volume). Although there were initial expectations that this genetic defect might provide an explanation for common developmental speech disorders, further analysis of the *FOXP2* gene in a large SLI cohort did not find this to be the case. As discussed by Newbury and Monaco, it seems unlikely that single-gene mutations are implicated in the majority of cases of SLI; rather, the genetic risk arises from the combined influence of many genes of small effect.

PRENATAL EXPOSURE TO ENVIRONMENTAL HAZARDS

The taking by mothers of antiepileptic drugs in pregnancy can have an adverse effect on the fetus, including prematurity, low birth weight, congenital malformations, and developmental delay. Fetal effects appear to be dose- and polypharmacy-related, but sodium valproate seems to pose the highest risk—as high as 14% (Meador et al., 2006). Dysmorphic features and orofacial defects are among the major malformations associated with taking the antiepileptic drug sodium valproate. Neurodevelopmental delays, particularly communication delays and autism spectrum disorders, have also been reported. Children exposed to valproate had a significantly lower verbal IQ in one retrospective study (Kini et al., 2006). Ongoing prospective studies of the outcome of antiepileptic drugs will help to determine more precise risks.

Fetal alcohol syndrome is diagnosed on the basis of maternal alcohol abuse and examination of the child; it is likely that in milder form it is commoner than is usually diagnosed. Fetal alcohol syndrome is a continuum ranging from mild intellectual and behavioral impairments to an extreme that often leads to profound disabilities or premature death (Mukherjee, Hollins, & Turk, 2006; O'Leary, 2004). Features of fetal alcohol syndrome—which may not all be present—include:

- prenatal or postnatal growth retardation—height and weight below the 10th centile for age or gestational age
- central nervous system (CNS) dysfunction—any neurological abnormality, developmental delay, or moderate learning difficulties
- characteristic craniofacial abnormalities (deformities in the growth of the skull and facial bones), including at least two of the following:
  - microcephaly (head circumference below the 3rd centile)
  - microphthalmia or other structural eye abnormality
  - poor development of the upper lip and flattening of the midfacial area.

STRUCTURAL BRAIN ABNORMALITIES

Although uncommon, polymicrogyria (literally many small folds on the surface of the brain) are implicated in some speech and language impairments. The polymicrogyria syndromes result from several different causes that are both genetic and nongenetic (Jansen & Andermann,

2005). When the perisylvian region is involved (see Dick, Richardson, & Saccuman, chapter 4, this volume), speech and language is impaired. Affected children may have learning difficulties, cerebral palsy, and seizures; the spectrum is broad, and severity depends on the extent of cortical involvement. Problems using the muscles of the face, throat, jaws, and tongue are common; if mild, they may lead to just a speech impediment or a tendency to drool, but if more severe, they can lead to difficulties with feeding as a baby. The abnormalities in the perisylvian regions may be seen on magnetic resonance imaging (MRI) scans, and the above features should prompt investigation using neuroimaging techniques (see chapter 4). It is bilateral perisylvian polymicrogyria that is now thought to be responsible for the congenital suprabulbar paresis first described by Worster-Drought (Clark, Carr, Reilly, & Neville, 2000). Features of this syndrome include severe speech impairment, history of feeding problems, drooling inappropriately, delay in gross motor function, learning impairment, pyramidal features on examination, and seizures (in a third of cases). Electroencephalogram (EEG) abnormalities—that is, variation from the electrical brainwave pattern appropriate to the age of the child—are commonly found.

Speech impairment, often with more general learning difficulties, may also be found in conditions causing cerebellar hypoplasia, including various forms of Joubert's syndrome, a rare developmental disorder that causes coordination and movement problems, mental retardation, and speech impairment. Two gene mutations have been identified as causing Joubert's syndrome.

In SLI without additional handicaps, it is uncommon to find evidence of brain lesions, although there is evidence of subtle abnormalities in the proportions and symmetry of different cortical regions from structural neuroimaging studies (e.g., Herbert et al., 2005; Leonard, Eckert, Given, Virginia, & Eden, 2006). Localized cortical dysplasia (neurons that have not migrated to the correct place in the cortex) may also be associated with specific language impairment (Webster & Shevell, 2004). Functional imaging provides some support for the idea that SLI is associated with a lack of the normal brain asymmetry thought to indicate lateralized specialization of language function (Bernal & Altman, 2003). However, these are research findings and not yet clinically useful routine tests.

ACQUIRED NEUROLOGICAL DAMAGE

Acquired causes of speech and language impairment include infections such as meningitis, trauma such as head injuries, or other intracerebral problems such as strokes affecting general brain function or localized areas of speech and language processing. Recovery from unilateral brain injury affecting the speech areas—as, for example, a middle cerebral artery thrombosis—depends upon the age of the child. Those under 6 or 7 years of age with a left middle cerebral artery infarction (damage caused by loss of blood supply) will usually show no difference in language competence by mid-childhood compared with other children, even though the damage is presumed to affect the normally dominant left-hemisphere language learning center. This illustrates a phenomenon known as plasticity—the ability of the brain to reorganize neural pathways based on new experiences. In the developing brain, the other hemisphere can take over language functions if the left is damaged, but only up to a certain age (Lenneberg, 1967).

A condition such as cerebral palsy may affect the bulbar apparatus and so lead to dysarthria. Cerebral palsy is easily diagnosed if movement of the limbs is involved. Cortical impairments affecting the speech motor areas of the brain may result in the Worster-Drought syndrome described above with minimal limb involvement. A number of disorders involving degeneration of areas affecting motoric speech output—for example, cerebellar tumors and Friedreich's ataxia—may present with dysarthria. These are rare, and other neurological physical abnormalities will prompt referral for neurological investigation.

Acute cerebellar damage may present as acquired mutism. This is rare but due most commonly to cerebellar damage from infection or by surgery, when the cerebellar mutism is accompanied by irritability and other features and may last days or months. The outcome depends to some extent upon the underlying pathology (Mewasingh, Kadhim, Christophe, Christiaens, & Dan, 2003).

EPILEPSY

Localized epilepsy, especially in the perisylvian region, which may or may not present as overt seizures, can have a devastating effect upon language development. Termed Landau–Kleffner syndrome (LKS), this most commonly occurs in children aged 4–7 years; in such cases parents may gradually or suddenly notice considerably diminished language use, accompanied by a profound receptive language impairment. The receptive difficulties may be severe enough to include poor response to environmental sounds. Overt seizures are frequently not part of the initial presentation, but they can occur. Sleep EEG shows a continuous spike wave activity, in some definitions more than 80% of the time, and it is the abolition of the interference this causes that is associated with improvement and recovery of speech and language (Robinson, Baird, Robinson, & Simonoff, 2001). Treatment to stop the epilepsy is therefore essential and might include surgery if the epilepsy does not respond to medication. Clinically, language regression or marked fluctuation of language comprehension and speech should trigger the request for a sleep EEG. Epilepsy localized to other areas—for example, Rolandic epilepsy—may also be associated with language impairment (Northcott et al., 2005).

A clear epileptic syndrome such as LKS is, however, rare. More common is the finding of epileptiform EEG abnormalities in sleep in children with speech and language impairment (Picard et al., 1998). These are distinctive waves or complexes seen on the EEG, distinguished from background activity, and resembling those recorded in a proportion of human subjects suffering from epileptic disorders. They are of uncertain significance; the current view is that they are as likely to be epiphenomena rather than etiologically significant (McVicar, Ballaban-Gill, Rapin, Moshé, & Shinnar, 2005).

STRUCTURAL DEFICITS AFFECTING SPEECH—FOR EXAMPLE, CLEFT PALATE AND MIDLINE SUBMUCOUS CLEFTS

Cleft palate should be considered when there are specific features of speech sound production and a history of palatal dysfunction, such as food coming down the nose. This should prompt close examination, with palpation of the soft palate if necessary. A bifid (split) uvula is another physical sign that should prompt referral to a specialist cleft palate team. Children with cleft lip and palate experience increased middle ear problems, and treatment with ventilation tubes is often warranted. It is particularly important that hearing and the impact of any impairment is monitored and treated. Jocelyn, Penko, and Rode (1996) reported that, even in the absence of other neurodevelopmental abnormalities, children with cleft lip and palatal problems achieved significantly lower scores on tests of cognition, comprehension, and expressive language abilities at 12 and 24 months of age than did matched control children.

SYNDROMES IN WHICH SPEECH AND LANGUAGE ARE IMPAIRED

Autism spectrum disorders

An autism spectrum disorder (ASD) is an important differential diagnosis to make in a child presenting with speech and language delay. An ASD is characterized by a qualitative impairment in sociability, empathy, and the ability to infer another person's feelings and perspective, the communicative use of language, creative and imaginative play, a restricted range of interests and activities, and limited cognitive and behavioral flexibility. There may also be altered sensory responses to the environment. ASD has been found to be more likely in children identified as having SLI compared with the general population (Conti-Ramsden, Simkin, & Botting, 2006). Whether this represents misdiagnosis earlier, a changing clinical picture, or both is not clear. A developmental history and examination specifically looking for features of autism should be part of any assessment, using the screening instruments mentioned above and/or structured parent interviews (see Le Couteur & Gardner, 2008, for overview). Features of speech and language in autism are shown in Exhibit 1.4.

Tager-Flusberg (2006) reported that verbal children with autism can be divided into three groups on the basis of standardized language test performance: impaired, borderline, or normal. The impaired and borderline groups had language profiles similar to those found in SLI. Brain imaging revealed that reduced or absent hemispheric asymmetry often associated with SLI is also to be found in children with autism, but only in those children with autism who also had LI (cf. Herbert et al., 2005).

Tager-Flusberg's work suggests that one cannot differentiate between autistic spectrum disorder and SLI on the basis of language profile alone. This echoes a conclusion reached by Rapin and Allen (1983). They devised a linguistic nosology of language problems in children that categorized them on the basis of the domain of language affected. Rapin and Allen concluded that all types of language problems that are found in SLI (which they termed *developmental dysphasia*) can also be found in children with autism.

It is sometimes assumed that social impairments in children are a consequence of LI; however, longitudinal studies indicate that language may improve without a concomitant improvement in social interaction. This is especially the case if there are other features of ASD present (Michelotti, Charman, Slonims, & Baird, 2002).

EXHIBIT 1.4: Typical language and communication profile in autistic spectrum disorder

- Delayed onset of first words and phrases without compensatory gesture
- Language comprehension deficits (often early apparent deafness to speech but not music or favorite household sounds)
- Unusual nonspeech sounds
- Echolalia; whole sentences learned as chunks
- Use of one word rather than sentences, even when capable of producing sentence
- Repetitive and ritualistic use of language
- Odd use of words: for example, referring to object by color or number and not by name
- Persistent context-bound or associative use of language
- Disassociation between good articulation and grammar and poor functional use
- Pedantic or precise use of language
- Overliteral interpretation; for example, would take literally an injunction to "pull your socks up"
- Lack of social chat
- Can talk nonstop "at people"; lack of reciprocity and conversation
- Poor assumption of listener knowledge

Selective mutism

Selective mutism is considered to be a form of anxiety disorder with a particular manifestation. Children with selective mutism have greater social anxiety and other internalizing symptoms compared with controls. However, in contrast with children who present with social phobia only, children with selective mutism may also have some subtle speech and language impairments (Manassis et al., 2003; Steinhausen, Wachter, Laimbock, & Metzke, 2006). The criteria for this disorder are :

1. a marked and consistent selectivity in speaking—that is, a failure to speak in social situations;

2. a normal or near-normal level of language comprehension;

3. a level of expressive language competence sufficient for social communication;

4. evidence that the child can and does speak normally or almost normally in some situations.

Prevalence refers to the total number of cases of a disease in a defined population at any given moment in time. Prevalence rates vary depending upon populations studied but are approximately 1% (Bergman, Piacentini, & McCracken, 2002), with onset at age 3–4 years. The problem must exist for at least 4 weeks, and in the DSM criteria (American Psychiatric Association, 1994) there are exclusions if another disorder—for example, a communication disorder—is present.

Follow-up studies show that the overt symptoms may improve considerably. However, in a study of adults there were significantly higher rates of phobic disorder and other psychiatric disorders compared with controls. High levels of individual psychopathology and family psychopathology predicted poorer outcome (Cunningham, McHolm, Boyle, & Patel, 2006).

It is recommended that children with selective mutism are referred to appropriate services for active intervention and treatment. Treatments shown to be effective are both behavioral (e.g., cognitive behavior therapy) and pharmacological (e.g., Fluoxetine/Prozac) (Steinhausen et al., 2006).

A SYSTEMATIC APPROACH TO MEDICAL ASSESSMENT AND INVESTIGATION OF SPEECH AND LANGUAGE PROBLEMS

The principle for history taking, physical examination, and subsequent investigations is that treatable conditions need to be identified and a high priority given to any condition with genetic implications for the child or for other family members. The impact of false negative and false positive tests, the time taken and discomfort associated with some examinations and investigations, and economic constraints mean that a valuable skill is that of knowing when further investigations are warranted and when they are not. Differences in training, seniority, and experience will affect the level of an individual's threshold between examining and investigating him/herself and referring to another specialist colleague. In what follows, reference is made to evidence helpful in decisions about which investigation is worthwhile for a particular child; but sometimes evidence is lacking, and clinical opinion is substituted.

Clinicians have become increasingly familiar with the concepts outlined by Sackett, Haynes, Tugwell, and Guyatt (1991) that the likelihood of any particular investigation—be it physical examination or laboratory test—giving a positive result can be informed by the pretest probability, which is derived from the prevalence of the condition in the particular population under investigation and altered by the findings that accrue during the process of history and examination. As is discussed more fully below, it is not appropriate to instigate detailed medical work-ups for all children with speech and language problems; rather, such investigations should be prompted by findings of specific diagnostic features. For example, a marked speech impairment plus dysmorphic features of the mouth and face areas, combined with epilepsy, would increase the likelihood of finding cortical dysplasia on MRI scan of the brain.

Questions to ask in the case history

Parents are good informants of current development and can also be usefully asked to estimate the overall functioning age of their child. Signs and symptoms of any general learning difficulty should be noted. Parents may be less good at remembering particular milestones (although the age of walking is usually recalled), but they do remember whether a child's development was delayed or not. Asking parents to bring the parent health record to an appointment is a good aide memoire, provided key information has been documented.

Pregnancy

Enquiry should be directed at the prenatal environment and exposure to alcohol, anticonvulsants, and any history of rashes and fever during pregnancy, which may indicate exposure to a congenital viral infection.

Birth and neonatal history

Parents are frequently concerned that any difficulty at birth is the cause of subsequent developmental problems, and hence it is important to establish the gestational age at birth, the birth weight, and whether the baby is "small for dates"—that is, below the 10th centile at birth for the appropriate ethnic group. Premature delivery has been associated with speech and language delay (Bhutta, Cleves, Casey, Cradock, & Anand, 2002), but significant delays after the second year should not be assumed to be due solely to prematurity.

Birth details need to include the type of delivery, the state of the baby at birth, and subsequent neonatal course. Although a difficult birth may be significant, it can also be a marker of preexisting fetal difficulties. The Apgar score—where 10 corresponds to optimal condition—is a widely used measure of the infant's state at birth. Persistent Apgar scores below 5 with any symptoms of neonatal encephalopathy (for example, seizures), early imaging evidence, general metabolic disturbance, requirement for breathing support and the period for which that was needed would all be relevant in considering whether a difficult birth was a risk factor for subsequent developmental problems.

Although multiple pregnancies are associated with increased neonatal risk and early language delay, the longer-term outcome for twins compared with singletons in mental ability and educational performance is positive (Christensen et al., 2006)

Family history

Speech and language impairments have long been known to recur in families (Conti-Ramsden, Simkin, & Pickles, 2006) and frequently co-occur with reading and spelling impairments (Flax et al., 2003). Males are more commonly affected than females. Relevant family history concerns any problem with speech, language, reading, or spelling in parents or siblings; often it is spelling that remains impaired into adult life. In a study of children at a special school for speech and language impairments, over 40% had a relative with such problems—28% had a parent or sibling (Robinson, 1991). A family history of other developmental problems may also be relevant—for example, autism spectrum disorders are reported more commonly in families where a child has a developmental language problem (Tomblin, Hafeman, & O'Brien, 2003).

Postnatal history

Key features for inquiry are any major illness, trauma, accident involving head injury, or any other event, such as a seizure, that could indicate a reason for neurological dysfunction, including acquired hearing loss.

Language environment

While a bilingual environment is unlikely to be a sole cause of significant continuing delay, it may exacerbate another causative problem. Nursery placements with frequently changing and poor staff/child ratios are also environments that predispose to constant colds or ear infections. Maternal mental health problems can affect maternal responsiveness and will impact on the child and therapeutic plans.

General examination

This encompasses watching the child moving about playing as well as any specific physical examination. Most information about any motor difficulty can be gained from observation. Physical examination then confirms any suspicions of motor impairment and should include being alert to other problems, including neglect or abuse. Head circumference, height, and weight should be plotted on appropriate centile charts. Single measures, unless at extremes, are seldom diagnostically helpful but are essential for plotting trajectories that may be more diagnostically indicative. Dysmorphologies, especially of the face, may indicate specific diagnoses, especially in a child with learning difficulties. Physical examination should also include an inspection of the skin for café au lait patches for neurofibromatosis and for white patches best elicited by the use of Wood's light for tuberous sclerosis. Oral examination should be undertaken in a child with severe speech impairment but may be best left until the end! Specific neurological examination without clear indications of abnormality is unlikely to add to diagnosis; although in the past it has been suggested that neurological examination can detect "soft signs" of neurological immaturity, this has not proved to be valid.

Specific tests

Karyotype and cytogenetic tests

Karyotyping refers to the process of obtaining an organized profile of a person's chromosomes to evaluate the size, shape, and number. There is a limited evidence base for judging the value of routine karyotypic estimation in language impairment, but certain dysmorphic features will increase the pretest probability of finding an abnormality—for example, those of 22q deletion outlined above. The routine requesting of karyotype in nondysmorphic developmental delay/mental retardation continues to be questioned, quoting abnormal karyotype findings of <1% but fragile

X morphology of 3% (Macayran, Cederbaum, & Fox, 2006). New techniques, such as array comparative genomic hybridization, may alter both the yield and advice about tests.

Metabolic tests

Routine metabolic screening is not indicated in developmental delays. Thyroid function tests are not indicated unless there are physical symptoms. Serum lead should be restricted to those children with identifiable risk factors.

Neuroimaging

In the absence of physical signs, there is no indication for routine MRI in developmental speech and language problems.

Electroencephalography

This should be requested if there is regression of language without clinical autism and, of course, as part of the investigation of any epilepsy. Routine EEG is not otherwise indicated in developmental speech and language problems.

THE ETIOLOGICAL YIELD IN ISOLATED DEVELOPMENTAL SPEECH AND LANGUAGE PROBLEMS

The term "etiological yield" refers to the probability that a medical investigation will uncover a cause for a disorder. One study has addressed the issue of the yield of investigations for developmental problems where only one problem exists. Shevell, Majnemer, Rosenbaum, and Abrahamowicz (2000a) assessed consecutive referrals to a tertiary assessment service for children younger than 5 years of age with developmental language disorders. After examination and laboratory tests (metabolic, cytogenetic, imaging), an etiological diagnosis was made in only 4% (3/72) of the children. Absence of dysmorphic features and dysarthria make the yield of investigations low in speech impairment.

Selection of subjects may alter the yield of investigation, highlighting the point that the context of the practice of the professional will alter the approach to tests. For example, in the SLI Consortium Genetic Study, 89 families with 252 children were assessed; of these, only eight children were found to have karyotype abnormalities. These included 3 XYY, 2 siblings and a parent with del(10)(q11.2q11.2), one child with XXX, a son and mother with 46XY,t(2.11)(q35,p15.1)mat, and one other child with a translocation not apparent in either parent. This corresponds to a yield of greater than 5% on karyotype alone (SLI Consortium, unpublished data). Features that were more common in those with chromosome abnormalities were IQ at the low end of the normal range or below and dysmorphic features. In two children IQ was in the normal range but there was challenging behavior.

In special schools for children with speech and language impairments, etiological diagnoses are more common, reflecting the obvious point that more severe and persistent impairments are more likely to have identifiable causes. Robinson (1991) described a secondary school population of 82 children; etiology was established in 26% of the total (11% prenatal, 12% postnatal). A similar study in 2007 in the same school found an etiology in 16% (5% postnatal) (Baird, unpublished data).

ASSESSMENT WHEN THERE IS A GENERAL LEARNING DIFFICULTY (MENTAL RETARDATION)

Speech and language impairment is often the first sign of a general global learning problem (mental retardation), which should then prompt fuller physical examination and assessment. The minimal investigation in the absence of any signs on physical examination is karyotype and DNA test for fragile X. A high index of suspicion should prompt testing creatine phosphokinase to screen for muscular dystrophy in the young preschool boy (not all are delayed in walking—later than 18 months—but running is always a problem), and serum ferritin if there is a dietary abnormality to test for iron deficiency. More specific genetic tests are indicated for children with particular dysmorphic features—for example, Angelman syndrome.

Shevell, Majnemer, Rosenbaum, and Abrahamowicz (2000b) evaluated the etiological yield of investigation in children with global developmental delay. The case records of all children less than 5 years of age referred consecutively to a single outpatient setting for global developmental delay were systematically reviewed. An underlying cause was found in 37% of children. Commonest etiological groupings were genetic syndrome/chromosomal abnormality, intrapartum asphyxia, cerebral dysgenesis (disruption of the normal organization of the brain), psychosocial deprivation, and toxin exposure. Factors associated with the ability to eventually identify an underlying cause included female gender, abnormal prenatal/perinatal history, absence of autistic features, presence of microcephaly, abnormal neurologic examination, and dysmorphic features. In children without any abnormal features identified on history or physical examination, routine screening investigations (karyotype, fragile X molecular genotyping, and neuroimaging) revealed an underlying etiology in only 16%. Shevell et al. concluded that the etiological yield in an unselected series of young children with global developmental delay is close to 40% overall and 55% in the absence of any coexisting autistic features. Readily apparent clinical features increased the likelihood of an identified etiology.

Autism as an additional impairment does not by itself indicate further medical investigations or tests, since the yield is low, although alertness is needed with regard to epilepsy (Shevell et al., 2000b; Srour, Mazer, & Shevell, 2006)

REGRESSION OF SPEECH AND LANGUAGE

Although rare, regression of speech and language at any stage in a child's development should prompt referral for further investigation. The com-

monest time for regression to occur is at the time the child has fewer than 10 words in his or her repertoire—usually between the ages of 1 and 2 years. Regression is more likely if the child also shows symptoms of autism; between 15 and 30% of cases of autism report language regression. In one of the largest studies of language regression (Shinnar et al., 2001), over 90% of children who regressed when younger than 3 years of age received diagnoses of autism. In contrast, language regression is very rare in developmental speech/language impairment (Pickles et al., 2007).

In general, investigations to date have been unhelpful in elucidating the cause or affecting the management of such children, although epileptiform activity on the EEG is widely reported. Epileptiform EEGs occur in children with and without regression but are of uncertain significance, though there is a trend to greater epileptiform activity with regression than with no regression (Baird, Robinson, Boyd, & Charman, 2006; McVicar et al., 2005; Tuchman, Rapin, & Shinnar, 1991). It is not even clear that epileptiform is the most helpful terminology for these EEG manifestations. In autism regression occurs equally in those with and without epilepsy. As noted above, epileptiform EEGs are also found in SLI but with unclear relevance (Picard et al., 1998). However, in older children language regression without such clear-cut behavioral symptoms of autism does occur in association with, and is probably caused by, epilepsy in the perisylvian regions of the brain (Landau–Kleffner syndrome: see above).

SUMMARY OF MEDICAL INVESTIGATIONS IN SPEECH AND LANGUAGE PROBLEMS

- Hearing testing is mandatory.
- Routine tests—such as karyotype, imaging—have a low yield in children whose only symptom is language impairment.
- Comorbid mental retardation (learning problems), dysmorphic features, or neurological

signs increase the yield from imaging and karyotype.

- Presence of autism reduces the yield from tests.
- Specific speech disorder with physical examination abnormalities (e.g., skin lesions, neurological signs, structural abnormalities, dysmorphology) or specific syndromes increases the yield from imaging and karyotype.

Loss of language without autism should prompt investigation with sleep EEG to look for epilepsy with electrical status epilepticus during slow sleep (ESES).

REFERENCES

American Psychiatric Association (1994). *Diagnostic and Statistical Manual of Mental Disorders* (4th ed.). Washington, DC: Author.

Baird, G., Robinson, R. O., Boyd, S., & Charman, T. (2006). Sleep electroencephalograms in young children with autism with and without regression. *Developmental Medicine & Child Neurology, 48,* 604–608.

Barton, M., Robins, D., & Fein, D. (1999). *Modified Checklist for Autism in Toddlers (M-CHAT) Form.* Retrieved on March 18, 2008 from http://www2 .gsu.edu/~wwwpsy/faculty/robins.htm

Bates, E. A. (2004). Commentary. Explaining and interpreting deficits in language development across clinical groups: Where do we go from here? *Brain and Language, 88,* 248–253.

Beitchman, J., Wilson, B., Johnson, C., Atkinson, L., Young, A., Adlaf, E., et al. (2001). Fourteen-year follow-up of speech/language-impaired and control children: Psychiatric outcome. *Journal of the American Academy of Child and Adolescent Psychiatry, 40,* 75–82.

Bergman, R. L., Piacentini, J., & McCracken, J. T. (2002). Prevalence and description of selective mutism in a school-based sample. *Journal of the American Academy of Child and Adolescent Psychiatry, 41,* 938–946.

Bernal, B., & Altman, N. R. (2003). Speech delay in children: A functional MR imaging study. *Radiology, 229,* 651–658.

Bhutta, A. T., Cleves, M. A., Casey, P. H., Cradock, M. M., & Anand, K. J. S. (2002). Cognitive and behavioral outcomes of school-aged children who were born preterm: A meta-analysis. *Journal of the American Medical Association, 288,* 728–737.

Bishop, D. V. M. (2003). *The Children's Communication Checklist* (Version 2). London: The Psychological Corporation.

Bishop, D. V. M., & Edmundson, A. (1987). Language-impaired 4-year-olds: Distinguishing transient from persistent impairment. *Journal of Speech and Hearing Disorders, 52,* 156–173.

Brock, J. (2007). Language abilities in Williams syndrome: A critical review. *Development and Psychopathology, 19,* 97–127.

Broomfield, J., & Dodd, B. (2004). Children with speech and language disability: Caseload characteristics. *International Journal of Language and Communication Disorders, 39,* 303–324.

Christensen, K., Petersen, N., Skytthe, A., Herskind, A. M., McGue, M., & Bingley, P. (2006). Comparison of academic performance of twins and singletons in adolescence: Follow-up study. *British Medical Journal, 333,* 1095–1097.

Clark, M., Carr, L., Reilly, S., & Neville, B. G. R. (2000). Worster-Drought syndrome, a mild tetraplegic perisylvian cerebral palsy: Review of 47 cases. *Brain, 123,* 2160–2170.

Clegg, J., Hollis, C., Mawhood, L., & Rutter, M. (2005). Developmental language disorders—a follow-up in later adult life: Cognitive, language and psychosocial outcomes. *Journal of Child Psychology and Psychiatry, 46,* 128–149.

Conti-Ramsden, G., Simkin, Z., & Botting, N. (2006). The prevalence of autistic spectrum disorders in adolescents with a history of specific language impairment (SLI). *Journal of Child Psychology and Psychiatry, 47,* 621–628.

Conti-Ramsden, G., Simkin, Z., & Pickles, A. (2006). Estimating familial loading in SLI: A comparison of direct assessment versus parental interview. *Journal of Speech, Language, and Hearing Research, 49,* 88–101.

Cunningham, C., McHolm, A., Boyle, M., & Patel, S. (2006). Behavioral and emotional adjustment, family functioning, academic performance, and social relationships in children with selective mutism. *Journal of Child Psychology and Psychiatry, 45,* 1363–1372.

Fenson, L., Dale, P. S., Reznick, J. S., Bates, E., Thal, D. J., & Pethick, S. J. (1994). Variability in early communicative development. *Monographs of the Society for Research in Child Development, 59*(5).

Flax, J. F., Realpe-Bonilla, T., Hirsch, L. S., Brzustowicz, L. M., Bartlett, C. W., & Tallal, P. (2003). Specific language impairment in families: Evidence for co-occurrence with reading problems. *Journal of Speech, Language, and Hearing Research, 46,* 530–543.

Glascoe, F. P., & Robertshaw, N. S. (2006). *Parents' Evaluation of Developmental Status: Developmental Milestones (PEDS: DM).* Nashville, TN: Ellsworth & Vandermeer.

Herbert, M. R., Ziegler, D. A., Deutsch, C. K., O'Brien, L. M., Kennedy, D. N., Filipek, P. A., et al. (2005). Brain asymmetries in autism and developmental language disorder: A nested whole-brain analysis. *Brain, 128,* 213–226.

Hill, E. L. (2001). Non-specific nature of specific language impairment: A review of the literature with regard to concomitant motor impairments. *International Journal of Language & Communication Disorders, 36,* 149–171.

Howlin, P., & Cross, P. (1994). The variability of language test scores in 3- and 4-year-old children of normal non-verbal intelligence: A brief research report. *European Journal of Disorders of Communication, 29,* 279–288.

Jansen, A., & Andermann, E. (2005). Genetics of the polymicrogyria syndromes. *Journal of Medical Genetics, 42,* 369–378.

Jocelyn, L. J., Penko, M. A., & Rode, H. L. (1996). Cognition, communication, and hearing in young children with cleft lip and palate and in control children: A longitudinal study. *Pediatrics, 97,* 529–534.

Jusczyk, P. W. (1997). *The discovery of spoken language.* Cambridge, MA: MIT Press.

Kennedy, C. R., McCann, D. C., Campbell, M. J., Law, C. M., Mullee, M., Petrou, S., et al. (2006). Language ability after early detection of permanent childhood hearing impairment. *New England Journal of Medicine, 354,* 2131–2141.

Kini, U., Adab, N., Vinten, J., Fryer, A., Clayton-Smith, J., on behalf of the Liverpool and Manchester Neurodevelopmental Study Group. (2006). Dysmorphic features: An important clue to the diagnosis and severity of fetal anticonvulsant syndromes. *Archives of Disease in Childhood: Fetal and Neonatal Edition, 91,* F90–95.

Koomen, I., Grobbee, D. E., Roord, J. J., Donders, R., Jennekens-Schinkel, A., & van Furth, A. M. (2003). Hearing loss at school age in survivors of bacterial meningitis: Assessment, incidence, and prediction. *Pediatrics, 112,* 1049–1053.

Kuhl, P. K. (2004). Early language acquisition: Cracking the speech code. *Nature Reviews Neuroscience, 5,* 831–843.

Law, J., Boyle, J., Harris, F., Harkness, A., & Nye, C. (1998). Screening for speech and language delay: A systematic review of the literature. *Health Technology Assessment, 2.*

Law, J., Garrett, Z., & Nye, C. (2004). The efficacy of treatment for children with developmental speech and language delay/disorder: A meta-analysis. *Journal of Speech, Language, and Hearing Research, 47,* 924–943.

Laws, G., & Bishop, D. V. M. (2004). Verbal deficits in Down's syndrome and specific language impairment: A comparison. *International Journal of Language and Communication Disorders, 39,* 423–451.

Le Couteur, A., & Gardner, F. (2008). Use of structured interviews and observational methods in clinical settings. In M. Rutter, D. Bishop, D. Pine, S. Scott, J. Stevenson, E. Taylor, & A. Thapar (Eds.), *Rutter's child and adolescent psychiatry* (5th ed.). Oxford: Blackwell.

Lenneberg, E. H. (1967). *Biological foundations of language.* New York: Wiley.

Leonard, C., Eckert, M., Given, B., Virginia, B., & Eden, G. (2006). Individual differences in anatomy predict reading and oral language impairments in children. *Brain, 129,* 3329–3342.

Macayran, J. F., Cederbaum, S. D., & Fox, M. A. (2006). Diagnostic yield of chromosome analysis in patients with developmental delay or mental retardation who are otherwise nondysmorphic. *American Journal of Medical Genetics, 140A,* 2320–2323.

Manassis, K., Fung, D., Tannock, R., Sloman, L., Fiksenbaum, L., & McInnes, A. (2003). Characterizing selective mutism: Is it more than social anxiety? *Depression and Anxiety, 18,* 153–161.

McVicar, K. A., Ballaban-Gil, K., Rapin, I., Moshé, S. L., & Shinnar, S. (2005). Epileptiform EEG abnormalities in children with language regression. *Neurology, 65,* 129–131.

Meador, K., Baker, G., Finnell, R., Kalayjian, L., Liporace, J., Loring, D., Mawer, G., Pennell, P., Smith, J., Wolff, M., for the NEAD Study Group. (2006). In utero antiepileptic drug exposure: Fetal death and malformations. *Neurology, 67,* 407–412.

Mewasingh, L., Kadhim, H., Christophe, C., Christiaens, F., & Dan, B. (2003). Nonsurgical cerebellar mutism (anarthria) in two children. *Pediatric Neurology, 28,* 59–63.

Michelotti, J., Charman, T., Slonims, V., & Baird, G. (2002). Follow-up of children with language delay and features of autism from preschool years to middle childhood. *Developmental Medicine & Child Neurology, 44,* 812–819.

Mukherjee, R., Hollins, S., & Turk, J. F. (2006). Fetal alcohol spectrum disorder: An overview. *Journal of the Royal Society of Medicine, 99,* 298–302.

Mutton, D., & Lea, J. (1980). Chromosome studies of children with specific speech and language delay. *Developmental Medicine & Child Neurology, 22,* 588–594.

Nation, K., Clarke, P., Marshall, C. M., & Durand, M. (2004). Hidden language impairments in children: Parallels between poor reading comprehension and specific language impairment? *Journal of Speech, Language, and Hearing Research, 47,* 199–211.

National Initiative for Autism Screening and Assessment. (2003). *National autism plan for children (NAPC).* London: National Autistic Society.

Nelson, H. D., Nygren, P., Walker, M., & Panoscha, R. (2006). Screening for speech and language delay in preschool children: Systematic evidence review for the US Preventive Services Task Force. *Pediatrics, 117,* e298–319.

Northcott E., Connolly, A. M., Berroya, A., Sabaz, M., McIntyre, J., Christie, J., et al. (2005). The neuropsychological and language profile of children with benign Rolandic epilepsy. *Epilepsia, 46*(6), 924–930.

O'Leary, C. (2004). Fetal alcohol syndrome: Diagnosis, epidemiology, and developmental outcomes. *Journal of Pediatrics and Child Health, 40,* 2–7.

Óskarsdóttir, S., Persson, C., Eriksson, B., & Fasth, A. (2005). Presenting phenotype in 100 children with the 22q11 deletion syndrome. *European Journal of Pediatrics, 164,* 146–153.

Paul, R. (1996). Clinical implications of the natural history of slow expressive language development. *American Journal of Speech-Language Pathology, 5,* 5–21.

Picard, A., Heraut, F. C., Bouskraoui, M., Lemoine, M., Lacert, P., & Delattre, J. (1998). Sleep EEG and developmental dysphasia. *Developmental Medicine & Child Neurology, 40,* 595–599.

Pickles, A., Simonoff, E., Conti-Ramsden, G., Falcaro, M., Simkin, Z., Charman, et al. (2007). *Loss of language in early development of autism and specific language impairment.* Manuscript submitted for publication.

Pruden, S. M., Hirsh-Pasek, K., & Golinkoff, R. M. (2006). The social dimension in language development: A rich history and a new frontier. In P. Marshall & N. Fox (Eds.), *The development of social engagement: Neurobiological perspectives* (pp. 118–152). New York: Oxford University Press.

Rapin, I., & Allen, D. (1983). Developmental language disorders: Nosologic considerations. In U. Kirk (Ed.), *Neuropsychology of language, reading, and spelling* (pp. 155–184). New York: Academic Press.

Ratcliffe, S. (1999). Long term outcome in children of sex chromosome abnormalities. *Archives of Disease in Childhood, 80,* 192–195.

Renfrew, C. (1991). *The Bus Story: A test of continuous speech.* Bicester, UK: Winslow Press.

Roberts, J. E., Rosenfeld, R. M., & Zeisel, S. A. (2004). Otitis media and speech and language: A meta-analysis of prospective studies. *Pediatrics, 113,* e238–248.

Robinson, R. J. (1991). Causes and associations of severe and persistent specific speech and language disorders in children. *Developmental Medicine & Child Neurology, 33,* 943–962.

Robinson, R. O., Baird, G., Robinson, G., & Simonoff, E. (2001). Landau–Kleffner syndrome: Course and correlates with outcome. *Developmental Medicine & Child Neurology, 43,* 243–247.

Rosenfeld, R. M., Culpepper, L., Doyle, K. J., Grundfast, K. M., Hoberman, A., Kenna, M. A., et al. (2004). Clinical practice guideline: Otitis media with effusion. *Otolaryngology—Head and Neck Surgery, 130*(5, Suppl. 1), S95–S118.

Rutter, M., Bailey, A., & Lord, C. (2003). *Social Communication Questionnaire (SCQ).* Los Angeles, CA: Western Psychological Services.

Sackett, D., Haynes, R., Tugwell, P., & Guyatt, G. (1991). *Clinical epidemiology: A basic science for clinical medicine* (2nd ed.). Boston, MA: Little Brown.

Semel, E., Wiig, E. H., & Secord, W. A. (2004). *Clinical evaluation of language fundamentals* (4th ed.). San Antonio, TX: Harcourt Assessment.

Shevell, M. I., Majnemer, A., Rosenbaum, P., & Abrahamowicz, M. (2000a). Etiologic yield in single domain developmental delay: A prospective study. *Journal of Pediatrics, 137,* 633–637.

Shevell, M. I., Majnemer, A., Rosenbaum, P., & Abrahamowicz, M. (2000b). Etiologic yield of subspecialists' evaluation of young children with global developmental delay. *Journal of Pediatrics, 136,* 593–598.

Shevell, M. I., Majnemer, A., Webster, R. I., Platt, R. W., & Birnbaum, R. (2005). Outcomes at school age of preschool children with developmental language impairment. *Pediatric Neurology, 32,* 264–269.

Shinnar, S. S., Rapin, I., Arnold, S., Tuchman, R., Shulman, L., Ballaban-Gil, K., et al. (2001). Language regression in childhood. *Paediatric Neurology, 24,* 183–189.

Shriberg, L. D., Tomblin, J. B., & McSweeny, J. L. (1999). Prevalence of speech delay in 6-year-old children and comorbidity with language impairment. *Journal of Speech, Language, and Hearing Research, 42,* 1461–1481.

Silva, P., McGee, R., & Williams, S. (1983). Developmental language delay from 3 to 7 years and its significance for low intelligence and reading difficulties at age seven. *Developmental Medicine & Child Neurology, 25,* 783–793.

Snowling, M., Bishop, D. V. M., & Stothard, S. E. (2000). Is preschool language impairment a risk factor for dyslexia in adolescence? *Journal of Child Psychology and Psychiatry, 41,* 587–600.

Spaulding, T. J., Plante, E., & Farinella, K. A. (2006). Eligibility criteria for language impairment: Is the low end of normal always appropriate? *Language, Speech, and Hearing Services in Schools, 37,* 61–72.

Srour, M., Mazer, B., & Shevell, M. I. (2006). Analysis of clinical features predicting etiologic yield in the assessment of global developmental delay. *Pediatrics, 118,* 139–145.

Steinhausen, H. C., Wachter, M., Laimbock, K., & Metzke, C. W. (2006). A long-term outcome study of selective mutism in childhood. *Journal of Child Psychology and Psychiatry, 47,* 751–756.

Stevenson, J., & Richman, N. (1978). Behaviour, language and development in three-year-old children. *Journal of Autism and Childhood Schizophrenia, 8,* 299–313.

Tager-Flusberg, H. (2006). Defining language phenotypes in autism. *Clinical Neuroscience Research, 6(3–4),* 219–224.

Tomblin, J. B., Hafeman, L. L., & O'Brien, M. (2003). Autism and autism risk in siblings of children with specific language impairment. *International Journal of Language and Communication Disorders, 38,* 235–250.

Tomblin, J. B., Records, N. L., Buckwalter, P., Zhang, X., Smith, E., & O'Brien, M. (1997). Prevalence of specific language impairment in kindergarten children. *Journal of Speech, Language, and Hearing Research, 40,* 1245–1260.

Tuchman, R. F., Rapin, I., & Shinnar, S. (1991). Autistic and dysphasic children: II. Epilepsy. *Journal of Pediatrics, 88,* 1219–1225.

Wake, M., Poulakis, Z., Hughes, E., Carey-Sargeant, C., & Rickards, F. (2005). Hearing impairment: A population study of age at diagnosis, severity, and language outcomes at 7–8 years. *Archives of Disease in Childhood, 90,* 238–244.

Webster, R. I., Erdos, C., Evans, K., Majnemer, A., Kehayia, E., Thordardottir, E., et al. (2006). The clinical spectrum of developmental language impairment in school-aged children: Language, cognitive, and motor findings. *Pediatrics, 118,* E1541–E1549.

Webster, R. I., & Shevell, M. I. (2004). Neurobiology of specific language impairment. *Journal of Child Neurology, 19,* 471–481.

2

Short-term memory in children with developmental language disorder

Maggie Vance

INTRODUCTION

Many practitioners working with children with language impairments (LI) report the difficulty that these children appear to have with retaining verbal information. Research confirms these observations: as a group, children with LI do less well across a range of short-term memory (STM) and working memory (WM) tasks than do typically developing children (Archibald & Gathercole, 2006a; Montgomery, 2003). Findings also suggest that any difficulty children with LI have with retaining information in the short term may not be confined to verbal material (Archibald & Gathercole, 2006a; Bavin, Wilson, Maruff, & Sleeman, 2005).

A key issue of debate has been the nature of the relationship between STM/WM difficulties and LI. In particular, are STM deficits a cause or a consequence of LI, or do STM deficits and LI both arise as correlated symptoms of some other underlying factor (see Figure 2.1)? It has been suggested (cf. Gathercole & Baddeley, 1990) that STM deficits have a limiting effect on language learning and play a causal role in LI. However, more recent work indicates that not all children with poor STM skills have language difficulties (Gathercole et al., 2005). Bishop (2006; see also chapter 5, this volume) has argued that there is no single cause of LI, so that limitations to STM in itself may not be sufficient to "cause" language impairment. It is also possible that the development of STM might be affected by a child's

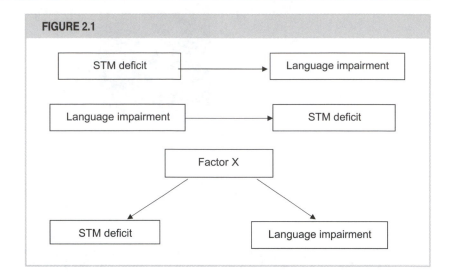

FIGURE 2.1

Possible relationships between STM deficits and language impairment

language. The STM skills of children with LI were found by van der Lely and Howard (1993) to be poorer than those of children of the same age, but similar to those of younger children with the same level of language skills. A third possibility is that some underlying difficulty (Factor X in Figure 2.1) will have an impact on both language and STM development. The research literature indicates that the ability to process speech—to recognize what is heard, store information about spoken words, and produce speech relatively accurately—impacts on STM and WM skills. In this chapter I explore the role of speech processing in STM and WM and highlight some of the findings demonstrating that children with LI process spoken material less efficiently.

MODELS OF MEMORY

The terminology used to describe memory deficits in children with LI is a potential source of confusion. Many terms are used, including STM, phonological STM, auditory memory, auditory-verbal memory, verbal STM, WM, phonological WM, and verbal WM. It would be helpful to

clarify what aspects of memory these terms refer to. It is possible to be clear about the distinction between STM and WM. STM generally refers to the temporary storage and recall of untransformed material—for instance, when a child repeats verbatim what she or he has heard. WM is used to describe the storage and recall of material that has been processed in some way. The difference between these two types of memory is best demonstrated by considering two tasks used to measure them. In a STM task such as digit recall, the child is asked to repeat a series of digits in the order they were heard. However, for backwards digit recall the child is asked to repeat the digits in reverse order. This is, therefore, a WM task, as the material being recalled is processed—that is, the order is changed, and not repeated verbatim. WM is involved in complex tasks such as comprehension, learning, and reasoning (Baddeley, 2000).

STM and WM are mechanisms for storage and recall of a range of material, including visuospatial information. The terms *verbal* and *phonological* STM or WM indicate storage and recall of speech-based material, although use of verbal and phonological to describe STM and WM do not appear to be used differentially in the literature. This chapter focuses on the recall of spoken material, as this is the more pertinent in work with LI children.

This chapter also addresses immediate recall of material, and it is important to clarify STM or WM in the context of longer-term memory. One observation often made about children with LI is that they do not remember, from one day to the next, vocabulary or concepts that have been presented. Remembering something that was done the day before, or even the lesson before, relies on long-term memory. STM is temporary and measured in seconds, generally not more than a minute or two, not hours or days. However, STM skills do impact on long-term memory. For learning to take place, material needs to be held temporarily in STM, while long-term representations are being established, so that information can be stored in long-term memory. In the case of word learning—a difficulty for many children with LI—the child has to temporarily store phonological and semantic information about an item while lexical representations are being laid down.

Working memory model

In order to better understand the difficulties faced by children with LI, it is helpful to consider current theoretical frameworks used to explore STM and WM. Much recent research has focused on the Working Memory Model first described by Baddeley and Hitch in 1974. The model had three components. The central executive is described as regulating and directing the flow of information through the STM system, and as retrieving information from long-term memory. There are two facilities for untransformed recall: the phonological loop for verbal material, and the visuo-spatial sketchpad for visual material (see Figure 2.2). The phonological loop functions as verbal or phonological STM, as material stored here is not processed. Speech-based material is held in a phonological store and actively rehearsed through the subvocal rehearsal mechanism. As indicated above, functioning of the phonological loop can be assessed by asking children to repeat a series of digits or words. Another measure that has been used is the repetition of nonwords. Children's digit or word span and/or their ability to repeat nonwords has been found to be significantly correlated with their vocabulary and grammatical development (Adams & Gathercole, 1995; Gathercole, Service, Hitch, Adams, & Martin, 1999; Masoura, Gathercole, & Bablekou, 2004).

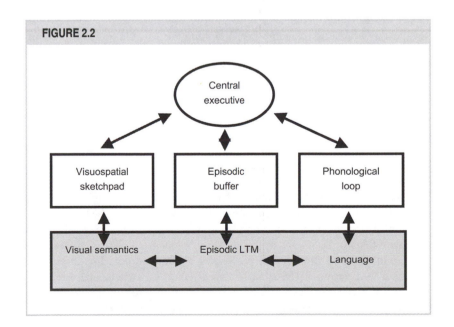

FIGURE 2.2

Central executive

Visuospatial sketchpad

Episodic buffer

Phonological loop

Visual semantics

Episodic LTM

Language

Revised Working Memory Model (this figure was published in Baddeley, 2000; copyright Elsevier, 2000).

Research findings indicate that both speech input and speech output factors, such as speech perception and speech rate, are related to STM span. For example, Norrelgen, Lacerda, and Forssberg (2001) reported that children's ability to discriminate similar-sounding single-syllable nonwords is significantly correlated with their ability to carry out a similar task for nonwords of increasing length, in which the perceptual differences were easy to identify but the memory demands were greater. A large body of literature has suggested that speech rate is significantly correlated with STM skills. Jarrold, Hewes, and Baddeley (2000) found that the speed at which children could articulate pairs of words was a significant predictor of their ability to recall a list of words. Key researchers in this field have suggested that functioning of the phonological loop relies on the same processing mechanisms as speech (Baddeley, 2000; Snowling & Hulme, 1994).

If this hypothesis is true, then it is likely that the integrity and efficiency of speech processing skills will have an impact on STM span, and that performance on STM tasks might reflect speech processing limitations as much as memory limitations. The interaction of STM with speech processing skills is also evident when we consider that children's ability to recall lists of words is affected by a range of phonological features of those words. This includes how phonologically similar the words are to each other, how long the words are (Henry, 1991), and the phonological complexity of the words (Service, 1998; Vance, 2001). However, any influence of speech processing on STM does not seem to require peripheral speech output processing skills. Evidence from Bishop and Robson (1989) shows that individuals with either no speech or impaired speech output, as a result of anarthria or dysarthria, respond to STM tasks in the same way as those with normal speech. These authors suggest that STM processes rely on abstract phonological representations rather than on the ability to actually articulate the words.

As well as reflecting speech processing skills for input and output, STM span is also affected by stored lexical representations. Children are able to recall more words when the words are more familiar and occur more frequently in the language (Majerus & van der Linden, 2003). They are also able to recall more words than nonwords; however, this is only observable in children over 5 years (Turner, Henry, & Smith, 2000). Hulme et al. (1997) accounted for these findings by describing a redintegration process in STM. Partially degraded memory traces are "reconstructed" or "filled in" using long-term knowledge and "best guess" as to what the word is. These top-down processes rely on existing lexical representations.

Baddeley, Gathercole, and Papagno (1998) argued that the role of the phonological loop is to support learning of the phonological structure of language, vocabulary in particular, and that children with language learning problems are likely to have a phonological loop deficit. Numerous studies report that children with LI perform poorly on tasks purporting to measure phonological loop functioning, such as word recall, digit recall, and nonword repetition (NWR) (see Montgomery, 2003, for a review). However, children with LI also have poor speech processing skills, such as greater difficulty in recognizing differences between similar-sounding syllables (Ziegler, Pech-Georgel, George, Alario, & Lorenzi, 2005) and in inaccurate speech production (Yont, Miccio, & Hewitt, 2002). In addition, children with LI also have impoverished vocabularies (Hick, Botting, & Conti-Ramsden, 2005) and so are less able to use top-down processes to support recall. Maniela-Arnold and Evans (2005) reported that degraded lexical representations underlie the difficulty in recall for LI children, as they had greater difficulty with recall of low-frequency words, but not with high-frequency words.

The central executive is the component of this model involved in WM, rather than STM. It does not have a storage function but, rather, is involved in the processing of material being held in the phonological loop or the visuospatial sketchpad. It has been difficult to identify the role of the central executive very precisely (Towse & Houston-Price, 2001). Baddeley (1996) suggested that it coordinates performance across separate tasks, switches between different retrieval strategies for recall, directs attention selectively to one source of information, and accesses long-term memory.

Central executive functioning is considered to affect tasks that require simultaneous processing and storage of material; it is assessed by tasks such as backward digit recall. There has been little research to date about the relationship between central executive functioning and language development. Adams, Bourke, and Willis (1999) found that children's performance on a task purporting to reflect the central executive significantly predicted their spoken language comprehension. However, the task used was a verbal fluency task that required retrieval of information from long-term memory and relied on existing language knowledge, which would also be implicated in language comprehension.

There is some evidence that children with LI have difficulties with central executive functioning. Children with LI have difficulty with simultaneous processing in a task involving sentence comprehension and nonword repetition (Marton & Schwartz, 2003). Archibald and Gathercole (2006a) report that children with LI perform poorly on both phonological loop (STM) and central executive (WM) tasks. Gathercole et al. (2005) suggested that children with STM deficits but adequate WM abilities early in development had age-appropriate language skills by age 8. On the other hand, children with poor WM but intact STM were experiencing a range of learning difficulties by that age. They suggested that children diagnosed with LI have both STM and WM deficits. Gathercole and colleagues (2005; Gathercole, Willis, Emslie, & Baddeley, 1992) have argued that STM skills are more critical for language development early in development, but factors such as conceptual ability and exposure to spoken and written language override any influence from STM as children get older.

The Working Memory Model has more recently been refined (Baddeley, 2000) to include a component called the *episodic buffer* (see Figure 2.2). This is described as a limited-capacity system that provides temporary storage of information in a multimodal code. It integrates information from the subsidiary WM systems and from long-term memory into a unitary "episodic" representation. The process focuses on the integration of information, rather than on separate subsystems. There is

a flow of information in both directions between long-term memory and the episodic buffer, which suggests that this component of WM may be involved in learning (Alloway, Gathercole, Willis, & Adams, 2004). Sentence recall is described as demonstrating the functioning of the episodic buffer because it "involves the integration of information from temporary memory subsystems (to support the verbatim recall of individual words and their order) with the products of semantic and syntactic analysis by the language processing system" (Alloway et al., 2004, p. 89). There is limited evidence that children's sentence recall performance is significantly associated with language, literacy, and a range of other measures (Alloway et al., 2005); however, the functioning of the episodic buffer and the role it plays in LI is as yet uncertain.

Capacity theory

The capacity theory of language comprehension has also been investigated in relation to LI. This theory describes working-memory capacity as being shared between processing and storage (Just & Carpenter, 1992) and is typically assessed using a Competing Language Processing task (Gaulin & Campbell, 1994). In this task, children hear a series of sentences such as "Carrots can *dance*," "Water is *dry*," and "sugar is *sweet*." The processing component of the task requires them to make a true-or-false judgment to each sentence in turn. After hearing sentence sets of varying lengths, the storage component is measured by asking the children to recall the last word at the end of each sentence in the set—for example, "dance, dry, sweet."

This model is compatible with the Working Memory Model described above. It corresponds approximately to the central executive and does not incorporate modality-specific storage systems. It is more explicit in terms of how the two functions of processing and storage interact. Within this theory, attention is given to how early parts of a sentence may be forgotten if later parts of the sentence demand extra processing. It refers to simultaneous processing of material, so that several elements of a sentence are being processed at the same time. If, in the course of an activity, the available capacity is exceeded, then processing will slow down, and some elements may be forgotten, described by Just and Carpenter (1992) as "capacity constrained comprehension." If mental processes are efficient, then more information or material can be retained. The model predicts that when a task is easy, there is less difference in performance between individuals with different WM capacities, but when the task is complex or demanding, there may be large differences in performance.

Within capacity theory, individual differences in working memory are seen as reflecting differences in capacity available for storage and the amount of processing involved in the task being carried out. Thus, if processing of material is more demanding, then less capacity will be available for storage. Examples from studies with adults show that fewer words are recalled when presented against a white-noise background, in an unfamiliar dialect, or in synthetic speech (Luce, Feustel, & Pisoni, 1983; Mattingly, Studdert-Kennedy, & Megan, 1983; Rabbitt, 1968; all cited in Brady, 1991). Figure 2.3 depicts this trade-off: If a quarter of the available capacity is used for processing (Figure 2.3a), then three-quarters is available for storage. However, if processing is more difficult, then half of the capacity may be used for

processing, with only half left for storage (Figure 2.3b). Finally, if little of the capacity is needed for processing, then much more is available for storage (see Figure 2.3c). Extrinsic factors, such as listening conditions and the material presented, or intrinsic factors, such as an individual's processing speed and efficiency, may affect the ease or difficulty of language processing.

In contrast to this view, Hitch and Baddeley (1976) suggest that processing and storage are distinct operations. Evidence for this came from an experiment in which they gave individuals a list of items, then presented a true–false judgment task, and finally asked them to recall the series of items. Processing of more complex true–false judgments did not have a negative effect on recall of the items. However, when participants were asked to rehearse the series of items they were recalling at the same time they carried out the true–false judgment task, performance on the more complex sentences was adversely affected. This suggests that when attention has to be divided between the separate processes of the judgment task and STM, there is an effect on the individual's ability to process the information.

Few studies have examined the relationship between working memory, as described by the capacity theory and typical language development,

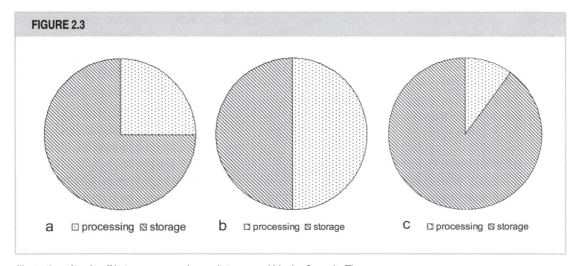

FIGURE 2.3

a   □ processing ☒ storage   b   □ processing ☒ storage   c   □ processing ☒ storage

Illustration of trade-off between processing and storage, within the Capacity Theory.

although Gaulin and Campbell (1994) found that children's performance on the Competing Language Processing task was significantly correlated with their receptive vocabulary. A greater body of work has explored the memory capacity (sometimes called *functional working memory*) of children with LI within this framework. For example, Montgomery (2000a, 2000b) found that children with LI had a reduced capacity when compared with age-matched peers, but a capacity similar to that of younger children with the same language level. The predicted trade-off between processing and storage was reported in children with LI who had reduced recall when processing demands were increased (Montgomery, 2000a). Ellis Weismer, Evans, and Hesketh (1999) found that children with LI were as accurate in processing sentences in the Competing Language Processing task as typically developing children, but they recalled fewer words. Children with SLI may be experiencing greater difficulty processing input, for example, when listening to speech against background noise (Ziegler et al., 2005), or they may have difficulty processing the content of utterances because they are unfamiliar with the vocabulary and sentence structures used in the task. Both deficits could potentially constrain how much information children with LI are able to retain.

In typically developing children, global processing speed, as measured by scanning of figures and pictures, has been found to be directly related to memory span (Ferguson & Bowey, 2005). Miller, Kail, Leonard, and Tomblin (2001) found that LI children were slower to respond to both linguistic and nonlinguistic tasks than were typically developing children. Response times were measured for a range of linguistic tasks, including naming pictures, sentence comprehension, and grammaticality judgments. Children with LI were able to learn new words as well as typically developing children could, but only when these words were presented at a slow rate. They also produced significantly fewer new words that had been presented at a fast rate than did children of the same age and younger children who had a similar level of vocabulary knowledge (Ellis Weismer & Hesketh, 1996). A beneficial effect of a slower input

rate for children with LI was confirmed by Montgomery (2005). Children with LI were quickest to identify target words in a sentence when sentences were presented slowly, rather than at a normal or fast rate. They were also significantly slower than typically developing children to recognize the words when the sentences were presented at a normal or fast rate. These findings suggest that children with LI are less able to process language quickly, and that their processing is facilitated by slower presentation of language. If LI children do have inefficient or slow processing of verbal material, then the capacity theory would predict reduced storage of material.

MEMORY LIMITATIONS IN LI: A CLINICAL MARKER?

There is evidence that children with LI have both STM and WM difficulties (Archibald & Gathercole, 2006a), but the direction of causation is unclear. Poor STM may affect the ability to learn phonological forms of the language, and poor WM may constrain the ability to process and store verbal-based material in the course of language processing and other learning activity. On the other hand, our exploration of the models above indicates that either a processing difficulty or a language knowledge deficit would have some impact on STM and WM performance. Montgomery (2002) described how many children with LI are less efficient at processing language that is within the bounds of their linguistic knowledge, while others simply have poor language knowledge. Resources may be taken up to process this less familiar content.

However, there is some evidence that deficits in STM and/or WM cannot be attributed wholly to language deficit, as the memory limitations of children with LI appear to extend to nonverbal material. Bavin et al. (2005) reported that children with LI were less accurate in performing nonverbal visuospatial tasks relative to typically developing children. Archibald and Gathercole (2006a) also found poorer performance on visuospatial STM tasks in a substantial minority of their LI cohort. These authors found that the children's performance on visuospatial tasks was consistent with their language level. However, further investigations using a wider range of visuospatial memory tasks did not reveal differences between children with LI and their typically developing peers. Archibald and Gathercole (2006b) argued, therefore, that the memory deficits of children with LI are specific to the verbal domain.

Two specific tasks have been identified as clinical markers for LI: nonword repetition and sentence recall. Both of these tasks are considered to tax STM and are taken as evidence that children with LI have STM deficits. However, both tasks also rely on speech processing skills and existing language knowledge and may therefore reflect an interaction between memory and language.

Nonword repetition

A consistent finding in the literature is that children with LI have a particular deficit in NWR, and this deficit is apparent even when the initial LI has resolved itself (Bishop, North, & Donlan, 1996). NWR performance has been found to discriminate well between children with and without LI (Dollaghan & Campbell, 1998). Furthermore, in a comparison of several linguistic processing tasks, NWR was found to be one of the best predictors of LI in young children (Conti-Ramsden, 2003).

For a number of years NWR was considered a measure of phonological loop integrity; difficulties with NWR were taken to indicate a phonological STM or phonological WM deficit (Gathercole & Baddeley, 1990). It was argued that such a deficit could impair language learning because NWR taps the child's ability to accurately hold novel phonological information in store (Baddeley et al., 1998). Indeed, there is substantial evidence for a relationship between NWR and improvement in vocabulary in typical development, particularly at earlier stages (Gathercole, Willis, Emslie, & Baddeley, 1992; Jarrold, Baddeley, Hewes, Leeke, & Phillips, 2004). However, NWR also involves speech processing skills (Dollaghan, Biber, & Campbell, 1995; Leitao, Hogben, & Fletcher, 1997; Snowling, Chiat, & Hulme, 1991). Our own studies have shown that NWR was significantly correlated with speech output, as measured by picture naming, and speech input, as measured by a mispronunciation detection task, in typically developing children aged 3 to 7 years (Vance, Donlan, & Stackhouse, 1999). These measures of speech input and output were at a single-word level, and a picture was present, minimizing STM or WM requirements. The correlations with NWR are therefore unlikely to reflect common memory demands. This suggests that children's NWR accuracy is determined to some extent by the accuracy of their speech processing skills.

Research also suggests that existing vocabulary knowledge supports NWR. Regardless of the child's native language, when nonwords are rated as being more word-like (e.g., prindle), young children repeat them more accurately than they do when the nonwords are less word-like (e.g., woogalamic) (Gathercole, 1995; van Bon & van der Pijl, 1997). Dollaghan et al. (1995) found that children repeated nonwords containing stressed syllables that corresponded to real single-syllable words (e.g.,/'bleɪməfət/) more accurately than nonwords in which no syllables corresponded to a real word (/'bliməfət/). These findings confirm that a process like redintegration, in which existing linguistic knowledge supports temporary storage, is likely to be involved in NWR.

More recent research has demonstrated that NWR taps a wider range of skills than does STM. For example, Archibald and Gathercole (2006a), who studied a group of children with LI who were much more impaired at NWR than other STM tasks, suggest that the NWR deficit in LI "does not originate solely from an impairment in verbal STM" but, rather, reflects "multiple indices of language impairment" (p. 687). The NWR difficulties that seem to be evident in very many children with LI may be as much a reflection of speech processing difficulties and reduced vocabulary knowledge, as of a STM deficit per se.

Sentence repetition

Another measure reported to be a clinical marker for LI is sentence repetition (Conti-Ramsden, Botting, & Faragher, 2001), which is considered to tap the functioning of the episodic buffer (Alloway et al., 2004). STM skills have been found to be related to children's sentence recall (Alloway et al., 2004; Blake, Austin, Cannon, Lisus, & Vaughan, 1994; Willis & Gathercole, 2001). However, Marshall and Nation (2003) suggested that sentence recall can be affected by processes other than STM; they found that children with poor reading comprehension showed intact digit span recall but poor sentence recall.

Sentence recall highlights the interaction between STM and the language processing system. For example, many more words can be recalled if they are grouped in meaningful sentences than those in unrelated word lists (e.g., Miller & Selfridge, 1950; cited in Willis & Gathercole, 2001). When errors do occur in recalling the verbatim form of sentences, the gist of the sentence is often preserved (Marshall & Nation, 2003), and substitutions tend to be with a synonym rather than an unrelated word (Alloway & Gathercole, 2005a). This suggests that existing language knowledge supports recall of sentences in a way similar to the redintegration process described for word recall. Findings from Vance and Drake (2007) support hypotheses that sentence recall reflects both language knowledge and STM skills. They found that sentence recall was highly correlated with both STM and receptive language skills in typically developing children. If sentence recall particularly reflects an interaction between language and STM, then LI children, who have reduced language knowledge and possibly a STM deficit, may be "doubly" disadvantaged. A recent body of research by Alloway and colleagues explores sentence recall in children with and without LI. For children with special educational needs, sentence recall was a better predictor of language skills than WM measures (Alloway & Gathercole, 2005b). Children with poorer phonological STM were also poorer at sentence recall (Alloway & Gathercole, 2005a)

ASSESSMENT

There are a number of published standardized assessments that measure aspects of STM and WM in children (Table 2.1). On the WMTB–C, children with LI perform at about 1 standard deviation below the normative mean on digit recall, word recall, nonword recall, listening recall, and backward digit recall (Archibald & Gathercole, 2006a). As a group, they achieved higher scores on the Word List Matching task, but lowest scores on Counting Recall (1.9 *SD* below the mean).

A number of standardized language assessments include a sentence recall task. While the child's overall score will indicate the presence/absence of a deficit, qualitative analysis of the errors they make might be more helpful in identifying whether recall is affected more by limitations in STM or by language knowledge. Vance and Drake (2007) propose a simple level of error analysis. Errors that indicate STM limitations on recall include those in which the order of items in the sentence has been changed: for example, "The ball was not thrown by the boy or the girl" becomes "*The ball was not thrown by the girl or the boy*." Memory for the surface form of the sentence is also implicated when the sentence is grammatically and semantically intact and the meaning is intact: for example, "The man in the house next door promised to water our flowers during our holiday" becomes "*The man who lived next door promised to water our flowers when we were on our holiday*." However, where meaning changed, this might indicate that the child did not understand the sentence: for example, "The man stopped to pick up some milk even though he was late for work" becomes "*The man who picked up some milk was too late for work*." Other language knowledge limitations are indicated if the child produces a sentence that is semantically or grammatically incorrect, such as "If she would have baked some biscuits, they would have been eaten" becoming the ungrammatical "*If she baked some biscuits, they would have been eateaned*."

It can be difficult to interpret the performance of children with LI on memory assessments. It is possible that a child may perform poorly on some tasks due to speech processing difficulties, limited language knowledge, and/or a lack of understanding of the task and of the concepts involved. For example, with the Listening Span task (WMTB–C; Pickering & Gathercole, 2001),

TABLE 2.1

Standardized assessments of aspects of STM and WM

Assessment	Task	Aspect of memory
Wechsler Intelligence Scale for Children (Wechsler, 2004)	Digit span	STM
	Backward digit span	WM
British Ability Scales (Elliott, Murray, & Pearson, 1983)	Digit span	STM
Working Memory Test Battery for Children (WMTB–C) (Pickering & Gathercole, 2001)	Digit span	Phonological loop
	Word span	Phonological loop
	Nonword span	Phonological loop
	Word-list matching [a]	Phonological loop
	Backwards digit span	Central executive
	Listening recall [b]	Central executive
	Counting recall [c]	Central executive
Children's Test of Non-Word Repetition (CNRep) (Gathercole & Baddeley, 1996)	Nonword repetition	STM
Test of Language Development (TOLD P–3) (Newcomer & Hammill, 1997)	Sentence recall	Episodic buffer
Clinical Evaluation of Language Fundamentals (CELF 4) (Semel, Wiig, & Secord, 2006)	Sentence recall	Episodic buffer

Note. STM = short-term memory; WM = working memory.

[a] The child hears a list of two or more words, which is then repeated either in the same order, e.g., "bed dot," "bed dot," or a different order, e.g., "rock dip," "dip rock." [b] Similar to Competing Language Processing task described earlier. [c] The child counts the number of dots in a series of arrays and then recalls the total number in each array.

if the child does not understand the notion of the sentences being correct or incorrect, or that they have to remember and repeat the *last* word in each sentence, their poor performance may not be the result of poor WM capacity. It is also important to ascertain that the child is familiar with the stimuli or material used—for example, digits for digit recall—as any lack of the necessary language knowledge, or a reduced familiarity with the words, will affect recall. It would be prudent to consider at what age a typically developing child is considered able to complete a memory task, to ensure that a child with LI has an equivalent level of verbal comprehension.

INTERVENTION

There are three strands to management and intervention for children with STM/WM deficits: developing phonological skills to support phonological loop functioning, developing strategies to support recall, and adapting the way in which material to be learnt or remembered is presented. There are few studies that address effectiveness of interventions for STM/WM either on memory or on language. The practitioner should consider the rationale for working on STM or WM skills as part of the intervention offered for each individual child. Depending on the child's profile, the aim of intervention may be to improve memory skills per se in a child who is presenting with STM difficulties but not with spoken language difficulties. For children with LI, increasing STM may or may not have an effect on a child's language. However, it may facilitate the child's functioning and ability to learn, through more efficient transfer to long-term memory (Vance & Mitchell, 2005). If the rationale for working on STM is to facilitate language development, then in addition to measurement of increases in STM span, the outcome should include some measurement of, for example, new word learning/vocabulary development.

Phonological skills

This approach is not considered to address phonological STM, but does address one of the potential consequences of poor STM: word learning. De Jong, Seveke, and van Veen (2000) trained children, aged 4–6 years, in phonological awareness skills, and this led to significantly better performance in learning new words. These authors suggest that phonological awareness training enhances the child's ability to analyze the phonological structure of new words. Gillam and van Kleeck (1996) argued that it is more useful to train phonological awareness than to train phonological WM directly, in that this can support the phonological coding and recoding needed for WM, and for reading. They found that improving phonological awareness skills in young children with LI using rhyme tasks improved the children's NWR abilities. However, neither of these studies demonstrated an improvement in STM or WM per se.

Strategy use

Turley-Ames and Whitfield (2003) defined strategies as "techniques intended to facilitate process-

ing and/or storage" (p. 447). They suggested that use of strategies accounts for individual variation in working memory and higher order cognitive tasks. Typically developing children appear to make increasingly greater use of rehearsal strategies as they get older, resulting in better performance on STM tasks (Henry & Millar, 1993). Intervention with typically developing children and adults suggests that teaching strategies to support recall is effective. Several different strategies have been reported to improve recall in students and adults.

A semantic strategy in which a sentence or story is created using the words to be remembered was found to be successful (McNamara & Scott, 2001; Turley-Ames & Whitfield, 2003). Verbal rehearsal requires the person recalling the material to repeat it to him/herself either overtly or subvocally, presumably maintaining material within the phonological loop. Turley-Ames and Whitfield (2003) found this had a beneficial effect on recall and, in particular, had a greater effect on students who had lower STM spans prior to the strategy training. These authors suggest that individuals with higher spans are already using effective strategies. A third strategy is visualization, in which the individual creates a visual image of the material to be recalled.

It appears that strategy training needs to be specific in order to improve recall. McNamara and Scott (2001) found that STM practice did not improve recall without strategy training. Schneider, Krin, Hunnerkopf, and Krajewski (2004) reported a wide range of variability in young children's recall following nonspecific teaching of strategy use. The children were just instructed to "do whatever they wanted to do with the items to improve recall" (p. 197). They found that children either spontaneously adopted one or more strategies and used them successfully, or they did not use any strategy at all, and consequently did not improve recall.

Few studies have reported the effect of strategy teaching with children with LI. Visual imagery was found to have more effect on improving STM than did developing verbal rehearsal for children with generalized language difficulties, but for children with reading difficulties the reverse was true, with use of a verbal rehearsal strategy having the greatest effect (Brady & Richman, 1994). Gill, Klecan-Aker, Roberts, and Fredenburg (2003) found that children with LI (aged 7–11 years) who were taught a rehearsal strategy or a rehearsal/ visualization strategy were better able to follow directions immediately posttraining than were those receiving traditional language therapy. However, in longer term follow-up, only the combined approach had an effect on performance. Others have found that teaching the use of visualization and verbal rehearsal strategies was no more effective for improving language comprehension than traditional intervention (Dixon, Joffe, & Bench, 2001). These authors suggest that the use of strategies places heavy demands on WM, and this may limit the effectiveness of this approach.

One potential difficulty is that strategy training and many of the strategies advocated are themselves mediated by language, and this may pose difficulties for children with LI. Nevertheless, strategies are potentially useful for word learning, by helping to maintain phonological information in temporary storage for longer, and in exploring the semantic properties of items. The use of strategy intervention to support STM and WM is further explored in Vance and Mitchell (2005), and therapy materials, such as memory bricks (Mitchell, 1994) and *Mastering Memory* (Mitchell, 2001), are commercially available.

Delivery of material

Consideration should be given to the way in which material is presented for language learning and other learning activities. The implications of capacity theory are that reducing the processing load increases the capacity available for storage. Processing load can be reduced by presenting new or less familiar material within familiar contexts. New vocabulary can be taught using short sentences with a familiar structure. New sentence structures should be introduced using familiar vocabulary. All learning can make use of familiar activities and routines, so that the child is not trying to work out the rules of a new game, or what he or she is being asked to do, while learning new vocabulary. It will also be helpful to in-

crease familiarity with the language the child does know, because well-known, established language will require less processing. Teachers and therapists often introduce new vocabulary or sentence structures too quickly, once a child appears to have mastered items taught earlier. However, the child may only have a tenuous knowledge of this earlier material, and it will require increased processing for some time. Use of a slower speaking rate, emphatic stress on key words, and frequent repetition has been shown to be beneficial in new word learning (Ellis Weismer & Hesketh, 1996; Montgomery, 2005).

A study by Riches, Tomasello, and Conti-Ramsden (2005) of verb-learning found that LI children needed twice as many presentations of the new items than typically developing children. They also benefited from learning activities being spaced over four days, rather than all being presented in a single day. This distributed learning across time is similar to the reviewing technique advocated by Mitchell (2000), in which new material is reviewed over slowly increasing time frames. The act of trying to recall material appears to help the development of long-term representations.

The use of visual material to reduce the need to retain information in STM while trying to complete a classroom task can be supported by the use of icons and self-generated visual material that aid recall, as described by Bristow, Cowley, and Daines (1999). Gathercole, Lamont, and Alloway (2006) made suggestions for presenting material and activities within the classroom to support children with WM difficulties, many of which are already considered good practice in working with LI children:

- keep instructions brief and simple, breaking them down into smaller constituents
- repeat instructions frequently
- ask the child to repeat an instruction back
- use external memory aids, such as unifix blocks in mathematics
- reduce the processing load of the task—for example, in sentence writing, by modifying the length and/or complexity of the sentence.

CONCLUSION

It seems that both STM and WM are affected by processing ability and/or language knowledge. There is also an interaction between memory and existing language knowledge. It is, therefore, unsurprising that children with LI tend to show reduced STM and WM. However, it is not clear whether memory deficits cause LI or are a consequence of language difficulties. It may be that difficulties with memory and with language are both symptoms of an underlying cognitive deficit, such as the ability to process speech.

Providing memory practice is unlikely to improve language skills. However, developing the use of strategies may improve a child's ability to recall verbal information. Reducing the processing load may also support language learning and recall.

REFERENCES

Adams, A. M., Bourke, L., & Willis, C. (1999). Working memory and spoken language comprehension in young children. *International Journal of Psychology, 34,* 364–373.

Adams, A. M., & Gathercole, S. E. (1995). Phonological working memory and speech production in pre-school children. *Journal of Speech and Hearing Research, 38,* 403–404.

Alloway, T. P., & Gathercole, S. E. (2005a). Working memory and short-term sentence recall in young children. *European Journal of Cognitive Psychology, 17,* 207–220.

Alloway, T. P., & Gathercole, S. E. (2005b). The role of sentence recall in reading and language skills of children with learning difficulties. *Learning and Individual Differences, 5,* 271–282.

Alloway, T. P., Gathercole, S. E., Adams, A. M., Willis, C., Eaglen, R., & Lamont, E. (2005). Working memory and phonological awareness as predictors of progress towards early learning goals at school entry. *British Journal of Developmental Psychology, 23,* 417–426.

Alloway, T. P., Gathercole, S. E., Willis, C., & Adams, A. M. (2004). A structural analysis of working memory and related cognitive skills in young children. *Journal of Experimental Child Psychology, 87,* 85–106.

Archibald, L. M. D., & Gathercole, S. E. (2006a). Short-term memory and working memory in specific language impairment. *International Journal of Language & Communication Disorders, 41,* 675–693.

Archibald, L. M. D., & Gathercole, S. E. (2006b). Visuospatial immediate memory in specific language impairment. *Journal of Speech Language and Hearing Research, 49,* 265–277.

Baddeley, A. (1996). Exploring the central executive. *Quarterly Journal of Experimental Psychology, 49A,* 5–28.

Baddeley, A. (2000). The episodic buffer: A new component of working memory. *Trends in Cognitive Sciences, 4,* 417–423.

Baddeley, A., Gathercole, S., & Papagno, C. (1998). The phonological loop as a language learning device. *Psychological Review, 105,* 158–173.

Baddeley, A., & Hitch, G. J. (1974). Working memory. In G. Bower (Ed.), *The psychology of learning and motivation* (Vol. 8, pp. 47–90). New York: Academic Press.

Bavin, E. L., Wilson, P. H., Maruff, P., & Sleeman, F. (2005). Spatio-visual memory of children with specific language impairment: Evidence for generalised processing problems. *International Journal of Language and Communication, 40,* 319–332.

Bishop, D. V. M. (2006). Developmental cognitive genetics: How psychology can inform genetics and vice versa. *Quarterly Journal of Experimental Psychology, 59,* 1153–1168.

Bishop, D. V. M., North, T., & Donlan, C. (1996). Nonword repetition as behavioural marker for inherited language impairment: Evidence from a twin study. *Journal of Child Psychology and Psychiatry, 37,* 391–405.

Bishop, D. V. M., & Robson, J. (1989). Unimpaired short-term memory and rhyme judgement in congenitally speechless individuals: Implications for the notion of "articulatory coding." *Quarterly Journal of Experimental Psychology, 41A,* 123–140.

Blake, J., Austin, W., Cannon, M., Lisus, A., & Vaughan, A. L. (1994). The relationship between memory span and measures of imitative and spontaneous language complexity in pre-school children. *International Journal of Behavioral Development, 1,* 91–107.

Brady, H. V., & Richman, L. C. (1994). Visual versus verbal mnemonic training effects on memory-deficient and language deficient sub groups of children with reading disability. *Developmental Neuropsychology, 10*, 335–347.

Brady, S. A. (1991). The role of working memory in reading disability. In S. A. Brady & D. Shankweiler (Eds.), *Phonological processes in literacy: A tribute to Isabelle Y. Liberman* (pp. 129–151). Hillsdale, NJ: Lawrence Erlbaum Associates.

Bristow, J., Cowley, P., & Daines, B. (1999). *Memory and learning: A practical guide for teachers*. London: David Fulton.

Conti-Ramsden, G. (2003). Processing and linguistic markers in young children with specific language impairment (SLI). *Journal of Speech Language and Hearing Research, 46*, 1029–1037.

Conti-Ramsden, G., Botting, N., & Faragher, B. (2001). Psycholinguistic markers for specific language impairment. *Journal of Child Psychology and Psychiatry and Allied Disciplines, 42*, 741–748.

De Jong, P. F., Seveke, M. J., & van Veen, M. (2000). Phonological sensitivity and the acquisition of new words in children. *Journal of Experimental Child Psychology, 76*, 275–301.

Dixon, G., Joffe, B., & Bench, R. J. (2001). The efficacy of visualising and verbalising: Are we asking too much? *Child Language Teaching and Therapy, 17*, 127–141.

Dollaghan, C., Biber, M. E., & Campbell, T. E. (1995). Lexical influences on nonword repetition. *Applied Psycholinguistics, 16*, 211–222.

Dollaghan, C., & Campbell, T. E. (1998). Nonword repetition and child language impairment. *Journal of Speech, Language, and Hearing Research, 41*, 1136–1146.

Elliott, C. D., Murray, D. J., & Pearson, L. S. (1983). *British Ability Scales*. Swindon, UK: NFER Nelson.

Ellis Weismer, S., Evans, J. L., & Hesketh, L. J. (1999). An examination of verbal working memory capacity in children with specific language impairment. *Journal of Speech, Language, and Hearing Research, 42*, 1249–1260.

Ellis Weismer, S., & Hesketh, L. J. (1996). Lexical learning by children with specific language impairment: Effects of linguistic input presented at varying speaking rates. *Journal of Speech and Hearing Research, 39*, 177–190.

Ferguson, A., & Bowey, J. A. (2005). Global processing speed as a mediator of developmental changes in children's auditory memory span. *Journal of Experimental Child Psychology, 91*, 89–112.

Gathercole, S. E. (1995). Is nonword repetition a test of phonological memory or long-term knowledge? It all depends on the nonwords. *Memory and Cognition, 23*, 83–94.

Gathercole, S. E., & Baddeley, A. D. (1990). Phonological memory deficits in language disordered children: Is there a causal connection? *Journal of Memory and Language, 29*, 336–360.

Gathercole, S. E., & Baddeley, A. (1996). *The Children's Test of Non-Word Repetition*. London: The Psychological Corporation.

Gathercole, S. E., Lamont, E., & Alloway, T. P. (2006). Working memory in the classroom. In S. Pickering (Ed.), *Working memory and education* (pp. 219–240). San Diego, CA: Elsevier.

Gathercole, S. E., Service, E., Hitch, G. J., Adams, A. M., & Martin, A. J. (1999). Phonological short-term memory and vocabulary development: Further evidence on the nature of the relationship. *Applied Cognitive Psychology, 13*, 65–77.

Gathercole, S. E., Tiffany, C., Briscoe, J., Thorn, A., & The ALSPAC Team. (2005). Developmental consequences of poor phonological short-term memory function in childhood: A longitudinal study. *Journal of Child Psychology and Psychiatry, 46*, 598–611.

Gathercole, S. E., Willis, C. S., Emslie, H., & Baddeley, A. D. (1992). Phonological memory and vocabulary development during the early school years: A longitudinal study. *Developmental Psychology, 28*, 887–898.

Gaulin, C. A., & Campbell, T. F. (1994). Procedure for assessing verbal working memory in normal school-age children: Some preliminary data. *Perceptual and Motor Skills, 79*, 55–64.

Gill, C. B., Klecan-Aker, J., Roberts, T., & Fredenburg, K. A. (2003). Following directions: Rehearsal and visualization strategies for children with specific language impairment. *Child Language Teaching and Therapy, 19*, 85–101.

Gillam, R. B., & van Kleeck, A. (1996). Phonological awareness training and short term memory: Clinical implications. *Topics in Language Disorders, 7*, 72–81.

Henry, L. (1991). The effects of word length and phonemic similarity in young children's STM. *Quarterly Journal of Experimental Psychology, 43A*, 35–52.

Henry, L. A., & Millar, S. (1993). Why does memory span improve with age? A review of the evidence for two current hypotheses. *European Journal of Cognitive Psychology, 5*, 241–287.

Hick, R. F., Botting, N., & Conti-Ramsden, G. (2005).

Short-term memory and vocabulary development in children with Down syndrome and children with specific language impairment. *Developmental Medicine & Child Neurology*, 47, 532–538.

Hitch, G. D., & Baddeley, A. D. (1976). Verbal reasoning and working memory. *Quarterly Journal of Experimental Psychology*, 28(4), 603–621.

Hulme, C., Roodenrys, S., Schweickart, R., Brown, G. D. A., Martin, S., & Stuart, G. (1997). Word frequency effects on short-term memory: Evidence for a redintegration process in immediate serial recall. *Journal of Experimental Psychology: Learning, Memory and Cognition*, 23, 1217–1232.

Jarrold, C., Baddeley, A. D., Hewes, A. K., Leeke, T. C., & Phillips, C. E. (2004). What links verbal short-term memory performance and vocabulary level? Evidence of changing relationships among individuals with learning disability. *Journal of Memory and Language*, 50, 134–148.

Jarrold, C., Hewes, A. K., & Baddeley, A. (2000). Do two separate speech measures constrain verbal short-term memory in children. *Journal of Experimental Psychology: Learning, Memory and Cognition*, 26, 1626–1637.

Just, M. A., & Carpenter, P. A. (1992). A capacity theory of comprehension: Individual differences in working memory. *Psychological Review*, 99(1), 122–149.

Leitao, S., Hogben, J., & Fletcher, J. (1997). Phonological processing skills in speech and language impaired children. *European Journal of Disorders of Communication*, 32, 91–111.

Luce, P. A., Feustel, T. C., & Pisoni, D. B. (1983) Capacity demands in short-term memory for synthetic and natural speech. *Human Factors*, 25, 17–32.

Majerus, S., & van der Linden, M. (2003), Long-term memory effects on verbal short-term memory: A replication study. *British Journal of Developmental Psychology*, 21, 303–331.

Maniela-Arnold, E., & Evans, J. L. (2005). Beyond capacity limitations: Determinants of word recall performance on verbal working memory span tasks in children with SLI. *Journal of Speech, Language, and Hearing Research*, 48, 897–909.

Marshall, C. M., & Nation, K. (2003). Individual differences in semantic and structural errors in children's memory for sentences. *Educational and Child Psychology*, 20, 7–18.

Marton, K., & Schwartz, R. G. (2003). Working memory capacity and language processes in children with specific language impairment. *Journal of Speech, Language, and Hearing Research*, 46, 1138–1153.

Masoura, E. V., Gathercole, S. E., & Bablekou, Z. (2004). Contributions of phonological short-term memory to vocabulary acquisition. *Psychology: The Journal of the Hellenic Psychological Society*, 11, 341–355.

Mattingly, I. G., Studdert-Kennedy, M., & Megan H. (1983, May). Paper presented at the meeting of the Acoustical Society of America. Cincinnati, Ohio.

McNamara, D. S., & Scott, J. L. (2001). Working memory capacity and strategy use. *Memory and Cognition*, 29, 10–17.

Miller, C. A., Kail, R., Leonard, L. B., & Tomblin, J. B. (2001). Speed of processing in children with specific language impairment. *Journal of Speech, Language, and Hearing Research*, 44, 416–433.

Miller, G., & Selfridge, J. (1950). Verbal context and the recall of meaningful material. *American Journal of Psychology*, 63, 176–187.

Mitchell, J. E. (1994). *Enhancing the teaching of memory using memory bricks*. London: Communication and Learning Skills Centre.

Mitchell, J. E. (2000). *Time to revise*. London: Communication and Learning Skills Centre.

Mitchell, J. E. (2001). *Mastering memory* (3rd ed.). London: Communication and Learning Skills Centre.

Montgomery, J. W. (2000a). Verbal working memory and sentence comprehension in children with specific language impairment. *Journal of Speech, Language, and Hearing Research*, 43, 293–308.

Montgomery, J. W. (2000b). Relation of working memory to off-line and real-time sentence processing in children with specific language impairment. *Applied Psycholinguistics*, 21, 117–148.

Montgomery, J. W. (2002). Understanding the language difficulties of children with specific language impairments: Does verbal working memory matter? *American Journal of Speech-Language Pathology*, 11, 77–91.

Montgomery, J. W. (2003). Working memory and comprehension in children with specific language impairment: What we know so far. *Journal of Communication Disorders*, 36, 221–231.

Montgomery, J. W. (2005). Effects of input rate and age on the real-time language processing of children with specific language impairment. *International Journal of Language & Communication Disorders*, 40, 171–188.

Newcomer, P. L., & Hammill, D. D. (1997). *Test of*

language development: Primary (3rd ed.). Austin, TX: PRO-ED.

Norrelgen, F., Lacerda, F., & Forssberg, H. (2001). Temporal resolution of auditory perception in relation to perception, memory, and language skills in typical children. *Journal of Learning Disabilities, 34*, 359–369.

Pickering, S., & Gathercole, S. (2001). *Working Memory Test Battery for Children*. London: The Psychological Corporation.

Rabbitt, P. M. (1968). Repetition effects and signal classification strategies in serial choice-response tasks. *Quarterly Journal of Experimental Psychology, 2*, 232–240.

Riches, N. G., Tomasello, M., & Conti-Ramsden, G. (2005). Verb learning in children with SLI: Frequency and spacing effects. *Journal of Speech, Language, and Hearing Research, 48*, 1397–1411.

Schneider, W., Krin, V., Hunnerkopf, M., & Krajewski, K. (2004). The development of young children's memory strategies: First findings from the Wurzburg Longitudinal Memory Study. *Journal of Experimental Child Psychology, 88*, 193–209.

Semel, E., Wiig, E. H., & Secord, W. A. (2006). *Clinical evaluation of language fundamentals* (4th ed.). London: The Psychological Corporation.

Service, E. (1998). The effect of word-length on immediate serial recall depends on phonological complexity, not articulatory duration. *Quarterly Journal of Experimental Psychology, 51A*, 283–304.

Snowling, M., Chiat, S., & Hulme, C. (1991). Words, nonwords, and phonological processes: Some comments on Gathercole, Willis, Emslie & Baddeley. *Applied Psycholinguistics, 12*, 369–373.

Snowling, M., & Hulme, C. (1994). The development of phonological skills. *Philosophical Transactions of the Royal Society of London, Series B: Biological Sciences, 346*, 21–27.

Towse, J. N., & Houston-Price, C. M. T. (2001). Reflections on the concept of the central executive. In J. Andrade (Ed.), *Working memory in perspective* (pp. 240–260). Hove, UK: Psychology Press.

Turley-Ames, K., & Whitfield, M. M. (2003). Strategy training and working memory performance, *Journal of Memory and Language, 49*, 446–468.

Turner, J. E., Henry, L. A., & Smith, P. T. (2000). The development of the use of long-term knowledge to assist short-term recall. *Quarterly Journal of Experimental Psychology, 53A*, 457–478.

van Bon, W. H. J., & van der Pijl, J. M. L. (1997). Effects of word length and wordlikeness on pseudoword repetition by poor and normal readers. *Applied Psycholinguistics, 18*, 101–114.

Vance, M. (2001). *Speech processing and short-term memory in children with normal and atypical speech and language development*. Unpublished doctoral dissertation, University of London, London, UK.

Vance, M., Donlan, C., & Stackhouse, J. (1999). Speech processing limitations on non-word repetition in children. In M. Garman, C. Letts, B. Richards, C. Schelletter, & S. Edwards (Eds.), *The New Bulmershe Papers series* (pp. 40–50). Reading, UK: Faculty of Education and Community Studies, University of Reading.

Vance, M., & Drake, J. (2007). *Sentence repetition in children: An interaction between short-term memory and language skills*. Manuscript in preparation.

Vance, M., & Mitchell, J. E. (2005). Short term memory: Assessment and intervention. In M. Snowling & J. Stackhouse (Eds.), *Dyslexia, speech and language: A practitioners handbook* (2nd ed.). London: Whurr.

van der Lely, H. K. J., & Howard, D. (1993). Children with specific language impairment or short-term memory deficit? *Journal of Speech and Hearing Research, 36*, 1193–1207.

Wechsler, D. (2004), *Wechsler Intelligence Scale for Children* (4th ed.). Oxford, UK: Harcourt Assessment.

Willis, C. S., & Gathercole, S. E. (2001). Phonological short-term memory contributions to sentence processing in young children. *Memory, 9*, 349–363.

Yont, K. M., Miccio, A. W., & Hewitt, L. E. (2002). Phonological breakdowns in children with specific language impairment. In F. Windsor, M. L. Kelly, & N. Hewlett (Eds.), *Investigations in clinical phonetics and linguistics* (pp. 161–168). Mahwah, NJ: Lawrence Erlbaum Associates.

Ziegler, J. C., Pech-Georgel, C., George, F., Alario, F. X., & Lorenzi, C. (2005). Deficits in speech perception predict language learning impairment. *Proceedings of the National Academy of Sciences USA, 102*, 14110–14115.

3

Using eye movements to investigate developmental language disorders

Kate Nation

INTRODUCTION

If a child is suspected to have a difficulty with comprehending language, there are many tools one could use to assess the nature and severity of their impairment. For example, one could administer standardized tests that require children to define words, to match pictures to words or to sentences, to follow a series of instructions, or to listen to sentences or dialogues and answer questions about their content. A suite of well-chosen assessments, in combination with close observation of a child in interaction with others, typically provides a wealth of information. It may reveal, for example, that the child has low vocabulary knowledge, or a difficulty interpreting complex sentences, or problems understanding figurative language. Such observations provide the clinician with a starting point for intervention and are used by researchers to define, characterize, and categorize the children who participate in their research studies. Beyond surface description and quantification, however, standard assessment instruments are quite blunt tools. They cannot reveal the underlying cause of a child's comprehension impairment—they cannot determine *why* a child has low vocabulary knowledge, difficulty interpreting complex sentences, or problems understanding complex sentences. *Why* questions can be addressed at many levels, as reflected in the broad range of perspectives brought together in this volume. For example, we can consider the biological bases of language impairment and ask what genetic factors are implicated (Bishop, chapter 5, and Newbury & Monaco, chapter 6, this volume), or ask about its neural basis (Dick, Richardson, & Saccuman, chapter 4, this volume). The aim of this chapter is to highlight the need to think about the nature of language *processing*, if we are to understand *why* some people find language comprehension so difficult.

The chapter is organized into four sections. First, we consider what is meant by "on-line" language processing, why it is important, and how this is best measured. We then turn to evidence from the psycholinguistics literature that serves to (a) highlight the complexities of language comprehension and (b) demonstrate the utility of eye movement paradigms as a tool to explore spoken language comprehension in skilled adults. Next we review the small number of published studies that have used these methods with children, before finally turning our attention to studies of language processing in people with language learning difficulties.

WHAT IS MEANT BY LANGUAGE PROCESSING?

Even the simplest utterances can be ambiguous. Individual words may be ambiguous if they have more than one meaning (e.g., the word *bank* can refer to a money bank or a river bank). Sentences can be syntactically ambiguous. For example, in the sentence "The French bottle smells," should *bottle* be interpreted as part of a noun phrase *French bottle* that happens to smell, or is *bottle* a verb, with French people doing the bottling of smells? Often, language is nonliteral. If we were to hear "Chomsky is on the shelf" in conversation, we are more likely to interpret this as one of Chomsky's books being on a bookshelf, rather than literally Chomsky himself. Our language is littered with figurative expressions, such as "pull your socks up": expressions that have mean-

ings quite different to their literal interpretations; newspaper headlines can make us smile with their accidental ambiguities such as "Drunk gets nine months in violin case" or "Juvenile court to try shooting defendant" (Pinker, 1994). Importantly, however, it is not just badly written headlines that are ambiguous, nor individual rogue words like *bank*, well-known idioms, or figurative expressions. As we listen to language as it unfolds in real time, ambiguities are everywhere. One hundred milliseconds or so into the acoustic realization of the word "Robert," the token is perfectly compatible with other lexical items, including robber and robin, to name but a few. Until we hear "in the box," the instruction "put the apple on the towel in the box" is ambiguous, as it could refer to an apple that is on the towel (which needs to be moved to the box) or the final destination for an apple. The magnitude of ambiguity that our language system has to cope with is illustrated by Gerry Altmann in his analysis of the phrase "time flies like an arrow" (Altmann, 1997, p. 85). We are all familiar with this as a figurative expression, but there are, in fact, at least 50 interpretations of the phrase; if we hear the phrase rather than see it written down, this rises to at least 100.

Thus, as language unfolds, its meaning is temporarily ambiguous and undetermined. Language processing can be defined as the set of mechanisms and sources of knowledge that we draw upon to resolve these local and (hopefully) temporary ambiguities. Language processing is complex, requiring sensitivity to phonological, syntactic, semantic, and pragmatic factors. As skilled users of our language, these sources of knowledge are so well tuned that we are rarely troubled by ambiguity, or even notice it. Typically developing children appear to take language learning in their stride, despite the deftness of skills they need to learn and quantity of knowledge they need to amass. For those children who have difficulty with comprehension, however, how do we begin addressing the question of *why* they have problems with processing language?

Traditionally, many studies have used what can be termed off-line tasks that measure the end point of comprehension. For example, we might ask a child what a word means, or ask him or her to listen to a story and then answer questions, or to listen to a word and point to the picture that matches the word. These tasks are complicated: they require children to follow instructions and to understand the task, to work out the language, and then to organize and output a response. If children fail such a task, it is impossible to know why they did: was it that they did not have the necessary knowledge, or were they unable to demonstrate their knowledge due to the metalinguistic or meta-cognitive demands of the task? Even if children give the correct answer, satisfactory processing can still not be assumed—it may be that they worked out the correct solution, but it took them a very long time. This would not be indicative of typical language processing, nor be any guarantee that they would be able to cope with the dynamics of language and the to-and-fro of conversational exchange.

In contrast to off-line tasks, on-line tasks allow inferences to be made about the processing of language itself, not just its endpoint. Our understanding of the temporal dynamics of sentence processing in skilled adults has long been informed by on-line measures such as reading time (Rayner, 1998). To borrow an example from Altmann (1997, p. 95), when participants read a sentence such as "Sam told the writer that he couldn't understand to get some help from a decent editor," eye movements during the reading of "to get" are disturbed, relative to when they read the same words in the almost identical sentence: "Sam asked the writer that he couldn't understand to get some help from a decent editor." This is because in the first sentence, the verb "told" sets up an expectation that the word "that" will introduce a message, rather than an embedded clause. Disruptions to eye movements are indicative of the processing difficulty participants experience as they read something that is not expected. As this method demands fluent reading ability, it is of limited utility for exploring processing in children with poor language, many of whom have concomitant difficulties with reading (Snowling & Hulme, chapter 11, this volume).

A small number of studies have used other on-line methods to investigate language processing in children with poor language (e.g., Montgom-

ery, 2000, 2006; Nation & Snowling, 1998, 1999; Tyler & Marslen-Wilson, 1981). However, the experimental methods they use still require participants to complete a task or make a decision, and none of the methods is well suited to exploring language processing in more naturalistic contexts. One paradigm that offers much promise to those interested in investigating language processing in children with poor language is the so-called visual world paradigm. This builds on work initially described by Cooper (1974) and introduced to the psycholinguistics community by Tanenhaus, Spivey-Knowlton, Eberhard, and Sedivy (1995). The method involves participants wearing a lightweight head-mounted eye-tracker,[1] or facing a remote tracking camera that sits beneath a computer monitor (Figure 3.1). The eye-tracker records their eye movements as they view a visual scene (which might comprise an array of real objects or of objects presented on

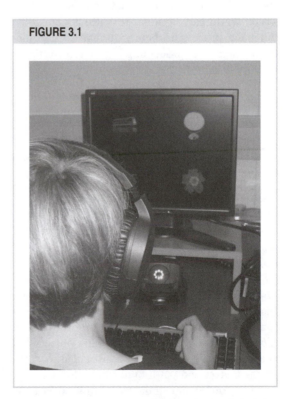

FIGURE 3.1

Remote eye-tracking system and picture displays typical of those used in visual world paradigms.

screen). At the same time, they are spoken stimuli that describe aspects al scene. As participants tend to look that serve as potential referents for the linguistic expressions they hear, eye movements can reveal how long participants take to establish reference. Experimental manipulations (of the language, or of the scene) then allow the experimenter to compare processing in different conditions, moment by moment, as the language unfolds in real time, allowing competing hypotheses to be evaluated.

Over the past decade, experiments using the visual world paradigm have done much to inform our understanding of language comprehension and language production in skilled listeners and speakers. A comprehensive review is beyond the scope of this chapter, but interested readers are referred to Henderson and Ferreira (2004) for a thorough review and discussion of topics, theories, and methods. Nevertheless, it is useful to consider some of these studies to ask what the visual world paradigm has revealed about skilled language processing before turning to consider on-line language processing in children with poor comprehension.

THE VISUAL WORLD PARADIGM AND SKILLED LANGUAGE PROCESSING

Word recognition and lexical access in spoken language comprehension

Allopenna, Magnuson, and Tanenhaus (1998) had participants view and interact with arrays of objects displayed on a computer screen. Ostensibly, the task required participants to pick up objects and move them around the screen, using the computer mouse. For example, while viewing an array that included a picture of a *beaker*, a *beetle*, and a *speaker*, among other objects and shapes, participants might be instructed to "pick up the beaker and put it on the triangle." Clearly, this is a simple and straightforward task. What is of interest, however, is where participants chose to look as the spoken instructions unfolded in

real time. In this example, the target item *beaker* shares its onset with *beetle*, also depicted in the array. Thus, during the initial unfolding of the acoustic token *beaker*, the signal is ambiguous, as potentially it could refer to either the *beaker* or the *beetle*. Allopenna and colleagues reasoned that this temporary ambiguity would cause eye movements to the target (*beaker*) to be delayed, relative to looks to the *beaker* when the array does not contain a lexical competitor such as *beetle*. As the target word unfolded, participants were as likely to look at the *beetle* as the *beaker*. Approximately 400 milliseconds after word onset, however, the pattern of eye movements began to diverge, with fixations to the *beaker* becoming much more probable than to the *beetle*. These findings are consistent with models of lexical access that propose that listeners dynamically evaluate incoming speech against an activated set of lexical candidates that are consistent with the speech input (for a review, see Cutler, 1995). Traditionally, these models place heavy emphasis on the onsets of words. In the cohort model, for example (Marslen-Wilson, 1987), the onset of a word activates a set of items (the cohort) that share an onset and therefore compete for recognition. As more information becomes available over time, the cohort is reduced until lexical access is achieved. Thus, once the second consonant of *beaker* has been registered, *beetle* is no longer a competing lexical candidate, resulting in fewer fixations to it and more fixations to the beaker. Interestingly, however, about 300 milliseconds after the target word onset, just as fixations to *beetle* were starting to decline, Allopenna et al. observed an increase in fixations to *speaker*, a word that shares a rhyme overlap with the target item. This suggests that listeners are not just sensitive to cohort overlap at the beginnings of words, but, instead, multiple activations to multiple words occur throughout the processing of speech, consistent with continuous mapping models (e.g., McClelland & Elman, 1986).

The appropriate interpretation of these data for models of lexical access continues to be debated and refined further by data from other experiments (e.g., Dahan & Gaskell, 2007; Dahan, Magnuson, Tanenhaus, & Hogan, 2001). For present purposes, however, even this brief overview of Allopenna et al.'s study demonstrates that examining what participants do when presented with a relatively pared-down bit of language—"to pick up the beaker . . ."—reveals the interactive and highly dynamic nature of language processing.

Allopenna et al.'s study focused on how listeners use phonological information in speech to identify words. However, listeners also need to activate the meanings of words they hear. Eye movement experiments have shown that listeners do not wait for phonological analysis to be complete before semantic analysis begins. Instead, word meanings become active very early during processing, before phonological analysis is complete and while multiple candidates are still being considered. Yee and Sedivy (2006) asked participants to view visual arrays on a computer screen depicting four objects. At the same time, participants heard the name of one of the objects, and they were instructed to point to the named object on the screen. For example, participants heard the word *lock* while viewing an array comprising a picture of a *lock*, a *key*, a *deer,* and an *apple*. Not surprisingly, as the auditory token *lock* unfolded in time, participants were most likely to fixate the target picture, the lock. However, Yee and Sedivy also observed elevated looks to the picture of a key, relative to the control items (deer and apple). This suggests that the meaning of the spoken target *lock* was activated, causing the temporary activation of words semantically related to *lock*, such as *key*, leading to a temporary increase in eye movements to the *key* in the visual array. A follow-up experiment showed an even more striking result. As participants heard the target word *logs*, eye movements to a visual array comprising pictures of some logs, along with three other objects (a key, a deer, and an apple), were monitored. During the processing of *logs*, more fixations were made to the picture of the key than to the other distracters (deer and apple). Yee and Sedivy offer the following explanation: hearing the word *logs* activates phonological competitors that are plausible—but only temporarily so—candidates for the actual item, including the word *lock*; the activation of *lock* as a potential candidate then activates items that are semantically related,

including *key*, resulting in looks to the picture of the key. This "semantic competitor" effect is short-lived, lasting only approximately 200 milliseconds, suggesting that the semantic activation of unintended candidates quickly decays once the input is no longer consistent with their forms; additionally (or alternatively) more active candidates may inhibit less active candidates over time. While more research is needed to inform these hypotheses, Yee and Sedivy's study once again demonstrates that language processing is dynamic and highly interactive (see Huettig & Altmann, 2005, for converging evidence).

From words to sentences (and beyond)

So far, this review has considered the processing of single words only. Clearly, however, language is typically experienced in sentences that form a connected discourse. Over recent years language-mediated eye movement studies have informed our understanding of these aspects of language processing. Altmann and Kamide (1999) found that listeners are highly sensitive to information contained in verbs and that this information is used to guide subsequent processing. When listening to a sentence such as "Jane watched her mother eat the cake," participants fixated the picture of the cake (the only edible object in the array) well before the acoustic onset of the word *cake*. In more neutral sentences such as "Jane watched her mother choose the cake," the probability of looking at the cake (relative to other objects in the visual array that were also chooseable) only increased once the acoustic token of the word *cake* began to unfold. In a follow-up experiment, Kamide, Altmann, and Haywood (2003) demonstrated that listeners combine information from the verb and the subject of a sentence in order to predict the likely object. For example, while hearing the verb *drink* in a sentence with *the man* as the subject, participants were more likely to fixate the picture of some beer in the visual array, rather than the picture of some milk. In contrast, while hearing the verb *drink* in a sentence with *the girl* as subject, looks toward the milk were much more common than looks to the beer. These findings demonstrate that listeners are highly sensitive both to the semantic information contained in verbs *and* the relative plausibility of what that information might apply to, given the subject of the sentence (man vs. girl) and the potentially drinkable objects (beer vs. milk) in the visual array.

Similar conclusions can also be made concerning listeners' interpretation of syntax. Consider a sentence such as "put the apple on the towel into the box." This sentence in ambiguous because as listeners hear the prepositional phrase "on the towel," it could refer to the desired end location for the apple, or it could refer to additional information to modify the noun phrase, the apple, indicating that the apple that needs to go into the box is the apple that is currently on the towel, rather than some other apple. Many experiments have asked how listeners choose to interpret sentences such as these, and a full discussion is beyond the scope of this chapter (for a review, see Spivey, Tanenhaus, Eberhard, & Sedivy, 2002). However, it is useful to describe a traditional account of syntactic ambiguity resolution in a little detail in order to demonstrate the utility of the visual word paradigm in generating data to inform our understanding of syntactic processing. According to a "syntax-first" type of account (e.g., Frazier & Clifton, 1996), listeners have biases that initially lead them to interpret sentences so that they obey certain syntactic principles. Should this result in an incomprehensible outcome, the language is then reevaluated, perhaps taking into account contextual or lexical constraints. This takes time, and this is why in traditional reading time experiments, participants are slower to read syntactically ambiguous sentences if they disobey the preferred syntactic solution. To illustrate, consider again the sentence " put the apple on the towel into the box." In the absence of other cues, we tend to interpret the phrase "on the towel" as a goal argument—that is, we conclude that the towel is the final location on which the apple is to be put. If we subsequently encounter "into the box," we realize that we may have misinterpreted the prepositional phrase "on the towel" and rather than serving as a goal argument, it is a noun modifier, alerting the listener that it is the apple that is on the towel that needs to go into the box.

In contrast, other theorists have argued that a strong preference to interpret "on the towel"

as goal argument only occurs in the absence of other information—most crucially, information from context. If—as might be the case in natural language—listeners are aware that there are two apples, then it may be that this information prevents initial misinterpretation and instead leads the listener to interpret the syntax as modifying the noun—that is, indicating that it is the apple on the towel that needs to be moved. While there is some empirical support that knowledge of referential context can indeed override syntactic biases from reading time studies (e.g., Altmann & Steedman, 1988), this sort of evidence is limited, as contextual information can only be introduced via linguistic manipulations (i.e., prior discourse that sets up the presence of two apples). Potentially, this may lead to patterns of behavior that are distinct from those seen when language is referring to real-world contexts, many of which are not explicitly described in the language.

Spivey et al. (2002) used a visual world paradigm to address whether sensitivity to nonlinguistic cues (i.e., the presence of two apples in the visual world) influences processing of sentences containing syntactic ambiguities. They obtained clear evidence that referential context does disambiguate sentences that would otherwise be temporarily ambiguous. As participants heard the phrase "on the towel," if there was an apple already on a towel in the visual array, there were no looks to the empty towel, suggesting that contrary to "syntax-first" accounts, a towel was never considered as a location for a goal argument. Instead, the findings are consistent with a view of "a broad theoretical framework in which real-time language comprehension immediately takes into account a rich array of relevant nonlinguistic context" (Spivey et al., 2002, p. 448).

Over the past decade or so, a number of experiments in domains other than syntax have reported findings that echo Spivey et al.'s conclusions. Sedivy, Tanenhaus, Chambers, and Carlson (1999) investigated the role of context in on-line semantic interpretation of sentences containing scalar adjectives that disambiguated between potential referents in the visual scene (e.g., a tall glass and a short glass). Listeners were very sensitive to this information, suggesting that (a) semantic interpretation is conducted incrementally, and (b) contextual information is integrated into semantic interpretation very early in processing. Similarly, listeners rapidly integrate paralinguistic cues into on-line interpretation. For example, a speaker's prosody and intonation influence the listener's incremental interpretation of discourse (Snedeker & Trueswell, 2003; Weber, Grice, & Crocker, 2006); listeners are also sensitive to common ground—that is, knowledge of what a conversational partner knows or understands (Hanna & Tanenhaus, 2004) and to the desired goals (or affordances) of the situation within which they are interpreting the language (Chambers, Tanenhaus, & Magnuson, 2004).

This selective review of some of the studies that have used the visual world paradigm to explore issues in language comprehension in skilled processing highlights a number of points and allows a number of conclusions to be drawn. First, some methodological points: it is clear that the relationship between looking and listening is closely time-locked, making the paradigm a sensitive tool with which to explore the time course of language comprehension. It also allows language to be observed implicitly—participants do not need to make metacognitive or meta-linguistic judgments—and it enjoys ecological validity, with participants being free to move and interact with others or with objects, thus allowing language to be observed in relatively naturalistic circumstances. Turning to more theoretical issues, data from language-mediated eye movement studies make very clear that language processing is incremental and highly dynamic. It is referentially driven, with listeners' sensitivity to context (both linguistic context and context supplied by referents or situations in the visual world) exerting an immediate effect on real-time comprehension. Language comprehension is extraordinarily interactive. Studies of word recognition show that as listeners hear language, words that share phonological overlap with the target may be activated, as well as semantic associates of these words. At the same time, information from context is impacting on the listeners' unfolding interpretation, influencing and interacting with information gleaned from the speech signal. Even when processing individual words, many lexical items may be active, although they are unlikely to be referents, and, as Yee and Sedivy (2006) state,

> Such rampant activation would seem to threaten chaos, yet the subjective experience of word recognition is not at all chaotic. This suggests that the mechanisms involved maintain a careful balance between activation and deactivation: widespread activation must be counteracted with swift deactivation. (p. 11)

These complexities must multiply when listening to sentences or extended discourse or engaging in dialogue. In addition, factors such as sensitivity to speakers' eye gaze, gestures, postures, tone of voice, and facial expression can help us to comprehend the intended message. This adds up to a language processing system that is complex, rich and dynamic, and well tuned to helping us comprehend the intended message as quickly as possible. Most of us, most of the time, are not aware of the complexities of what we are doing, or of the massive ambiguity our language systems are dealing with. But given this complexity, it is perhaps not surprising that some children experience substantial language impairments.

USING EYE MOVEMENTS TO INVESTIGATE CHILDREN'S LANGUAGE PROCESSING

There is a long tradition of inferring cognitive and linguistic skills in preverbal infants from their eye movements (Aslin, 2007). Studies in this tradition have tended to rely on global looking measures to ascertain whether infants prefer (i.e., spend longer) looking at the named object, allowing the researcher to infer whether or not the name of the object has been recognized or discriminated from a foil. More recently, however, researchers have recognized the potential for eye movement experiments to provide a more continuous measure of language interpretation. This approach has revealed that the emerging vocabulary of very young infants encodes substantial phonetic and phonological detail (Swingley, 2005; Swingley & Aslin, 2000), that infants and young children can recognize words on the basis of partial phonological information (Fernald, Swingley, & Pinto, 2001), and that, by 18 months of age, infants are faster to recognize a word if it is presented in a sentence frame rather than in isolation (Fernald & Hurtado, 2006). Taken together, these studies suggest that infants process language incrementally and are sensitive to cues in the language input that allow them to "listen ahead" and make predictions about the upcoming language.

Given the rich literature generated by the visual world paradigm exploring language processing in adults, and the increasing sophistication of our understanding of how infants process language, it is striking that only a handful of published studies have used eye movements to investigate on-line language processing in older children, and of these, only two have examined individual differences in language processing. Although small in number, these studies, reviewed below, demonstrate the utility of using eye movements to explore a range of language behaviors in children across the domains of phonology, semantics, syntax, and pragmatics. Generally, these studies show children to be remarkably adult-like in their language processing, albeit with some important differences.

Exploring the phonological domain, Desroches, Joanisse, and Robertson (2006) used the visual world paradigm to investigate issues of lexical access in typically developing children and in children with developmental dyslexia. Echoing Allopenna et al.'s (1998) findings, reviewed earlier, Desroches et al. found that children, like adults, were slower to recognize a target word such as *candle* when either an onset competitor (*candy*) or a rhyme competitor (*sandal*) were also present in the visual array. Interestingly, children with dyslexia showed interference from onset competitors, but they failed to show interference from rhyming words. It is not clear why this should be case, and therefore this finding awaits replication and further study. In the meantime, however, this experiment demonstrates the utility of the paradigm for exploring individual differences in phonological processing in both typical development and in dyslexia.

Turning to the semantic domain, Nation, Marshall, and Altmann (2003) used the visual world paradigm to investigate individual differences in children's sensitivity to verb argument structure. Like the adults observed by Altmann and Kamide (1999), 10-year-old children were sensitive to verb semantics such that they were much faster to launch an eye movement toward a picture of an edible object while hearing a sentence containing the verb *eat*, relative to a neutral verb such as *move* or *choose*. Children with poor language comprehension also showed this effect, suggesting that they too were very rapidly able to integrate information contained in the verb with contextual information provided by the visual scene. Interestingly, however, although the less-skilled comprehenders showed equal sensitivity to the contextual constraints offered by verbs, they also made more eye movements overall. Nation et al. suggested that this may reflect difficulties in memory (with more looks being needed to "refresh" traces either of the language or of the objects in the scene), or possibly differences in allocation of attentional resources in children. Potentially, these cognitive limitations may be related to their difficulties with language comprehension.

In the first published study to use the visual world paradigm with children, Trueswell, Sekerina, Hill, and Logrip (1999) investigated syntactic ambiguity resolution in typically developing 5-year-old children. The study was inspired by Spivey et al.'s (2002) finding that adults' sensitivity to referential context (number of apples in the scene) disambiguates sentences such as "put the apple on the towel in the box," as reviewed earlier. In contrast to adults, 5-year-old children interpret the sentence with little regard to referential context. Instead, they show a strong preference to interpret "on the towel" as the goal of "put" (i.e., the location where the apple should be moved to), rather than as a modifier (i.e., which particular apple), even when two apples were in the visual array, one of which was on a towel. When the syntactic ambiguity was removed, as in "put the apple that is on the towel in the box," children showed an adult-like pattern of eye movements. These data show that young children are well tuned to the local lexical properties of the verb *put* (i.e., that *put* is usually followed by a goal rather than a modifier), but not at all tuned to referential context. Follow-up studies reported by Snedeker and Trueswell (2004) confirmed this pattern of results, with 5-year-old children being highly sensitive to verb-specific semantic information: when a particular verb is more frequently predictive of a modifier (e.g., "choose the cow with the stick"), children's eye movements showed a preference for looking at the modifier in the scene (i.e., a cow holding a stick, rather than a stick), relative to sentences where the preference of the verb is biased to take an instrument (i.e., "tickle the pig with the fan" resulted in a greater proportion of looks toward the fan, rather than a pig holding a fan).

Why might 5-year-old children be so resistant to referential context when adults' sensitivity to referential context is so great that it can override our normal bias to interpret certain syntactic structures in a certain way (Spivey et al., 2002)? Trueswell et al. argued that it is highly unlikely that children do not have an appreciation of the referential principle; instead, they speculated that children are unable to apply it under certain processing conditions. Given their limited processing capacities, it might be that 5-year-olds are unable to contemplate uncommon or complex syntactic alternatives, or are unable to compute or integrate relevant contextual constraints (extracted from the visual scene) quickly enough to impact on on-line processing. Further work is needed to address these possibilities, as well as to address the obvious questions as to when children become adult-like in their processing, and what changes in their cognitive or linguistic abilities are needed to afford this change.

The final visual world study with children to be reviewed highlights the utility of the paradigm to address more pragmatic or communicative aspects of language processing. Nadig and Sedivy (2002) asked whether children were sensitive to the speaker's visual perspective as they listened to the speaker give an instruction, and whether this information was available on-line, as the language they were listening to unfolded in real-time. Children's (aged 5–6 years) eye movements were monitored as they listened to potentially ambiguous instructions such as "pick up the glass." The instruction was potentially ambiguous, as sometimes there were two glasses (one tall, one small) in the scene. In one condition (the common ground condition), both glasses could be seen by both the speaker and the child; in a second condition (the privileged ground condition), the child could see both glasses, but the speaker could only see one. If children are sensitive to common vs. privileged ground perspectives, they should find it easier to attend to the instruction "pick up the glass" when one of the glasses is occluded from the speaker, as they should be aware that this removes any potential ambiguity in the instruction. By contrast, when the speaker can see both glasses, the instruction "pick up the glass" requires further clarification if the child is to know which glass they ought to pick up. Nadig and Sedivy found that 5-year-old children were very sensitive to common vs. privileged ground and that they were able to use this information with striking speed: by the offset of the word *glass* in the spoken instruction, looking patterns differed between the two conditions. Specifically, in the privileged ground condition children do not consider the glass that they could see but the speaker could not as a potential referent; instead, they looked immediately at the glass that was also in the speaker's perspective. In the common ground condition, however, they looked back and forth between the two potential referents before choosing one at random or requesting further clarification. Contrary to more traditional views that see 5-year-old children as being egocentric, these findings show that children are extremely sensitive to speaker perspective, and that this information impacts on their on-line processing at the earliest possible opportunity during processing.

Although the visual world approach with children is in its infancy, these studies showcase the range of issues in on-line language processing that can be explored, from phonology through to semantics, syntax, and pragmatics. They also highlight the great potential that this paradigm has to understand language processing in atypical populations—a potential that is yet to be fully exploited but is sure to be so in the coming years. To illustrate, this chapter ends with an overview of one of our current studies investigating language processing in children with language and communication difficulties.

A VISUAL WORLD STUDY OF LANGUAGE PROCESSING IN CHILDREN WITH POOR LANGUAGE COMPREHENSION

Difficulties with language comprehension are prevalent in children with specific language impairment (SLI). For these children, it is assumed that impairments in some or all of the systems that support the basic building blocks of language (phonology, semantics, and syntax) lead to problems with understanding language (Bishop, 1997). Difficulties with language comprehension are also prevalent in children with autism. Such deficits are often considered to be a consequence of autistic cognition and, in particular, a tendency to process information in a piecemeal style (e.g., Happé, 1999). On this view, the focusing of attention toward local detail at the expense of attending to overall context and global meaning would have devastating consequences for language comprehension. Consistent with this, numerous studies have shown that people with autism are poor at using context when processing language (e.g., Happé, 1997; Jolliffe & Baron-Cohen, 1999, 2000; Lopez & Leekam, 2003).

There is now strong evidence indicating that many children with autism have structural language problems—that is, impairments in some or all of the basic building blocks of language, very reminiscent of what is seen in nonautistic children with SLI (e.g., Tager-Flusberg & Joseph, 2003). This raises the interesting possibility that some of the problems that autistic children have with processing language in context may be a consequence of language impairment, rather than of an autism-specific cognitive style. A series of studies by Norbury (2004, 2005a, 2005b) has investigated this possibility. In these studies, Norbury recruited

two samples of children with autism: one group had normal structural language skills (ALN), the other group had concomitant language impairment (ALI). A group of nonautistic children with language impairment (LI) and a typically developing (TD) control group were also recruited. Using a picture judgment task, Norbury (2005a) examined how well children in these four groups were able to use contextual information to resolve lexical ambiguities in two different tasks: one tapping contextual facilitation and one contextual suppression. In the facilitation task, children heard either a neutral sentence ("he ran from the bank") alongside a picture of a river bank or a money bank, or a supportive sentence ("he fished/stole from the bank) alongside the relevant picture. If sensitive to the context, children should be faster at judging that the picture is related to the sentence following supportive sentences relative to neutral sentences. In the suppression task, children heard sentences that biased meaning toward one meaning of an ambiguous word—for example "he stole from the bank"—and were again asked to judge whether a picture (pointing to the alternative meaning of the ambiguous word, i.e., a river bank) was congruent with the meaning of the sentence. If children are sensitive to linguistic context, they should respond no; if, however, they are less sensitive to the meaning of the sentence, or if they attend to local detail (i.e., the word *bank*), they may find it difficult to reject the picture. Across both tasks, Norbury found that both groups of children with poor language skills (ALI and LI) showed less sensitivity to context, regardless of whether or not they also had autism. More strikingly, those children with autism who had normal language ability (ALN) were just as sensitive to context as were typically developing children.

These findings are important, as they suggest that it is the presence of language impairment rather than an autistic "cognitive style" that is associated with lack of sensitivity to contextual constraints. As the experiment was off-line and required children to make metacognitive judgments, it was not able to elucidate on the source of the comprehension impairment, or its timing. Potentially, children with language impairment may have difficulty with the task because of the demands it places on memory, or because of its metacognitive demands, rather than lack of sensitivity to context per se.

Building on Norbury's (2005a) study, we have been exploring language processing in children with autism who differ in language ability as well as in children with language impairment and in typically developing controls, using the visual world paradigm (Brock, Norbury, Einav, & Nation, 2007). Our experiment integrated two well-established phenomena discussed above: adults' and children's sensitivity to cohort competitors that share phonological overlap with a target word (e.g., Allopenna et al., 1998; Desroaches et al., 2006) and their sensitivity to verb selection restrictions (e.g., Altmann & Kamide, 1999; Nation et al., 2003). Our participants were 24 adolescents with autism and a control group of adolescents with equivalent language scores. In both groups, there was a wide range of language ability, allowing us to investigate the relationship between language skills and eye movements.

Participants viewed visual scenes comprising pictures of four objects (e.g., hamster, hammer, trumpet, and gun), with two of the objects (hamster and hammer) sharing phonological overlap. We monitored eye movements as they listened to sentences that were neutral (e.g., "Joe chose the hamster," with all potential referents in the visual scene being chooseable) or constraining (e.g., "Joe stroked the hamster," with only the hamster being a plausible referent, given the verb stroke). Before discussing the children's data, it is worth describing the pattern of eye movements made by skilled adults in this experiment. In the neutral verb condition, adults were sensitive to the presence of the cohort competitor such that eye movements to both the hamster and the hammer were enhanced relative to the other two objects in the scene, until enough of the word "hamster" had unfolded to identify the referent as hamster rather than hammer. In the constraining verb condition, however, a very different pattern of eye movements was observed. Shortly after hearing the verb stroke, participants were already more likely to be looking toward the hamster; our data suggest that in the constraining context, hammer is not considered as a potential referent, despite its acoustic overlap with the target word hamster. These findings suggest that adults are remarkably adept at integrating information from the linguistic context (the verb) with knowledge of the visual scene and that this is used to guide subsequent processing of the sentence (see Dahan & Tanenhaus, 2004) for similar but not identical findings).

We found that, overall, participants were more likely to look toward the hamster much sooner following the constraining verb stroke than after the neutral verb choose. This was a highly significant and very strong effect. Of greater interest here is whether performance differed across the two groups of participants. It did not: young people with autism were as sensitive to contextual information provided by the verb, as revealed by a reduced cohort effect when sentences provided contextual cues.

A second experiment used the same stimuli and the same participants but made an important methodological change. Previously, the hamster had actually been present in the scene. As the participants were looking at the hamster, they were, of course, unable to be looking at the cohort competitor, the hammer. An interesting question is what would people look at if the target were not present in the visual scene? Would hearing a constraining verb such as stroke prevent looks to the hammer, or would participants consider the hammer a potential referent, given its phonological overlap with the target word? Our data from adults (Brock & Nation, 2007) suggest that as skilled language users listen to a sentence such as "Joe stroked the hamster," looks to hammer are not enhanced relative to the three other (unrelated) objects also present in the scene. In contrast, when hearing the neutral sentence "Joe chose the hamster," as the word "hamster" begins to unfold, hammer is considered a potential referent.

Consistent with these observations, our adolescent participants showed the same effect: following constraining verbs, looks to the cohort competitor were less likely than when the sentence contained a neutral verb. This suggests that the lack of looks to the hammer in the first experiment was not entirely a consequence of the participants looking at the hamster and therefore being unable to simultaneously look at the *hammer*. Instead, information from the verb serves to impact on the likelihood of considering a cohort competitor as a potential referent. Interestingly, there was no difference between the two groups of participants: overall, both the adolescents with autism and the nonautistic comparison group showed the same pattern of eye movements. However, there was a clear and strong relationship between the individual participants' language ability (as measured by a battery of standardized tests) and the patterns of eye movements they made. Poor language was particularly associated with increased fixation time to the contextually inappropriate cohort competitor. This suggests that in the absence of support from visual context (i.e., a picture of a hamster), adolescents with poor language were less sensitive to linguistic constraints (i.e., the verb). In contrast, adolescents with stronger language skills were sensitive to the verb constraints, such that looks to the cohort competitor were suppressed.

Our results do not support the idea that people with autism have difficulty integrating context, either linguistic context or the context provided by the visual scene. Only individuals with poor language (with or without autism) performed differently from their peers. These findings echo Norbury's (2004, 2005a, 2005b) observations and reinforce her conclusion that it is very important to control for individual difference in structural language skills in studies exploring autistic cognition. Our data also highlight that people with language impairment are perhaps not as sensitive to contextual constraints as their peers, although further experiments are needed to explore this finding in more detail.

CONCLUSION

This chapter has described the visual world paradigm—a relatively new psycholinguistic tool that has the potential to help us to understand a lot more about how children with atypical language process and comprehend language in real time. Our selective review of some of the studies that have used the paradigm with skilled adults reveals its utility—from investigations of phonological representation through to how listeners and speakers coordinate their dialogue, from resolving syntactic anomalies through to interpreting language "in the real world." All of these studies demonstrate that language comprehension is "referent-driven," with listeners rapidly seeking out cues to help them to interpret language so as to derive the most appropriate meaning. The fact that the paradigm offers excellent temporal resolution and enables a range of linguistic (e.g., verb constraints, syntax, anaphoric devices) and nonlinguistic (e.g., eye gaze, gesture, intonation) cues to be manipulated makes it an ideal tool with which to explore many issues in both typical and atypical processing. In sum, it provides tantalizing promise of revealing precisely why different children may fail to comprehend language for different reasons.

ACKNOWLEDGMENTS

I would like to thank Gerry Altmann, Jon Brock, and Courtenay Norbury for their many contributions to the work and ideas described in this chapter. Our work is supported by The Wellcome Trust, The Medical Research Council, and The Nuffield Foundation.

NOTE

1 For other examples of eye-trackers used in this field, see http://www.sr-research.com and http://www.a-s-l.com

REFERENCES

Allopenna, P. D., Magnuson, J. S., & Tanenhaus, M. K. (1998). Tracking the time course of spoken word recognition using eye movements: Evidence for continuous mapping models. *Journal of Memory and Language, 38*(4), 419–439.

Altmann, G. (1997). *The ascent of Babel: An exploration of language, mind and understanding.* Oxford, UK: Oxford University Press.

Altmann, G., & Kamide, Y. (1999). Incremental interpretation at verbs: Restricting the domain of subsequent reference. *Cognition, 73,* 247–264.

Altmann, G., & Steedman, M. (1988). Interaction with context during human sentence processing. *Cognition, 30*(3), 191–238.

Aslin, R. N. (2007). What's in a look? *Developmental Science, 10*(1), 48–53.

Bishop, D. V. M. (1997). *Uncommon understanding.* Hove, UK: Psychology Press.

Brock, J., & Nation, K. (2007, January). *Contextual suppression in spoken language comprehension: Evidence from eye-tracking.* Paper presented at the Experimental Psychology Society, London.

Brock, J., Norbury, C. F., Einav, S., & Nation, K. (2007). *Eye-movements reveal sensitivity to sentence context is associated with language ability not autism.* Manuscript submitted for publication.

Chambers, C. G., Tanenhaus, M. K., & Magnuson, J. S. (2004). Actions and affordances in syntactic ambiguity resolution. *Journal of Experimental Psychology: Learning, Memory, and Cognition, 30*(3), 687–696.

Cooper, R. M. (1974). Control of eye fixation by meaning of spoken language: New methodology for real-time investigation of speech perception, memory, and language processing. *Cognitive Psychology, 6*(1), 84–107.

Cutler, A. (1995). Spoken word recognition and production. In J. L. Miller & P. D. Eimas (Eds.), *Handbook of perception and cognition: Vol. 11. Speech, language, and communication* (pp. 97–136). San Diego, CA: Academic Press.

Dahan, D., & Gaskell, M. K. (2007). The temporal dynamics of ambiguity resolution: Evidence from spoken-word recognition. *Journal of Memory and Language, 57*(4), 483–450.

Dahan, D., Magnuson, J. S., Tanenhaus, M. K., & Hogan, E. M. (2001). Subcategorical mismatches and the time course of lexical access: Evidence for lexical competition. *Language and Cognitive Processes, 16*(5–6), 507–534.

Dahan, D., & Tanenhaus, M. K. (2004). Continuous mapping from sound to meaning in spoken-language comprehension: Immediate effects of verb-based thematic constraints. *Journal of Experimental Psychology: Learning, Memory, and Cognition, 30,* 498–513.

Desroches, A. S., Joanisse, M. F., & Robertson, E. K. (2006). Specific phonological impairments in dyslexia revealed by eyetracking. *Cognition, 100*(3), B32–B42.

Fernald, A., & Hurtado, N. (2006). Names in frames: Infants interpret words in sentence frames faster than words in isolation. *Developmental Science, 9*(3), F33–F40.

Fernald, A., Swingley, D., & Pinto, J. P. (2001). When half a word is enough: Infants can recognize spoken words using partial phonetic information. *Child Development, 72*(4), 1003–1015.

Frazier, L., & Clifton, C. (1996). *Construal.* Cambridge, MA: MIT Press.

Hanna, J. E., & Tanenhaus, M. K. (2004). Pragmatic effects on reference resolution in a collaborative task: Evidence from eye movements. *Cognitive Science, 28*(1), 105–115.

Happé, F. G. E. (1997). Central coherence and theory of mind in autism: Reading homographs in context. *British Journal of Developmental Psychology 15,* 1–12.

Happé, F. G. E. (1999). Autism: Cognitive deficit or cognitive style? *Trends in Cognitive Sciences, 3*(6), 216–222.

Henderson, J. M., & Ferreira, F. (Eds.). (2004). *The interface of language, vision and action.* New York: Psychology Press.

Huettig, F., & Altmann, G. T. M. (2005). Word meaning and the control of eye fixation: Semantic competitor effects and the visual world paradigm. *Cognition, 96*(1), B23–B32.

Jolliffe, T., & Baron-Cohen, S. (1999). A test of central coherence theory. Linguistic processing in high-functioning adults with autism or Asperger syndrome: Is local coherence impaired? *Cognition, 71*(2), 149–185.

Jolliffe, T., & Baron-Cohen, S. (2000). Linguistic processing in high-functioning adults with autism or Asperger syndrome: Can global coherence be achieved? A further test of central coherence theory. *Psychological Medicine, 30,* 1169–1187.

Kamide, Y., Altmann, G. T. M., & Haywood, S. L. (2003). Prediction and thematic information in incremental sentence processing: Evidence from anticipatory eye movements. *Journal of Memory and Language, 49,* 133–156.

Lopez, B., & Leekam, S. R. (2003). Do children with autism fail to process information in context?

Journal of Child Psychology and Psychiatry and Allied Disciplines, 44(2), 285–300.

Marslen-Wilson, W. D. (1987) Functional parallelism in spoken word-recognition. *Cognition, 25*, 71–102.

McClelland, J. L., & Elman, J. L. (1986). The Trace Model of Speech-Perception. *Cognitive Psychology, 18*(1), 1–86.

Montgomery, J. W. (2000). Verbal working memory and sentence comprehension in children with specific language impairment. *Journal of Speech, Language, and Hearing Research, 43*(2), 293–308.

Montgomery, J. W. (2006). Real-time language processing in school-age children with specific language impairment. *International Journal of Language & Communication Disorders, 41*(3), 275–291.

Nadig, A. S., & Sedivy, J. C. (2002). Evidence of perspective-taking constraints in children's on-line reference resolution. *Psychological Science, 13*(4), 329–336.

Nation, K., Marshall, C. M., & Altmann, G. T. M. (2003). Investigating individual differences in children's real-time sentence comprehension using language-mediated eye movements. *Journal of Experimental Child Psychology, 86*, 314–329.

Nation, K., & Snowling, M. J. (1998). Individual differences in contextual facilitation: Evidence from dyslexia and poor reading comprehension. *Child Development, 69*(4), 996–1011.

Nation, K., & Snowling, M. J. (1999). Developmental differences in sensitivity to semantic relations among good and poor comprehenders: Evidence from semantic priming. *Cognition, 70*(1), B1–B13.

Norbury, C. F. (2004). Factors supporting idiom comprehension in children with communication disorders. *Journal of Speech, Language, and Hearing Research, 47*(5), 1179–1193.

Norbury, C. F. (2005a). Barking up the wrong tree? Lexical ambiguity resolution in children with language impairments and autistic spectrum disorders. *Journal of Experimental Child Psychology, 90*(2), 142–171.

Norbury, C. F. (2005b). The relationship between theory of mind and metaphor: Evidence from children with language impairment and autistic spectrum disorder. *British Journal of Developmental Psychology, 23*, 383–399.

Pinker, S. (1994). *The language instinct*. New York: Penguin.

Rayner, K. (1998). Eye movements in reading and information processing: 20 years of research. *Psychological Bulletin, 124*(3), 372–422.

Sedivy, J. C., Tanenhaus, M. K., Chambers, C. G., & Carlson, G. N. (1999). Achieving incremental semantic interpretation through contextual representation. *Cognition, 71*(2), 109–147.

Snedeker, J., & Trueswell, J. (2003). Using prosody to avoid ambiguity: Effects of speaker awareness and referential context. *Journal of Memory and Language, 48*(1), 103–130.

Snedeker, J., & Trueswell, J. C. (2004). The developing constraints on parsing decisions: The role of lexical-biases and referential scenes in child and adult sentence processing. *Cognitive Psychology, 49*(3), 238–299.

Spivey, M. J., Tanenhaus, M. K., Eberhard, K. M., & Sedivy, J. C. (2002). Eye movements and spoken language comprehension: Effects of visual context on syntactic ambiguity resolution. *Cognitive Psychology, 45*(4), 447–481.

Swingley, D. (2005). 11-month-olds' knowledge of how familiar words sound. *Developmental Science, 8*(5), 432–443.

Swingley, D., & Aslin, R. N. (2000). Spoken word recognition and lexical representation in very young children. *Cognition, 76*(2), 147–166.

Tager-Flusberg, H., & Joseph, R. M. (2003). Identifying neurocognitive phenotypes in autism. *Philosophical Transactions of the Royal Society of London, Series B: Biological Sciences, 358*(1430), 303–314.

Tanenhaus, M. K., Spivey-Knowlton, M. J., Eberhard, K. M., & Sedivy, J. C. (1995). Integration of visual and linguistic information in spoken language comprehension. *Science, 268*(5217), 1632–1634.

Trueswell, J. C., Sekerina, I., Hill, N. M., & Logrip, M. L. (1999). The kindergarten-path effect: Studying on-line sentence processing in young children. *Cognition, 73*(2), 89–134.

Tyler, L. K., & Marslen-Wilson, W. D. (1981). Children's processing of spoken language. *Journal of Verbal Learning and Verbal Behavior, 20*(4), 400–416.

Weber, A., Grice, M., & Crocker, M. W. (2006). The role of prosody in the interpretation of structural ambiguities: A study of anticipatory eye movements. *Cognition, 99*(2), B63–B72.

Yee, E., & Sedivy, J. C. (2006). Eye movements to pictures reveal transient semantic activation during spoken word recognition. *Journal of Experimental Psychology: Learning, Memory, and Cognition, 32*(1), 1–14.

4

Using magnetic resonance imaging to investigate developmental language disorders

Frederic Dick, Fiona Richardson, and Maria Cristina Saccuman

The last decade has seen explosive growth in the use of magnetic resonance imaging (MRI) to explore human brain structure and function in healthy and clinical adult populations. MRI is also increasingly used to conduct research studies of typically and atypically developing children, from the first days of infancy and into the school years. MRI holds considerable promise as a research tool in the field of developmental speech and language disorders, and indeed in typical development as well. Already, studies of typically developing children have shown that the brain continues to develop and change throughout childhood and into adolescence, and that structural and functional change is possible through experience and environmental input. MRI studies of children with developmental language disorders have the potential to inform us about the pace and course of neurodevelopmental change in this population and to show us how "specific" language impairment might differ from other developmental disorders.

In the first half of this chapter we discuss the advantages of using MRI and also highlight some of the special challenges involved when using

MRI with children. In the second half we present a brief overview of MRI findings on typical neural development, summarize the MRI literature on developmental language disorders, and relate these findings to the larger literature on associated clinical syndromes such as autism. We end with some speculations about future findings and directions for research.

ADVANTAGES AND CHALLENGES OF PEDIATRIC MRI

MRI is a truly noninvasive imaging technique, something that is especially important for pediatric imaging. MRI uses strong magnetic fields and *nonionizing* radio frequency (RF) energy to generate a signal from the body. Nonionizing radiation—like that used for transmitting radio broadcasts or mobile phone signals—carries little energy and does not alter atomic or molecular structures. [In contrast, sufficient doses of *ionizing* radiation, as used in established imaging techniques such as computerized tomography (CT) and positron emission tomography (PET), can be harmful to cellular mechanisms.] The magnetic fields used in MRI are also safe— several decades of experiments have shown no deleterious effects of long-term exposure to high-strength magnetic fields in developing or adult organisms. (The background and safety of MRI is described in Exhibit 4.1; the basic components and mechanics are described in Exhibits 4.2 and 4.3 and in the Appendix.)

Magnetic resonance (MR) is also a flexible and fast imaging method. Less than one hour of scan time will provide a vast amount of data on various aspects of brain structure and function. Indeed, it can take as little as 4–5 minutes to acquire a single high-resolution scan showing the structure of the whole brain. Similarly, basic functional MRI protocols can be used to localize primary visual, auditory, motor, and sensory regions with 4–8 minutes of scanning. While using MRI with

---

Exhibit 4.1. Background and safety of magnetic resonance imaging

Magnetic resonance (MR) has been used as a basic research tool in the physical sciences for more than fifty years. However, it was only in the 1970s that innovations by Paul Lauterbur and Sir Peter Mansfield enabled MR to be used to create two-dimensional images of physical structures. MRI uses strong magnetic fields and nonionizing radio-frequency (RF) energy to generate a signal from the body. In contrast, the use of ionizing radiation is central to both CT (X-rays) and PET (injected radionuclides). When ionizing radiation passes through the body, it is energetic enough to strip electrons off atoms and molecules such as water. This can create free radicals in the form of ionized water, which can, in turn, remove electrons or hydrogen atoms from other molecules in the body. In sufficient doses, this process can cause damage or death to cell machinery. By contrast, nonionizing radiation—like that used for transmitting mobile phone signals, radio broadcasts, or microwave transmissions, as well as for MRI—transmits much less energy, and it only excites electrons to a higher energy state, rather than removing them from their orbits. When the electrons fall back to their less energetic state, they give off their excess energy in the form of heat. However, it takes a lot of RF or microwave energy to create significant heating, and MRI scanners are carefully calibrated to avoid depositing too much energy in a given amount of tissue. The magnetic fields used in MRI are also safe—several decades of experiments have shown no deleterious effects of long-term exposure to high-strength magnetic fields in developing or adult organisms (for an extensive list of studies, see http://mrisafety.com/research_summary .asp). In recognition of this evidence, the U.S. Food and Drug Administration has declared MRI safe for children and infants aged more than 1 month for magnetic field strengths up to 8 Tesla, and for neonates aged less than 1 month for magnetic field strength up to 4 Tesla (http://jerlab.psych.sc.edu/kidsMRIsite/mrisafety/ Abstracts_Pdfs/articlepdfs/USFDA_2003.pdf).

Exhibit 4.2. Basic components of MRI

While modern MRI scanners are extremely complex pieces of equipment, they can be broken down into four basic components.

The first of these is the main magnet itself. It is made of several thin large-diameter spools of coiled wire in a sealed cylinder, which is cooled by liquid helium so that the wire loses all electrical resistance and becomes "superconducting." To generate a magnetic field, a very strong electrical current (~300 A) is injected into the coil; remarkably, this current will continue to flow around the coil without any additional energy input, provided that the liquid helium keeps the coil sufficiently cool to retain its superconductivity. The electrical current moving around the coil generates a very strong magnetic field, measured in units of Tesla. Standard MRI scanners have magnetic field strengths of 1.5, 3.0, and sometimes 4.0 Tesla—as a comparison, the magnetic field right next to the pole of a small bar magnet is about 0.01 Tesla. Because the magnetic field is so strong, ferromagnetic metallic objects (keys, coins, tools) that are brought into the scanner room can be sucked in to the bore of the magnet at very high speeds, endangering whoever is near or in the magnet, as well as potentially damaging the scanner itself. This is one of the major safety concerns when using MRI; thus, when in the vicinity of an MRI scanner, it is important to remember that the magnet is always on, even when the scanner is not in operation.

In addition to the main magnet, MRI scanners also have three magnetic gradient coils that pulse on and off at different times, depending on the type of scan. The coils are arranged such that they generate gradients in the strength of the magnetic field in the left–right direction, the front–back direction, and the head-to-toe direction. The magnetic field generated by these coils is not as strong as the main magnet, but, unlike the main magnet, the magnetic field varies in strength from one end of the coil to another, for reasons explained in the Appendix. In the presence of the main magnetic field, the fast-switching electrical currents in these gradient coils generate a magnetic field that results in force on the coils, causing them to vibrate at the switching rate. This vibration in the gradient coils causes the loud "clanging" or "beeping" noises characteristic of MRI scanning. Fortunately, recent advances in scanner technology have helped to reduce this noise significantly.

The third major scanner component is the radiofrequency (RF) transmit coil, which sends out brief pulses of RF energy, much in the same way that mobile phones transmit signals back and forth.

The fourth component is the RF receiver coil. The position of this coil, or set of coils, will depend on the particular part of the body being imaged. For brain imaging, the coils tend to be arranged in a kind of "birdcage" configuration that surrounds the head of the participant. The coils pick up faint RF signals from the body, which are then amplified and processed by computers connected to the scanner.

children does present some special challenges (as we outline below), these qualities make it very attractive as a research tool for understanding links between brain and behavior and how these might change over developmental time.

Varieties of MR images

MRI is an especially powerful imaging technique partly because it can reveal so many different tissue properties. There are three general families of MR images that are commonly used in neuroscientific and clinical research: structural, functional, and diffusion-tensor imaging. Structural images can be thought of as a "snapshot" of the brain at one point in time. Structural scans for research purposes are usually of quite high resolution (often 1 mm^3 of tissue) and can be used to measure the volume, shape, and position of tissues of interest. These scans can also be used to reconstruct the cortical surface, which can then be measured in terms of its thickness and relative curvature at different locations in the brain.

Unlike the high-resolution, single-snapshot view of the brain provided by structural scans, functional MRI (fMRI) scans reflect transient changes in the brain occurring over a period of seconds and minutes, changes that are thought to reflect alterations in neuronal activity. Thus, fMRI

Exhibit 4.3. How are different MR images generated?

- *Structural imaging:* Just as in film photography, the relative brightness of a given tissue in a structural MR image is determined by how that tissue absorbs and gives off energy during the time the image is acquired. Furthermore, the choice of structural scan type will determine whether a given tissue shows up as bright or dark. For instance, in so-called T1-weighted scans, cortical gray matter (primarily composed of neuronal cell bodies, glial cells, capillaries, and dendrites) will look gray, whereas white matter (predominantly myelinated axons) will tend to look white, and cerebrospinal fluid (CSF) will be very dark. On the other hand, T2-weighted images will tend to show white matter as dark, gray matter as gray, and CSF as bright.

- *BOLD (functional) imaging:* The logic of BOLD imaging is as follows: about 2–3 seconds after a population of neurons increases its firing rate, there is a transient (12–20-second) change in the amount of oxygenated hemoglobin delivered to that region of tissue by the brain's circulatory system. This oxygenated hemoglobin replaces some of the deoxygenated hemoglobin that was previously in that region. This slight change in the ratio of oxygenated to deoxygenated hemoglobin can be picked up by a standard clinical MR scanner. Because deoxygenated hemoglobin is paramagnetic, it "spoils" the coherence of the MR signal to some extent. Oxygenated hemoglobin, on the other hand, is less paramagnetic, so when it replaces the deoxygenated blood, the overall coherence of the signal in that region increases. These small, transient increases and decreases in signal due to the influx of blood after neuronal activation are what allows us to visualize—albeit indirectly—changes in neural activation over time.

- *Diffusion tensor imaging:* DTI techniques take advantage of two basic facts: (1) water molecules move randomly (e.g., Brownian motion), and (2) water diffuses differently around white and gray matter. Water will meander slowly through gray matter, in many different directions, but will move more quickly along white-matter pathways and will not diffuse through them very easily, since they are ensheathed in water-repelling myelin. We can use MRI to track the diffusion of water molecules over time, in many different directions, and thereby reconstruct the likely location and orientation of white-matter tracts.

---

can be used to assess and compare the pattern of functional activation of brain regions during different cognitive tasks. By far the most frequently used fMRI method is that of "Blood oxygenation level dependent," or BOLD, imaging. This technique, discovered in the early 1990s, cleverly uses the change in the ratio of oxygenated to deoxygenated hemoglobin in the blood as an indirect measure of changes in the location of neuronal firing. In a typical fMRI experiment, participants will perform a task or see different stimuli while being scanned. By associating the change in the BOLD MRI signal over time with changes in task or stimuli, it is possible to unveil the brain regions involved in performing a specific task or perceiving specific stimuli.

The third type of MR imaging commonly used for brain research is diffusion-weighted, or diffusion tensor imaging (DTI). This MRI technique uses another physical phenomenon—the directions that water diffuses in brain tissue—in order to reveal the location and orientation of white matter tracts such as the corpus callosum and the superior longitudinal fasciculus, both very important for allowing different brain regions to "talk" to each other. This MRI technique has particular relevance for studies of children with language impairments, as we will see below.[1]

The challenges of studying children using MRI

While MRI is a powerful and versatile tool, it comes with its own set of challenges and limitations when applied to developmental cognitive neuroscience—like all other research methodologies. Many of these are practical difficulties. For instance, MRI is quite resource-intensive, both in terms of the cost per hour for scanning itself, and in the time and experience required to process and analyze MRI data. Furthermore, some children either cannot be scanned—for example, those with metal in their bodies, including orthodontic devices—or find the scanner environment aversive, either because of claustrophobia (the magnet bore can be quite narrow), the loud scanner noise, or the clinical atmosphere of many MRI suites. MRI also requires participants to remain still for 5–10-minute intervals. Not only is this difficult for some children, but also differences in the extent of head movement between age groups (leading to profound effects on image quality) can introduce major confounds in the experimental design and analysis. In functional imaging, participants must also attend for long periods of time: age differences in levels of attention or task compliance are sometimes difficult to detect in the scanner, but can have considerable impact on patterns of brain activation (Kotsoni, Byrd, & Casey, 2006). These and other issues are addressed in several recent reviews of the developmental neuroimaging literature, such as Munakata, Casey, and Diamond (2004).

STUDIES OF LANGUAGE DEVELOPMENT USING MRI

The study of structural and functional brain development using MR techniques in infants and young children presents methodological as well as practical challenges (Berl, Vaida, & Gaillard, 2006). Many of the techniques used in the analysis of neuroimaging data were developed for adult brains and had to be modified and adapted for use with children. It is only recently that tools have been devised to allow reliable group comparisons between younger children and adults. In this section we aim to outline the recent advances MRI and fMRI have made in the study of brain development and function in young children, with particular reference to developmental language disorders.

Overview of brain regions

Brain regions classically associated with language function in adults are illustrated schematically in Figure 4.1. This MRI-based reconstruction (Fischl, Sereno, & Dale, 1999) is a lateral view showing the folded cortex of a typical person's left hemisphere. The cortex is only 2–3 mm thick and is made of up neuronal bodies, glial cells, and capillaries, or "gray matter." Underneath the cortex is a vast network of interneuronal connections, composed primarily of myelin-wrapped neuronal axons or "white matter." Embedded within these white matter pathways are many ensembles of nuclei, such as the thalamus and basal ganglia. Since the early days of neurology, the brain has been divided up into the frontal, temporal, parietal, and occipital lobes; the approximate borders of these lobes are shown in Figure 4.1.

In the frontal lobe, the orbital (A), triangular (B), and opercular (C) parts of the left inferior frontal gyrus are traditionally associated with language production, with at least the opercular part, if not the whole gyrus, thought of as being "Broca's area."[2]

In the left temporal and parietal lobes, the anterior (D) and posterior (E) parts of the superior temporal gyrus and the supramarginal gyrus (F) are traditionally associated with language comprehension. "Wernicke's area" is made up of the most posterior part of the superior temporal gyrus plus the supramarginal gyrus—although the reader should note that definitions of both Broca's area and Wernicke's area are quite variable.[3] Finally, in both the right and left hemispheres, many parts of the occipital lobe, as well as the inferior temporal lobe, are often associated with more "visual" language tasks such as reading and object naming.

Structural brain development

Early language development is occurring in a brain that is massively reorganizing itself, something that MRI has been very useful in showing. In the first years of life, the progressive development of cognitive function is accompanied by ongoing structural change in the brain. In the first published studies of human brain development, MRI was used to describe the qualitative changes

FIGURE 4.1

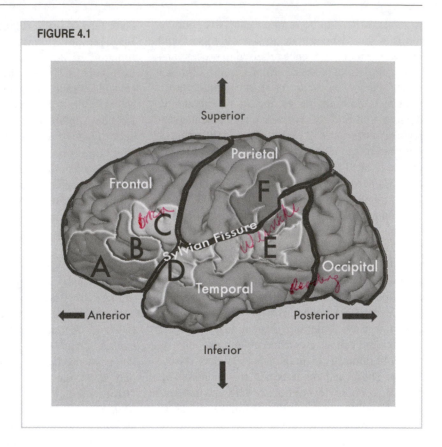

Brain regions classically associated with language processing.

of gray and white matter in the neonatal brain up to the first 2 years of life. These studies delineate the changes in cerebral tissue composition that take place in the first months, as myelination processes set in (Barkovich, Kjos, Jackson, & Norman, 1988; McArdle et al., 1987). More recently, MRI techniques have been used in quantitative longitudinal studies of brain development in children starting as young as 4 years of age, and up into young adulthood. These changes are typically quantified in terms of brain size, cortical thickness, and gray and white matter volume (see Lenroot & Giedd, 2006, for a review). A recent study by Sowell and colleagues (2004) found that in normally developing children between the ages of 5 and 11 years, brain volume expands at a rate of up to 1 mm per year. This expansion of brain volume, found predominantly in the prefrontal region, is accompanied by underlying changes in gray and white matter composition—namely, as brain size expands (in right-frontal and parietal and occipital regions bilaterally), gray matter thins out and white matter increases due to myelin proliferation, a process that improves the speed and efficiency of processing between cortical regions. In fact, cortical thinning of the frontal and parietal lobes was found to correlate with better performance on measures of verbal skill. Increases in cortical thickness also occur, but these are more selective and appear to be localized mainly within the left anterior and posterior perisylvian regions. Interestingly, these regions correspond to classical language areas such as Broca's and Wernicke's, with gray matter thickening also occurring in the right-hemisphere homologue of Wernicke's area.

As children mature, the proportion of gray and white matter in the brain changes. Approaching puberty, the rate of gray and white matter maturation accelerates. While white matter volume typically shows a linear increase throughout childhood, changes in gray matter volume are nonlinear, in that they decrease in postadolescence (Giedd et al., 1999; Gogtay et al., 2004; Sowell et al., 1999). Interestingly, gray matter volume peaks in the frontal and parietal regions of the brain approximately one year earlier in females than in males, which corresponds with the earlier onset of puberty in females, suggesting an influence of gonadal hormones upon brain development (Giedd et al., 1999). In tracking the sequence of gray matter development in different brain regions in young individuals aged 4 to 21 years, Gogtay et al. (2004) found that the process of gray matter maturation appears to follow a similar sequence to how the brain regions evolved, with phylogenetically older regions maturing first. Moreover, the sequence of structural development was also similar to that of functional development, whereby primary sensorimotor cortices and the frontal and occipital poles mature first, followed by the remainder of the cortex in a posterior-to-anterior direction, with the superior temporal cortex being the last area to mature.

fMRI and language development

In general, fMRI studies in children aim to establish the similarities and differences between patterns of functional activation found in children in comparison to adults, and how these relate to an increase in skill or proficiency over the course of development. In the study of language, imaging studies have sought to track the emergence of the language network across development in order to determine how, and at what rate, functional specialization for language emerges to resemble the left-lateralized language network typically found in adults. For example, Szaflarski, Holland, and Schmithorst (2006) explored the effect of age upon language lateralization using a covert verb generation task and found that a shift in lateralization toward the dominant (left) hemisphere occurs between the ages of 5 and 20 years and reaches its peak between the ages of 20 to 25. These data, along with two early imaging studies of auditory

language comprehension in young children, suggest that early language processing is predominantly bilateral, activating the inferior frontal gyrus (IFG) and the temporal cortices (Booth et al., 1999; Ulualp, Biswal, Yetkin, & Kidder, 1998). However, as we discuss below, studies by other groups (summarized in Ahmad, Balsamo, Sachs, Xu, & Gaillard, 2003) appear to show that left-lateralization is established relatively early on in development (Ahmad et al., 2003; Holland et al., 2001; Saccuman et al., 2007)

The activation pattern of the inferior frontal gyrus and the temporal cortices found in children is consistent with the activation patterns found in adults and has been replicated across child studies of language processing (Ahmad et al., 2003; Balsamo et al., 2002; Brown et al., 2005; Gaillard et al., 2000, 2001; Holland et al., 2001; Schlaggar et al., 2002; Szaflarski et al., 2006). However, more recent studies carried out across a range of language tasks, including verbal fluency, auditory response naming, and passive listening, suggest that although children do show more extensive patterns of activity overall, with significantly more activation occurring in the right hemisphere in comparison to adults, calculations to determine language lateralization (known as lateralization indices) indicate a dominance in activation in the left hemisphere (Ahmad et al., 2003; Balsamo et al., 2002; Gaillard et al., 2000), which increases with age, consolidating language within the left hemisphere (Holland et al., 2001). In support of this more recent perspective on language lateralization in children, a functional imaging study carried out by Dehaene-Lambertz, Dehaene, and Hertz-Pannier (2002) in 3-month-old infants listening to meaningful and reversed speech while asleep and awake, found activity in left lateralized language regions, including the superior temporal and angular gyri—suggesting a bias for speech processing in these regions prior to the onset of speech production (Dehaene-Lambertz, Hertz-Pannier, & Dubois, 2006).

In addition to the issue of lateralization, fMRI studies of language development attempt to describe changes in the patterns of functional activations distinguishing between age- and performance-related effects. For example, a study carried out by Brown et al. (2005) used a series of three lexical association tasks presented in both auditory and visual modalities in order to track the maturation of functional activity, identifying 40 brain regions that showed age-related effects even when performance was matched across ages. In the majority of these regions (primarily in bilateral occipital and temporal cortices), activity decreased over age; the ten regions showing age-related increases in activity were mainly found in left frontal and parietal cortex. Perhaps more importantly, the developmental trajectory of these up- and down-regulations in activation was nonlinear, and varied considerably across region, suggesting that no global "maturational" process could easily account for such changes.

In another recent study (Saccuman et al., 2007), fMRI was used to compare children's (10–12 years old) and young adults' functional organization for two well-characterized language tasks—overt picture naming and auditory sentence interpretation—which preferentially tap processes of lexical access and syntactic interpretation. In order to assess potential interactions between task complexity and age, pictures and sentences were classed into two levels of difficulty based on previous behavioral studies. While adults and children showed similar overall activation patterns, there were significant differences in activation modulated by age, task, and task difficulty. In picture naming, adults showed greater activation than children in frontal, parietal, and inferior temporal-occipital networks involved in lexical retrieval. Conversely, in sentence comprehension, children showed greater activation than young adults in prefrontal and superior temporal regions; only in the left parietal lobe did adults show more activation than children. These developmental shifts could not easily be accounted for by differences in behavioral performance. Moreover, areas of increased activation in children did not generally overlap with those upregulated when stimulus complexity increased. These results highlight the complex and multifaceted nature of language development; and, perhaps more importantly, they suggest that global "maturational" changes cannot be

the sole driver of functional reorganization over development. Rather, they suggest that functional organization is the result of an interplay between general maturation patterns, task-related differences, and strategic differences.

BRAIN IMAGING IN DEVELOPMENTAL LANGUAGE DISORDERS

Imaging techniques have been used to delineate the neuroanatomical and functional characteristics of developmental language disorders, including specific language impairment (SLI), developmental dyslexia (DD), and autism. We focus on the studies published so far on specific language impairment, a behaviorally defined condition in which areas of language processing are affected in the context of otherwise "normal" development. While most children seem to acquire language effortlessly, a few experience significant and persistent difficulties that may result in a diagnosis of specific language impairment. English-speaking children with language impairment (henceforth, CLI) exhibit expressive and/or receptive language difficulties and struggle in particular with grammatical inflections, in spite of a nonverbal IQ within the normal range and the absence of frank neurologic impairment, mental retardation, hearing loss, autism, or severe social or emotional problems (Webster & Shevell, 2004).

Studies of brain structure in CLI

Although there is a rich literature on language profiles of CLI, until recently only a handful of studies (Gauger, Lombardino, & Leonard, 1997; Jernigan, Hesselink, Sowell, & Tallal, 1991; Trauner, Wulfeck, Tallal, & Hesselink, 2000) had attempted to delineate the neurological, neuroanatomical, or neurophysiological status of CLI, revealing significant but subtle and heterogeneous abnormalities. Structural imaging studies of CLI have identified regions of abnormal asymmetry in brain structure, in particular the planum temporale, an area that is known to be involved in the processing of speech and acoustic information (Griffiths & Warren, 2002). Slight deviations of the planum temporale have been seen in many studies involving young children with LI, although the nature of these abnormalities has been somewhat inconsistent, with some studies finding reversed asymmetry or a more symmetrical planum temporale in individuals with SLI (Plante, Swisher, Vance, & Rapcsak, 1991), more exaggerated asymmetry (Gauger et al., 1997), or even greater leftward asymmetry (Herbert et al., 2005). The heterogeneity of SLI as a disorder (Hill, 2001; Mengler, Hogben, Michie, & Bishop, 2005) could potentially account for some of these differences. However, more studies are required to establish whether this is the case. Additional atypical anatomical features reported in LI include a significantly smaller and atypically symmetric triangular part of the inferior frontal gyrus, and prefrontal abnormalities, particular in motor regions (De Fossé et al., 2004; Gauger et al., 1997; Jaencke, Siegenthaler, Preis, & Steinmetz, 2007; Jernigan et al., 1991; Leonard et al., 2002).

Several recent studies have used quantitative analyses of structural MRI data to compare children with LI with children with other clinical diagnoses. For instance, Herbert et al. (2004) compared a group of 5–11-year-old children with LI to a matched sample of children with autism. Strikingly, overall white matter volume was found to be selectively *enlarged* in both groups of impaired children compared to controls, with the enlargement only observed in the late-myelinating "radiate" white matter in frontal, temporal, and occipital lobes. The fact that these anatomical differences were found across three of the four cerebral lobes but only in late-myelinating white matter regions suggests that the etiology of both language impairment and autism might be linked to alterations in a more general neurodevelopmental process, rather than a disruption in specific brain circuits or regions (Herbert et al., 2004). This point is bolstered by findings in the same sample of multiple localized abnormalities in the relative symmetry of gray matter, with asymmetries that are again quite similar across the children with LI and autism (Herbert et al., 2005).

Another comparison across clinical developmental groups is that of Leonard et al. (2006), who compared cortical morphology in 11–16-year-old children with language impairment with 11–16-year-olds with DD. Here, Leonard, Eckert, Given, Berninger, and Eden (2006) showed that these two clinical groups differed on a set of anatomical "risk factors": children with LI showed smaller and more symmetrical cortical structures, whereas children with DD tended to show more exaggerated cortical asymmetries. These results show the promise of using MRI to assist "differential diagnosis," as distinguishing between specific language impairment and developmental dyslexia on the basis of behavioral measures alone has proved challenging (Bishop & Snowling, 2004).

Studies of brain function in CLI

Hugdahl et al. (2004) investigated language processing in 5 Finnish family members with SLI and an age-matched sample of 6 controls in a passive listening task in which participants listened to real words, vowel sounds, and pseudowords. Overall, SLI participants showed smaller and weaker patterns of activation in left-hemisphere language regions in comparison to controls. Activations for the SLI group were concentrated within the upper posterior region of the superior temporal gyrus, with no significant activation in the superior temporal sulcus and medial temporal gyrus as seen in control participants. Friederici (2006) has suggested that the reduced activation may be related to the difficulties individuals with SLI have in decoding the phonological structure of words and pseudowords.

In another study, Saccuman et al. (2007) used the same two tasks described above for typically developing children and adults to explore the functional underpinnings of language processing in school-age children with LI engaged in naturalistic language tasks involving production and comprehension. Children with LI performed well on both tasks, particularly on picture naming, where their speed and accuracy approached the performance of normally developing children, but they showed patterns of activation that were significantly different from those of controls. The patterns observed did not dramatically diverge from those of normal children but could, rather, be described in terms of diffuse reductions in activation, with more accentuated signal loss in frontal, temporal, and parietal regions. Remarkably, LI children showed significantly more deactivation than did normal children, especially for picture naming—a pattern that could be interpreted as a sign of limitation in processing resources for the LI group. Right-hemisphere activation that could be interpreted as "compensatory" of left-hemisphere deficits was observed only in the fusiform gyrus for picture naming. In contrast, areas contralateral to activated left-hemisphere regions often showed a small deactivation. This pattern was observed in children with normal language, but was significantly more frequent in the LI group.

It is important to note that the structural and functional differences between children with LI and typically developing children are relatively subtle ones and are quantitative rather than qualitative—for example, even the most experienced investigator cannot "eyeball" a structural or functional scan and determine whether it is of a child with language impairment. More fundamentally, it is currently unclear what direction the "causal pathways" of language impairment run. Are structural brain differences such as those observed by Herbert et al. the underlying cause of language impairments, or are these brain differences at least partly due to differences in the child's language use and his or her effect on the language environment? Similarly, are the functional differences between language-impaired and typically developing children (such as those observed in the study of Saccuman et al., 2007) the result of aberrant structural connectivity, or are they perhaps part of the cause of that aberrant connectivity? It is particularly difficult to answer these questions given the small sample sizes of all of the above studies, as well as the highly heterogeneous character of the samples themselves in terms of diagnostic criteria, age, and gender.

Further studies with more epidemiological sample sizes (cf. Brown et al., 2005) and more targeted comparisons between potentially related clinical groups (similar to the Herbert et al. and Leonard et al. studies) will be extremely useful in teasing apart these causal factors. One promising approach to untangling causal pathways that has been used recently with other clinical groups is a combination of diffusion tensor, structural, and functional imaging. (For a useful overview of such a "converging methodologies" approach, see Schlaggar & McCandliss, 2007.) Early identification and scanning of language-impaired children—preferably at multiple points across development—will be crucial for uncovering potentially wayward developmental pathways (as suggested by the results of Herbert et al.) Finally, a synthesis of neuroimaging and behavioral results should not only allow for a richer understanding of the clinical underpinnings of language impairment, but should also lead to new ideas for treatment and early intervention.

ACKNOWLEDGMENTS

FD is supported by an MRC New Investigator Award (G0400341) to Frederic Dick; FR is supported by an MRC Career Establishment Grant (GO300188) and British Academy Grant (SG-40400) awarded to Michael Thomas. We would like to thank Rob Leech, Marty Sereno, Angelica Ronald, and Evelyne Mercure for extremely helpful suggestions; many thanks to Courtenay Norbury for her comments on earlier versions of this chapter, and Afasic for its support of children with developmental language disorders.

NOTES

1 For more information on MRI physics, we can recommend several excellent websites (www.e-fmri.org and www.cis.rit.edu/htbooks/mri/) and books (Buxton, 2001; Huettel, Song, & McCarthy, 2004).
2 The orbital part of the inferior frontal gyrus is often thought of as part of the "prefrontal" cortex.

3 This group of regions involved in language processing is often referred to as "perisylvian" cortex, in that they lie around the Sylvian fissure separating the temporal from the parietal and frontal lobes (see Figure 4.1).

REFERENCES

Ahmad, Z., Balsamo, L. M., Sachs, B. C., Xu, B., & Gaillard, W. D. (2003). Auditory comprehension of language in young children: Neural networks identified with fMRI. *Neurology, 60,* 1598–1605.

Balsamo, L. M., Xu, B., Grandin, C. B., Petrella, J. R., Braniecki, S. H., Elliot, T. K., & Gaillard, W. D. (2002). A functional magnetic resonance imaging study of left hemisphere language dominance in children. *Archives of Neurology, 59,* 1168–1174.

Barkovich, A., Kjos, B., Jackson, D., Jr., & Norman, D. (1988). Normal maturation of the neonatal and infant brain: MRI imaging at 1.5 T. *Radiology, 166,* 173–180.

Berl, M., Vaida, C., & Gaillard, W. (2006). Functional imaging of developmental and adaptive changes in neurocognition. *NeuroImage, 30,* 679–691.

Bishop, D. V. M., & Snowling, M. J. (2004). Developmental dyslexia and specific language impairment: Same or different? *Psychological Bulletin, 130,* 858–886.

Booth, J., MacWhinney, B., Thulborn, K., Sacco, K., Voyvodic, J., & Feldman, H. (1999). Functional organization of activation patterns in children: Whole brain fMRI imaging during three different cognitive tasks. *Progress in Neuro-Psychopharmacology & Biological Psychiatry, 23,* 669–682.

Brown, T. T., Lugar, H. M., Coalson, R. S., Miezin, F. M., Petersen, S. E., & Schlaggar, B. L. (2005). Developmental changes in human cerebral functional organization for word generation. *Cerebral Cortex, 15,* 275–290.

Buxton, R. (2001). *Introduction to functional magnetic resonance imaging: Principles and techniques.* Cambridge, UK: Cambridge University Press.

De Fossé, M. S., Hodge, S. M., Makris, N., Kennedy, D. N., Caviness, V. S., McGrath, L., et al. (2004). Language-association cortex asymmetry in autism and specific language impairment. *Annals of Neurology, 56,* 757–766.

Dehaene-Lambertz, G., Dehaene, S., & Hertz-Pannier, L. (2002). Functional neuroimaging of speech perception in infants. *Science, 6,* 2013–2015.

Dehaene-Lambertz, G., Hertz-Pannier, L., & Dubois, J. (2006). Nature and nurture in language acquisition: Anatomical and functional brain-imaging studies in infants. *Trends in Neuroscience, 29*(7), 367–373.

Fischl, B., Sereno, M. I., & Dale, A. (1999). Cortical surface-based analysis. II: Inflation, flattening, and a surface-based coordinate system. *NeuroImage, 9*(2), 195–207.

Friederici, A. D. (2006). The neural basis of language development and its impairment. *Neuron, 52,* 941–952.

Gaillard, W. D., Hertz-Pannier, L., Mott, S. H., Barnett, A. S., LeBihan, D., & Theodore, W. H. (2000). Functional anatomy of cognitive development. *Neurology, 54,* 180–185.

Gaillard, W. D., Pugliese, M., Grandin, C. B., Braniecki, S. H., Kondapaneni, P., Hunter, K., et al. (2001). Cortical localization of reading in normal children. *Neurology, 57,* 47–54.

Gauger, L. M., Lombardino, L. J., & Leonard, C. M. (1997). Brain morphology in children with specific language impairment. *Journal of Speech, Language, and Hearing Research, 40,* 1272–1284.

Giedd, J. N., Blumenthal, J., Jeffries, N. O., Castellanos, F. X., Liu, H., Zijdenbros, A., et al. (1999). Brain development during childhood and adolescence: A longitudinal MRI study. *Nature Neuroscience, 2,* 861–863.

Gogtay, N., Giedd, J. N., Lusk, L., Hayashi, K. M., Greenstein, D., Vaituzis, A. C., et al. (2004). Dynamic mapping of human cortical development during childhood through early adulthood. *Proceedings of the National Academy of Sciences, 101*(21), 8174–8179.

Griffiths, T. D., & Warren, J. D. (2002). The planum temporale as a computational hub. *Trends in Neuroscience, 25,* 348–353.

Herbert, M. R., Ziegler, D. A., Deutsch, C. K., O'Brien, L. M., Kennedy, D. N., Filipek, P. A., et al. (2005). Brain asymmetries in autism and developmental language disorder: A nested whole-brain analysis. *Brain, 128,* 213–226.

Herbert, M. R., Ziegler, D. A., Makris, N., Filipek, P. A., Kemper, T. L., Normandin, J. J., et al. (2004). Localization of white matter volume increase in autism and developmental language disorder. *Annals of Neurology, 55,* 530–540.

Hill, E. L. (2001). Non-specific nature of specific language impairment: A review of the literature with regard to concomitant motor impairments. *International Journal of Language & Communication Disorders*, *36*, 149–171.

Holland, S. K., Plante, E., Weber Byers, A., Strasburg, R. H., Schmithorst, V. J., & Ball, Jr., S. (2001). Normal fMRI activation patterns in children performing a verb generation task. *NeuroImage*, *14*, 837–843.

Huettel, S., Song, A., & McCarthy, G. (2004). *Functional magnetic resonance imaging*. Sunderland, MA: Sinauer Associates.

Hugdahl, K., Gundersen, H., Thomsen, T., Rimol, L. M., Ersland, L., & Niemi, J. (2004). fMRI brain activation in a Finnish family with specific language impairment compared with a normal control group. *Journal of Speech, Language, and Hearing Research*, *47*, 162–172.

Jaencke, L., Siegenthaler, T., Preis, S., & Steinmetz, H. (2007). Decreased white-matter density in a left-sided fronto-temporal network in children with developmental language disorder: Evidence for anatomical anomalies in a motor-language network. *Brain and Language, 102*(1), 91–98.

Jernigan, T. L., Hesselink, J. R., Sowell, E. R., & Tallal, P. A. (1991). Cerebral structure on magnetic resonance imaging in language- and learning-impaired children. *Archives of Neurology*, *48*(5), 539–545.

Kotsoni, E., Byrd, D., & Casey, B. J. (2006). Special considerations for functional magnetic resonance imaging of pediatric populations. *Journal of Magnetic Resonance Imaging*, *23*(6), 877–886.

Lenroot, R., & Giedd, J. (2006). Brain development in children and adolescents: Insights from anatomical magnetic resonance imaging. *Neuroscience and Behavioral Reviews*, *30*, 718–729.

Leonard, C., Eckert, M., Given, B., Berninger, V., & Eden, G. (2006). Individual differences in anatomy predict reading and oral language impairments in children. *Brain, 129*(12), 3329–3342.

Leonard, C. M., Lombardino, L. J., Walsh, K., Eckert, M. A., Mockler, J. L., Rowe, L. A., et al. (2002). Anatomical risk factors that distinguish dyslexia from SLI predict reading skill in normal children. *Journal of Communication Disorders*, *35*, 501–531.

McArdle, C., Richardson, C., Nicholas, D., Mirfakhraee, M., Hayden, C., & Amparo, E. (1987). Developmental features of the neonatal brain: MR imaging. Part I. Gray–white matter differentiation and myelination. *Radiology*, *162*, 223–229.

Mengler, E., Hogben, J., Michie, P., & Bishop, D. (2005). Poor frequency discrimination is related to oral language disorder in children: A psychoacoustic study. *Dyslexia, 11*(3), 155–173.

Munakata, Y., Casey, B. J., & Diamond, A. (2004). Developmental cognitive neuroscience: Progress and potential. *Trends in Cognitive Sciences*, *8*(3), 122–126.

Plante, E., Swisher, L., Vance, R., & Rapcsak, S. (1991). MRI findings in boys with specific language impairment. *Brain and Language*, *41*, 52–66.

Saccuman, M. C., Wulfeck, B., Müller, R.-A., Krupa-Kwiatkowski, M., Moses, P., & Dick, F. (2007). *Learning to speak, and learning to listen: fMRI reveals differential developmental changes in functional organization for expressive and receptive language*. Manuscript submitted for publication.

Schlaggar, B. L., Brown, T. T., Lugar, H. M., Visscher, K. M., Miezin, F. M., & Petersen, S. E. (2002). Functional neuroanatomical differences between adults and school-age children in the processing of single words. *Science*, *296*, 1476–1479.

Schlaggar, B. L., & McCandliss, B. (2007). Development of neural systems for reading. *Annual Review of Neuroscience, 30*, 475–503.

Sowell, E. R., Thompson, P. M., Holmes, C. J., Batth, R., Jernigan, T. L., & Toga, A. W. (1999). Localizing age-related changes in brain structure between childhood and adolescence using statistical parametric mapping. *NeuroImage*, *9*, 587–597.

Sowell, E. R., Thompson, P. M., Leonard, C. M., Welcome, S. E., Kan, E., & Toga, A. W. (2004). Longitudinal mapping of cortical thickness and brain growth in children. *Journal of Neuroscience*, *24*(38), 8223–8231.

Szaflarski, J. P., Holland, S. K., & Schmithorst, V. J. (2006). fMRI study of language lateralisation in children and adults. *Human Brain Mapping*, *27*, 202–212.

Trauner, D., Wulfeck, B., Tallal, P., & Hesselink, J. (2000). Neurological and MRI profiles of children with developmental language impairment. *Developmental Medicine & Child Neurology*, *42*, 470–475.

Ulualp, S. O., Biswal, B. B., Yetkin, Z., & Kidder, T. M. (1998). Functional magnetic resonance imaging of auditory cortex in children. *Laryngoscope*, *108*, 1782–1786.

Webster, R. I., & Shevell, M. I. (2004). Neurobiology of specific language impairment. *Journal of Child Neurology*, *19*, 471–481.

APPENDIX. Mechanics of MRI

- ***Basic physics of MRI:*** How do the four components of the MRI scanner work together to create such a wide variety of functional and structural images of the brain and body? The answer to this question lies in some fundamental properties of atoms and their interactions with each other. Medical MRI exploits the fact that the nucleus of the most abundant element in the body—hydrogen, with only one proton—acts like a small magnet, with a north and a south pole. The magnetic dipoles of the billions and billions of hydrogen protons in a small tissue volume are usually oriented randomly, meaning that they do not have an overall net magnetization. But when the tissue is placed in a very strong magnetic field like the one in an MRI scanner, a tiny proportion of the hydrogen protons in the tissue will align with the field, thereby forming a very weak but detectable magnetization that is aligned with the magnet's bore (the "longitudinal" magnetization).

  Each hydrogen proton also has an intrinsic property called "spin," somewhat like a top or dreidel spinning on a hard surface. Just like a top in the earth's gravitational field, the spinning protons will tend to be oriented within the main magnetic field. If a top is spinning rapidly on a table and is then tilted away from the main axis of the earth's gravitational field (e.g., straight up and down), it will start to swivel slowly around that axis. Constantly "spinning" hydrogen protons do the same thing in a magnetic field. Interestingly, the speed with which the protons precess is completely predictable given the strength of the main magnetic field; this precession rate is termed the "Larmor frequency."

  Even though the hydrogen protons aligned with the magnetic field are rotating or precessing at the same rate or frequency around the magnetic axis, they are not all in sync. Instead, they are out of phase with each other, and not all pointing in the same direction at the same time. However, if we beam in an electromagnetic pulse (an RF pulse) that oscillates at the same frequency as the protons are precessing, then they will all start to point in the same direction as they swivel around.

  If the RF pulse is the correct length, it will tip all of the spinning protons completely over so that they are swiveling around in sync in the plane perpendicular to the main magnetic orientation. (Imagine a table full of spinning tops that have been tipped over on their sides and are miraculously swiveling just above the table's surface, all in unison.) Recall that when the hydrogen protons are aligned, they generate their own small magnetic field. When the precessing protons are tipped over on their sides, their net magnetization is rotating perpendicular to the main magnetic field. As long as they are tipped over and are not aligned with the main magnetic field, this little rotating magnetization will induce electrical current in a surrounding coil of wire. This is the signal that MRI scanners detect. (Electric generators work on the same principle— e.g., a magnet rotating quickly within a wire coil or vice versa.)

  Eventually, the protons will start to tip back up (or relax) and align with the main magnetic field, and they will also get out of phase with each other. (This is a little more difficult to visualize with real tops: it is as if the proton "tops" have no friction and never slow down, but are constantly colliding with each other, with the end result that their coordinated swiveling returns to an uncoordinated swiveling.) This means that the electrical current that they induce will also decrease and eventually disappear. The speed with which the spinning protons dephase and relax—and therefore the speed with which the electrical signal decays— depends upon the chemical composition of the surrounding tissue. This difference in the rate of decay of the protons' signal is what makes it possible for MRI to detect different tissue types, in that the signal from the precessing protons in white matter, gray matter, and cerebrospinal fluid will decay at different rates.

  The above describes the layout of the most basic MR experiment. An object—in our case, a person—is put into a large magnetic field, the person's protons become slightly more aligned with the magnetic field, and a RF pulse is applied at the Larmor frequency, making the spinning protons tip over and precess in unison. This, in turn, generates a small electrical current in the wire coil around the person, and the speed with which that current decays tells us something about the chemical composition of the tissue surrounding the hydrogen protons.

- ***How are MR images generated?*** While the MR experiment above is very useful for finding out the chemical properties of a given sample, it does not tell us anything about the spatial layout of different substances within that sample. As we noted previously, it was Mansfield's and Lauterbur's innovations in the 1970s that made it possible to use magnetic resonance techniques to create 2D pictures of objects like the human body. The key insight into creating MR "pictures" was taking advantage of the lawful relationship between magnetic field strength and precession (Larmor) frequency. As MRI scanners have not only a very strong static magnetic field, but also three magnetic gradient coils arranged at perpendicular axes (X, Y, Z) along the main bore of the magnet, introduction of current into one of these coils creates a magnetic gradient that is slightly weaker at one end, and slightly stronger at the other end. This means that the Larmor frequency will change from one end of the magnetic gradient to the other.

  This systematic change in the hydrogen protons' precession frequency can be used to encode spatial information in the MRI signal in what is generally a three-stage process. The first is the "slice-select" stage, where one magnetic gradient is switched on, thus creating a "gradient" of Larmor frequencies along the Z-axis parallel with the bore of the magnet. A precisely calibrated RF pulse is then delivered that will only tip over protons with a narrow range of Larmor frequencies—and thus excite protons in a thin slice of tissue. After these protons within one slice are tipped and are precessing in unison, a second, perpendicular magnetic gradient is turned on momentarily, thereby changing the phase of the precessing protons systematically along the Y-axis. Finally, the last perpendicular gradient is turned on along the X-axis, again systematically changing the Larmor frequency along the X-axis while the MR signal is collected.

  By repeating this process many times, with many different variants of magnetic gradient, the spatial composition of the entire sample can be recorded. Perhaps the most remarkable thing about the process is the decoding of this signal. The brain image is reconstructed by simply applying a Fourier transform to the entire set of measurements. A Fourier transform reconstructs an image (like a brain slice) by adding together a large number of stripe patterns of different spacings and different orientations (Fourier components), each with a particular weighting. Each data point coming from the head coil corresponds to a single Fourier component and represents the extent to which the brain slice resembles a stripe pattern of a certain orientation and spacing. Remarkably, even though each such measurement comes from the whole head, a detailed picture can nevertheless be reassembled. The gradients are essentially used to create all the different stripe patterns.

5

Specific language impairment, dyslexia, and autism: Using genetics to unravel their relationship

Dorothy V. M. Bishop

Language impairment is not something that is obvious at birth; rather, awareness that all is not well creeps up on a parent insidiously over months and years, as it becomes apparent that the child is not talking like other children do. The typical reaction of professionals to a parent of a late-talking toddler is to offer reassurance that all will be well, given time. And, indeed, very often this advice is appropriate, because there are many late bloomers who catch up rapidly after a slow start (Paul, 2000). Our concern, though, is with those children who don't catch up but, instead, continue to lag behind their peers in talking and/or understanding. Parents then want to know two

things: what can be done to help the child to communicate, and what is the cause of the language difficulties. In this chapter I focus on the second question. This can be a source of considerable concern to parents, who will ask why their child is having such difficulties when other children learn language so effortlessly. Is there anything they could have done differently to prevent language impairment? If they have other children, are they likely to have the same problems?

When I started research on specific language impairment (SLI) in the mid-1970s, very little was known about causes. I vividly remember a parent of one of my research participants complaining that the pediatrician would not tell her what had caused her child's problems, and I had to gently point out that this was probably because nobody knew. We have made enormous strides forward in piecing together the puzzle since that time, but there is still considerable uncertainty. We now know that genes play an important part in causing SLI, but there is no biological diagnostic test. In fact, the growing consensus is that in most cases of language impairment we will not be able to point the finger at a single causal factor: rather, SLI is regarded as a complex multifactorial disorder, in which a collection of risk factors conspires to disrupt language development. I start by briefly reviewing some environmental and biological factors that were thought to be potential causes of language impairment in the 1970s but have been shown to be relatively unimportant. I then move on to discuss studies of genetic risks for language impairment, outlining the research approaches that can throw light on this topic and presenting the major developments that have taken place over the past 20 years, since the first Afasic International Symposium, in Reading in 1987. One development since that meeting has been the integration of research into SLI and research into dyslexia, with a move from regarding them as distinct disorders to treating them, rather, as points on a continuum of severity. I shall consider how far the genetic research supports that view. Another intriguing insight from genetic research is that SLI and autistic disorder might have causal influences in common: the jury is still out on this question, but I review the evidence for and against this position. Finally, I consider implications for intervention.

THINGS THAT ONE MIGHT EXPECT TO CAUSE LANGUAGE IMPAIRMENT BUT DON'T

Quantity and quality of language input

Language is clearly something that is learned by hearing others talk. A child growing up in Kyoto learns Japanese, a child in Madrid learns Spanish, and one in Warwick learns English. When I started in this field, it was common to hear teachers comment that "he doesn't speak properly because his parents don't talk to him." However, while we would all agree that it is good to talk with your child, the notion that inadequate communication from parents can cause clinically significant language difficulties in their offspring has been shown to be unwarranted. There are plenty of children with SLI whose parents communicate plentifully and effectively with them, and plenty of children who receive relatively impoverished input from parents yet have no difficulties with language development (Mogford & Bishop, 1988). Unfortunately, the notion that parents are to blame for their children's language difficulties continues to resurface from time to time. A BBC report on an education conference in 2003 stated that "Parents who do little more than grunt at their children every day are damaging their language development, a literacy expert has said." Alan Wells, director of the Basic Skills Agency, says that parents no longer talk to their children; instead, they just let them sit in front of the television or computer for hours. He said: "At the age when they come into school, many children have very few language skills at all" (http://news.bbc.co.uk/1/hi/education/2638889.stm). It is unfortunate indeed that such unfounded speculation should be widely publicized; it is bad enough having to worry about one's child's language difficulties without being made to feel responsible for causing them.

In making this point, I am not implying that language input has no effect on children—indeed, the language environment may play an important part in the remediation of language difficulties, and many intervention programs work with parents to help achieve optimal communication with their child (McCauley & Fey, 2006). However, it is a common mistake to conclude that, because a parent's language level predicts a child's language level, one has caused the other. As we shall see, an alternative explanation exists for such an association, in terms of shared genetic risk.

Mild hearing loss

Another very plausible but unsubstantiated theory attributes SLI to the fluctuating hearing loss associated with otitis media, a common childhood ailment in which the middle ear becomes filled with fluid. We know that severe and profound hearing loss can dramatically impair the child's ability to learn spoken language, and so it seems reasonable to suppose that milder levels of hearing loss might make it difficult to hear speech clearly and so make it hard to learn to talk. In the 1960s, an influential paper by Holm and Kunze (1969) presented language test results from a group of children who had been treated for chronic otitis media, showing major problems in many of them. However, there was a subtle but important logical flaw in this study. Children were selected for the study on the basis that they had been referred for specialist treatment of their middle ear disease. Middle ear disease is extremely common in preschool children and is frequently left untreated, or is treated by a family doctor. So one has to ask oneself why this subset of children had been referred on for hospital treatment. One possible reason is that they were having language difficulties, and thus their ear problems were taken more seriously than if they had had no language problems. Thus the study sample may well have been biased. To test this explanation, one needs to do a large-scale study in which a whole population of children is screened for otitis media and then followed up, rather than just focusing on those referred for treatment. There have now been several studies of this kind, and they do not support the idea that otitis media has a major impact on children's language (Roberts, Rosenfeld, & Zeisel, 2004). This is not to say we should disregard middle ear disease in children. As I argue below, risk factors that do not normally have an adverse effect on language may assume importance if they occur in combination with other risks. But it seems unlikely that even persistent middle ear disease will be the sole cause of a child's language difficulties. More recent work supporting this conclusion comes from studies of children who have hearing loss because of damage to the cochlea. These sensorineural hearing losses do not fluctu-ate but will impair the child's ability to hear differences between speech sounds. Nevertheless, explicit comparisons between children with such hearing losses and those with SLI indicate that, provided consideration is restricted to children with losses in the mild-to-moderate range, only a minority of hearing-impaired children have poor language, and they seldom have the major grammatical difficulties that characterize many children with SLI (Briscoe, Bishop, & Norbury, 2001; Norbury, Bishop, & Briscoe, 2001; Wake et al., 2006).

Early brain injury

If an adult suffers brain damage, due to conditions such as stroke, tumor, or head injury, this can cause severe and selective language difficulties while leaving other mental faculties intact. The site of injury is critical: certain areas of the left cerebral hemisphere are crucial for language processing, and even small areas of damage in these regions can lead to serious language problems (Damasio & Damasio, 1992). It is therefore logical to suppose that language difficulties in children might be caused by damage to these same regions. Children with SLI typically do not have obvious indications of brain injury, but it is nevertheless possible that disease or trauma could have affected the brain before or around the time of birth without anyone being aware of this. Once again, we have a theory that seems entirely plausible but is no longer regarded as correct. There are two lines of evidence that are key: First, studies of birth histories of children with SLI do not find any evidence of increased rates of perinatal problems that might lead to subtle brain injury (Merricks, Stott, Goodyer, & Bolton, 2004; Tomblin, Smith, & Zhang, 1997). Second, when we look at children who have suffered brain injury affecting language regions, they do not look like cases of SLI. This point was first made over 40 years ago by Basser (1962), who noted that it was possible for language to develop normally despite removal of a left cerebral cortex that was diseased early in life. If similar surgery is conducted for disease acquired in adulthood, language is seriously impaired. More recent studies have shown that for children with focal injury of the left hemisphere, language usually develops along normal lines, though there may be a rather slow start (Bates & Roe, 2001). This demonstrates that the child's brain can recover from focal injury, with other regions taking over the functions of the damaged area. Subtle damage to the language regions of the brain does not, therefore, seem to be a plausible cause of SLI.

GENETIC RISK FACTORS

How do we know whether genes play a part?

In studying causes of disorders, a broad distinction is commonly drawn between genetic and environmental factors. In common parlance, we are used to thinking of "environmental" factors as referring to things like air pollution, background radiation, quality of housing, and so on; but for geneticists, the term has much broader connotations and includes anything and everything that is not genetic. This would include some of the factors discussed in previous sections: the quality of language spoken to the child, early brain damage, and ear disease. In contrast, a genetic cause is identified when the presence or absence of a condition depends on a person's genetic makeup. In fact, most of the genome is the same for all human beings: we have genes that are important for building bodies and maintaining biological functions, and these do not vary from one person to another. But some genes take different forms in different people—that is, they show allelic variation. Genes for eye color and blood group are of this kind.

How do we identify whether genetic variation is related to a condition such as SLI? One might imagine that the way to do this would be by comparing genetic variants (alleles) in people with SLI and people with normal language. This poses enormous problems, however, because there are so many genes that it is hugely demanding to identify all the allelic forms, and also it becomes impossible to tell whether an association between genotype and phenotype (i.e., observed charac-

teristics) is a real finding that will hold up for everyone, or something that turned up by chance in a specific sample. Newbury and Monaco (chapter 6, this volume) review developments in this area of molecular genetics. One important point that emerges is that if you want to discover genes associated with SLI, then the results you get will depend on how you define disorder (see also Newbury, Bishop, & Monaco, 2005). This is a point to which we return.

Other work on genetics of SLI does not involve looking directly at genes. Rather, we estimate whether genes are implicated in causing impairment by looking at people who differ in their genetic relatedness. Twins are invaluable in this regard, because you have two people who are the same age, exposed to many of the same environmental influences, and yet who vary in genetic relatedness. Monozygotic (MZ) or identical twins are formed by the splitting of a single fertilized ovum and are to all intents and purposes genetically identical. Dizygotic (DZ) twins, also known as fraternal or nonidentical twins, are formed when two ova are fertilized simultaneously, and they have 50% of their alleles in common.[1] We select twin children who have SLI and then ask whether their cotwins also have SLI. The first question of interest is whether there are any cases where one MZ twin has SLI and the cotwin does not. If so, this tells us that SLI cannot be accounted for just in terms of genes, because the two MZ twins are genetically identical. The next question is whether the MZ and DZ cotwins are equally likely to have SLI. If so, that suggests that genes are unimportant in causing disorder, and that similarity between twins is due to environmental influences that they share. On the other hand, if the likelihood of both twins being affected is greater for MZ than DZ pairs, then this tells us that genes are likely to be implicated in causing the disorder. The statistical procedures used to quantify the relative importance of genes and environment are complex, but they are derived from this basic logic and allow us to compute a statistic known as heritability (h^2), which ranges from 0 to 1 and indicates the relative importance of genetic vs. environmental factors (Plomin, DeFries, McClearn, & McGuffin, 2000). As noted above, the term *environmental factors* subsumes a huge range of possible influences, which are not differentiated by this method, though we can distinguish between *shared environment,* which refers to environmental influences that affect both members of a twin pair growing up together, and *nonshared environment,* which refers to influences that are specific to an individual child. For instance, if we assume that parents communicate in a similar fashion to both twins, then any effects of parent communicative style would come under shared environment; if the probability of suffering otitis media is independent for two members of a twin pair, then this would be a nonshared environmental influence.[2]

Twin studies of SLI

Twin studies of school-aged children have been remarkably consistent in showing significant genetic effects on SLI (Bishop, North, & Donlan, 1995; Lewis & Thompson, 1992; Tomblin & Buckwalter, 1998), though the precise results differ depending on how language impairment is measured. In general, there is rather little evidence that aspects of shared environment play a role in causing SLI. This agrees with the conclusions above showing that factors such as parental communicative style are less important than commonly thought. A striking exception to this pattern comes from analysis of in-home language test data from 4-year-olds in the Twins Early Development Study (TEDS; Hayiou-Thomas, Oliver, & Plomin, 2005), where the estimated heritability for SLI was not significantly greater than zero and shared environment appeared to play an important role in determining which children were affected. This study had a larger sample than prior studies, and the discrepancy with other studies was puzzling. Further analysis of this dataset proved illuminating (Bishop & Hayiou-Thomas, 2008). An important feature of this study was that the twins had been identified from a population-based study, in which a sample was screened for language skills, and those scoring in the SLI range were then selected for analysis. Most of the children with SLI (62%) had never been referred to a speech and language therapist for assessment or intervention. In this regard, the sample

was very different from previous twin studies, where children with language disorders had been identified on the basis of clinical concern. When we reclassified children from TEDS, we found that language impairment was highly heritable if defined in terms of contact with speech and language therapy services. This study, then, suggested that there is something distinctive about those children who attract clinical concern. Further analysis suggested that presence of speech difficulties was a key feature: speech problems were highly heritable and were more common in the children who had been clinically referred. This reanalysis meshed well with previous studies suggesting that language tests can miss some aspects of communicative impairment that are regarded as clinically significant (Conti-Ramsden, Crutchley, & Botting, 1997; Dunn, Flax, Sliwinski, & Aram, 1996). Such studies raise the intriguing possibility that we might find higher heritability for clinical samples than for population-based samples because the former have different types of language disorder which have a stronger genetic loading.

Multifactorial risk factors

Even for those studies showing strong genetic influence on SLI, many questions remain. One issue that causes much confusion is the nature of the genetic effect. If one says a condition is "genetic," people often assume that we will be able to identify a defective gene and eventually develop a diagnostic test. In fact, it seems unlikely that this will be the case for SLI. Much excitement was generated by the discovery of a genetic mutation that caused severe and specific speech and language problems in approximately half the members of a three-generation British family (Fisher, 2005). However, although some other cases of mutation of this gene, *FOXP2*, have been reported (MacDermot et al., 2005; Zeesman et al., 2006), it is now evident that this is very rare, and the gene is entirely normal in most people with SLI. Furthermore, although SLI does run in families, it does not normally show the clear-cut patterns of inheritance that you would expect to see if it were a single-gene disorder. It seems likely that, for most cases, genetic influences on

SLI are complex and are due to the combined influence of many genes of small effect, together with environmental risk factors. This kind of "complex multifactorial etiology" is widely found in common medical disorders, such as asthma, allergies, and diabetes, where it is clear that we are not going to find "the gene" for the disorder but, rather, need to identify genetic variants that exert small and probabilistic effects that increase the risk of disorder. This makes the task of identifying relevant genes that much harder.

One approach to this problem is to move away from studying SLI and to look, instead, for genetic influences on underlying language skills. It would be dangerous to assume that gene–behavior relationships will be clearer if we adopt this approach, but it is a reasonable working hypothesis that there might be distinct causal influences on different components of language development. In my own studies, I have focused on language measures that relate to current theories of SLI, and this has led to a series of studies using nonword repetition as a measure of impairment. Nonword repetition first attracted the attention of those working in SLI when Gathercole and Baddeley (1990) published a paper showing that this simple test was remarkably sensitive at distinguishing children with SLI from a control group. The child listens to spoken nonsense words that vary in length from 2 to 5 syllables, such as "hampent" (2 syllables) or "perplisteronk" (4 syllables). The task is to repeat back what is heard, and each nonword is scored right or wrong. Children with SLI make few errors on the shortest 2-syllable nonwords, but their performance declines markedly as the number of syllables increases and the memory demands of the task become greater. Baddeley, Gathercole, and Pagagno (1998) have argued that most humans have a remarkable ability to remember unfamiliar strings of speech sounds, and this is important for learning new vocabulary and syntax. Their theory is that this is mediated by a specific brain system that fails to develop normally in children with SLI. Bishop et al. (1996) confirmed that nonword repetition was very sensitive to SLI in a study of twins and also found that poor scores were obtained by children who had a history of speech and language therapy, even if they no longer had

obvious signs of SLI. Thus nonword repetition seems a good marker of residual problems (see also Stothard, Snowling, Bishop, Chipchase, & Kaplan, 1998). Most importantly, this twin study found that poor nonword repetition was highly heritable: thus the ability to do this simple task appeared to depend on a child's genetic makeup, rather than on environmental experiences. This work with nonword repetition has subsequently fed into molecular genetic studies, as described in chapter 6.

Bishop et al. (1999) considered whether poor nonword repetition might arise as a consequence of an auditory temporal processing (ATP) problem of the kind postulated by Tallal (2000). A group of twins, including some with SLI, were given both nonword repetition and an ATP task, and we expected that the two measures might be correlated, showing a common origin. We were surprised to find a quite different pattern of results. Poor ATP performance did not show any genetic influence but, rather, was affected by shared environment. There was some suggestion that performance on the ATP test was affected by the child's musical experience at home (Bishop, 2001a). Children with the worst SLI tended to do badly at both nonword repetition *and* ATP, but these two deficits had apparently different origins. This was the first clue to the complexity of the etiology of SLI: rather than looking for a single underlying cause, these data suggested that we should think of SLI as a disorder that arises when the child has two or more underlying problems.

According to Baddeley et al. (1998), a deficit in nonword repetition can lead to a whole range of language difficulties: vocabulary is difficult to acquire because the sounds of a new word are not retained adequately in short-term memory, and the child finds it hard to learn syntax because this requires sentences and sentence fragments to be held in memory while they are analyzed. We might therefore expect to see that children who are poor at nonword repetition are also bad at tests of vocabulary and syntax. This idea was tested in a subsequent twin study with 6-year-olds, but the results did not come out as expected (Bishop, Adams, & Norbury, 2006). There was little relationship between nonword repetition and vocabulary, with the latter showing much stronger influence of shared environment than of genes. Ability to do a specific syntax task that involved producing verb inflections to mark tense also showed high heritability, but performance on this test was not strongly associated with nonword repetition scores, and the two kinds of language deficit appeared to have different genetic origins. But once again, the children with the most severe language difficulties had *both* kinds of problem. This pattern of results, together with the earlier finding on ATP performance, fits with the idea that language development is usually quite robust and will develop in the teeth of various adverse circumstances. However, if for genetic or environmental reasons the child has a cumulation of two or more risk factors, then this can seriously hinder language development. It is results such as these that led me to argue that we should abandon the quest for a single underlying cause of SLI (Bishop, 2006). Even if we were to discover a single allelic variant of a gene that led to poor nonword repetition, this would not be "the cause" of SLI, and we would probably find many children who had this variant but had normal language skills. However, when this variant occurs together

with other genetic or environmental risks, then language may be disrupted (see Figure 5.1). If this causal model is correct, then we might expect to see high rates of poor nonword repetition in relatives of children with SLI, even if those relatives do not themselves have overt language difficulties. This is exactly what has been found in studies of relatives of children with SLI (Barry, Yasin, & Bishop, 2007; Clark et al., 2007).

ARE SLI AND DYSLEXIA DIFFERENT MANIFESTATIONS OF THE SAME DISORDER?

For many years, there was little contact between research on SLI and research on developmental dyslexia. There were several reasons for this. First, until the late 1970s, dyslexia was commonly believed to have a visual basis, with emphasis being placed on features such as a tendency to reverse letters or problems controlling eye movements when reading text. Second, children with reading difficulties were seen by specialists from education and psychology whereas those with

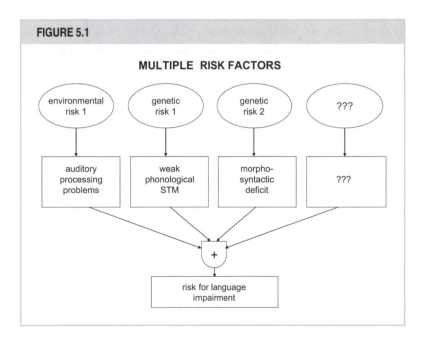

FIGURE 5.1

Model showing how different independent risk factors can combine to increase the risk of language impairment. The "???" box indicates that there are likely to be factors other than those already identified. The shield-shaped symbol indicates that the effects of the different risk factors are additive.

MULTIPLE RISK FACTORS

environmental risk 1 → auditory processing problems

genetic risk 1 → weak phonological STM

genetic risk 2 → morpho-syntactic deficit

??? → ???

+ → risk for language impairment

SLI were seen by speech-language pathologists, and there was little communication between these disciplines. In the past 30 or so years, there has been a dramatic change of perspective, with recognition that most children with reading disability have problems in identifying sound segments in words even when no written language is involved, and that it is these problems, rather than visual difficulties, that typically make it hard for them to learn to read (Bryant & Bradley, 1985; Liberman, Shankweiler, Camp, Blachman, & Werfelman, 1979). An important step was taken to integrate work on reading disability and SLI by Catts and Kamhi (1986), who noted that phonological awareness problems were seen in children with SLI as well as in those with dyslexia, and who suggested that there were many commonalities between these two disorders. These days it is not uncommon for SLI and dyslexia to be regarded as points on a continuum of severity rather than distinct conditions, and this view seems supported by studies finding that many children who are identified with dyslexia have a history of delayed speech, and, conversely, many children with SLI go on to develop literacy problems (for a review, see Bishop & Snowling, 2004).

This unifying account of the two disorders suggests that we might find similar heritable difficulties in nonword repetition in children with dyslexia as well as in those with SLI. This prediction has been confirmed in both twin studies (Bishop, 2001b) and family studies (Raskind, Hsu, Berninger, Thomson, & Wijsman, 2000). Furthermore, Bishop (2001b) and Bishop, Adams, and Norbury (2004) showed that heritability of reading skill was stronger in children who have low nonword repetition scores than in those with normal nonword repetition. This suggested that the same phonological deficit might be implicated in both SLI and some cases of dyslexia. However, it is clear that it would be oversimplistic to conclude that all problems with language and literacy have common genetic origins. As is reviewed in chapter 2, molecular genetic studies find some linkage sites that are associated with both language and literacy problems, but others are more specific. Also, the difference between SLI and dyslexia cannot be

fully captured by a single dimension of severity: children with SLI typically have problems with aspects of grammatical morphology and oral language comprehension that are not usually seen in developmental dyslexia. And there are some children who can read accurately despite having SLI. In integrating these findings, Bishop and Snowling (2004) concluded that we need at least two dimensions of impairment to characterize the range of clinical profiles that are observed in this field. Children who are impaired on a phonological processing dimension will have problems learning to read, and those who are impaired on other language dimensions, notably semantics and syntax, will have poor oral language skills and poor comprehension. Once again, it seems that children who have the most severe SLI are those who happen to have risk factors for several distinct difficulties and who are impaired on two or more of these dimensions.

DO AUTISTIC DISORDER AND SLI HAVE COMMON ORIGINS?

Given the intense interest in nonword repetition as a marker of a heritable phenotype in SLI, it was intriguing to read a report by Kjelgaard and Tager-Flusberg (2001) who found poor nonword repetition in a substantial subset of children with autistic disorder. Traditionally, autism and SLI have been regarded as separate disorders, but there has been much debate as to whether they should be regarded as differing only in severity, or whether they are qualitatively distinct. At the 1999 Afasic Symposium I reviewed the evidence for commonalities between autism and SLI: the existence of children who appear to have a condition intermediate between SLI and autism, the presence of language impairments in relatives of children with autism, and the convergence of clinical presentation for children with receptive SLI and autism when followed over time (Bishop, 2000). Undoubtedly, children with autism have far more widespread and pervasive difficulties than children with typical SLI, but the possibility was raised that there might be a common core deficit in both disorders. Bishop (2003) referred to this as the "autism as SLI plus" hypothesis: in both disorders there are common language difficulties, but those with autism have additional impairments. This hypothesis has potential importance for molecular genetic studies, which have traditionally treated SLI and autism as separate disorders.

The jury is still out on the "autism as SLI plus" hypothesis, but my own view is that the evidence is moving against it. In coming to this conclusion, I have been influenced by two family studies of autism. Bishop et al. (2004) looked at data from a nonword repetition test in Australian children with autism and their immediate family members. We confirmed the finding of Kjelgaard and Tager-Flusberg (2001) that many children with autism do very poorly on nonword repetition. However, this deficit was not familial—that is, the parents and siblings of children with autism did no worse than a control group at nonword repetition. Similar findings were obtained in a British sample studied by Whitehouse, Barry, and Bishop (2007), where parents of children with SLI were explicitly compared with parents of children with ASD and control parents. A double dissociation was found, such that the parents of children with SLI did poorly on nonword repetition and oromotor tasks but appeared normal on a self-report measure of social communication, whereas the parents of children with ASD had atypical scores on social communication but were unimpaired on nonword repetition. Once again, some children with ASD themselves did poorly on nonword repetition. However, the lack of deficit in relatives suggested that this was not genetically mediated. In both the Australian and UK studies, children who had ASD and poor nonword repetition had more widespread and severe problems in other domains. We suggested that the underlying cause of nonword repetition deficits in ASD was different from that in SLI, being more a consequence of having a combination of other deficits that interfered with task performance, rather than reflecting a primary problem with phonological short-term memory. If we are right, this means

that it would be a mistake to group together children with ASD and SLI in molecular genetic studies, because the similarities in their language deficits are superficial rather than indicative of shared etiology.

IMPLICATIONS FOR INTERVENTION

Whenever I write about genetic bases of SLI, I feel the need to stress that a heritable disorder is not an untreatable disorder. For many years, people were reluctant to countenance the possibility that genes may be implicated in common developmental disorders, because they feared that this might support the idea of a genetically inferior underclass whose deficits were immutable. I hope that I have made clear that the "genetic inferiority" notion is not just socially unacceptable but also scientifically untenable. My own work has barely scratched the surface in looking for genetic and environmental bases of different aspects of SLI, but it has already altered how I conceptualize this disorder. I had anticipated that we might find a handful of genetic variants that substantially increase the risk of SLI, but, with the notable exception of the *FOXP2* mutation, that has not been the case. Rather, it seems that the likelihood of SLI is determined less by the presence or absence of one specific allele and more by the specific combination of alleles that the child possesses. And it seems likely that there are allelic variants that are fairly common in the general population and are usually associated with mild language deficits that are of no clinical significance; it is only when these occur in combination with other risk alleles and environmental risk factors that language learning is seriously hindered.

The second issue concerns the efficacy of intervention. SLI is a very broad category, with some children having mild and transient expressive problems and others having severe and persistent difficulties with both receptive and expressive language. It would be disingenuous to suggest that it is easy to remediate cases of more severe SLI: there is no doubt that some children's language-learning difficulties remain severe even after intensive intervention from dedicated and knowledgeable professionals. But it would be a mistake to conclude that a disorder is untreatable because it has a genetic basis. There are numerous examples from physical medicine to the contrary. The potential value of genetic research lies in its ability to help us painstakingly reconstruct the path from gene to brain to language, so that with this greater understanding of mechanisms we will in future be able to intervene more effectively.

ACKNOWLEDGMENTS

The author is supported by a Principal Research Fellowship from the Wellcome Trust.

NOTES

1 This account is oversimplified in two ways. First, in females, in each cell one of the two copies of the X-chromosome undergoes inactivation, apparently at random, which means that MZ twin girls can have a different effective allelic constitution. Second, when we talk of "50% of alleles in common," this refers only to the small proportion of the genome that shows variation from one person to another. As noted in the text, most genes do not vary from person to person.

2 Once again, I have oversimplified to communicate the important point here. But in practice "shared" and "nonshared" environment are theoretical constructs and are not identified with specific measured variables. For instance, susceptibility to otitis media can be affected by factors at home (e.g., parental smoking) and genetic constitution, as well as by more child-specific influences, and thus could itself be decomposed into genetic, shared environment and nonshared environmental components.

REFERENCES

Baddeley, A., Gathercole, S., & Papagno, C. (1998). The phonological loop as a language learning device. *Psychological Review, 105*, 158–173.

Barry, J. G., Yasin, I., & Bishop, D. V. M. (2007). Heritable risk factors associated with language impairments. *Genes, Brain and Behavior, 6*, 66–76.

Basser, L. S. (1962). Hemiplegia of early onset and the faculty of speech with special reference to the effects of hemispherectomy. *Brain, 85*, 427–460.

Bates, E., & Roe, K. (2001). Language development in children with unilateral brain injury. In C. A. Nelson & M. Luciana (Eds.), *Handbook of developmental cognitive neuroscience* (pp. 281–307). Cambridge, MA: MIT Press.

Bishop, D. V. M. (2000). Pragmatic language impairment: A correlate of SLI, a distinct subgroup, or part of the autistic continuum? In D. V. M. Bishop & L. B. Leonard (Eds.), *Speech and language impairments in children: Causes, characteristics, intervention and outcome* (pp. 99–113). Hove, UK: Psychology Press.

Bishop, D. V. M. (2001a). Genetic and environmental risks for specific language impairment in children. *Philosophical Transactions of the Royal Society, Series B, 356*, 369–380.

Bishop, D. V. M. (2001b). Genetic influences on language impairment and literacy problems in children: Same or different? *Journal of Child Psychology and Psychiatry, 42*, 189–198.

Bishop, D. V. M. (2003). Autism and specific language impairment: Categorical distinction or continuum? In G. Bock & J. Goode (Eds.), *Autism: Neural basis and treatment possibilities. Novartis Foundation Symposium 251* (pp. 213–226). Chichester, UK: Wiley.

Bishop, D. V. M. (2006). Developmental cognitive genetics: How psychology can inform genetics and vice versa. *Quarterly Journal of Experimental Psychology, 59*, 1153–1168.

Bishop, D. V. M., Adams, C. V., & Norbury, C. F. (2004). Using nonword repetition to distinguish genetic and environmental influences on early literacy development: A study of 6-year-old twins. *American Journal of Medical Genetics, 129B*, 94–96.

Bishop, D. V. M., Adams, C. V., & Norbury, C. F. (2006). Distinct genetic influences on grammar and phonological short-term memory deficits: Evidence from 6-year-old twins. *Genes, Brain and Behavior, 5,* 158–169.

Bishop, D. V. M., Bishop, S. J., Bright, P., James, C., Delaney, T., & Tallal, P. (1999). Different origin of auditory and phonological processing problems in children with language impairment: Evidence from a twin study. *Journal of Speech, Language, and Hearing Research, 42,* 155–168.

Bishop, D. V. M., & Hayiou-Thomas, M. E. (2008). Heritability of specific language impairment depends on diagnostic criteria. *Genes, Brain and Behavior, 7,* 365–372.

Bishop, D. V. M., Maybery, M., Wong, D., Maley, A., Hill, W., & Hallmayer, J. (2004). Are phonological processing deficits part of the broad autism phenotype? *American Journal of Medical Genetics, 128B,* 54–60.

Bishop, D. V. M., North, T., & Donlan, C. (1995). Genetic basis of specific language impairment: Evidence from a twin study. *Developmental Medicine & Child Neurology, 37,* 56–71.

Bishop, D. V. M., North, T., & Donlan, C. (1996). Nonword repetition as a behavioural marker for inherited language impairment: Evidence from a twin study. *Journal of Child Psychology and Psychiatry, 37,* 391–403.

Bishop, D. V. M., & Snowling, M. J. (2004). Developmental dyslexia and specific language impairment: Same or different? *Psychological Bulletin, 130,* 858–886.

Briscoe, J., Bishop, D. V. M., & Norbury, C. F. (2001). Phonological processing, language, and literacy: A comparison of children with mild-to-moderate sensorineural hearing loss and those with specific language impairment. *Journal of Child Psychology and Psychiatry, 42,* 329–340.

Bryant, P., & Bradley, L. (1985). *Children's reading problems.* Oxford, UK: Blackwell.

Catts, H. W., & Kamhi, A. G. (1986). The linguistic basis of reading disorders: Implications for the speech-language pathologist. *Language, Speech, and Hearing Services in Schools, 17,* 329–341.

Clark, A., O'Hare, A., Watson, J., Cohen, W., Cowie, H., Elton, R., et al. (2007). Severe receptive language disorder in childhood—familial aspects and long-term outcomes: results from a Scottish study. *Archives of Disease in Childhood, 92,* 614–619.

Conti-Ramsden, G., Crutchley, A., & Botting, N. (1997). The extent to which psychometric tests differentiate subgroups of children with SLI. *Journal*

of Speech, Language, and Hearing Research, 40, 765–777.

Damasio, A. R., & Damasio, H. (1992). Brain and language. *Scientific American, 267,* 89–95.

Dunn, M., Flax, J., Sliwinski, M., & Aram, D. (1996). The use of spontaneous language measures as criteria for identifying children with specific language impairment: An attempt to reconcile clinical and research findings. *Journal of Speech and Hearing Research, 39,* 643–654.

Fisher, S. E. (2005). Dissection of molecular mechanisms underlying speech and language disorders. *Applied Psycholinguistics, 26,* 111–128.

Gathercole, S. E., & Baddeley, A. D. (1990). Phonological memory deficits in language disordered children: Is there a causal connection? *Journal of Memory and Language, 29,* 336–360.

Hayiou-Thomas, M. E., Oliver, B., & Plomin, R. (2005). Genetic influences on specific versus nonspecific language impairment in 4-year-old twins. *Journal of Learning Disabilities, 38,* 222–232.

Holm, V. A., & Kunze, L. H. (1969). Effect of chronic otitis media on language and speech development. *Pediatrics, 43,* 833–839.

Kjelgaard, M. M., & Tager-Flusberg, H. (2001). An investigation of language impairment in autism: Implications for genetic subgroups. *Language and Cognitive Processes, 16,* 287–308.

Lewis, B. A., & Thompson, L. A. (1992). A study of developmental speech and language disorders in twins. *Journal of Speech and Hearing Research, 35,* 1086–1094.

Liberman, I. Y., Shankweiler, D., Camp, L., Blachman, B., & Werfelman, M. (1979). Speech, the alphabet and teaching to read. In L. Resnick & P. Weaver (Eds.), *Theory and practice of early reading* (Vol. 2, pp. 109–134). Hillsdale, NJ: Lawrence Erlbaum Associates.

MacDermot, K. D., Bonora, E., Sykes, N., Coupe, A. M., Lai, C. S., Vernes, S. C., et al. (2005). Identification of *FOXP2* truncation as a novel cause of developmental speech and language deficits. *American Journal of Human Genetics, 76,* 1074–1080.

McCauley, R. J., & Fey, M. E. (Eds.). (2006). *Treatment of language disorders in children.* Baltimore: Paul H. Brookes.

Merricks, M. J., Stott, C. M., Goodyer, I. M., & Bolton, P. (2004). The aetiology of specific language impairment: No evidence of a role for obstetric complications. *Journal of Neural Transmission, 111,* 773–789.

Mogford, K., & Bishop, D. (1988). Five questions about language development considered in the light of exceptional circumstances. In D. Bishop & K. Mogford (Eds.), *Language development in exceptional circumstances* (pp. 239–260). Edinburgh, UK: Churchill Livingstone.

Newbury, D. F., Bishop, D. V. M., & Monaco, A. P. (2005). Genetic influences on language impairment and phonological short-term memory. *Trends in Cognitive Sciences, 9*, 528–534.

Norbury, C. F., Bishop, D. V. M., & Briscoe, J. (2001). Production of English finite verb morphology: A comparison of SLI and moderate hearing impairment. *Journal of Speech, Language, and Hearing Research, 44*, 165–178.

Paul, R. (2000). Predicting outcomes of early expressive language delay: Ethical implications. In D. V. M. Bishop & L. B. Leonard (Eds.), *Speech and language impairments in children: Causes, characteristics, intervention and outcome* (pp. 195–209). Hove, UK: Psychology Press.

Plomin, R., DeFries, J. C., McClearn, G. E., & McGuffin, P. (2000). *Behavioral genetics* (4th ed.). New York: Worth.

Raskind, W. H., Hsu, L., Berninger, V. W., Thomson, J. B., & Wijsman, E. M. (2000). Family aggregation of dyslexia phenotypes. *Behavior Genetics, 30*, 385–396.

Roberts, J. E., Rosenfeld, R. M., & Zeisel, S. A. (2004). Otitis media and speech and language: A meta-analysis of prospective studies. *Pediatrics, 113*, e238–248.

Stothard, S. E., Snowling, M. J., Bishop, D. V. M., Chipchase, B. B., & Kaplan, C. A. (1998). Language impaired preschoolers: A follow-up into adolescence. *Journal of Speech, Language, and Hearing Research, 41*, 407–418.

Tallal, P. (2000). Experimental studies of language learning impairments: From research to remediation. In D. V. M. Bishop & L. B. Leonard (Eds.), *Speech and language impairments in children: Causes, characteristics, intervention and outcome* (pp. 131–155). Hove, UK: Psychology Press.

Tomblin, J. B., & Buckwalter, P. R. (1998). Heritability of poor language achievement among twins. *Journal of Speech, Language, and Hearing Research, 41*, 188–199.

Tomblin, J. B., Smith, E., & Zhang, X. (1997). Epidemiology of specific language impairment: Prenatal and perinatal risk factors. *Journal of Communication Disorders, 30*, 325–344.

Wake, M., Tobin, S., Cone-Wesson, B., Dahl, H.-H., Gillam, L., McCormick, L., et al. (2006). Slight/mild sensorineural hearing loss in children. *Pediatrics, 118*, 1842–1851.

Whitehouse, A., Barry, J. G., & Bishop, D. V. M. (2007). The broader language phenotype of autism: A comparison with specific language impairment. *Journal of Child Psychology and Psychiatry, 48*, 822–830.

Zeesman, S., Nowaczyk, M. J. M., Teshima, I., Roberts, W., Oram Cardy, J., Brian, J., et al. (2006). Speech and language impairment and oromotor dyspraxia due to deletion of 7q31 that involves *FOXP2*. *American Journal of Medical Genetics, 140A*, 509–514.

6

The application of molecular genetics to the study of developmental language disorder

Dianne F. Newbury and Anthony P. Monaco

INTRODUCTION

Traditionally the field of genetics was considered a specialized discipline that focused upon severe but relatively rare disorders caused by mutations in single genes. The aim was to identify the genes involved by exploiting existing information regarding inheritance patterns and disease pathology. For example, the cloning of the gene causing Duchenne Muscular Dystrophy was aided by the characterization of chromosome abnormalities in affected patients, whereas the isolation of the β globin gene, which causes sickle-cell anemia, was facilitated by the purification of the damaged protein from red blood cells. Such research was often driven by the premise that gene identification would ultimately enable a cure either directly, via the correction of the genetic code or replacement of the damaged protein, or indirectly, through the development of pharmaceuticals that restored chemical balance to the affected pathway. As information regarding single-gene disorders grew and laboratory and computational techniques advanced, the interests of researchers broadened to include more common traits that are believed to be influenced by genetic factors. These complex, or polygenic, genetic disorders typically have more unpredictable and less pervasive presentation than classic single-gene disorders but nonetheless affect a large number of individuals and therefore represent a significant burden upon health services. In this chapter, we describe briefly the methods used to identify genes that contribute to complex genetic traits and, using SLI and dyslexia as examples, we discuss the difficulties of interpreting, applying, and integrating the information yielded by such studies. Finally, we use *FOXP2* to exemplify the ways in which gene mapping can aid our knowledge and understanding of neurodevelopmental disorders.

MAPPING GENETIC DISORDERS

Complex genetic traits are so called because they can be influenced by several genes that interact with each other and the environment in a multifaceted network. Each component of this network may operate at a variable level of efficiency both between individuals and over time, thus producing a wide range of phenomena. Single-gene diseases are directly caused by genetic mutations that alter the DNA coding sequence and prevent the production of a fully functioning protein. In contrast, complex disorders are caused by coincidental combinations of perfectly normal genetic variations (or alleles), which encode functional but slightly less efficient proteins. The most important characteristic of complex disorders is the involvement of intermingled genetic pathways and the environment. This means that the disorder under study is not necessarily caused by the same genetic variants in all affected individuals, and there is often no clear correlation between the genetic makeup of an individual (genotype) and his or her trait (phenotype). Thus when discussing complex genetic disorders, instead of categorizing people as affected or unaffected, we often refer to the risk of disorder, with certain genotype–environment combinations rendering some individuals more susceptible than others to disease onset. This subtle distinction is often overlooked but has important consequences in terms of the direction and implications of genetic studies. The fact that there is unlikely to be a single genetic entity that is sufficient to cause disorders such as SLI and dyslexia means that the prospect of diagnosis and cure—the very ideology that has driven ge-

netic research for so long—may be unattainable. Instead, the primary aim of studies into complex genetic disorders should be one of understanding. At the genetic level, such investigations enable characterization of genetic variability and understanding of the relationships between genetic makeup and individual phenotypes (behaviors). At the clinical level, this research will allow the identification of the biological pathways important to the development of these disorders, and this, in turn, will help us to better understand the etiology and enable us to begin to answer some of the many questions such as those posed in this book (e.g., Is SLI a unitary condition? What causes the overlaps between autism, dyslexia, and ADHD?). Ultimately, for disorders such as SLI and dyslexia, it is hoped that the information arising from this research, in combination with psycholinguistic and neurological data, will aid in the development of better predictive test batteries, thus allowing the early identification and better treatment of those individuals at risk of language impairments.

Positional cloning and recombination

A technique known as positional cloning can be used to identify the genetic mutation involved in simple single-gene disorders even when there is little prior knowledge regarding the biochemical basis of the disorder. The first step in a positional cloning strategy is usually a genome screen. This involves identification of DNA variants that are always present in affected individuals but are never found in unaffected individuals. Although a genome screen hypothetically involves the examination of the entire genome, it does not require the sequencing of every base or the study of every gene. Instead, it exploits the fact that DNA is inherited as mosaic blocks passed from parents to offspring. All individuals carry two copies of each chromosome, only one of which will be passed onto their offspring. During the production of gametes (sperm and egg cells), the chromosomes align along the middle of the cell and segregate to alternative poles producing two germ cells, each containing a random array of parental chromosomes. While they are aligned within the developing gamete, analogous chromosomes can become entangled and cross over with each other, exchanging genetic material between chromosome pairs. This recombination process is, for the most part, indiscriminate, and therefore the chromosomes carried within the germ cells are essentially random mosaic arrangements of the parental chromosomes. The distance separating any two genetic sequences (or loci) can be expressed in terms of the likelihood that they are separated by a recombination event; as the distance between them increases, the likelihood that they are inherited in separate mosaic blocks increases accordingly. Two loci that are very close on a chromosome and rarely separated by a recombination event are said to be in linkage disequilibrium (LD) with each other. As a consequence of this, we are able to say that if two siblings are genetically identical at any given locus, they are also likely to be sharing the same DNA at neighboring loci. Thus, by sampling regions of DNA along each chromosome, it is possible to infer the parental origin of the majority of the genome without the need to characterize every DNA base. The results of linkage analyses are traditionally reported as a logarithm of odds (LOD) score, which is given by the log of the probability of obtaining the given data in the presence of linkage against that of obtaining the given data in the absence of linkage. Thus the higher the LOD score, the more likely it is that the region identified contains a genetic variant that underlies the disorder in question. (For good overviews of genetics and linkage techniques, see Eley & Craig, 2005; Eley & Rijsdijk, 2005.)

Genome screens of complex disorders

For a single-gene disorder, a genome screen is usually performed within a single family. In this case all the affected people carry the same disease-causing mutation, and they will be reasonably uniform in terms of their genetic background, making it a relatively simple process to identify linkage. However, in a complex disorder, which is not caused by a single genetic mutation, there will be a weaker correlation between genotype and phenotype, and this has some important ramifications for linkage studies. Although a positional cloning approach can still be applied,

the study design and methodology require some adjustments to allow for these factors.

Linkage studies of complex disorders assume the presence of a single gene variant that accounts for the majority of disease susceptibility and is therefore present in a high proportion of affected individuals. Under this assumption, affected sib-pair methods can be applied to genetic data collected from large numbers of small families, identifying regions of the genome that are shared by affected siblings more than would be expected by chance alone.

A second complication caused by the involvement of several genetic factors is the variability of resultant phenotype. As discussed in other chapters of this book, SLI is a particularly diverse trait that varies over time and between individuals, shows considerable overlaps with other developmental disorders, and is, in these respects, typical of a complex disorder. However, it is impossible to say whether these variations are indicative of distinct genetic etiologies or whether they are simply random variations that exemplify the complexity of the genetic networks involved. For example, although a clinical division may be evident between those individuals with phonological, expressive, and mixed expressive-receptive language disorders, it does not necessarily follow that discrete genetic variants will underlie each of these subclasses. It may be that the distinction between these disorders reflects subtle environmental effects, or they may share a major gene but differ in their modifying genetic effects. A primary problem arising from phenotype variability is the classification of individuals for genetic studies. Complex traits usually present as continuous distributions, and while there are many cases who are clearly affected, there will be a similar number of individuals who fall on the borders of a category or possess additional complicating factors. Rather than trying to subdivide people into affected and unaffected cases, it may be preferable to treat the disorder as a continuum and directly analyze relevant quantitative measures within a linkage model. For instance, instead of dividing people into those with and those without SLI, one could use a quantitative measure of language ability. These quantitative-trait-loci (QTL) methods detect loci where there is a correlation between the genetic identity and phenotypic similarity of sibling pairs.

GENETIC STUDIES OF SPEECH SOUND DISORDERS

The success of any genetic study depends crucially on how people are selected for inclusion. In order to maximize the likelihood of the existence of a single major gene variant, one must ensure that selection criteria are consistent across families, while being relaxed enough to allow the collection of large samples but specific enough to ensure that the people in the study are representative of the clinical population. Often selection strategies are driven by the research interests of an individual group. For example, some researchers of language impairments have chosen to restrict their investigations to those individuals affected by speech sound disorder (SSD), characterized by developmentally inappropriate errors in speech production that occur in the absence of any physical abnormalities; thus, it is considered to be a phonological subtype of SLI (Smith, Pennington, Boada, & Shriberg, 2005; Stein et al., 2004, 2006). This approach assumes that different genetic factors independently contribute to impairments in different domains of speech and language, and thus the restriction in sample selection will be accompanied by a reduction in the number of genetic variants present. Interestingly, researchers who have employed this strategy have also restricted their genetic analyses by investigating selected regions of the genome. In their initial investigation, Stein et al. (2004) focused upon a region of chromosome 3 that had previously been implicated in dyslexia. They reasoned that since SSD and dyslexia share many surface features, it is likely that they also possess a common genetic etiology. In this study, probands and siblings were assessed using a range of quantitative tests, including measures of phonological memory, articulation, vocabulary (expressive and receptive), reading accuracy, and reading comprehension. The re-

searchers used the data from these tests to perform a factor analysis that showed that three factors could be calculated, which accounted for 64% of the variance in the individual test scores. These three factors loaded upon aspects of articulation, phonological short-term memory, and vocabulary. The three factor scores were then analyzed for linkage alongside six individual test scores. A significant level of linkage was found to the phonological factor score ($p = 5.6 \times 10^{-5}$), and this was supported by suggestive levels of linkage to the two individual traits contributing to this factor (single-word reading and nonword reading). The same set of families was then used in a subsequent investigation of chromosome 15, which has been linked to both autism and dyslexia (Stein et al., 2006). However, in contrast to the study described above, this investigation employed a binary affection status (i.e., affected or unaffected) for their linkage analyses. A modest level of linkage was found within a Caucasian subgroup of families ($p = 0.007$), which strengthened slightly when quantitative measures of oral-motor function, articulation, and phonological memory were included as covariates within the linkage model ($p = 0.004$). The suggestion of linkage on chromosome 15 corroborates that previously reported by another group who had explored the role of dyslexia loci on chromosomes 1, 6, and 15 in families affected by SSD (Smith et al., 2005). This study analyzed cases in terms of whether they were affected/unaffected but also looked at six quantitative measures of spoken language ability in these regions. They reported significant linkage to the affected/unaffected status on chromosome 6 ($p = 0.0006$) and to measures of nonword repetition and articulation on chromosome 15 ($p = 0.0053$). It therefore appears that studies of families affected by SSD support the existence of shared genetic variants on chromosomes 3 and 15 that predispose individuals to language and/or reading impairments. Since a diagnosis of dyslexia and SSD both rely heavily upon the presence of phonological deficits, one may postulate that these genes would be involved in biological pathways important for phonological processing. However, it should be noted that the correlation between SSD and dyslexia is not perfect, thus indicating the existence of additional modifying components that play more specific roles in each of the discrete disorders.

GENETIC STUDIES OF SPECIFIC LANGUAGE IMPAIRMENT

Other genetic investigations of language disorders have applied more liberal selection strategies, including individuals with expressive, receptive, and phonological impairments. In contrast to the above studies, this approach assumes the existence of general genetic variants that play a role in all forms of language impairment. Under such a hypothesis, all individuals carrying these alleles will be at risk of language disorders of some kind, but the actual presentation of the impairment will depend upon the presence of additional modifying factors, which may be genetic and/or environmental in nature.

The first of these studies by the SLI Consortium (SLIC) selected families containing a single affected individual with language skills >1.5 SD below the mean for their chronological age (SLI Consortium, 2002). Three quantitative measures of language ability—nonword repetition (NWR) and two scales of the Clinical Evaluation of Language Fundamentals (CELF-R), the expressive and receptive language composite scores—were used in a complete genome screen. Linkage was found between chromosome 16q and the nonword repetition phenotype (maximum LOD 3.55) and between chromosome 19q and the expressive language score (maximum LOD 3.55). The SLI Consortium has since replicated these findings in two further independent cohorts of families (Falcaro et al., 2008; SLI Consortium, 2004). However, while chromosome 16 appears to be consistently linked to NWR, chromosome 19 shows linkage to alternative traits across samples. In this region, linkage appears to be specific to the expressive language score in some cohorts, while in others it appears only in the analysis of NWR. Suggestive levels of linkage have also been demonstrated between a measure of spelling ability and chromosome 16 (maximum LOD 2.67) (SLI

Consortium, 2004). Shortly after the publication of the first SLIC study, a second group completed a full genome screen using families affected by SLI (Bartlett et al., 2002). In order to increase the likelihood of finding a single risk variant, these researchers selected individuals from 5 large Canadian pedigrees, thus giving a genetically more homogeneous sample. Each of these pedigrees contained at least two individuals with a spoken language score >1 SD below that expected for their age. In a similar approach to the Stein et al. study, these researchers collected data from a range of quantitative language and reading tests and collapsed them into three binary categories. They classified individuals as "reading impaired" if there was a discrepancy between their nonverbal IQ and reading test scores and/or as "language impaired" if they scored below a given threshold on a test of spoken language. They also defined a more relaxed "clinical impairment" category, which included all reading- and language-impaired individuals and also those who had good spoken language but scored significantly below the mean across a range of other receptive and expressive language tests. In addition, this category also included those who had a history of language problems that required speech therapy. Two regions of linkage were found, one on chromosome 13 in the analysis of the reading-impaired samples (maximum LOD 3.92) and a second on chromosome 2 in the language-impaired individuals (maximum LOD 2.86). The researchers found that their linkage on chromosome 13 overlapped with a locus previously implicated in autism, and so they went on to study other regions also thought to be important in autism—namely, chromosomes 2 and 7—within a second sample of 22 American families. Within this independent sample, linkage was again found between chromosome 13 (maximum LOD = 2.62) and the reading impairment affection status (Bartlett et al., 2004). Like the SSD studies, Bartlett et al. discussed the possibility that chromosome 13 may harbor genetic variants that play a role in the onset of both SLI and autism. However, the details of the methodology used here make these conclusions a little less intuitive. The families investigated in these studies were selected to have a spoken language deficit and showed linkage to chromosome 13 when defined as affected on the basis of a nonword reading test. While this group have produced considerable support for the existence of a chromosome 13 genetic variant that is involved in susceptibility to SLI, it is curious that the effects of this variant should only be reflected in the performance of individuals in a test of reading. Moreover, although there is no doubt of the overlaps between SLI and autism and there is some evidence that variants on chromosome 13 influence both disorders, it would be injudicious to conclude that there exists a shared etiological variant on the basis of these studies alone. Although it may seem desirable to consider multiple disorders together, this can complicate the conclusions drawn and obscure information that could elucidate the mechanisms behind one of those disorders.

QUANTITATIVE TRAITS AND REPLICATION

By the same token, although the consideration of multiple phenotypes is often used to avoid having to simply categorize people as affected or not, the interpretation of the results from the simultaneous investigation of many traits can create alternative issues. For example, the locus identified on chromosome 16 by SLIC is consistently linked to nonword repetition, which is primarily a measure of phonological short-term memory. This region has also been shown to be linked to a spelling measure, but does not show linkage to the two composite, and moderately correlated, measures of expressive or receptive language abilities employed by this group. A possible explanation for this may be that since NWR and spelling are single measures, they provide a cleaner representation of the processes underlying language ability than do the composite scores. Alternatively, this result may indicate that the gene variant that lies on chromosome 16 is not involved in the susceptibility to language impairments per se but instead plays some role in the development of phonological memory ability, which, when impeded to a

greater degree, may render individuals susceptible to the onset of language disorders. Explanations for the locus on chromosome 19, which has been shown to yield linkage that is apparently specific to different, albeit related, measures in alternative groups, are slightly harder to formulate. SLIC investigated additional psychometric measures within the chromosome 16 and 19 regions using a multivariate method that models the contribution of several phenotypic traits simultaneously at a given locus. They found that while the genetic effects on chromosome 16 could be captured by considering only NWR and single-word reading and spelling measures, the linkage on chromosome 19 could be attributed to a whole range of different measures (Monaco & SLI Consortium, 2007). In reality, phenomena such as these probably say more about our lack of understanding of the processes that underlie and interconnect various psychometric measures than they do about gene functions or the quality of the study itself. Remember that any given gene simply encodes a single protein that plays a limited biological role within a complex and multifarious network. Thus it is unrealistic to expect a one-to-one correlation between a genetic variant and a cognitive process or ability on a psychometric test that relies upon a whole series of neurological processes and, ultimately, many thousands of proteins.

Another issue that the above studies serve to illustrate is that of replication. It is important to remember that a genome screen simply allows the assessment of the likelihood that any given region contains a gene contributing to the disorder under study. For a single-gene disorder it is relatively straightforward to assess the significance of a locus. However, for complex disorders, variations in study design, sample and trait distributions, the sensitivity of tests, and random effects mean that the occurrence of false positives is common. For a sib-pair study, a suggestive linkage (LOD ≥ 2.2, $p \leq 7 \times 10^{-4}$) can be expected to occur randomly once per genome screen, and a significant linkage (LOD ≥ 3.6, $p \leq 2 \times 10^{-5}$) is expected to occur once in every 20 genome screens (Lander & Kruglyak, 1995). These figures will increase accordingly for each phenotype analyzed and every type of analysis performed. It is for this reason that replication studies are so important. The true value of a linkage result can be assessed only on the basis of subsequent studies of the same disorder. While the chromosome 15 locus is supported by both studies of SSD, it yielded a much weaker level of linkage than either of the investigations of chromosome 3 or chromosome 6. However, neither of these loci has been investigated by more than one group in relation to SSD. Furthermore, in the absence of a genome-wide report, the true validity of these results is difficult to measure accurately. Two groups have performed genome-wide screens using families affected by SLI; however, very little overlap was seen in the results of these studies. Since the loci on chromosome 13, 16, and 19 have since been replicated in additional sample sets, it would appear that they do represent true genetic loci for susceptibility to SLI; however, this is difficult to assess in the absence of any truly independent replication data.

GENE IDENTIFICATION WITHIN LINKAGE REGIONS

A genome screen allows researchers to narrow their investigation from an entire genome to a single stretch of DNA that is shared between affected individuals and harbors the disease-causing allele. The size of this region depends upon many factors, including the study design, sample ascertainment, and the nature of the genetic variant underlying the linkage, but it is typically over a million base pairs (megabase or Mb) and can contain hundreds of genes. Traditionally the identification of the causative gene involved the detection of a mutant DNA sequence within the linkage region that is carried only by affected individuals. This process would involve the positioning and characterization of all genes within the area of interest and the selection and sequencing of candidate genes on the basis of existing knowledge regarding their expression and function. The completion of the Human Genome Project, which aimed

to determine the sequence of the entire human genome and identify and position all the genes within this sequence, greatly facilitated the gene characterization step of this procedure, which can now primarily be completed using computer simulations. Nonetheless, the selection of a candidate gene and detection of a causative variant is by no means straightforward. For example, the study of the KE family, a three-generation large pedigree affected by a severe single-gene form of speech and language impairment, identified a linkage region approximately 6 Mb in length (Fisher, Vargha-Khadem, Watkins, Monaco, & Pembrey, 1998). This region contained about 100 genes, 20 of which had known functions or detailed expression data. Characterized genes included a neuronal cell adhesion molecule, a brain-specific potassium channel, and a gene that is upregulated in response to neuronal cell injury, all of which provided perfect candidates for the KE phenotype. In addition, the region incorporated a gene, then known as *CAGH44*, which was involved in lung development and, in contrast to the above genes, was not considered a good candidate for causing the KE linkage. However, the fortuitous referral of a patient with verbal dyspraxia who had a chromosome 7 translocation (a chromosomal rearrangement in which a segment of one chromosome is exchanged with material from another chromosome) that was found to disrupt *CAGH44* suddenly made this gene a more interesting prospect (Lai et al., 2000). Subsequent investigations revealed that *CAGH44* contained an amino acid sequence characteristic of the FOX family of proteins, and, accordingly, it was renamed *FOXP2*. Although studies showed that *FOXP2* was primarily expressed in the lung, some expression was also found in the brain, stomach, and heart. Furthermore, a screen of *FOXP2* in the KE family revealed a change in the DNA sequence that was found to cosegregate perfectly with the speech and language disorder (Lai, Fisher, Hurst, Vargha-Khadem, & Monaco, 2001). Thus, even for a severe single-gene disorder, the selection of a candidate gene on the basis of existing information is not always as simple as it may appear. For complex disorders this problem is amplified, since the expected function of the gene is often vague, and in most cases the presence of a mutation is not anticipated. For this reason, most researchers therefore follow linkage with a second, more accurate, gene-positioning strategy known as association analysis. In contrast to linkage analysis, which detects regions of DNA displaying increased sharing between siblings, in its simplest form, association analysis identifies specific sequence variations that are more common in cases affected by the disorder under study than in the general population. As with linkage, the basic association technique has been adapted and extended to enable application across various sample types and study designs. Although association affords a better resolution than does linkage, the fact that it investigates genetic variation at the population level demands the collection of comprehensive data from many genetic markers across large numbers of samples. These techniques are therefore more applicable to smaller genetic regions than for whole genome analyses. Nevertheless, as technology and knowledge progress, researchers are beginning to attempt association analyses of entire genomes for genes underlying complex disorders.

THE FINE MAPPING OF DYSLEXIA ON CHROMOSOME 6

When discussing dyslexia, we will restrict consideration to the chromosome 6 locus, which is the most consistently replicated linkage region in the genetic study of dyslexia and perfectly exemplifies the techniques used and issues encountered in a two-step linkage and association method. This region encompasses the Major Histocompatibility Complex, which encodes many human antigens and was initially investigated in a large sample of sib-pairs because of a reported comorbidity between dyslexia and autoimmune disorders (Cardon et al., 1994). The chromosome 6 linkage has been replicated by several studies, despite variation in sample selection, assessment

strategies, and linkage approaches (reviewed in Williams & O'Donovan, 2006). Although well characterized, the region of linkage was large (~16 Mb) and contained several hundred genes. Many groups therefore followed up the linkage by applying an association analysis. Initial association studies using sparse maps of markers enabled the refinement of the chromosome 6 region to an interval of approximately 600,000 base pairs (600 kilobases or Kb) containing 5 genes, which occur in two clusters. *VMP* and *DCDC2* are adjacent to each other and separated from a cluster of the remaining three genes *THEM2*, *TTRAP,* and *KIAA0319* by a gene-free region of 200 Kb (Deffenbacher et al., 2004; Francks et al., 2004; Kaplan et al., 2002). An initial follow-up study of this region saturated each of these five genes with genetic markers and appeared to demonstrate a clear association between dyslexia and two markers in the *KIAA0319* gene (maximum $p = 1 \times 10^{-5}$—Cope et al., 2005). However, this was closely followed by a second investigation, which, instead, implicated the *DCDC2* gene (maximum $p = 3 \times 10^{-4}$—Meng et al., 2005); subsequent reports have provided support for each of these associations in turn (*KIAA0319*, Harold et al., 2006; *DCDC2*, Schumacher et al., 2006), creating two groups, each supporting the importance of different genes in susceptibility to dyslexia. Intriguingly, a number of these replication studies utilized samples ascertained by the Colorado Learning Disabilities Research Center and thus had significantly overlapping cohorts but yet reported associations to alternative genes (Deffenbacher et al., 2004; Francks et al., 2004; Meng et al., 2005). As discussed in the previous section, this demonstrates the way in which small variations in sample structure and definition can have profound effects upon the outcomes of studies. Preliminary functional studies indicate that *DCDC2* and *KIAA0319* may both have similar roles in neuronal migration within the developing cortex (Meng et al., 2005; Paracchini et al., 2006), a function that can be easily integrated into current understandings of dyslexia pathology.

These studies of dyslexia illustrate the difficulties involved in identifying the gene variants that cause complex disorders. Although in the presence of a major gene variant association may be relatively easy to find, this is not always sufficient to prove the role of a gene in the onset of a complex disorder. Association between a genetic variant and a disorder implies either that the variant is directly responsible for the disorder, or that it lies very close to an allele that is causally implicated. Alternatively, the association may be a false positive or be caused by a bias in the study, samples, or analysis. Proof of causation requires the use of functional studies and model systems to demonstrate that the variant under study affects the expression levels of a protein that is both spatially and temporally relevant to the onset of dyslexia.

In the case of dyslexia, it is possible that both *DCDC2* and *KIAA0319* independently contribute to an increased risk of disorder. Alternatively, dyslexia susceptibility may be caused by another as yet unidentified locus that is in close proximity to the currently associated variants. A final, albeit increasingly unlikely, possibility is that both or either of the reported associations represent false positives. Nevertheless, the identification of the variants in *DCDC2* and *KIAA0319* and the investigation of the processes in which these genes are involved can increase our understanding of brain development and focus future studies of dyslexia and related disorders.

FOXP2 AND LANGUAGE DISORDERS

As we have seen above, linkage, association, and gene identification techniques, despite being much accelerated over the last decade, are by no means trouble-free. Similarly, although gene identification is the objective of many ongoing studies, it does not represent the end-point of genetic research. Positional cloning is followed by functional studies that, as the name suggests, elucidate the function of the gene identified and try to place this within a framework of prior knowledge regarding disorder pathology. The nature of the functional studies will depend somewhat upon the

identity of the isolated gene but will usually involve the isolation of interacting proteins and the characterization of the pathways and processes in which it functions.

In 2001, researchers demonstrated that mutations in the *FOXP2* gene result in a speech and language disorder characterized by severe impairments in the learning and production of complex articulatory movement accompanied by gross deficits in expressive and receptive language abilities (Lai et al., 2001). Although a handful of investigations have subsequently identified disruptions of the *FOXP2* coding sequence in individuals with comparable phenotypes (Lai et al., 2001; MacDermot et al., 2005; see also Feuk et al., 2006; Lennon et al., 2007; Shriberg et al., 2006; Zeesman et al., 2006), it appears unlikely that this gene plays a role in more common, genetically complex forms of language impairment or in associated disorders such as autism. However, it is hoped that the investigation of this gene may provide a gateway into the biological pathways involved in language impairments and thus facilitate the identification of genes that underlie more common language disorders.

IN SILICO FUNCTIONAL STUDIES

If the full coding sequence of a gene is known, then it is possible to gather a certain amount of functional information solely through the *in silico* manipulation of its sequence—that is, by using computer simulation to work out the likely function. The DNA sequence can be directly translated into an amino acid (protein) sequence, and both can be scanned for the presence of familiar patterns (conserved motifs) that may imply certain functional abilities. For example, analysis of the *FOXP2* sequence indicated that it belonged to a family of well-characterized molecules known as the forkhead (or FOX) proteins. This, in turn, indicated that it probably functions as a transcription factor, modulating the expression of specific genes by binding the DNA surrounding them. Computer programs were able to model the structure of the protein, illustrating the physical configuration of the identified domains. This modeling process indicated that the DNA binding motif of *FOXP2* is particularly short and probably confers only a relatively weak DNA binding ability (Stroud et al., 2006). It is therefore postulated that DNA binding by *FOXP2* requires the presence of auxiliary proteins and the creation of a transcription factor complex. It is further proposed that the function of this complex may be to connect physically remote DNA sequences that would otherwise be unable to interact (Stroud et al., 2006). The mutation described within the KE family is predicted to alter the electrostatic charge of the DNA interaction surface and thus reduce the already weak binding ability of the *FOXP2* protein (Banerjee-Basu & Baxevanis, 2004).

Using computational techniques and sequence manipulation, it is also possible to compare the DNA sequence of human genes of interest with similar genes in other species, thus inferring something about the evolution of the gene. Given the putative function of *FOXP2* in speech and language, this is of great interest to researchers in this area. Comparisons of DNA sequences show that the *FOXP2* gene is found in most organisms, from yeast to humans (Enard et al., 2002). Thus, while *FOXP2* may be involved in pathways important for speech and language in humans, it must also play a more basic role in a process that is required by a wide range of species. This concept demonstrates the complexity of gene regulation within and between species. Prior to the Human Genome Project, it was known that mice had approximately 20,000 genes; on this basis, it was predicted that humans were likely to have around 100,000. However, the estimate of human gene number currently stands at just 30,000. It is thought that this diminutive number reflects the ability of the human body to use the same protein products in many different roles. Although every cell in our bodies contains the same genes, each gene can be independently switched on and off or expressed at different levels or in different forms both between cell types and over time. Thus each cell will display a characteristic pattern of gene expression that can be regulated in response to

its specific circumstances. This process is chiefly controlled by regulatory elements that fall outside coding sequences and as yet remain poorly understood. The ability of individual cells to control their own gene expression allows the formation of complex regulatory pathways that are essential to the function of the human body.

LABORATORY FUNCTIONAL STUDIES

Although a surprising amount of work can be done using gene sequences alone, in order to fully elucidate the function of any gene, one must use "wet" laboratory methods that involve the investigation of proteins within model systems. Such techniques may involve the study of protein distribution and the identification of interacting proteins within in vitro cell lines or may investigate the role of the protein within certain organs or at given developmental time points using whole organisms such as mice and rats. Cell line investigations of *FOXP2* demonstrate that the encoded protein is usually localized to the nucleus, supporting its role in DNA binding (Mizutani et al., 2007). Furthermore, forms of the protein that carry the mutation found in the KE family enter the nucleus to a lesser extent, providing proof that this change is functionally relevant (Vernes et al., 2006). Support for the importance of *FOXP2* in developmental pathways comes from the breeding of mice with targeted disruptions of both copies of the gene (knockout mice) (Shu et al., 2005). Pups bred in this way have severe motor impairments that restrict their movements and lead to premature death. Interestingly, they are also reported to display a decreased incidence of vocalization compared to their normal siblings. Ultrasonic vocalizations are produced by mouse pups when they are removed from their mother and are thought to play an important role in mother–infant social interaction. In contrast to full knockouts, mice that carry a single disrupted copy of *FOXP2* are reported to have only modest developmental delays, but they also display this vocalization decrease (Shu et al., 2005). Similar investigations of *FOXP2* in the brains of song-birds show that it is highly expressed within a region that is known to be necessary for vocal learning (Area X). Furthermore, expression in this region increases at the time when chicks are learning to sing (Haesler et al., 2004). Postmortem examination of the brains from knockout mice found no gross structural abnormalities but did provide some evidence of subtle abnormalities (Shu et al., 2005). The expression of *FOXP2* in the brain appears to be tightly regulated temporally and spatially through development and occurs predominantly in brain circuits implicated in motor control (Lai, Gerrelli, Monaco, Fisher, & Copp, 2003; Ferland, Cherry, Preware, Morrisey, & Walsh, 2003). It is thought that *FOXP2* is probably involved in establishing and maintaining connections within neuronal circuits crucial for complex motor control and may be important in processes such as procedural learning (Takahashi, Liu, Hirokawa, & Takahashi, 2003) or the mirror system (Corballis, 2004). Although the gene is expressed in tissues other than the brain, it is believed that the brain is particularly sensitive to levels of *FOXP2,* and any alteration conferred by a mutation would therefore be expected to result in the abnormal development of those brain regions in which *FOXP2* is important. As discussed above, the fact that *FOXP2* is expressed across a wide range of tissues is normal and not only demonstrates the intricacy of gene regulation but also illustrates how the popular media can sometimes overly simplify a complex story. The use of terms such as "language gene" is misleading, and while the importance of the *FOXP2* gene product in biological pathways involved in the development of speech and language is not disputed, this should never be represented as the sole function of the protein.

We can see from the studies described above that the breadth of investigations that can be completed subsequent to gene identification is enormous, and for this reason functional studies are often driven by the interests of individual researchers (e.g., evolution, lung development, language ability, etc). While this enables the completion of a wide range of studies and the production of a comprehensive map that can be integrated across subject fields, it can often result in an overrepresentation of information in those areas that are considered the most provocative at that time point. For example, while our knowledge base regarding the evolution of *FOXP2* and its function in brain development has increased exponentially over the last five years, we are still relatively ignorant regarding its functions in tissues such as the lung. This serves to illustrate how the interest of the media and the public can have a great influence upon the perceived importance of certain research areas and can ultimately steer the direction of current research allocations.

In summary, this chapter provides a broad overview of how, even in the absence of any prior knowledge regarding the identity of a gene, it is possible to map associations between genes and common, genetically complex disorders such as SLI and dyslexia. These disorders serve to illustrate the complexities involved in the interpretation of results and the proof of causation. Finally, we hope to have implied the importance of the role of researchers and media alike when considering the terminology used and conclusions made in the treatment of results from such studies.

REFERENCES

Banerjee-Basu, S., & Baxevanis, A. D. (2004). Structural analysis of disease-causing mutations in the P-subfamily of forkhead transcription factors. *Proteins, 54,* 639–647.

Bartlett, C. W., Flax, J. F., Logue, M. W., Smith, B. J., Vieland, V. J., Tallal, P., & Brzustowicz, L. M. (2004). Examination of potential overlap in autism and language loci on chromosomes 2, 7, and 13 in two independent samples ascertained for specific language impairment. *Human Heredity, 57,* 10–20.

Bartlett, C. W., Flax, J. F., Logue, M. W., Vieland, V. J., Bassett, A. S., Tallal, P., & Brzustowicz, L. M. (2002). A major susceptibility locus for specific language impairment is located on 13q21. *American Journal of Human Genetics, 71,* 45–55.

Cardon, L. R., Smith, S. D., Fulker, D. W., Kimberling, W. J., Pennington, B. F., & DeFries, J. C.

(1994). Quantitative trait locus for reading disability on chromosome 6. *Science, 266,* 276–279.

Cope, N., Harold, D., Hill, G., Moskvina, V., Stevenson, J., Holmans, P., et al. (2005). Strong evidence that *KIAA0319* on chromosome 6p is a susceptibility gene for developmental dyslexia. *American Journal of Human Genetics, 76,* 581–591.

Corballis, M. C. (2004). *FOXP2* and the mirror system. *Trends in Cognitive Science, 8,* 95–96.

Deffenbacher, K. E., Kenyon, J. B., Hoover, D. M., Olson, R. K., Pennington, B. F., DeFries, & J. C., Smith, S. D. (2004). Refinement of the 6p21.3 quantitative trait locus influencing dyslexia: Linkage and association analyses. *Human Genetics, 115,* 128–138.

Eley, T., & Craig, I. (2005). Introductory guide to the language of molecular genetics. *Journal of Child Psychology and Psychiatry, 46,* 1039–1041.

Eley, T., & Rijsdijk, F. (2005). Introductory guide to the statistics of molecular genetics. *Journal of Child Psychology Psychiatry, 46,* 1042–1044.

Enard, W., Przeworski, M., Fisher, S. E., Lai, C. S., Wiebe, V., Kitano, T., et al. (2002). Molecular evolution of *FOXP2*, a gene involved in speech and language. *Nature, 418,* 869–872.

Falcaro, M., Pickles, A., Newbury, D. F., Addis, L., Banfield, E., Fisher, S. E., et al., & the SLI Consortium (2008). Genetic and phenotypic effects of phonological short-term memory and grammatical morphology in specific language impairment. *Genes, Brain and Behavior, 7,* 393–492.

Ferland, R. J., Cherry, T. J., Preware, P. O., Morrisey, E. E., & Walsh, C. A. (2003). Characterization of *FOXP2* and *FOXP1* mRNA and protein in the developing and mature brain. *Journal of Computational Neurology, 460,* 266–279.

Feuk, L., Kalervo, A., Lipsanen-Nyman, M., Skaug, J., Nakabayashi, K., Finucane, B., et al. (2006). Absence of a paternally inherited *FOXP2* gene in developmental verbal dyspraxia. *American Journal of Human Genetics, 79,* 965–972.

Fisher, S. E., Vargha-Khadem, F., Watkins, K. E., Monaco, A. P., & Pembrey, M. E. (1998). Localisation of a gene implicated in a severe speech and language disorder. *Nature Genetics, 18,* 168–170.

Francks, C., Paracchini, S., Smith, S. D., Richardson, A. J., Scerri, T. S., Cardon, L. R., et al. (2004). A 77-kilobase region of chromosome 6p22.2 is associated with dyslexia in families from the United Kingdom and from the United States. *American Journal of Human Genetics, 75,* 1046–1058.

Haesler, S., Wada, K., Nshdejan, A., Morrisey, E. E., Lints, T., Jarvis, E. D., & Scharff, C. (2004). *FOXP2* expression in avian vocal learners and non-learners. *Journal of Neuroscience, 24,* 3164–3175.

Harold, D., Paracchini, S., Scerri, T., Dennis, M., Cope, N., Hill, G., et al. (2006). Further evidence that the *KIAA0319* gene confers susceptibility to developmental dyslexia. *Molecular Psychiatry, 11,* 1085–1091.

Kaplan, D. E., Gayán, J., Ahn, J., Won, T.-W., Pauls, D., Olson, R. K., et al. (2002). Evidence for linkage and association with reading disability on 6p21.3–22. *American Journal of Human Genetics, 70,* 1287–1298.

Lai, C. S. L., Fisher, S. E., Hurst, J. A., Levy, E. R., Hodgson, S., Fox, M., et al. (2000). The *SPCH1* region on human 7q31: Genomic characterisation of the critical interval and localisation of translocations associated with speech and language disorder. *American Journal of Human Genetics, 67,* 357–368.

Lai, C. S. L., Fisher, S. E., Hurst, J. A., Vargha-Khadem, F., & Monaco, A. P. (2001). A novel forkhead-domain gene is mutated in a severe speech and language disorder. *Nature, 413,* 519–523.

Lai, C. S. L., Gerrelli, D., Monaco, A. P., Fisher, S. E., & Copp, A. J. (2003). *FOXP2* expression during brain development coincides with adult sites of pathology in a severe speech and language disorder. *Brain, 126,* 2455–2462.

Lander, E. S., & Kruglyak, L. (1995). Genetic dissection of complex traits: Guidelines for interpreting and reporting linkage results. *Nature Genetics, 11,* 241–247.

Lennon, P. A., Cooper, M. L., Peiffer, D. A., Gunderson, K. L., Patel, A., Peters, S., et al. (2007). Deletion of 7q31.1 supports involvement of *FOXP2* in language impairment: Clinical report and review. *American Journal of Medical Genetics, 143A:* 791–798.

MacDermot, K. D., Bonora, E., Sykes, N., Coupe, A. M., Lai, C. S., Vernes, S. C., et al. (2005). Identification of *FOXP2* truncation as a novel cause of developmental speech and language deficits. *American Journal of Human Genetics, 76,* 1074–1080.

Meng, H., Smith, S. D., Hager, K., Held, M., Liu, J., Olson, R. K., et al. (2005). *DCDC2* is associated with reading disability and modulates neuronal development in the brain. *Proceedings of the National Academy of Sciences USA, 102,* 17053–17058.

Mizutani, A., Matsuzaki, A., Momoi, M. Y., Fujita, E., Tanabe, Y., & Momoi, T. (2007). Intracellular distribution of a speech/language disorder associated *FOXP2* mutant. *Biochemistry Biophysics Research Communication, 353*, 869–874.

Monaco, A. P., & SLI Consortium. (2007). Multivariate linkage analysis of specific language impairment (SLI). *Annals of Human Genetics, 71*: 660–673.

Paracchini, S., Thomas, A., Castro, S., Lai, C., Paramasivam, M., Wang, Y., et al. (2006). The chromosome 6p22 haplotype associated with dyslexia reduces the expression of *KIAA0319*, a novel gene involved in neuronal migration. *Human Molecular Genetics, 15*, 1659–1666.

Schumacher, J., Anthoni, H., Dahdouh, F., Konig, I. R., Hillmer, A. M., Kluck, N., et al. (2006). Strong genetic evidence of *DCDC2* as a susceptibility gene for dyslexia. *American Journal of Human Genetics, 78*, 52–62.

Shriberg, L. D., Ballard, K. J., Tomblin, J. B., Duffy, J. R., Odell, K. H., & Williams, C. A. (2006). Speech, prosody, and voice characteristics of a mother and daughter with a 7;13 translocation affecting *FOXP2*. *Journal of Speech Language, and Hearing Research, 49*, 500–525.

Shu, W., Cho, J. Y., Jiang, Y., Zhang, M., Weisz, D., Elder, G. A., et al. (2005). Altered ultrasonic vocalization in mice with a disruption in the *FOXP2* gene. *Proceedings of the National Academy Sciences USA, 102*, 9643–9648.

SLI Consortium. (2002). A genomewide scan identifies two novel loci involved in specific language impairment. *American Journal of Human Genetics, 70*, 384–398.

SLI Consortium. (2004). Highly significant linkage to the *SLI1* locus in an expanded sample of individuals affected by specific language impairment. *American Journal of Human Genetics, 74*, 1225–1238.

Smith, S. D., Pennington, B. F., Boada, R., & Shriberg, L. D. (2005). Linkage of speech sound disorder to reading disability loci. *Journal of Child Psychology and Psychiatry, 46*, 1057–1066.

Stein, C. M., Millard, C., Kluge, A., Miscimarra, L. E., Cartier, K. C., Freebairn, L. A., et al. (2006). Speech sound disorder influenced by a locus in 15q14 region. *Behavior Genetics, 36*, 858–868.

Stein, C. M., Schick, J. H., Taylor, G., Shriberg, L. D., Millard, C., Kundtz-Kluge, A., et al. (2004). Pleiotropic effects of a chromosome 3 locus on speech-sound disorder and reading. *American Journal of Human Genetics, 74*, 283–297.

Stroud, J. C., Wu, Y., Bates, D. L., Han, A., Nowick, K., Paabo, S., et al. (2006). Structure of the forkhead domain of *FOXP2* bound to DNA. *Structure, 14*, 159–166.

Takahashi, K., Liu, F. C., Hirokawa, K., & Takahashi, H. (2003). Expression of *FOXP2*, a gene involved in speech and language, in the developing and adult striatum. *Journal of Neuroscience Research, 73*, 61–72.

Vernes, S. C., Nicod, J., Elahi, F. M., Coventry, J. A., Kenny, N., Coupe, A. M., et al. (2006). Functional genetic analysis of mutations implicated in a human speech and language disorder. *Human Molecular Genetics, 15*, 3154–3167.

Williams, J., & O'Donovan, M. C. (2006). The genetics of developmental dyslexia. *European Journal of Human Genetics, 14*, 681–689.

Zeesman, S., Nowaczyk, M. J., Teshima, I., Roberts, W., Cardy, J. O., Brian, J., et al. (2006). Speech and language impairment and oromotor dyspraxia due to deletion of 7q31 that involves *FOXP2*. *American Journal of Medical Genetics, 140A*, 509–514.

Validating diagnostic standards for specific language impairment using adolescent outcomes

J. Bruce Tomblin

For several years, there has been considerable discussion about evidence-based practice in health services and, more recently, education. Evidence-based practice begins with the acknowledgment that an important part of clinical work consists of decision making. The effectiveness of one's clinical practices will be determined by the quality of the decisions made and, of course, the skill involved in executing actions dictated by these decisions. A fortunate by-product of the emphasis on evidence-based practice is that the clinical decision-making process is receiving greater emphasis in clinically related research. This chapter is concerned with one of the first decisions made while serving a child with a language disorder. I examine some of the evidence that bears on the validity of two standards used to determine when an individual represents a clinical case and is, therefore, in need of clinical services. Specifically, I examine a standard my research group established several years ago concerning when poor language skills should represent a language impairment. We also consider whether there is support for requiring a discrepancy between performance IQ and language ability. These questions concern the issue of validity, and therefore we must establish the grounds upon which we validate these diagnostic standards. This chapter argues that socially valued outcomes should serve as the basis for justifying clinical services and that evidence concerning these outcomes can be obtained to test the validity of diagnostic standards.

STANDARDS FOR CASE SELECTION

Current clinical standards for the identification of children who have poor language abilities are varied within the United States and certainly worldwide. About 10 years ago, my colleagues and I reviewed the standards used at that time, including a sample of practicing speech-language clinicians in the United States (Tomblin, Records, & Zhang, 1996). We concluded that a child who fell below the 10th percentile in two or more areas of language was likely to be judged as language impaired by these clinicians. This criterion, referred to as the epiSLI standard, was then used in a large-scale study of the epidemiology of specific language impairment (SLI). This standard is very similar to one proposed by Paul (2001). In establishing this standard, we focused on the level of severity of poor language in reference to a child's age peers. Stark and Tallal (1981) argued that SLI represented a condition in which the child did not present with mental retardation, psychiatric problems, and neuromotor impairments. Additionally, they required that the child have a performance IQ greater than 85. This requirement for language abilities to be below cognitive level as represented by nonverbal IQ is referred to as cognitive referencing. Following this precedent, we incorporated this standard in our epidemiological study. Thus, SLI was defined as the absence of developmental disorders such as mental retardation, autism, or cerebral palsy, and of sensory disorders of hearing or vision. Additionally, language levels in accord with the epiSLI standard and a performance IQ of more than 85 were required. Our study also included children who had poor language skills but also had low nonverbal skills, to whom we shall refer as children with general delay (GD). Several authors (Cole, Dale, & Mills, 1990; Lahey, 1990; Plante, 1998) have argued that the use of cognitive referencing is neither conceptually well founded nor supported by empirical

data. Tomblin and Zhang (1999) have shown that language-impaired children with performance IQ levels above and below 85 have the same patterns of language deficits and differ only in terms of overall severity of impairment. Recently, a panel of experts convened by the National Institute on Deafness and Other Communication Disorders (NIDCD) has proposed that the use of a performance IQ be examined to determine whether this standard should be retained (Tager-Flusberg & Cooper, 1999). In light of this it is reasonable to ask whether the epiSLI standard identifies children who should be viewed as language impaired and whether we should distinguish between the GD and SLI groups.

Communication and health

If we are going to seek empirical evidence to support a clinical decision regarding a child's communication status, it is necessary to first establish what that decision actually represents. What is it that we mean when we say that a child has a communication disorder? A simple answer is that the child's communication skills are not what they *should* be. But on what grounds do we determine what should or should not be occurring in a child's communication development, so that we can determine the presence of a communication disorder? The answer to this question turns out to be the same as one to the question we can ask with regard to any form of ill health.

There is a modest literature within the philosophy of medicine that has addressed this topic. As one might expect within philosophy, there isn't a single answer but, rather, a range of viewpoints. These viewpoints, however, generally fall between two perspectives. The first viewpoint is one that claims that there is a design for each organism, and that design dictates certain functions. Thus, health is a condition congruent with the organism's design, and disorder[1] is a violation of this design. We can see this logic by analogy to artifacts we do design and build. Thus, my car is designed to move me and my passengers at certain speeds and has the capability to turn and stop as necessary. These functions are provided by designing and manufacturing wheels, brakes, an engine, and so forth. Violations of the designed properties of these components result in malfunction and thus in the car not working. In the case of humans and other organisms, we can attempt to discover what their design is and therefore the proper function through the use of natural science. This viewpoint is called naturalism. Boorse (1977, 1987) has advocated this view at least with regard to the notion of disease and health. Boorse argues that healthy function of an organism such as the human can be learned by determining the average structure and function of the organism. Disease can then be computed as a deviation from this average. Indeed, we rarely consider levels of average function to be instances of ill health. Thus, the naturalist assumes that with sufficient empirical study of the systems concerned with human function, we can discover those conditions that comprise ill health with regard to deviations from the average. The greatest criticism of neutralism has been its inability to address satisfactorily what constitutes how to determine when deviation from the average constitutes disease. Consider that in some situations deviation from the mean is considered healthier than an average level (the case of body mass or cholesterol). Also, the direction of the deviation is not the same. For some things, falling below the mean is unhealthy; for others, being above the mean is. If statistics alone can determine health states, then we need a statistical scheme to say which kind of variation is healthy and which is not. Thus, naturalism provides a means for defining what should be but struggles to help us to determine what should not be.

A contrasting position to naturalism is normativism. The term *norm* here refers to social values, not statistical properties. A normative account of health and ill health does not require that there be a standard design for an organism, nor does it assume that one can determine from studying the organism what it should be like. Instead, the source of what should or should not be found in an organism—in this case, humans—comes from social values regarding biological and behavioral functioning of the organism. These social expectations come from the values we obtain in our culture. Thus, we can consider health as a state in which one is functioning within the social expectations of our society, and ill health comprises a

situation in which one is not able to meet these expectations. Ill health or disorder is, therefore, not so much something that exists in nature and is discovered but, rather, an assigned status based on cultural values.

We are going to adopt this normative perspective in our effort to construct a framework for evaluating diagnostic standards for communication disorder and, in particular, language impairment. Very simply, we can state that a language disorder exists when the child's language achievement results in an unacceptable level of risk for undesirable outcomes. That is, language disorder represents a situation in which the child is unlikely to be able to meet the socially defined functional expectations either currently or in the future because of his or her current or future language abilities. In fact, I think this is what most clinicians actually mean when they determine that a child requires clinical intervention. Note that this viewpoint says nothing about why the child's language abilities are what they are. The causes of individual differences (environments, genes, etc.) in language development are different from those that cause us to be concerned about some of these individual differences. In this perspective, language disorder is defined not by underlying causal systems but, rather, by the socially evaluated outcomes, and thus we need to focus on where and when individual differences in language abilities are associated with and are likely causes of disvalued outcomes.

Developmental outcomes as competence

Within this perspective, socially important domains of function become a focal point of research. To define what these domains are and when function in these is viewed as compromised, we may use the concept of *competence*, as defined by researchers in child development and psychopathology. Masten defined competence as "adaptation success in the developmental tasks expected of individuals of a given age in a particular cultural and historical context" (Masten et al., 1999). Societal expectations of individuals change as they age. This variation in expectation is incorporated in Zigler and Gllick's (1986) notion of salient developmental tasks. Roisman,

Masten, Coatsworth, and Tellegen (2004) have stated that "salient developmental tasks represent the benchmarks of adaptation that are specific to a developmental period and are contextualized by prevailing sociocultural and historically embedded expectation" (p. 123). Because expectations vary with development, there are transitional points in life where old competencies are diminishing in saliency and new ones are emerging to become salient (Roisman et al., 2004). As these new competencies emerge, they build on the prior competencies and also upon new cultural supports that motivate growth. For instance, within many cultures it is likely that language development itself represents a salient developmental task of early childhood. Subsequently, during later childhood, academic and peer relations become salient tasks, but these will be influenced in part by the earlier language development. Masten has proposed that failures in the development of competence at a latter stage of development can often be traced to failures of development at earlier stages of development.

Our current interest is the developmental period of adolescence. Therefore we can ask, within the culture of the United States, what are the developmentally salient tasks of adolescence around which we can define good or poor competence? Masten and colleagues (1999) recognized three domains of adolescent competence: academic achievement, behavioral conduct, and social performance. The *academic competence* domain was measured by achievement test results, school grades, teacher ratings of school performance, and parent reports of school performance. *Conduct* was reflected in measures of rule following versus disruptive behavior and rule violations at home, at school, and in the community, based on parent, teacher, and child reports. *Social* competence was reflected in the adolescent and parent report of the adolescent's ability to develop close and lasting relationships with age mates. Although not a part of competence as such, these researchers also acknowledged a fourth area of function for the adolescence. This was termed *psychological well-being,* which was determined by the adolescent's report of self-worth, absence of psychological distress, and positive emotionality.

COMPETENCE IN ADOLESCENTS AND YOUNG ADULTS WITH SLI

Much of what we know about the outcomes of SLI in adolescence comes from a handful of longitudinal studies of children identified during earlier childhood with language impairment and then followed through the school years into or through adolescence (Aram & Nation, 1980; Beitchman et al., 1996b; Conti-Ramsden, Nicola, Simkin, & Botting, 2001; Johnson et al., 1999; Mawhood, Howlin, & Rutter, 2000; Stothard, Snowling, Bishop, Chipchase, & Kaplan, 1998). These studies have consistently shown that children with poor language abilities in the early school years are very likely to persist in having poor language ability throughout the school years.

Academic competence in adolescence

A few early studies reported academic outcomes in adolescence and adulthood of children with SLI (Hall & Tomblin, 1978; Nation & Aram, 1980). These studies found persistent depressed academic achievement, greater rates of children being held back in school (grade retention), and lower rates of post-secondary school attendance among children with language impairments than among those who had age-appropriate language status. Beitchman's longitudinal cohort (Young et al., 2002) revealed that, as young adults, children with early language impairment lagged significantly behind typically developing children in all areas of academic achievement, even after controlling for nonverbal intelligence. Rates of poor academic achievement despite normal intelligence (in the United States and Canada, this is referred to as learning disabilities) were significantly higher in the language-impaired group than in either the typically developing group or in community base rates. Such poor academic outcomes were not found for children with initial impairments of speech only. Reports of the adolescent outcomes of children who had participated in Bishop and Edmundson's (1987) study of preschool language impairment also indicated poorer academic outcomes for those children who had persisting language problems at the age of 5½, and even those who appeared to have recovered by school entry were doing somewhat more poorly than a typically developing group with no history of language impairment (Snowling, Adams, Bishop, & Stothard, 2001; Stothard et al., 1998). Thus, the pattern of compromised academic competence in children with language impairment extends throughout the school years.

Psychosocial outcomes in adolescence

A small set of studies have shown that children with language impairment are at risk for psychiatric and social difficulties in young adulthood. In fact, two studies (Baker & Cantwell, 1987; Rutter & Mawhood, 1991) have suggested that this risk increases in adulthood. In contrast with these studies, Beitchman et al. (1996a) reported that rates of behavior disorders were somewhat—although not significantly—lower in adolescence than when these children were in kindergarten. However, these authors noted differences in measurement as a possible cause for the somewhat lower rates. More recently, Beitchman et al. (2001b) followed this cohort into early adulthood and reported significantly higher rates of anxiety disorder compared with individuals who had age-appropriate language status as children. The majority of participants with anxiety disorders had a diagnosis of social phobia. Trends were found toward associations between language impairment (SLI and GD) and antisocial personality disorder rates. Males from the language-impaired group had significantly higher rates of antisocial personality disorder compared with males from the typically developing group. This research group (Beitchman et al., 2001a, 2001b) also studied substance abuse and behavior disorders in this cohort and found that a large proportion of the depressed drug abusers and those with antisocial behaviors had speech and/or language impairment at age 5.

This brief overview supports the general contention that children who enter school with poor language skills are likely to face poor competence in adolescence. However, these studies used a variety of diagnostic standards, and none of them examined the extent to which differences in outcome exist between children with or without discrepancies between language and nonverbal abilities. We have recently completed a 10-year longitudinal study that allows us to examine whether the epiSLI standards are associated with compromised adolescent competence and whether there is reason to incorporate cognitive referencing into our clinical decision making.

IOWA LONGITUDINAL STUDY

The longitudinal cohort for this research originated from a large sample of kindergarten-age children who participated in a cross-sectional epidemiologic study of SLI. Methods for the original cross-sectional sample are described by Tomblin et al. (1997), and the methods for selection of the longitudinal sample are provided in Tomblin, Zhang, and Buckwalter (2000). Members of this cohort, initially 604 children, were diagnosed with language impairment when they were in kindergarten (5–6 years old). These children were reevaluated two, four, eight, and ten years after kindergarten. When they were in kindergarten, these children were diagnosed using the Test of Language Development (TOLD:2-P; Newcomer & Hammill, 1988) and a narrative comprehension and retell task (Culatta, Page, & Ellis, 1983). Children who scored at or below $-1.25\ SD$ on two areas of this battery were considered to be language impaired. These children were also given the block design and picture completion test of the Wechsler Intelligence Scale for Children–III (Wechsler, 1989), and those who received scores below 75 ($n = 27$) were excluded. Children with nonverbal IQs above $-1\ SD$ (85) were assigned to the SLI or typically developing groups, depending on their language status. For the current analysis those with nonverbal IQs at or below $-1\ SD$ (<86) who also had language impairment as defined above were assigned to the general delay (GD) group. Table 7.1 provides a description of these children with respect to their language, nonverbal IQ status, sex distribution, and parental education background.

The typically developing comparison group

TABLE 7.1

Language scores, nonverbal IQ scores, and demographic data for the three groups of children diagnosed at kindergarten

	Kindergarten language		Kindergarten performance IQ		Male (%)	Parent school attendance[a]
	IQ	SS	IQ	SS		
TD	100.35	13.09	99.17	12.32	57	13.5
SLI	76.64	5.65	99.78	7.26	59	13
GD	73.53	6.99	82.65	3.52	49	12

Note. IQ = IQ scores; SS = standard score units. TD = typically developing; SLI = specific language impairment; GD = general delay.

[a] Median parent school attendance, in years.

has language and nonverbal abilities in the normal range, and on average the language and nonverbal scores are equivalent. The SLI and GD group have similar levels of depressed language abilities, but the SLI group has normal nonverbal skills similar to the typically developing group, with a clear discrepancy between language and nonverbal abilities, whereas the GD group has much less of a discrepancy between their language and nonverbal abilities. The SLI and GD groups also do contrast somewhat with regard to their parent's education, with the GD children coming from homes with a lower educational background. Parental education can serve as a good indicator variable for the socioeconomic characteristics of the home. Table 7.2 shows the sample size and age at each observational interval. All participants were from monolingual English-speaking homes

TABLE 7.2

Ages and numbers of children for each group across the five grade levels at which data were collected

Grade level	TD			SLI			GD		
	N	M[a]	SD	N	M[a]	SD	N	M[a]	SD	N
Kindergarten	577	5.9	0.33	372	6.0	0.29	123	6.0	0.29	82
Second	577	7.9	0.41	372	8.0	0.34	123	8.0	0.35	82
Fourth	545	9.89	0.42	356	10.0	0.36	117	10.0	0.38	72
Eighth	503	13.9	0.40	333	13.9	0.38	106	13.9	0.40	64
Tenth	481	15.8	0.38	319	15.8	0.37	102	15.8	0.37	60

Note. TD = typically developing; SLI = specific language impairment; GD = general delay.

[a] Mean ages in years.

and predominately either of European background or African–American.

Our focus in this chapter is on outcomes that are associated with these children's language status as kindergarteners. We have shown that their diagnostic status does not remain stable across time (Tomblin et al., 2003). This instability was shown to be largely due to measurement error— that is, the fact that test scores are never perfect indicators of ability and will vary from one occasion to another. Our previous study showed that around 46% of the children identified as language impaired (LI)—either GD or SLI—in our initial diagnosis were likely to be false positive cases who did not really have any problems. Thus, it should not be surprising to find that only 52% of the children in our initial sample of children with LI in kindergarten met the same standard for LI at 16 years. Also not surprisingly, a larger percentage of children with GD (67%) continued to qualify as LI at 16 years, compared with fewer (42%) children with SLI. It is natural to ask at this point whether we should exclude children who were likely to be false positives in the first place. In practice this is not possible, as we cannot establish which children are clearly false-positive cases. Thus, our results here describe the outcomes of children who met our initial criteria for LI, despite the attendant uncertainty of the diagnosis.

We focus on the data obtained from tenth-grade adolescents, who represent a substantial proportion of the children who were initially enrolled in this longitudinal study. The greatest attrition can be found within the GD group, where we lost contact with 26% of the sample.

COMPETENCE IN ADOLESCENCE

A wide range of data were gathered on adolescent outcomes. These included questionnaires administered to the parents, teachers, and the young people themselves. We also obtained direct measures of academic competence in the form of reading and school examination scores. Col-lectively, these instruments provided information concerning the four domains of competence outlined by Masten and colleagues for adolescence and young adulthood. For each domain, we examine the relationship of our initial diagnostic categories and these outcomes and consider whether the distinction between SLI and GD is justified. We report effect sizes when we find statistical significance: these allow us to tell not just whether a difference was reliable, but whether it is important. The terms used are in accord with Cohen's terminology (strong, medium, small) reflecting the strength of the association.

Academic competence

The literature already provides a strong case for our expectation that the two groups of children with language impairment are likely to have poor academic outcomes as they near the end of their mandatory schooling (age 16 in the United States). According to parent report, the adolescents with language impairment were much more likely to be receiving special education services than the typically developing group. During the 11 years of this follow-up study, 37% of the children with SLI and 34% of the children with GD had received some form of special education placement. Given that the children with SLI had normal nonverbal IQs, it is somewhat surprising that they were receiving more special education services than the GD group, but this difference was not statistically significant, $\chi^2(1, N = 137) = .36$, $p = .55$. The rate of special education services for the typically developing group was substantially lower than that for the two LI groups at 9%.

Reading is usually viewed as a crucial academic skill. We have previously reported that the children with SLI and GD in this longitudinal study had difficulties with reading by the second grade (7–8 years) and that these reading difficulties persisted through the eighth grade (13–14 years; Catts, Adlof, & Weismer, 2006; Catts, Fey, Tomblin, & Zhang, 2002; Catts, Fey, Zhang, & Tomblin, 1999, 2001). As shown in Figure 7.1, these reading problems persist into the tenth grade (15–16 years). A single composite scale score (mean = 100, *SD* = 15) for reading

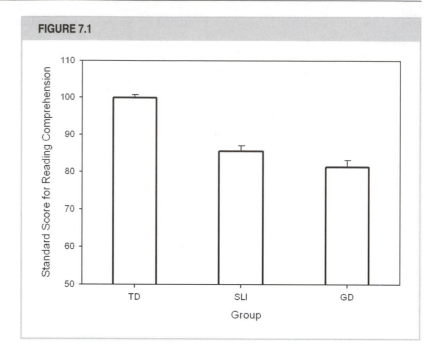

FIGURE 7.1

Mean and standard error (standard score scale) for reading comprehension for the children with age-appropriate levels of spoken language in kindergarten (TD), children with specific language impairment (SLI), and children with general delay (GD).

comprehension was formed from the Gray Oral Reading Comprehension Subtest (Wiederholt & Bryant, 1992) and the Passage Comprehension subtest of the Woodcock Reading Mastery test (Woodcock, 1998). The children with SLI were significantly below the typically developing group (mean difference = 14.34, Tukey LSD, p < .05), as was the GD group (mean difference = 18.56, Tukey LSD, p < .05). The effect size for these differences was strong (r^2 = .24). In contrast, the SLI and GD groups did not differ (mean difference = 0.22, Tukey LSD, ns).

These values indicate that the two groups of language-impaired adolescents were often doing poorly in reading. We can attach more meaning to these outcomes by examining their reading ability levels. We defined functional illiteracy as having a reading level below 11 years. Using this criterion for the Passage Comprehension subtest of the Woodcock Reading Mastery test, 19% of the children with SLI and 31% of the GD children are functionally illiterate, in comparison with 5% of the typically developing group. The difference in the rates between the SLI and GD was not significant, $\chi^2(1, N = 158) = 3.19, p = .07$, but the differ-

ence between the two language-impaired groups and the typically developing group was, $\chi^2(1, N = 462) = 35.60, p < .0001, \mathbf{w} = .28$. According to Cohen's (1988) criteria, the relationship between early language status and later poor literacy is strong.

Reading is certainly a very important aspect of academic performance; however, reading might be expected to be closely related to language ability. To look at indicators of academic performance that are not specific to reading, we can consider parent reports on the Child Behavior Checklist (CBCL; Achenbach, 1991a) and teacher reports on the Teacher Report Form (TRF; Achenbach, 1991b). These scales provides a subscale score concerned with academic performance (TRF) and school performance (CBCL), respectively. These scores (see Figure 7.2) are represented in the form of T scores with a mean of 50 ($SD = 10$) for peers of the same age and gender. We can see that the teachers generally had a more positive view of the individual's school performance than did the parents; however, the contrasts across groups were quite similar. Those who entered school with language skills in the normal range were rated

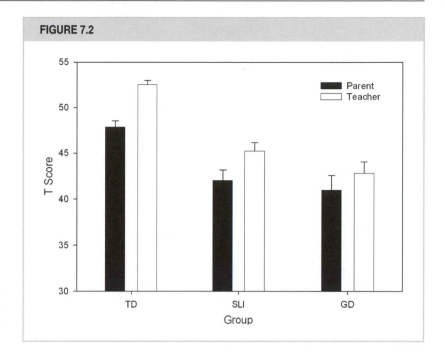

FIGURE 7.2

Mean and standard deviation (T score scale), for parent report (CBCL) and teacher report of tenth-grade academic performance in children with typical language development at kindergarten (TD), children with specific language impairment (SLI), and children with general delay (GD).

by both their teachers and their parents as significantly better students at tenth grade than those with SLI or with GD at school entry ($p < .05$). Furthermore there was no difference between the SLI and GD groups with respect to either teacher or parent ratings.

One additional source of information concerning school performance was obtained from the school administered Iowa Tests of Educational Development (ITED; Feldt, Forsyth, Ansley, & Alnot, 1994). These tests were not mandatory at the time of this study, and therefore not all of the schools that the students attended administered the tests. However, we were able to obtain results from 240 of the typically developing group, 72 of the students with SLI, and 47 of the students with GD. Although the ITED contains several subtests, for our purposes we can focus on just two. One of these consists of the mathematics concepts test, which is described as measuring the students' ability to use correct mathematical reasoning, but did not measure computational ability under time pressure. Thus, this provides a measure of applied mathematical problem solving. The other subtest is the overall composite score. Figure 7.3

reveals a pattern across the groups on these tests that is very similar to that shown in the prior measures. Again, significant differences were found between the typically developing group and the SLI and GD groups for both the mathematics concepts test and the overall composite measure ($p < .05$), and no significant difference was shown between the SLI and GD groups.

We can see, however, that the magnitude of the group differences is smaller for these measures than for the reading comprehension measure shown in Figure 7.1. Whereas an r^2 value of .24 was found for the effect of the three groups on reading comprehension, r^2 values of .09 and .12 (medium strength) were found for the mathematics concepts and composite scores, respectively. Thus the effect of initial language status at school entry was more than twice as strong for reading comprehension as it was for mathematics problem solving or for general educational achievement. Further analysis showed that this was not a consequence of using different subgroups of children for the different measures.

The high-school academic competence results from this study are consistent with prior studies

FIGURE 7.3

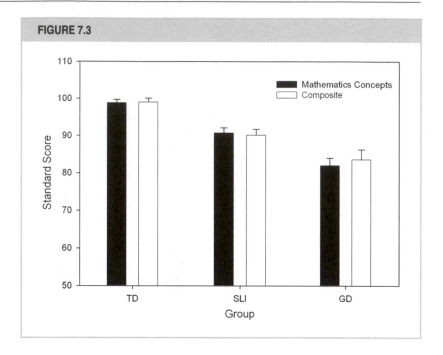

Average scores and standard error for mathematics concepts and overall composite score from the Iowa Tests of Educational Development (ITED) for children with typical language at kindergarten (TD), children with specific language impairment (SLI), and children with general delay (GD).

and with the prior academic performance of these students. Early language impairment is consistently associated with poorer school outcomes and, in particular, poor reading ability. We also see that although the trend is for the students with SLI to have somewhat better school performance than that found for the GD students, these trends are not statistically significant. In fact, it is likely that the trend toward better school performance for the SLI group is attributable to the fact that they also have somewhat better language skills. Thus, as far as school performance is concerned, spoken language abilities appear to have a substantial impact on a child's outcomes, and the impact of the child's nonverbal IQ is quite small. In fact, if we perform a stepwise multiple regression of tenth-grade reading comprehension onto kindergarten composite language and nonverbal IQ for the total group of students, we find that language accounts for 43% of the variance of reading comprehension, whereas nonverbal IQ only contributes 3%. Furthermore, if we incorporate the discrepancy between language and nonverbal IQ in the form of an interaction term, this does not account for any significant amount of variance.

Thus, insofar as school performance is concerned, a discrepancy-based definition of SLI receives no support.

Social outcomes

Academic achievement is a competence domain that is highly valued by most adults in many societies, but it may not be as widely valued among young people. However, it is very clear that adolescence represents a period in development where social relationships, particularly among peers, are very salient to young people. We were able to measure social competence in our adolescents via measures of youth and parent reports. The Youth Self Report (YSR) and the CBCL both provided a measure of the social competence of our cohort members at age 15–16. Social competence on each of these questionnaires reflected the extent of the adolescent's friendships and social activities. Also, the parents completed the Social Skills Rating System (SSRS; Gresham & Elliott, 1990), which provides an "assertion" subscale based on questions regarding friendships and group participation. Thus, these three measures reflect the quantity of social activity. Another questionnaire, the UCLA Loneliness Scale, was used to tap the students' perception of their adequacy of social relationships (Russell, 1996). In order to allow us to compare the scores on these scales, we created local norms based on the total sample of adolescents in our study. These norms were placed on a T scale with a mean of 50 and a standard deviation of 10 in order to remain consistent with the scores used with the CBCL and YSR.

Table 7.3 summarizes the status of our three groups with regard to social participation of the adolescents based on their initial kindergarten diagnosis. We can see a familiar pattern where, once again, the two groups with language impairment fall below the typically developing group. We can also see that the size of the differences for these outcomes is not as large as those in the academic areas. These impressions are supported by ANOVAs performed on each scale. The two parent report scales both resulted in similar findings. The typically developing group was significantly better than either the SLI (Tukey LSD: CBCL mean difference = -6.89, $p < .05$; SSRS = -5.39, $p < .05$) or the GD group (Tukey LSD CBCL mean difference = -6.89, $p < .05$; SSRS = -4.71, $p < .05$); the two groups with language impairment were not different from each other.

The YSR, which reflects level of social activity, paralleled the parent reports in that both groups of language-impaired children fared more poorly than the typically developing group (Tukey LSD:

SLI mean difference = -4.92, $p < .05$; GD mean difference = -4.60, $p < .05$), but these two groups with language impairment were not different from each other. Since the three scales reflecting social participation were all similar, they were scaled to be T scores and averaged (see Figure 7.4). We can also consider the proportion of extremely low rates of social participation. Scores at or below 33 on these scales, which represent clinically significant deviations, were reported by 1.98% of typically developing groups, 5.43% of the SLI group, and 8.89% of the GD group. Likewise, parents reported scores at these levels for 3.52% of the typically developing groups, 8.14% for the SLI group, and 19.57% for the GD group. In each case, the typically developing groups were significantly less likely to have scores as low as the LI group—youth report, $\chi^2(1, N = 389) = 5.38$, $p = .02$, and parent report, $\chi^2(1, N = 388) = 10.70$, $p = .001$. In both cases more adolescents with GD reported low levels of participation; however, the difference in these rates was not significant, no doubt in part because the number of individuals with low scores was small.

Figure 7.4 also provides the results of the UCLA Loneliness Scale, scaled in T score units where higher scores reflect less loneliness or what might be viewed as social affiliation. We see that the GD group had significantly poorer outcome than the typically developing group (Tukey LSD, mean difference = -5.24, $p < .05$) and the SLI

TABLE 7.3

T scores and standard deviations for levels of social participation for adolescents

	TD		SLI		GD	
	T score	*SD*	*T score*	*SD*	*T score*	*SD*
Youth Self Report Form	51.4	8.66	46.78	8.24	47.10	9.94
CBCL	52.38	9.69	45.48	7.99	45.22	10.73
Social Skills Rating Scale	50.81	10.18	46.32	10.25	46.99	10.22

Note. TD = adolescents with typical language development at kindergarten; SLI = adolescents with specific language impairment; GD = adolescents with general delay. CBCL = Child Behavior Checklist.

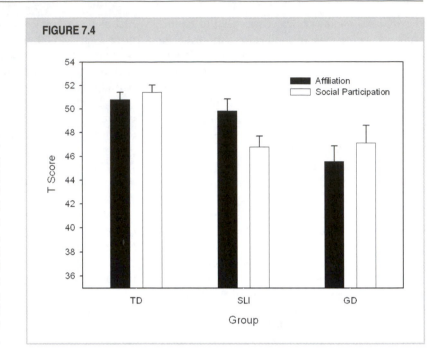

FIGURE 7.4

Mean and standard error for measures of social participation (averaged scores from the Youth Self Report), and self-reported levels of social affiliation as measured by the UCLA Loneliness Scale for children with typical language at kindergarten (TD), children with specific language impairment (SLI), and children with general delay (GD).

group (Tukey LSD, mean difference = –4.47, $p < .05$), and no difference was seen between the SLI and the typically developing group. Thus, it appears that even though their social participation is similar, the adolescents with SLI did not feel as socially isolated as the GD adolescents.

Because, as we have seen above, the measures of social participation as measured by the YSR, CBCL, and SSRS result in similar patterns, we computed an average T score across these scales in order to provide an overall measure of the effect size of these social effects. Using this mean T score, we found an effect size of $r^2 = .10$, which represents a moderate relationship. In contrast, the UCLA Loneliness Scale yielded a smaller effect size of $r^2 = .03$. These data would suggest that language status has more bearing on adolescents' rates of social participation than on how they perceive and evaluate their social involvement.

So far we have not considered whether these social outcomes are associated with gender. Figure 7.5 shows these data with regard to average social participation. We can see that indeed there were significant gender differences for social par-

ticipation across the diagnostic groups $F(2, 476) = 25.23$, $p < .006$. The males with SLI scored significantly lower than did the females with SLI, $F(1, 100) = 4.65$, p $< .03$, $r^2 = .04$, whereas the opposite pattern was found for the GD group, $F(1, 59) = 5.35$, $r^2 = .08$. The typically developing group showed no gender differences. We also tested for a gender effect on the UCLA scale and found no main effect for gender and no interaction with diagnostic groups. The Gender × Diagnosis difference found for the social participation scales does not have an obvious explanation.

Conduct

Conduct refers to compliance with the rule systems within social institutions spanning the home, school, and community. We obtained information concerning this domain of competence from the parent and teacher reports reflected on the subscale termed "rule breaking" on the Achenbach scales (CBCL, TRF). The distribution of scores on this scale was not normal, because overall scores were very low. This makes the usual (parametric) statistical analysis questionable. Instead

FIGURE 7.5

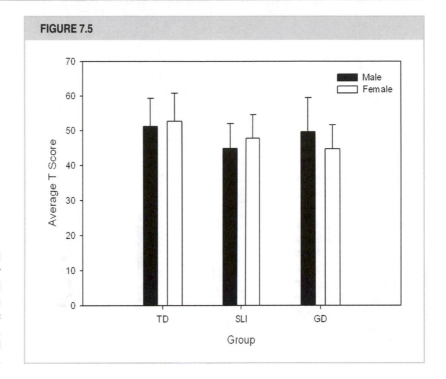

Average levels of social participation by gender for children with typical language at kindergarten (TD), children with specific language impairment (SLI), and children with general delay (GD).

of using the scores themselves, we used a cut-off at the level where rule breaking is considered to be clinically significant (T scores > 66; see Figure 7.6). There was a significant difference among the groups in the numbers of adolescents engaged in serious rule breaking as reported by parents $\chi^2(2, N = 399) = 5.81$, $p = .05$, and teachers $\chi^2(2, N = 286) = 7.76$, $p = .02$, $\mathbf{w} = .04$, but according to Cohen's criteria this effect is quite small.

Teachers reported higher rates of rule breaking in the children with language impairment than did the parents. An inspection of Figure 7.6 also suggests that from the perspective of the parents the students in the GD group were more prone to serious rule breaking (18.75%) than were those in the SLI group (10%); however, this difference in rate was not significant. Evidence that scores from the SLI group were somewhat lower than the GD is shown by a nonsignificant difference between the SLI and the typically developing group in the rate of parent report of rule breaking, whereas the GD group was different from the typically developing group, $\chi^2(1, N = 241) = 05.86$, $p = .015$. Finally,

the differences in rates of rule breaking by the two groups as reported by the teachers was not significant $\chi^2(2, N = 97) = 0.15$, $p = .90$. Thus, we do not have evidence that the two groups were reliably different with respect to problems of conduct. The T scores on these scales are normed for the child's gender, and so it is not surprising that no gender effects were found.

The parent and teacher scales ask about misconduct such as stealing, lying, cheating, skipping school, and alcohol and drug use. Another indicator of conduct problems pertains to difficulty with the law. A separate questionnaire was mailed out to these young people a year later, when they were aged 17–18, which asked them whether they had ever been arrested or in trouble with the law. Here we found no significant differences in the rates of affirmative answers across the three groups of children. Thus, it does not appear that early language problems serve as risk factors for conflict with legal authorities; however, the children with both SLI and GD do seem to have more difficulty with compliance at home and at school.

FIGURE 7.6

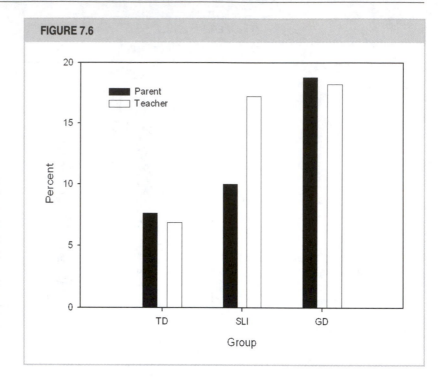

Percent of participants displaying clinically significant levels of rule violation as measured by the Child Behavior Checklist (Parent) and Teacher Report Form (Teacher) for children with normal language at kindergarten (TD), children with specific language impairment (SLI), and children with general delay (GD).

Subjective well-being

The broad concept of self-perceived quality of life (QOL) has become a crucial dimension of health outcomes research. Numerous QOL questionnaires have been developed to examine the impact of various illnesses on QOL. Usually, these questionnaires emphasize the impact of the illnesses on daily life activities and the person's sense of loss or unhappiness with regard to the functional difficulties imposed by the illness. In parallel with QOL research in health outcomes, there has been growth in research in social psychology, often referred to as "positive psychology" (Seligman & Csikszentmihalyi, 2000). Central to positive psychology is a broad umbrella of subjective well-being (SWB) that encompasses the constructs of happiness, satisfaction with life, and self-esteem. These notions of positive well-being are the things that we often hear parents expressing as what they hope to see in their children throughout life. Obviously these positive aspects of well-being can also have their negative counterparts, such as depression, anxiety, and low self-esteem—undesirable outcomes, all of which parents would like their

children to avoid. The notion of well-being has been examined by several scholars who have asked whether there are subcomponents to well-being. This research has resulted in a common distinction between the construct of satisfaction with life as a whole versus self-esteem or self-worth. Satisfaction with life has been characterized as one's judgment about one's life circumstances based upon self-imposed standards (Pavot & Diener, 1993). A construct that is similar to satisfaction with life is that of self-worth, which concerns one's satisfaction with one's behavior and personal characteristics (Harter, 1996). Despite their similarity, several studies have shown that measures of these two constructs are not strongly related (Huebner, Gilman, & Laughlin, 1999; Lucas, Diener, & Suh, 1996). Furthermore, self-concept or self-esteem has usually been found to have both a global quality and specific subdimensions that apply to particular aspects of one's performance, and these dimensions appear to have a developmental quality that leads to increasing differentiation across childhood (Harter, 1990).

We sought to measure these aspects of subjective well-being—both the negative and positive—in our study. In order to do this, we employed several self-report questionnaires. Some of these were standard questionnaires such as the YSR, which provided information on depression and anxiety. We also used the Satisfaction with Life Scale (SWLS; Pavot & Diener, 1993; Pavot, Diener, Colvin, & Sandvik, 1991), which is a simple 5-item scale that asks for ratings on statements such as "I am satisfied with life" or "If I could live my life over, I would change almost nothing."

We also developed a scale for perceived self-worth based upon Harter's measures of self-esteem and self-worth in adolescents (Harter, 1988). Harter's scales employ a 4-point scale formatted as shown in Figure 7.7. In this case the student is given two polar examples of self-perception and asked to determine which kind of student he or she is more like. Then the student indicates how closely he or she feels similar to this student. Because some of our children were poor readers, we adapted this scale by presenting it in both auditory and text form via ePrime software running on a computer. The student then entered the responses on a button box.

We selected items from the Harter Self-Perception Profile for Adolescents (Harter, 1988), as shown in the "Items" column in Table 7.4. These were selected because they loaded most heavily on the principal factors on this scale. We then added several of our own items to increase the content regarding communication competence and to provide some items that children who had poor academic and social skills might still feel they could endorse positively (driving, dancing, video games). We subjected the items to a principal components analysis, which is a method for identifying groups of items (factors) that go together. A three-factor solution accounted for most of the variance. The factor loadings for each item on each of these components are shown in Table 7.4, and those loadings that are sizable are in bold. We have assigned names to these, as shown in the table, based on the nature of the items that loaded most heavily on each factor.

Self-worth

The three dimensions of self-worth just described provided three factor scores for each student. These factor scores were transformed into a

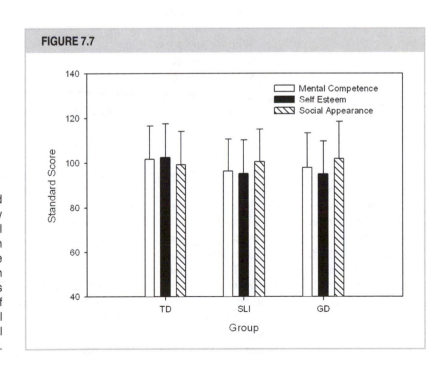

Average and standard deviations obtained by adolescents with typical language at kindergarten (TD), with specific language impairment (SLI), and with general delay (GD) on scales measuring self-perception of mental competence, global self-esteem, and social appearance.

FIGURE 7.7

TABLE 7.4

Item content on the Self Perception scale and three principal components

Components	Items	Factor 1	Factor 2	Factor 3
Mental competence	Confident in schoolwork	**64**	22	1
	Like writing papers	**61**	−10	−11
	Smart	**61**	18	15
	Inventive	**54**	−7	0
	Do well in school work	**48**	**41**	−18
	Want to answer teacher's questions	**47**	12	5
	Like TV watching rather than reading	**46**	10	**−41**
	Comfortable talking	**45**	16	**41**
	Creative	26	18	0
Global self-esteem	Satisfied with self	7	**63**	26
	Don't get lonely	5	**63**	3
	Get along with parents	5	**56**	−3
	Trouble understanding teacher	**39**	**52**	7
	Don't get teased a lot	−1	**54**	24
	Good communicators	29	**39**	22
	Are bright	28	**48**	−16
	Like themselves	16	**46**	**44**
Social appearance	Like physical appearance	10	24	**61**
	Romantic relationship	6	0	**65**
	Good at video games	1	−17	**40**
	Good dancer	24	−13	**35**
	Will be a good driver	−2	12	**51**
	Good at sports	−7	15	**56**
	Close friends	6	23	29

Note. Values in bold represent factor loadings >35 and thus are considered as loading on the factor.

standard score scale with a mean of 100 and standard deviation of 15. These factor scores were examined to determine whether there were diagnostic group effects, gender effects, and interactions between gender and diagnostic groups. Beginning with the first factor, which we termed *mental competence* (see Figure 7.7), we found a significant diagnostic group effect, $F(2, 493) = 5.34$, $p < .005$, $r^2 = .02$, but no significant effect of gender and no Group × Gender interaction. The diagnostic group effect was the product of a significant difference between the SLI group

and the typically developing group, Tukey LSD, mean difference $= -5.08$, $p < .05$, $r^2 = 02$. The GD group was not significantly different from either group. Thus, the children with SLI had poorer self-worth with regard to their mental abilities than did the typically developing students, but a level of perceived mental self-worth comparable with that of the GD group. Similar results were obtained for the second factor, which was labeled *global self-esteem*. The diagnostic group effect was found to be significant $F(2, 493) = 14.40$, $p < .0001$, but in this case both the GD (Tukey LSD, mean difference = –7.49, $p < .05$, $r^2 = .04$) and the SLI (Tukey LSD, mean difference = –7.49, p < .05, $r^2 = .04$) groups had lower ratings for self-esteem than did the typically developing group. There was no significant gender difference, nor did gender interact with diagnostic group. In contrast with the findings for the first two factors, the third factor, labeled *social appearance*, revealed no significant diagnostic group effects, but there was a significant gender effect, $F(1, 493) = 38.01$, $p < .0001$, $r^2 = .07$; there was, however, no significant Gender × Diagnostic group interaction. The girls obtained an average score of 95.58 (*SD* = 14.04), whereas the boys averaged 103.51 (*SD* = 14.83). Collectively, these data demonstrate that adolescent self-worth is compromised in children entering school with poor language abilities, and it appears that perception of mental competence is particularly compromised in students with SLI. However, the effect sizes were small.

Satisfaction with life

The results of the *SWLS* questionnaire are shown in Figure 7.8. Unlike the data on self-worth, we found no differences among the diagnostic groups, and none by gender. The scores represent total raw scores on this scale, and these average levels are very similar to those found for young adults reported in previous studies (Pavot & Diener, 1993). These findings are also consistent with previous findings from our lab with a different group of young people with histories of language impairment, where very similar questions about life satisfaction were asked (Records, Tomblin, & Freese, 1992). These findings would appear to be in conflict with the results just reported, suggesting group differences on self-worth; however, this scale focuses upon life circumstances rather than self-concept. It appears that language status does not affect the life situations that these young people find themselves in. Given that the life situation of these students is largely controlled by their parents, it may not be surprising that this aspect of well-being is not associated with language status at this stage.

Depression

The construct of well-being often also contains the construct of personal affective state. This emotional state, as reported on the YSR, was reflected in the Affective Disorder scale. Because distributions of scores on scales of problem emotions and

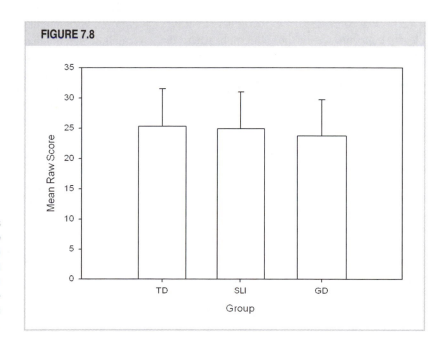

FIGURE 7.8

Average (SD) raw scores on the Satisfaction with Life Scale (Pavot & Diener, 1993) for adolescents with typical language at kindergarten (TD), specific language impairment (SLI), and general delay (GD).

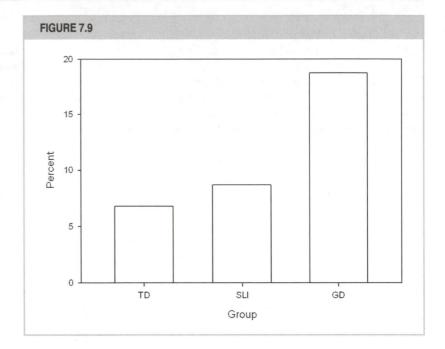

FIGURE 7.9

Percentage of adolescents at kindergarten, with specific language impairment (SLI), with general delay (GD), or who were typically developing (TD), who reported signs on the Youth Self-Report suggestive of clinically significant depression.

behaviors are highly skewed (i.e., non-normal), only the rates of clinically significant levels (T scores > 66) of affective problems were examined; these are presented in Figure 7.9. We can see that the rates of clinical levels of low affect were significantly different across the three groups, $\chi^2(2, N = 405) = 7.36$, $p = .025$. This effect was clearly concentrated in the GD group, where the rate of depression was 2.8 times as great as in the typically developing group, $\chi^2(2, N = 313) = 7.37$, $p = .025$, $\mathbf{w} = 0.15$, which, according to Cohen, represents a small effect.

SUMMARY OF FINDINGS AND CONCLUSIONS

The data presented in this chapter provide a generally coherent picture of the adolescent outcomes of children who enter school with poor language in comparison with their classmates who had age-appropriate levels of language. The findings from this study are largely consistent with those that have preceded it. Table 7.5 summarizes the results

in the form of levels of effects for each group of children with language impairment across the different outcome domains. These results show that there were statistically demonstrable associations of these early language abilities and adolescent outcomes in several areas for both groups of children with language impairment. Thus, we can conclude that the diagnostic standard employed is reasonable with regard to identifying children at risk for poor adolescent outcomes.

In most instances the outcomes were similar for the two groups of students with language impairment. Despite differences in nonverbal intellect, school performance was similarly compromised in both groups of children with poor language abilities. In particular, reading outcomes were strongly associated with early language problems. Of particular concern was the fact that a substantial minority of these adolescents had reading levels that are indicative of literacy abilities that would allow them to perform only the most basic literacy tasks. It would appear that normal nonverbal intelligence did not provide a means for young people with SLI to compensate in reading or in mathematics, and the extent to which the groups differed at all appeared to be due to differences

TABLE 7.5

Strength of relationships between outcomes in adolescence and contrasts of language status in typically developing adolescents and adolescents with language impairment

		Strength of relationship	
Outcome domains		*SLI*	*GD*
Academic	Reading	strong	strong
	Illiteracy	strong	strong
	General achievement	moderate	moderate
Social	Social participation	moderate	moderate
	Friendships	none	small
Conduct	Rule-following	none	small
	Legal troubles	none	small
Well-being	Mental competence	small	none
	Self-esteem	small	small
	Social appearance	none	none
	Satisfaction with life	none	none
	Depression	none	small

Note. SLI = adolescents with specific language impairment; GD = adolescents with general delay.

in the severity of language deficits between the groups. There were also similar results across the groups with regard to the amount of social participation. Both groups revealed lower rates of social participation than the typically developing groups. Despite this, when we measured their self-perception of social appeal, the two groups were similar to the typically developing group, and, in fact, the GD group had the highest mean score. Thus, their reduced rate of social participation does not appear to be the result of a belief that they are not socially appealing. Consistent with the depressed rates of social participation, we did find that self-esteem was lower in both groups. Whether social participation and self-esteem are related such that low self-esteem results from or in reduced social participation remains as an open question.

It can be seen from this summary that across the domains, the outcomes of the two language-impaired groups was often similar; however, there were some instances in which the two groups did differ. Within the social domain we found that the students with GD were less likely than the students with SLI to have satisfying close friendships. As shown in Table 7.5, the strength of this association within the GD students was small, but it does suggest that insofar as social isolation is a troubling outcome, the GD children are at somewhat greater risk and thus warrant greater clinical concern. Accompanying this pattern of greater perceived social isolation in the GD group was also a higher rate of depression in this group than in the SLI or typically developing group, and greater rates of rule breaking. Taken together, it would appear that children with GD comprise a group that should be monitored by psychological and psychiatric services. The measure of self-perceived mental competence provided the only instance in which children with SLI had a poorer outcome than the GD group and the typically developing group. Recall that with regard to measured school achievement, the two groups were similar, although the GD group had slightly lower school-achievement levels than the students with SLI. It is possible that the children with SLI have a stronger sense of underachievement as a result of the discrepancy between nonverbal and language abilities. In this case the discrepancy would directly cause the lower self-perception. Alternatively, it is possible that the students with SLI were placed in educational settings with higher expectations on the basis of their stronger overall intellectual status. If so, the causal relationship between the discrepancy and well-being is indirect.

The data provided by this study clearly support the viewpoint that children who enter school with poor language face compromised adolescent competence. In this respect, they warrant the provision of a range of clinical services that would improve their competence in school and in social domains. There is very little evidence that would suggest that the inclusion of performance IQ criteria into a clinical diagnosis of developmental language impairment is warranted. When group differences between SLI and GD were found, they were small and showed the GD children to be at somewhat greater risk. Only in the case of perceived mental competence was it shown that SLI results in poorer outcomes. Thus, these findings join others in arguing against discrepancy-based definitions for clinical case selection.

This study focused on whether the outcomes of children with SLI were different from those of children with GD. We noted above that many of these children may represent cases that could be considered to be false positives. These are children who on retesting fall above the cut-off scores used for diagnosis in this study. Some would consider these children as having "resolved" their language impairment; however, we have shown that much of this change is more likely to be due to measurement error than to a true improvement in their language status. These false positive cases often have language abilities that are near the cut-off value for LI and therefore have generally better language abilities than those children who repeatedly test below the cut-off. It is likely that the outcomes of these children who may be false positives will be better than those of the "true positives." Therefore the findings of this study may be viewed as a conservative estimate of the true relationship between early language status and outcomes; however, they are likely to be an accurate reflection of the risk to children upon failing a language diagnostic battery such as that used in this study.

NOTE

1 I follow Fulford's (2001) lead in using disorder as a cover term for illness, disease, disability, dysfunction.

REFERENCES

Achenbach, T. M. (1991a). *Integrative guide for the 1991 CBCL 4–18, YSR, and TRF profiles.* Burlington, VT: University of Vermont.

Achenbach, T. M. (1991b). *Manual for the Teacher's Report Form and 1991 Profile.* Burlington, VT: University of Vermont, Department of Psychiatry.

Aram, D. M., & Nation, J. (1980). Preschool language disorders and subsequent language and academic difficulties. *Journal of Communication Disorders, 13,* 159–170.

Baker, L., & Cantwell, D. P. (1987). A prospective psychiatric follow-up of children with speech/language disorders. *Journal of the American Academy of Child & Adolescent Psychiatry, 26,* 546–553.

Beitchman, J. H., Adlaf, E. M., Douglas, L., Atkinson, L., Young, A., Johnson, C. J., et al. (2001a). Comorbidity of psychiatric and substance use disorders in late adolescence: A cluster analytic approach. *American Journal of Drug and Alcohol Abuse, 27,* 421–440.

Beitchman, J. H., Brownlie, E. B., Inglis, J., Wild, J., Ferguson, B., & Schachter, D. (1996a). Seven year follow-up of speech/language impaired and control children: Psychiatric outcome. *Journal of Child Psychology and Psychiatry, 37,* 961–970.

Beitchman, J. H., Wilson, B., Brownlie, E. B., Walters, H., & Lancee, W. (1996b). Long-term consistency in speech/language profiles: I. Developmental and academic outcomes. *Journal of the American Academy of Child & Adolescent Psychiatry, 35,* 804–814.

Beitchman, J. H., Wilson, B., Johnson, C. J., Atkinson, L., Young, A., Adlaf, E., et al. (2001b). Fourteen-year follow-up of speech/language-impaired and control children: Psychiatric outcome. *Journal of the American Academy of Child & Adolescent Psychiatry, 40,* 75–82.

Bishop, D. V. M., & Edmundson, A. (1987). Language-impaired 4-year-olds: Distinguishing transient from persistent impairment. *Journal of Speech and Hearing Disorders, 52,* 156–173.

Boorse, C. (1977). Health as a theoretical concept. *Philosophical Science, 44,* 542–573.

Boorse, C. (1987). Concepts of health. In *Health care ethics: An introduction* (pp. 359–393). Philadelphia, PA: Temple University Press.

Catts, H. W., Adlof, S. M., & Weismer, S. E. (2006). Language deficits in poor comprehenders: A case for the simple view of reading. *Journal of Speech, Language, and Hearing Research, 49,* 278–293.

Catts, H. W., Fey, M. E., Tomblin, J. B., & Zhang, X. (2002). A longitudinal investigation of reading outcomes in children with language impairments. *Journal of Speech, Language, and Hearing Research, 45,* 1142–1157.

Catts, H. W., Fey, M., Zhang, X., & Tomblin, J. B. (1999). Language bases of reading and reading disabilities: Evidence from a longitudinal investigation. *Journal of the Scientific Study of Reading, 3,* 331–361.

Catts, H. W., Fey, M., Zhang, X., & Tomblin, J. B. (2001). Estimating the risk of future reading difficulties in kindergarten children: A research-based model and its clinical implementation. *Language, Speech, and Hearing Services in Schools, 32,* 38–50.

Cohen, J. (1988). *Statistical power analysis for the behavioral sciences.* Hillsdale, NJ: Lawrence Erlbaum Associates.

Cole, K. N., Dale, P. S., & Mills, P. E. (1990). Defining language delay in young children by cognitive referencing: Are we saying more than we know? *Applied Psycholinguistics, 11,* 291–302.

Conti-Ramsden, G., Nicola, B., Simkin, Z., & Botting, N. (2001). Follow-up of children attending infant language units: Outcomes at 11 years of age. *International Journal of Language & Communication Disorders, 36,* 207–219.

Culatta, B., Page, J., & Ellis, J. (1983). Story retelling as a communicative performance screening tool. *Language, Speech, and Hearing Services in Schools, 14,* 66–74.

Feldt, L. S., Forsyth, R. A., Ansley, T. N., & Alnot, S. D. (1994). *Iowa Tests of Educational Development: Interpretive guide for teachers and counselors.* Chicago: Riverside.

Fulford, K. W. (2001). "What is (mental) disease?" An open letter to Christopher Boorse. *Journal of Medical Ethics, 27,* 80–85.

Gresham, F., & Elliott, S. (1990). *Social Skills Rating System.* Circle Pines, MN: American Guidance Service.

Hall, P. K., & Tomblin, J. B. (1978). A follow-up study of children with articulation and language disorders. *Journal of Speech and Hearing Disorders, 43,* 227–241.

Harter, S. (1988). *Manual for the Self-Perception Profile for adolescents.* Denver, CO: University of Denver.

Harter, S. (1990). Developmental differences in the nature of self-representations: Implications for the understanding, assessment, and treatment of maladaptive behavior. *Cognitive Therapy & Research, 14,* 113–142.

Harter, S. (1996). Historical roots of contemporary issues involving self-concept. In B. A. Bracken (Ed.), *Handbook of self-concept* (pp. 1–37). New York: Wiley.

Huebner, E. S., Gilman, R., & Laughlin, J. E. (1999). A multimethod investigation of the multidimensionality of children's well-being reports: Discriminant validity of life satisfaction and self-esteem. *Social Indicators Research, 46,* 1–22.

Johnson, C. J., Beitchman, J., Young, A., Escobar, M. D., Atkinson, L., Wilson, B., et al. (1999). Fourteen-year follow-up of children with and without speech/language impairments: Speech/language stability and outcomes. *Journal of Speech, Language, and Hearing Research, 42,* 744–760.

Lahey, M. (1990). Who shall be called language disordered? Some reflections and one perspective. *Journal of Speech and Hearing Disorders, 55,* 612–620.

Lucas, R. E., Diener, E., & Suh, E. (1996). Discriminant validity of well-being measures. *Journal of Personality and Social Psychology, 71,* 616–628.

Masten, A. S., Hubbard, J. J., Gest, S. D., Tellegen, A., Garmezy, N., & Ramirez, M. (1999). Competence in the context of adversity: Pathways to resilience and maladaptation from childhood to late adolescence. *Development and Psychopathology, 11,* 143–169.

Mawhood, L., Howlin, P., & Rutter, M. (2000). Autism and developmental receptive language disorder: A comparative follow-up in early adult life. I: Cognitive and language outcomes. *Journal of Child Psychology and Psychiatry and Allied Disciplines, 41,* 547–559.

Nation, J. E., & Aram, D. M. (1980). Preschool language disorders and subsequent language and academic difficulties. *Journal of Communication Disorders, 13,* 159–179.

Newcomer, P., & Hammill, D. (1988). *Test of Language Development* (2nd ed., primary). Austin, TX: PRO-ED.

Paul, R. (2001). *Language disorders from infancy through adolescence.* St Louis, MO: Mosby.

Pavot, W., & Diener, E. (1993). Review of the Satisfaction with Life Scale. *Psychological Assessment, 5,* 164–172.

Pavot, W., Diener, E., Colvin, C. R., & Sandvik, E. (1991). Further validation of the Satisfaction with Life Scale: Evidence for the cross-method convergence of well-being measures. *Journal of Personality Assessment, 57,* 149–161.

Plante, E. (1998). Criteria for SLI: The Stark and Tallal legacy and beyond. *Journal of Speech, Language, and Hearing Research, 41,* 951–957.

Records, N. L., Tomblin, J. B., & Freese, P. R. (1992). Quality of life in adults with histories of specific language impairment. *American Journal of Speech-Language Pathology, 1,* 44–53.

Roisman, G. I., Masten, A. S., Coatsworth, J. D., & Tellegen, A. (2004). Salient and emerging developmental tasks in the transition to adulthood. *Child Development, 75,* 123–133.

Russell, D. (1996). The UCLA Loneliness Scale (Version 3): Reliability, validity, and factor structure. *Journal of Personality Assessment, 66,* 20–40.

Rutter, M., & Mawhood, L. (1991). The long-term psychosocial sequelae of specific developmental disorders of speech and language. In M. C. P. Rutter & P. Casaer (Eds.), *Biological risk factors for psychosocial disorders* (pp. 233–259). Cambridge, UK: Cambridge University Press.

Seligman, M. E. P., & Csikszentmihalyi, M. (2000). Positive psychology: An introduction. *American Psychologist, 55,* 5–14.

Snowling, M. J., Adams, J. W., Bishop, D. V. M., & Stothard, S. E. (2001). Educational attainments of school leavers with a preschool history of speech-language impairments. *International Journal of Language & Communication Disorders, 36,* 173–183.

Stark, R., & Tallal, P. (1981). Selection of children with specific language deficits. *Journal of Speech and Hearing Disorders, 46,* 114–122.

Stothard, S. E., Snowling, M. J., Bishop, D. V. M., Chipchase, B. B., & Kaplan, C. A. (1998). Language-impaired preschoolers: A follow-up into adolescence. *Journal of Speech, Language, and Hearing Research, 41,* 407–418.

Tager-Flusberg, H., & Cooper, J. (1999). Present and future possibilities for defining a phenotype for specific language impairment. *Journal of Speech, Language, and Hearing Research, 42,* 1275–1278.

Tomblin, J. B., Records, N. L., Buckwalter, P., Zhang, X., Smith, E., & O'Brien, M. (1997). The prevalence of specific language impairment in kindergarten children. *Journal of Speech, Language, and Hearing Research, 40,* 1245–1260.

Tomblin, J. B., Records, N. L., & Zhang, X. (1996). A system for the diagnosis of specific language impairment in kindergarten children. *Journal of Speech and Hearing Research, 39,* 1284–1294.

Tomblin, J. B., & Zhang, X. (1999). Are children with SLI a unique group of language learners? In H. Tager-Flusberg (Ed.), *Neurodevelopmental disorders: Contributions to a new framework from the cognitive neurosciences* (pp. 361–382). Cambridge, MA: MIT Press.

Tomblin, J. B., Zhang, X., & Buckwalter, P. (2000). The association of reading disability, behavioral disorders, and language impairment among second-grade children. *Journal of Child Psychology & Psychiatry & Allied Disciplines, 41,* 473–482.

Tomblin, J. B., Zhang, X., Buckwalter, P., & O'Brien, M. (2003). The stability of primary language impairment: Four years after kindergarten diagnosis. *Journal of Speech-Language-Hearing Research, 46,* 1283–1296.

Wechsler, D. (1989). *Wechsler Intelligence Scale for Children* (3rd ed.). San Antonio, TX: The Psychological Corporation.

Wiederholt, J. L., & Bryant, B. R. (1992). *Gray Oral Reading Tests.* Austin, TX: PRO-ED.

Woodcock, R. (1998). *Woodcock Reading Mastery Tests* (Revised/normative update). Circle Pines, MN: American Guidance Service.

Young, A. R., Beitchman, J. H., Johnson, C., Douglas, L., Atkinson, L., Escobar, M., et al. (2002). Young adult academic outcomes in a longitudinal sample of early identified language impaired and control children. *Journal of Child Psychology and Psychiatry, 43,* 635–645.

Zigler, E., & Gllick, M. (1986). *A developmental approach to adult psychopathology.* New York: Wiley.

8

Heterogeneity of specific language impairment in adolescent outcomes

Gina Conti-Ramsden

Children and young people with specific language impairment (SLI) represent a group of individuals who have deficits in language ability while "everything else" appears to be normal. That "everything else" includes, by definition, adequate input from the senses (i.e., normal hearing and normal/corrected vision), an adequate biological basis to develop language (i.e., no obvious signs of brain damage), and an adequate basis for learning (i.e., nonverbal abilities similar to those of peers of the same age). A desire to engage socially is also important; children and young people with SLI seek to interact socially with adults and peers, and as such are not like children with autism, who are not as socially engaged. This commonly used definition of SLI has a number of key implications for our understanding of the impairment.

First, SLI is considered a primary difficulty with language. Indeed, all young children who are likely to have SLI are "late talkers"—that is, the appearance of their first words is delayed compared to what is expected of most young children. Word combinations such as "want juice" and "bye-bye teddy" also appear at a later age than would be expected, and this is true for children learning not just English, but any language. Generally, across languages, children with SLI are described as having more difficulty with talking (producing words) than with understanding what is said to them (comprehending language). Although difficulties with talking attract the most attention and can occur in isolation, many children present with difficulties in both talking and understanding. Children who have problems understanding what is said to them but can talk normally are rare (except in the case of children with autism).

Second, in SLI there is a common assumption that a selective deficit in a language learning mechanism plays a causal role in the disorder. By definition, other possible causes of a language difficulty are excluded: the child with SLI does *not* have hearing impairment sufficient to cause the language difficulty, nor does he or she have general learning difficulties that could impede language development. In addition, children with SLI appear to be social and want to communicate, and thus interpersonal, social difficulties are not the cause of the language delay.

Third, SLI is not a diagnosis that one can "grow out" of. We acknowledge that SLI is a developmental condition, that it can be persistent, and that it is heterogeneous. Yet SLI is most commonly considered in a static way, and current definitions do not explicitly tell us about what to expect as children with SLI grow up.

In this chapter we examine precisely this issue: what are the developmental outcomes for adolescents with SLI, and what do these outcomes tell us about the nature of the disorder itself? We base our observations on our longitudinal investigation of SLI, the Manchester Language Study (MLS).

THE MANCHESTER LANGUAGE STUDY

This investigation began with an original cohort of 242 children who represented a random 50% of all children attending language units in Year 2 (7-year-olds) across England. Language units in England are classes attached to mainstream schools that offer specialist language environments for children with SLI. The staff/student ratio in these mixed-aged classes is high, at one staff member for approximately 10 students. Staff include a specialist teacher and a classroom or speech therapy assistant as well as regular, intensive speech and language therapy input (for details see Conti-Ramsden & Botting, 2000; Dockrell & Lindsay, chapter 9, this volume).

In the MLS, children reported by teachers to have frank neurological difficulties (brain damage), diagnoses of autism, known hearing impairment, or general learning impairments were excluded. All children had English as a first language, but 12% had exposure to languages other than English at home. In the original sample, 53.1% of participants came from households earning less than the average family wage for that year. The cohort was assessed at 8 years of age (n = 234), 11 years of age (n = 200), and 14 years of age (n = 130). Here, we report data on 139 adolescents who agreed to participate at age 16 years; these adolescents did not differ on any early variables of language, behavior, cognition, or socioeconomic status (SES) relative to those who did not participate. The adolescents presented with a variety of different language profiles, but the majority are described as having both receptive and expressive difficulties.

At age 16 years, the MLS expanded to include a comparison group of adolescents from a broad background who did not have a history of special educational needs or speech and language therapy provision. In total, 124 young people with typical language development (TD) aged between 15 years 2 months and 16 years 7 months (mean age 15;11 years) agreed to participate. Census data reported in the 2001–2002 General Household Survey (UK Office of National Statistics, 2004) were consulted in order to target adolescents who were representative of the range and distribution of households in England in terms of household income and maternal education. Initial analyses confirmed that there were no significant differences between TD adolescents and adolescents with SLI in maternal education levels, $\chi^2(2) = 1.756$, $p = .416$, or household income bands, $\chi^2(3) = 4.391$, $p = .222$. Groups were also matched for gender (number of girls/total number: SLI = 42/139, TD = 47/124; Fisher's exact $p = 0.20$). Table 8.1 presents the characteristics of the adolescents with SLI and the TD adolescents in terms of their age and their current language and cognitive functioning. As can be seen, mean scores of adolescents with SLI fell below −1 *SD* of the normative mean on all three measures.

TABLE 8.1

Participant characteristics

Participants	N	Age M	Age SD	Nonverbal abilities[a] M	Nonverbal abilities[a] SD	Talking[b] M	Talking[b] SD	Understanding[c] M	Understanding[c] SD
SLI	139	15;10	0;5	84.1	18.8	74.1	11.0	83.9	16.9
TD	124	15;11	0;4	99.9	15.8	97.2	15.0	99.5	13.2

Note. Mean age, nonverbal IQ, and expressive and receptive language scores are reported. Standard scores are reported for measures that have a normative mean of 100 and a *SD* of 15. Scores for children with specific language impairment (SLI) are significantly lower than scores for typically developing (TD) peers for each of the three measures.

[a]Nonverbal IQ. [b]Language expression. [c]Language comprehension.

From language units to mainly mainstream contexts

Adolescents with SLI were selected for participation in the study on the basis of their language unit attendance at 7 years. However, there was considerable movement during the intervening years from specialized units, to special schools catering for those with more global impairments, to mainstream schools catering for a variety of individuals, including those with special educational needs. Figure 8.1 shows the individual stability and change in educational placement across the educational lifespan of these children. These data are discussed more fully in Durkin, Simkin, Knox, and Conti-Ramsden (in press).

At 11 years (secondary-school entry), the majority (63%) were attending mainstream schools (47% with support; 16% without support). Around a fifth (19%) were attending special schools, and 18% were attending language units/schools. At 14 years, the proportions in different educational placements remained similar to that at 11 years. In total, 62% were attending mainstream schools (41% with support; 21% without support). Around one quarter (26%) were attending special schools, and 13% were in language units/language schools. Finally, at 16 years, 69% were attending mainstream schools (45% with support; 24% without

support). Around a quarter (24%) were attending a special unit/school, and only 7% were found to be attending a language unit/school. Therefore, at the end of compulsory schooling, three-quarters of the adolescents (76%) were attending placements with some form of special educational support. They had all received a statement of special educational needs (SEN) at age 7 years, and this figure remained high throughout secondary schooling: 79% at 11 years, 73% at 14 years, and 71% at 16 years. This provides further evidence of the persisting difficulties of the large majority of adolescents with SLI (Stothard, Snowling, Bishop, Chipchase, & Kaplan, 1998; Young et al., 2002). These data tell us that the majority of adolescents in our sample have continued educational needs throughout their academic careers and that these needs are being met mainly in mainstream schools during secondary schooling (cf. Dockrell & Lindsay, chapter 9, this volume).

Outcomes at 16 years: Literacy, academic achievement, friendships, and emotional health

Given the definition of SLI currently in use, we would expect these adolescents to have selective impairments in language functioning. Any deficits outside the language system are frequently

FIGURE 8.1

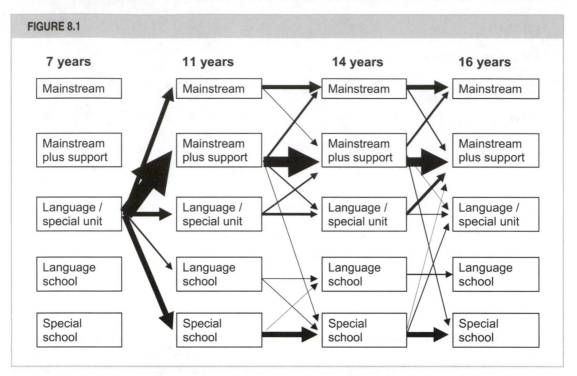

Change in educational placements during schooling for adolescents with SLI. The differences in arrow thickness depict the numbers of children moving from placement to placement across time: a thick arrow represents a high proportion of children, whereas a thin arrow represents relatively small numbers of children.

considered to be a causal consequence of impaired language development. In other words, we would expect there to be an association between the extent of the language difficulty and the extent of difficulties in related areas of functioning. In this chapter we examine four such areas of related functioning: literacy, academic achievement, friendships, and emotional health. The strength of the association between language and other areas of functioning can be examined in two ways: via correlation analyses, which measure the strength of association between two variables (e.g., oral language and literacy), and via regression analysis, whereby a number of different influencing factors are evaluated in relation to each other (e.g., how much variation in literacy attainment can be explained by phonological or grammatical skill). However, it is important to note that in complex behaviors there is no expectation that 100% of the variance will be explained.

Literacy outcomes

Recent evidence increasingly suggests that children with SLI are likely to experience literacy problems (e.g., Catts, 1991; Catts, Fey, Tomblin, & Zhang, 2002; Conti-Ramsden, Donlan, & Grove, 1992; Snowling, Bishop, & Stothard, 2000), and children who have reading problems—that is, dyslexia—are likely to experience difficulties with oral language skills beyond the area of phonology (Joanisse, Manis, Keating, & Seidenberg, 2000; McArthur, Hogben, Edwards, Heath, & Mengler, 2000). The literature suggests that there is an overlap between the two disorders of about 50% (McArthur et al., 2000). As noted by Snowling and Hulme (chapter 11, this volume), literacy builds on a foundation of oral language skills. Decoding skills are closely related to phonological abilities, whereas reading comprehension is more closely allied to nonphonological language skills (Bishop & Snowling, 2004). Thus, it is not surprising that the results of a number of studies suggest an association between reading skills and the language profiles of children with SLI. Some investigators have focused on global measures such as the severity of the language impairment. Performance on standardized tests of language expression and language understanding is closely associated with reading achievement (e.g., Bishop & Adams, 1990; Tallal, Dukette, & Curtiss, 1989; Wilson & Risucci, 1988). Furthermore, Bishop (2001) argues that the risk of developing literacy difficulties increases with the number of impaired language domains the child experiences. For example, Bishop found that 29% of children with SLI who were impaired in one language domain had difficulties with reading. In contrast, a much larger proportion of children with SLI (72%) impaired in two or more language domains had difficulties with reading. Thus, there appears to be substantial evidence that children with SLI are likely to experience reading difficulties at school age. In addition, it appears that children with SLI who have severe impairments or impairments in more than one domain of language appear to be at higher risk of developing reading difficulties.

We investigated two different types of reading outcome: reading accuracy and reading compre-

hension (see also Botting, Simkin, & Conti-Ramsden, 2006). While in typical development these two skills progress in tandem, reading accuracy and reading comprehension may be dissociated in atypical development. This includes those with dyslexia, whose decoding/accuracy skills tend to be poorer than comprehension skills (Bishop & Snowling, 2004), and poor comprehenders who (by definition) show average reading accuracy in the context of poor text comprehension (Cain & Oakhill, 1996). These two aspects of reading may also show different rates of impairment in children with SLI. In line with previous research (Snowling et al., 2000), we found that adolescents with SLI had more difficulties with reading comprehension than with reading accuracy (see Table 8.2).

We then examined predictors of reading outcome to determine the extent to which concurrent language skills predict reading outcome and whether concurrent language skills predict more variance in reading outcome than other factors such as nonverbal IQ.

Our results suggest that language expression and language understanding were associated with reading accuracy and reading comprehension. Language was the strongest predictor, explaining

---

TABLE 8.2

Mean standard scores on measures of reading accuracy and reading comprehension for adolescents with SLI and typically developing peers

| | Standard score for age | | | | < 1 SD from mean for age (%) | |
| | SLI | | TD | | | |
	M	SD	M	SD	SLI	TD
Reading accuracy	83.4	17.8	98.0	13.0	49	9
Reading comprehension	75.7	14.3	91.4	11.4	74	28

Note: SLI = adolescents with specific language impairment; TD = typically developing adolescents. N = 69 for TD adolescents. Standard scores have a normative mean of 100 and a SD of 15. The percentage of adolescents with scores >1 SD below the normative mean is also reported.

30% of the variance in reading outcome; however, nonverbal IQ also influenced reading ability.

Figure 8.2 illustrates that there was also variability in literacy outcomes within our sample of adolescents with SLI. Although the majority of young people with a history of SLI have significant literacy difficulties relative to TD peers, a proportion of our adolescents are competent readers.

In summary, these results show that impairment of both language understanding and production in SLI is associated with poorer outcome in literacy skills at 16 years of age, even when nonverbal IQ is taken into account. These findings are in line with a number of studies demonstrating an association between oral language skills and reading comprehension. For instance, Tallal, Curtiss, and Kaplan (1988) and Wilson and Risucci (1988) found that spoken language comprehension deficits predicted later reading difficulties in children with SLI. In addition, the present study indicates that *expressive* language skills also show associations with reading comprehension ability, in line with previous studies of younger children in which mean length of utterance (MLU) was found

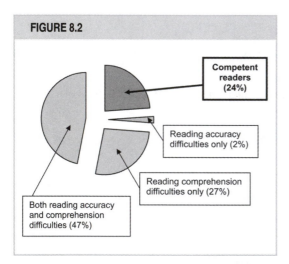

FIGURE 8.2

Competent readers (24%)

Reading accuracy difficulties only (2%)

Reading comprehension difficulties only (27%)

Both reading accuracy and comprehension difficulties (47%)

Pie chart illustrating the proportion of adolescents with a history of SLI who have impairments (score of −1 *SD* below the normative mean) on measures of reading comprehension and/or reading accuracy at age 16. The chart indicates that almost a quarter of this group (24%) score within normal limits on both reading outcomes.

to be a predictor of reading ability in children with SLI (Bishop & Adams, 1990). Although there is variation in outcome, our findings indicate that this population of young people are at very great risk of reading impairment in adolescence: 75% of our participants showed reading difficulties. Only a relatively small minority of "competent readers" were found in our group, demonstrating a strong association between oral language skills and literacy abilities in adolescence. In terms of competent readers, it was found that 63% had age-appropriate concurrent language scores as measured by the Clinical Evaluation of Language Fundamentals (CELF-R; Semel, Wiig, & Secord, 1987). The remainder had specific difficulties with expressive language as measured by the Recalling Sentences subtest of the CELF–R.

Academic achievement

The National Curriculum outlines the core subjects to be studied in English state schools and divides the curriculum into key stages, which specify the program of study for children of different ages (see also Dockrell & Lindsay, chapter 9, this volume). Key Stage 4 (KS4) subjects are studied in school years 10–11, when children are between 14 and 16 years old. KS4 examinations were completed by participants at around 16 years of age. These are national examinations, usually General Certificates of Secondary Education (GCSE) but also vocational examinations such as General National Vocational Qualifications (GNVQ). GCSE grades are awarded from A* (highest level) to G (lowest level). National Qualifications Framework (NQF) Level 2 is the expected level for adolescents at 16 years of age and is equivalent to GCSE grades A*–C or GNVQ Intermediate. NQF Level 1 is equivalent to GCSE grades D–G or GNVQ Foundation. NQF entry level is below Level 1. Figure 8.3 presents the highest academic qualification level achieved at 16 years (for further details see Conti-Ramsden, Durkin, Simkin, & Knox, in press).

A total of 44% of young people with SLI obtained at least one of the expected Level 2 qualifications, although twice as many in the TD group achieved this (88%). None of the TD adolescents left school with only entry-level qualifications,

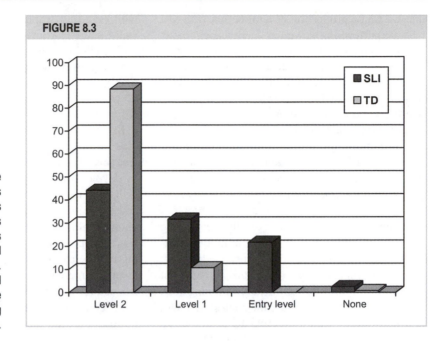

FIGURE 8.3

Bar chart depicting the proportion of group members in the SLI and TD groups achieving different levels of academic attainment, as specified by the UK National Qualifications Framework. Level 2 is the expected level for pupils aged 16 and at the end of compulsory schooling in the United Kingdom.

but this was true of 19% of the adolescents with SLI. A small proportion (11%) of the TD adolescents gained only Level 1 qualifications, with a third of the language-impaired sample having this as their highest educational level. We also examined predictors of academic achievement such as concurrent language skills and other factors such as nonverbal IQ. Our results suggest that oral language abilities and literacy skills were associated with academic achievement, explaining 27% of the variance in academic attainment. However, this time language was *not* the strongest predictor, nonverbal IQ was. There was also an influence of maternal education, but this factor made a smaller contribution than language and literacy. Thus, in order of explanatory power, the predictor variables were nonverbal IQ, language and literacy, and maternal education.

There was also evidence of variability in academic achievement. Figure 8.4 illustrates the fact

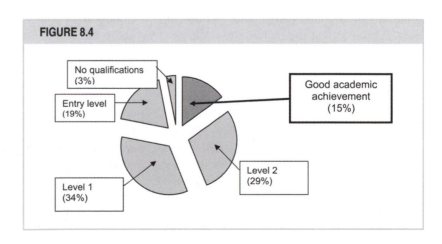

FIGURE 8.4

Pie chart illustrating the level of academic attainment for adolescents with a history of SLI. The chart indicates that approximately one-sixth of the adolescents performed academically as expected for their age (national figures; five or more passes A*–C, Ofsted, 2005).

that we find a proportion of adolescents with SLI who are performing as well as peers academically. Interestingly, it was found that of those young people with age-appropriate academic attainment, around two-thirds had current language skills within the normal range while the remaining one-third had more circumscribed problems with expressive language skills.

In summary, this report illustrates the heterogeneity of SLI in that a wide range of educational outcomes were found among our sample. Our data reflect the full range of findings reported in the literature previously, from good outcomes equivalent to comparable typically developing peers, to poor outcomes with few or no qualifications obtained at the end of compulsory education. Language skills do play a role in this outcome but not as strongly as other areas of functioning such as nonverbal IQ. As a group, the adolescents with SLI had lower mean nonverbal IQ scores at 16 years relative to TD peers (cf. Botting, 2005), and these nonverbal abilities were more closely linked to academic achievement than to the severity of the language impairment per se.

As an aside, it is of interest to note that our sample was entered for GCSE examinations or their equivalent in 2004 and 2005, 10 years on from the last relevant UK study in this area (Snowling, Adams, Bishop, & Stothard, 2001) and 20 years after earlier studies carried out in the 1980s (Clegg, Hollis, & Rutter, 1999; Haynes & Naidoo, 1991; Mawhood, Howlin, & Rutter, 2000). Although there is heterogeneity in attainment, our findings suggest an improvement in academic achievement in young people with SLI over the last 25 years in that the majority of adolescents with a history of SLI are obtaining some academic national qualifications at the end of compulsory education.

Friendships

Durkin and Conti-Ramsden (2007) describe friendships as being a vital dimension of child development. They are key markers of the selectivity of interpersonal relations, providing social and cognitive scaffolding (Hartup, 1996), serving variously as sources of support and information as well as buffers against many of life's problems,

with enduring implications for self-esteem and well-being (Hartup & Stevens, 1999; Shulman, 1993). Children and adolescents without friends, or with poor friendship quality, are at risk of loneliness and stress (Bagwell et al., 2005; Hartup & Stevens, 1999; Ladd, 1990; Ladd, Kochenderfer, & Coleman, 1996).

Friendship relations are complex, and this reflects in part the ways in which they interweave with other developmental processes, such as developing interpersonal and communicative skills, increasing social cognitive competence, and changing personal needs. For example, very young children form friendships largely on the basis of proximity and shared activities; during middle childhood friendships involve greater levels of interchange and awareness of individual attributes; and in adolescence many people seek via friendships to satisfy psychological needs for intimacy, shared outlooks, and identity formulation (Buhrmester, 1990, 1996; Hartup & Stevens, 1999; Parker & Gottman, 1989; Steinberg & Morris, 2001).

We examined friendship quality in our sample of adolescents with SLI and their TD peers at age 16 years. We asked them a series of questions regarding friends and acquaintances—for example, how easy do you find it to get on with other people? If you were at a party or social gathering, would you try to talk to people you had not met before? Based on a number of questions, we devised a scale ranging from 0 to 16 points, with scores closer to zero representing good-quality of friendships. Adolescents in the SLI group ranged from 0 to 14 points while adolescents in the TD group had scores between 0 and 2. As a group, adolescents with SLI were at risk of poorer quality of friendships.

We then examined predictors of friendships. Our results suggest that spoken language abilities (expression and understanding of language) as well as literacy skills (reading) were associated with friendship quality. But language was *not* the strongest predictor: these were difficult behavior and prosocial behavior. We found that, in the sample as a whole, language and literacy measures accounted for a small but significant 7% of variance associated with friendship scores. Thus, language ability is predictive of adolescents' friendship quality when other behavioral characteristics known to influence peer relations—problem behavior, prosocial behavior—have been taken into account, but the overall influence of language ability on friendship is small. Predictor variables in order of importance were difficult behavior, prosocial behavior, language and literacy, and nonverbal IQ.

As with our other measures, there was also evidence of variability in friendship quality within the SLI group. Figure 8.5 demonstrates that we find a large proportion of adolescents with SLI reporting good quality of friendships. Durkin and Conti-Ramsden (2007) examined the factors that potentially distinguish between those with good-quality friendships (60%) and those with poor-quality friendships (40%) in detail. Briefly, the findings suggest a marked developmental consistency in the pattern of poor language for the poor friendships group across a 9-year span, from 7 to 16 years of age.

SLI itself appears to be a risk factor for poorer friendship development. SLI is associated with social problems in childhood and adolescence, and it is reasonable to assume that these bear on peer relations and friendship development. At the same time, there are individual differences in the nature and severity of problems experienced; by age 16, many adolescents with SLI (60%) reported having a good quality of friendships.

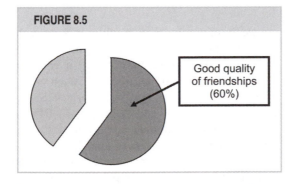

FIGURE 8.5

Good quality of friendships (60%)

Pie chart illustrating the percentage of adolescents with a history of SLI reporting good quality of friendships at age 16.

These data suggest that poor quality of friendships may not be simply a consequence of the severity of the language problem experienced but is an additional difficulty present in SLI that is particularly evident during adolescence.

Emotional health

A handful of studies have examined quality of life and psychiatric outcomes in young people with SLI (Beitchman et al., 2001; Cantwell & Baker, 1987; Clegg, Hollis, Mawhood, & Rutter, 2005). Beitchman and colleagues assessed a group of children with SLI from the age of 5 to 19 years and assessed them for the presence of possible psychiatric difficulties throughout this period. They found that children with SLI were at greater risk of having attention-deficit/hyperactivity disorders (Beitchman et al., 1996) and in later years had higher rates of anxiety disorders (Beitchman et al., 2001), aggressive behavior (Brownlie et al., 2004), and increased substance abuse (Beitchman et al., 2001). Rutter and colleagues (Clegg, Hollis, Mawhood, & Rutter, 2005) followed a cohort of children with receptive language impairments from 4 years to mid-adulthood and found an increased risk of psychiatric impairment compared to both peers and siblings. This cohort had symptoms particularly concerning depression, social anxiety, and schizoform/personality disorders. Other studies have examined language in populations referred primarily for psychiatric difficulties. Cohen, Barwick, Horodezky, Vallance, and Im (1998), for example, found a higher-than-expected rate of undiagnosed language impairment (40%) in their clinic sample. However, it needs to be noted that a recent study on SLI (Snowling, Bishop, Stothard, Chipchase, & Kaplan, 2006) did not identify increased risk of emotional disorders in a heterogeneous population of adolescents identified as having SLI at age 4. Thus, there is relatively little consensus about the long-term emotional health outcomes for children with SLI. Therefore, we investigated the occurrence of emotional symptoms such as anxiety and depression in our cohort at 16 years of age (Conti-Ramsden & Botting, 2008).

As can be seen from Table 8.3, adolescents with SLI had higher scores on measures assessing

TABLE 8.3

Scores on measures of anxiety and depression for adolescents with a history of SLI and for typically developing peers

| Adolescents | N | Anxiety[a] | | Depression[b] | |
		M	SD	M	SD
SLI	139	10.3	6.1	6.7	5.5
TD	124	7.0	4.9	3.9	4.2

Note. SLI = adolescents with specific language impairment; TD = typically developing peers. Higher scores on these measures are indicative of greater impairment.

[a] Maximum score for anxiety = 28. [b] Maximum score for depression = 26.

both anxiety and depression. In addition, the proportion of adolescents scoring above the clinical threshold for these disorders was larger in the SLI group than in the TD group for both anxiety (12% vs. 2%) and depression (39% vs. 14%).

We then examined predictors of emotional health. Our results suggest that there were virtually no associations between language ability and the development of emotional health symptoms. Examination of earlier factors (at 7 years) suggested that those with emotional problems at the age of 7 also showed increased anxiety at 16 years. Earlier language once again showed remarkably few associations with measures of mental and emotional health. Thus language ability was not a predictor of emotional health for these adolescents with SLI.

There was also evidence of variability within the group in terms of emotional health symptoms. Figure 8.6 illustrates that a large proportion of adolescents with a history of SLI has adequate emotional health.

In summary, the results of the above investigation raise a number of key issues that relate to emotional health in young people with SLI. First, our data clearly show an increased risk for mental health concerns in our SLI population as they near adulthood compared to TD peers. This finding replicates other studies that have shown raised

FIGURE 8.6

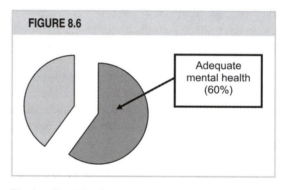

Adequate mental health (60%)

Pie chart illustrating the percentage of adolescents with a history of SLI reporting adequate mental health outcome. Two-thirds of the group report few, if any, symptoms of anxiety or depression.

prevalence of psychiatric difficulties in those with communication impairments (Clegg et al., 2005) and increased language impairment in children referred for psychiatric evaluation (Cohen et al., 1998; see also review by Toppelberg & Shapiro, 2000). Beitchman and colleagues (2001), in particular, found increased anxiety in a similar cohort with SLI at 19 years of age. The association has often been assumed to be causal in that either long-term language impairment may lead to (or exacerbate) wider difficulties, or psychiatric impairment may constrain communication skill.

However, in our cohort, surprisingly few direct associations were seen between language ability and the development of emotional health symptoms (cf. Clegg et al., 2005). The lack of association with language scores thus makes it more difficult to interpret the nature of the relationship; severity of language impairment does not appear to make an adolescent with SLI increasingly depressed or anxious per se. Thus, other factors are likely to play a role in making some individuals more vulnerable. From our own work we suggest these can range from a family history of anxiety and depression (Conti-Ramsden & Botting, 2008) to environmental factors such as being bullied (Knox & Conti-Ramsden, 2007). Interestingly, poor quality of friendships does not appear to be strongly associated with mental health difficulties. We found that in our sample, only 7% of adolescents showed difficulties with both friendships and mental health; 32% showed difficulties with friendships in the context of adequate mental health and 4% had the reverse pattern; 57% of the sample did not show difficulties in either area.

WHAT DO OUTCOMES IN ADOLESCENCE TELL US ABOUT THE NATURE OF SLI?

The findings presented briefly above point to the heterogeneity in outcomes in SLI. This heterogeneity is present both across individuals (i.e., different adolescents have different types of difficulties of different severity), as well as within an individual (i.e., there appears to be variation in the constellation of difficulties an adolescent may experience and in the severity of these difficulties). In a large sample such as ours, we see a wide variation in outcomes—from competent readers to very poor readers, from good academic achievement to significantly poor educational outcomes at the end of secondary schooling, from those enjoying good quality of friendships to those with difficulties developing such relationships, from those experiencing anxiety and/or depressive symptoms to those having adequate

emotional health. In terms of co-occurrence, it was found that 8% of adolescents had no difficulties in any of the four areas, while 5% had difficulties in all four areas. Most adolescents (41%) had difficulties in two areas, 32% had difficulties in three areas, and 14% had isolated difficulties in one area. Of those with difficulties in two areas, the most common pattern was to have literacy and academic difficulties together (90%). Of those with difficulties in three out of the four areas, the most common pattern was to have literacy, academic, and friendship difficulties (86%). Finally, of those adolescents with difficulties in just one area, the most common was to have isolated academic difficulties (63%).

Parents and practitioners will recognize this variability and heterogeneity as "messy." Heterogeneity increases complexity in practice. It becomes more difficult to predict from the individual's language profile other likely associated difficulties. Associations between skill areas vary from being very strong, as in the association between language and literacy, to virtually nonexistent, as in the association between language ability and emotional health. Yet, very importantly, a greater risk of poor outcome in all the domains discussed above is strongly associated with the diagnosis of SLI itself. In contrast, absolute level of language ability may be an important indicator of some outcomes but not others. In addition, the relative importance of language ability in predicting outcome varies across different skill sets. The complex relationship between our four outcome measures, language ability, and SLI is illustrated in Figure 8.7.

The concern that SLI is not a pure disorder of language is not a new idea (e.g., Leonard, 1987, 1991, 1998). What is less well established is the suggestion that we want to make here: at least some of the associated difficulties present in SLI are *not* directly related to the language difficulties present in SLI. We argue that the heterogeneity observed in the outcomes of adolescents with SLI, both within and across individuals, is a reflection of SLI being more than a language problem. The evidence points to a need to redefine SLI. First, SLI is a developmental disorder

FIGURE 8.7

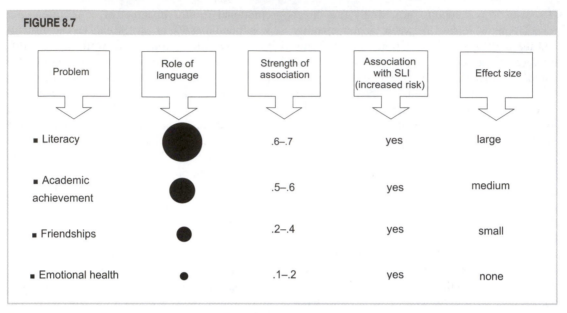

The nature and strength of relationships between diagnosis, language ability, and four outcome measures for adolescents with a history of SLI.

for which language is a primary manifestation in early childhood. It is the case that there are a number of children (7% of 5-year-olds; Tomblin et al., 1997) who present with primary language problems in the context of otherwise normal development. The issue is that this view of SLI is not accurate for a large proportion of children as they grow up. Deficits emerge in other areas of functioning, including areas that cannot be related directly to language per se. SLI is associated with difficulties that become more evident with development; only some of these are related to the severity and type of language problem experienced. A second assumption about SLI is that the primary difficulty with language is causally related to deficits in other areas. The evidence presented in this chapter of outcomes at age 16 years suggests that factors outside the language domain may well be crucial in understanding the range of deficits that individuals with SLI experience throughout their childhood and adolescence. Finally, in SLI the primary difficulty with language is assumed to be a defining

characteristic that, if persistent, stays with children as they grow into adolescence and young adulthood. This may well be the case for some individuals. The key issue raised by the findings reported above is that other areas of functioning may well be at least as bad (or worse) as the language deficit at 16 years. Thus for adolescents with SLI, language may no longer be a primary deficit, nor the most important factor for realizing optimal outcome.

ACKNOWLEDGMENTS

Writing of this chapter was made possible by an Economic and Social Research Council (ESRC) fellowship to the author (RES-063-27-0066). The author also gratefully acknowledges the support of the Nuffield Foundation (Grants AT 251 [OD], DIR/28 and EDU 8366) and the Wellcome Trust (Grant 060774). Thanks also to the Research

Assistants who were involved with data collection and the schools and families who gave their time so generously. Special thanks go to Zoë Simkin for her help with the preparation of the manuscript.

REFERENCES

Bagwell, C. L., Bender, S. E., Andreassi, C. L., Kinoshita, T. L., Montarello, S. A., & Muller, J. G. (2005). Friendship quality and perceived relationship changes predict psychosocial adjustment in early adulthood. *Journal of Social and Personal Relationships 22*, 235–254.

Beitchman, J. H., Brownlie, E. B., Inglis, A., Ferguson, B., Schachter, D., Lancee, W., et al. (1996). Seven-year follow-up of speech/language impaired and control children: Psychiatric outcome. *Journal of Child Psychology and Psychiatry, 37*, 961–970.

Beitchman, J. H., Wilson, B., Johnson, C. J., Atkinson, L., Young, A., Adlaf, E., et al. (2001). Fourteen year follow-up of speech/language impaired and control children: Psychiatric outcome. *Journal of the American Academy of Child & Adolescent Psychiatry, 40*, 75–82.

Bishop, D. V. M. (2001). Genetic influences on language impairment and literacy problems in children: Same or different? *Journal of Child Psychology and Psychiatry, 42*, 189–198.

Bishop, D. V. M., & Adams, C. (1990). A prospective study of the relationship between specific language impairment, phonological disorders and reading retardation. *Journal of Child Psychology and Psychiatry, 31*, 1027–1050.

Bishop, D. V. M., & Snowling, M. J. (2004). Developmental dyslexia and specific language impairment: Same or different? *Psychological Bulletin, 130*, 858–886.

Botting, N. (2005). Non-verbal cognitive development and language impairment. *Journal of Child Psychology and Psychiatry, 46*, 317–327.

Botting, N., Simkin, Z., & Conti-Ramsden, G. (2006). Associated reading skills in children with a history of specific language impairment (SLI). *Journal of Reading and Writing, 19*(1), 77–98.

Brownlie, E. B., Beitchman, J. H., Escobar, M., Young, A., Atkinson, L., Johnson, C., et al. (2004).

Early language impairment and young adult delinquent and aggressive behavior. *Journal of Child Psychology and Psychiatry & Allied Disciplines, 32*, 453–467.

Buhrmester, D. (1990). Intimacy of friendship, interpersonal competence, and adjustment during pre-adolescence and adolescence. *Child Development, 61*, 1101–1111.

Buhrmester, D. (1996). Need fulfillment, interpersonal competence and the developmental contexts of early adolescent friendship. In W. M. Bukowski, A. F. Newcomb, & W. W. Hartup (Eds.), *The company they keep: Friendship in childhood and adolescence* (pp. 158–185). New York: Cambridge University Press.

Cain, K., & Oakhill, J. (1996). The nature of the relation between comprehension skill and the ability to tell a story. *British Journal of Developmental Psychology, 14*, 187–201.

Cantwell, D. P., & Baker, L. (1987). Clinical significance of childhood communication disorders: Perspectives from a longitudinal study. *Journal of Child Neurology, 2*(4), 257–264.

Catts, H. (1991). Early identification of dyslexia: Evidence from a follow-up study of speech-language impaired children. *Annals of Dyslexia, 41*, 163–177.

Catts, H., Fey, M., Tomblin, J., & Zhang, X. (2002). A longitudinal investigation of reading outcomes in children with language impairments. *Journal of Speech, Language, and Hearing Research, 45*, 1142–1157.

Clegg, J., Hollis, C., Mawhood, L., & Rutter, M. (2005). Developmental language disorders—a follow-up in later adult life: Cognitive, language and psychosocial outcomes. *Journal of Child Psychology and Psychiatry, 46*, 128–149.

Clegg, J., Hollis, C., & Rutter, M. (1999, November). Life sentence: What happens to children with developmental language disorders in later life? *Bulletin of the Royal College of Speech and Language Therapists, 16–18*.

Cohen, N. J., Barwick, M., Horodezky, N., Vallance, D. D., & Im, N. (1998). Language, achievement, and cognitive processing in psychiatrically disturbed children with previously identified and unsuspected language impairments. *Journal of Child Psychology and Psychiatry, 36*(6), 865–878.

Conti-Ramsden, G., & Botting, N. (2000). Educational placements for children with specific language impairments. In D. V. M. Bishop & L. B. Leonard (Eds.), *Speech and language impairments in children: Causes, characteristics, intervention and outcome* (pp. 211–226). Hove, UK: Psychology Press.

Conti-Ramsden, G., & Botting, N. (2008). Emotional health in adolescents with and without a history of specific language impairment (SLI). *Journal of Child Psychology and Psychiatry, 49*, 516–525.

Conti-Ramsden, G., Donlan, C., & Grove, J. (1992). Characteristics of children with specific language impairment attending language units. *European Journal of Disorders of Communication, 27*, 325–342.

Conti-Ramsden, G., Durkin, K., Simkin, Z., & Knox, E. (in press). Specific language impairment and school outcomes I: Identifying and explaining variability at the end of compulsory education. *International Journal of Language & Communication Disorders*

Durkin, K., & Conti-Ramsden, G. (2007). Friendships, language, social behavior, and the quality of friendships in adolescents with and without a history of specific language impairment. *Child Development, 78*, 1441–1457.

Durkin, K., Simkin, Z., Knox, E., & Conti-Ramsden, G. (in press). Specific language impairment and school outcomes II: Educational context, student satisfaction and post-compulsory progress. *International Journal of Language & Communication Disorders*

Hartup, W. W. (1996). The company they keep: Friendships and their developmental significance. *Child Development, 67*, 1–13.

Hartup, W. W., & Stevens, N. (1999). Friendships and adaptation across the lifespan. *Current Directions in Psychological Science, 8*, 76–79.

Haynes, C., & Naidoo, S. (1991). *Children with specific speech and language impairment.* Oxford, UK: Blackwell.

Joanisse, M. F., Manis, F. R., Keating, P., & Seidenberg, M. S. (2000). Language deficits in dyslexic children: Speech perception, phonology and morphology. *Journal of Experimental Child Psychology, 71*, 30–60.

Knox, E., & Conti-Ramsden, G. (2007). Bullying in young people with a history of specific language impairment. *Educational and Child Psychology, 24*, 130–144.

Ladd, G. W. (1990). Having friends, keeping friends, making friends, and being liked by peers in the classroom: Predictors of children's early school adjustment? *Child Development, 61*, 1081–1100.

Ladd, G. W., Kochenderfer, B. J., & Coleman, C. C. (1996). Friendship quality as a predictor of young children's early school adjustment. *Child Development, 67*, 1103–1118.

Leonard, L. B. (1987). Is specific language impairment a useful construct? In S. Rosenberg (Ed.), *Advances in applied psycholinguistics: Vol. 1. Disorders of first-language development* (pp. 1–39). New York: Cambridge University Press.

Leonard, L. B. (1991). Specific language impairment as a clinical category. *Language, Speech, and Hearing Services in Schools, 22*, 66–68.

Leonard, L. B. (1998). *Children with specific language impairment.* Cambridge, MA: MIT Press.

Mawhood, L., Howlin, P., & Rutter, M. (2000). Autism and developmental receptive language disorders—a comparative follow-up in early adult life. I. Cognitive and language outcomes. *Journal of Child Psychology and Psychiatry, 41*, 547–559.

McArthur, G. M., Hogben, J. H., Edwards, S. M., Heath, S. M., & Mengler, E. D. (2000). On the "specifics" of specific reading disability and specific language impairment. *Journal of Child Psychology and Psychiatry, 41*, 869–874.

Ofsted (2005). *The annual report of Her Majesty's Chief Inspector of Schools 2004/2005.* London: The Stationery Office.

Parker, J. G., & Gottman, J. M. (1989). Social and emotional development in a relational context: Friendship interaction from early childhood to adolescence. In T. J. Berndt & G. W. Ladd (Eds.), *Peer relationships in child development* (pp. 95–131). New York: Wiley.

Semel, E., Wiig, E. H., & Secord, W. (1987). *Clinical evaluation of language fundamentals—revised.* San Antonio, TX: The Psychological Corporation.

Shulman, S. (1993). Close relationships and coping behavior in adolescence. *Journal of Adolescence, 16*, 267–283.

Snowling, M. J., Adams, J. W., Bishop, D. V. M., & Stothard, S. E. (2001). Educational attainments of school leavers with a preschool history of speech-language impairments. *International Journal of Language & Communication Disorders, 36*, 173–183.

Snowling, M., Bishop, D. V. M., & Stothard, S. E. (2000). Is preschool language impairment a risk factor for dyslexia in adolescence? *Journal of Child Psychology and Psychiatry, 41*, 587–600.

Snowling, M. J., Bishop, D. V. M., Stothard, S. E., Chipchase, B., & Kaplan, C. (2006). Psychosocial outcomes at 15 years of children with a preschool history of speech-language impairment. *Journal of Child Psychology and Psychiatry, 47,* 759–765.

Steinberg, L., & Morris, A. S. (2001). Adolescent development. *Annual Review of Psychology, 52,* 83–110.

Stothard, S. E., Snowling, M. J., Bishop, D. V. M., Chipchase, B. B., & Kaplan, C. (1998). Language impaired preschoolers: A follow-up into adolescence. *Journal of Speech and Hearing Research, 41,* 407–418.

Tallal, P., Curtiss, S., & Kaplan, R. (1988). The San Diego Longitudinal Study: Evaluating the outcomes of preschool impairments in language development. In S. G. Berber Mencher (Ed.), *International perspectives on communication disorders* (pp. 86–126). Washington, DC: Gallaudet University Press.

Tallal, P., Dukette, K., & Curtiss, S. (1989). Behavioral/emotional profiles of pre-school language impaired children. *Development and Psychopathology, 1,* 51–67.

Tomblin, J. B., Records, N. L., Buckwalter, P., Zhang, X., Smith, E., & O'Brien, M. (1997). Prevalence of specific language impairment in kindergarten children. *Journal of Speech, Language, and Hearing Research, 40,* 1245–1260.

Toppelberg, C. O., & Shapiro, T. (2000). Language disorders: A 10-year research update review. *Journal of the American Academy of Child & Adolescent Psychiatry, 39*(2), 143–152.

UK Office of National Statistics (2004). *2001–2002 General Household Survey.* London: The Stationery Office.

Wilson, B., & Risucci, D. (1988). The early identification of developmental language disorders and the prediction for the acquisition of reading skills. In R. Marsland & M. Marsland (Eds.), *Preschool prevention of reading failure* (pp. 187–203). Parkton, MD: York Press.

Young, A. R., Beitchman, J. H., Johnson, C., Douglas, L., Atkinson, L., Escobar, M., & Wilson, B. (2002). Young adult academic outcomes in a longitudinal sample of early identified language impaired and control children. *Journal of Child Psychology and Psychiatry, 43,* 635–646.

9

Inclusion versus specialist provision for children with developmental language disorders

Julie E. Dockrell and Geoff Lindsay

INTRODUCTION

There is a growing debate about the ways in which education of children and young people with special educational needs should be met (Cigman, 2007; House of Commons Education and Skills Committee, 2006). Debates revolve around the rights to be educated in mainstream settings (Lindsay, 2003; Rustemier, 2002), the most appropriate educational placement to raise achievements and well-being (Dyson, Farrell, Polat, Hutcheson, & Gallannaugh, 2004; Zigmond, 2003), and evidence-based pedagogical practices

(Lewis & Norwich, 2005; Lindsay, 2007). The issues raised impact directly on the ways in which the needs of children with specific speech and language difficulties (SSLD) are addressed. This debate was reflected in a UK national study that highlighted the differences between the views of education and health professionals regarding how best to develop services for children with SSLD. Typically education staff emphasized the development of inclusive education practices (Lindsay, Dockrell, Mackie, & Letchford, 2005a), while speech and language therapy services highlighted the need to develop more specialist provision (Dockrell, Lindsay, Letchford, & Mackie, 2006). The implicit assumption from both groups of respondents was that, independent of the causal origins of language problems, intervention can mediate or modify the effects of a developmental language disorder. Importantly, in both cases the focus was on the children's educational placement: mainstream or specialist provision.

Children with SSLD have a primary language problem, one that is not attributable to moderate learning difficulties,[1] severe or profound hearing loss, or lack of linguistic opportunity (Leonard, 1997). Various terms are used to describe these problems; here SSLD is used to reflect the term in common usage in educational settings in the United Kingdom at the time of the studies reported. These children are educated in a range of different settings, including mainstream and special schools and also special provision within mainstream schools for which different local authorities use different terms. The term *integrated resource* is used in this chapter to describe such specialist provision.

Currently in the United Kingdom the educational and speech and language needs of pupils with SSLD are met in a range of ways. At one end of the continuum, pupils are placed in specialist residential settings, but, as we demonstrate, the majority are in mainstream schools, with varying levels of additional support. The ways in which this support is provided varies across schools, services, and educational phase. In the first instance, children may be provided with additional teaching, but if their need is deemed to be greater than can be met by the school's resources, a statement of special educational needs is actioned. Statements may specify the numbers of hours of additional support a child is entitled to. How this additional support is provided will vary according to the child's needs and the school's resources. The ultimate aim is to personalize the support provided to meet the child's learning needs. Speech and language therapy is an additional resource and must be specified. Many speech and language therapists (SLTs) are employed by the health authority, and the ways in which speech and language therapy is provided will often depend on the organization of the child's health trust. Increasingly, education services are employing SLTs. Pupils in special schools are likely to receive regular and intensive speech and language therapy (Lindsay, Dockrell, Mackie, & Letchford, 2005b), while pupils in other settings may get some support in schools or clinics.

In this chapter we explore the challenges raised for the education system by children with SSLD. We argue that a focus on educational placement alone is unhelpful and examine the ways in which teaching and intervention can be systematically developed to meet the language learning needs of children with SSLD (Justice, 2006).

INCLUSION VERSUS SPECIALIST PROVISION

The respondents in the national survey focused on two different strategies for developing educational provision for children with SSLD (Dockrell et al., 2006; Lindsay et al., 2005a). Prima facie, these appear to be opposite; in practice, the distinction is not straightforward. Both inclusion and specialist provision have multiple meanings (Cigman, 2007). For some practitioners and academics, placement in a mainstream school is a necessary but not a sufficient condition for inclusion. This position is based on a view that children have a right to inclusive education (Lindsay, 2003). An alternative position argues that in addition to consideration of rights, which are value-driven, there is a need for evidence of the efficacy of the educational placements in terms of meeting children's needs (Lindsay, 2007). From this perspective inclusion can best be described as a process by which a school attempts to respond to all pupils as individuals, reconsidering its curricula, organization, and provision (Sebba & Sachdev, 1997), and so "inclusion" may be different for each individual child (Tomlinson, 1997). This definition allows a way of examining the evidence base for children with special educational needs. We can ask what a child's individual needs are, how provision addresses these needs, and what the best ways are to meet these needs. The answers to these questions will vary across individuals and will depend on an interaction between the child, the environment, and time (Wedell, 2005).

Children and young people can be excluded in mainstream classrooms or special classrooms from appropriate support, access to externally recognized qualifications, an appropriate curriculum, and friendship groups. For example, a child with SSLD in a mainstream setting may not have access to the appropriate supports to help with peer relations and may, as a result, remain relatively isolated. By corollary, a child with SSLD in a special school may be isolated from mainstream peers and mainstream social activities but have close friendships with other pupils and regular access to speech and language therapy (SLT). Thus inclusion is not simply a question of location but a process and, as such, exceedingly complex to evaluate (Lindsay, 2007).

Mainstream schools are not homogeneous: they vary greatly in their social mix, levels of achievement, and behavioral ethos (Office of Her Majesty's Chief Inspector, 2005). Mainstream schools drawing from similar populations may differ greatly in their levels of educational attainment, ethos, and levels of inclusion. Integrated resources also vary in their size, admissions policy, and working ethos. Although previous research suggested that language units were relatively homogeneous in the children who were placed there (Conti-Ramsden & Botting, 1999), more recent work challenges this assumption (Archibald & Gathercole, 2006). Special schools are similarly diverse. Special schools for children with language difficulties report that the children in their services experience a broad range of needs (Lindsay et al., 2005a). Thus there is considerable heterogeneity in the populations served by these different systems, and the extent of overlap between the systems in relation to the pupils' level of need is largely unknown.

WHY CHILDREN WITH LANGUAGE DIFFICULTIES RAISE CHALLENGES FOR THE EDUCATION SYSTEM

Children who enter schools with poor language skills are disadvantaged both academically and socially. In contrast to many of their peers, they will find the oral learning environment in the classroom challenging. Moreover, they will be disadvantaged in terms of the necessary building blocks required to develop their literacy and numeracy skills in the classroom. These challenges can be exacerbated when school staff are unfamiliar with their language learning needs (Dockrell & Lindsay, 2001; Mroz, 2006) and the ways to support oral language skills.

There are significant numbers of children with SSLD. The most commonly reported prevalence rate is 7.4% for children at school entry (Tomblin et al., 1997). In England, statements of special educational need (SEN) will be required for entry into most integrated resources and special schools. Currently approximately 3% of all pupils receive statements of SEN, although there is some variation by age and local authority (Department for Education and Skills, 2005). The majority of all children with statements of SEN (60%) are educated in mainstream schools, 7.7% of them in resourced provision, integrated resources, and special classes in mainstream schools (Department for Education and Skills, 2005). Children with SSLD will be a minority of all children with statements of SEN, and relative to other categories of SEN there are proportionally fewer children whose primary need is a function of speech language and communication difficulties in special schools (Department for Education and Skills, 2005). From the analysis of current prevalence rates of SSLD and current practice for all children with SEN, it follows that most children with SSLD are educated in mainstream settings. This is consistent with data from the Manchester Language Study, where we have estimated that only 0.07% of Year 2 children in England had spent time in language units—a substantially smaller number than the estimated prevalence of SLI by Tomblin et al. (1997). Thus, teachers, special educational needs coordinators (SENCOs), and teaching assistants in mainstream settings will be addressing the needs of children with SSLD on a daily basis. It is not simply the extent of the problem that challenges education staff. The terms used to describe the pupil's difficulties, the nature of their language problems, and the associated difficulties are problematic for staff who are not prepared by their initial training for meeting the needs of pupils' with language learning difficulties.

Identifying and understanding children's needs is a complicating factor. Debates about the utility of the terminology used for children with language difficulties are long-standing (Aram, Morris, & Hall, 1993) and continue to concern the profession (Walsh, 2005). The range of terms used can lead to confusion within the field (Kamhi, 1998). The lack of consistent terminology and of a common framework leads to miscommunication among education staff and misunderstanding about children's needs (Dockrell, George, Lindsay, & Roux, 1997). In a recent study of health trusts in England and Wales, ten different terms were being used by different speech and language services to refer to the same group of children (Dockrell et al., 2006).

The terms themselves do not necessarily provide details about the nature of the child's specific language difficulties. There is variability in both the criteria and the procedures used to identify the children (Kamhi, 1998; Lahey, 1990), which affects the nature of the population. Operational definitions that use nonverbal ability as an exclusionary criterion differ in their use of cutoff points, with standard scores ranging from 85 to 70 (Kamhi, 1998). Defining SSLD with exclusionary criteria does not identify a unique homogeneous group of language needs. Subtypes of language difficulties have been identified in clinical groups (Rapin & Allen, 1987) and by standardized assessments (Conti-Ramsden, Crutchley, & Botting, 1997). The extent to which these reflect valid clinical groupings with implications for educational interventions is less clear. Indeed, there are questions about the ways in which tests intended to tap different domains actually reflect the same underlying language dimensions (Tomblin & Zhang, 2006; van Weerdenburg, Verhoeven, & Van Balkom, 2006) and the ways in which test use can alter a child's eligibility for services (Cole, Dale, & Mills, 1992; Dockrell & Law, 2007). The importance of subgroups for educational provision is further questioned by

the significant movement between groups over relatively short periods of time (Conti-Ramsden & Botting, 1999).

Many children with SSLD have problems that are not specific to oral language but can be associated with oral language problems and can directly affect access to the curriculum. Children experience a range of problems with literacy, including inefficiencies in decoding (Catts, Fey, Tomblin, & Zhang, 2002; Stothard, Snowling, Bishop, Chipchase, & Kaplan, 1998) and deficits in reading comprehension (Nation, Clarke, Marshall, & Durand, 2004), spelling (Lewis & Freebairn, 1992), and writing (Bishop & Clarkson, 2003; Dockrell, Lindsay, Connelly, & Mackie, 2007). Problems with numeracy are also increasingly documented (Cowan, Donlan, Newton, & Lloyd, 2005). Difficulties that are indirectly related to the children's performance in the classroom—poor motor coordination (Hill, 2004) and social, emotional, and behavioral difficulties (Beitchman, Wilson, Brownlie, Inglis, & Lancee, 1996; Fujiki, Brinton, & Clarke, 2002; Lindsay, Dockrell, & Strand, 2007)—are also common. Thus both teachers and learning support staff need to consider a profile of competencies beyond the pupil's specific language problems.

Patterns of performance vary over time in terms of linguistic skills (Law, Boyle, Harris, Harkness, & Nye, 2000), nonverbal ability (Botting, 2005), and academic attainment (Dockrell et al., 2007; Young et al., 2002). As children develop, earlier problems in areas such as phonology and morphosyntax may improve; however, more detailed testing may show problems with higher-level language—for example, understanding of humor and idioms (Norbury, 2004). In UK post-16 educational contexts difficulties with basic skills serve as barriers to future educational and occupational opportunities (Dockrell et al., 2007). The relative importance of these factors will vary over the educational phases and with respect to the curricular demands being placed on the children.

A final complicating factor in meeting the needs of children with SSLD in the UK is the necessary interplay between health and education professionals. Effective collaboration between the key agencies to provide for the children's needs is advocated, but there are significant difficulties in achieving this (Dockrell et al., 1997; Dunsmuir, Clifford, & Took, 2006). Major decisions on provision, facilities, or patterns of practice are typically not taken collaboratively (Palikara, Lindsay, Cullen, & Dockrell, 2007). Some of these problems reflect different underlying philosophies. The conventional view of SLT practice places greater emphasis on factors within the child, while educational models focus on the influence of the learning environment. Recommendations from the different professionals for specific interventions and patterns of educational provision will reflect these different perspectives and may lead to a dichotomy between the views of education and health staff about the ways to meet the educational needs of children with SSLD.

THE CURRENT CONTEXT

UK provision

Debates about the nature and extent of provision for children with language difficulties are not new. Concern in the United Kingdom in the 1980s highlighted the scarcity of language units for junior-school-aged children (Key Stage 2, ages 3–11 years) as opposed to infants (Key Stage 1, 5–7 years) and the lack of specialist provision at secondary-school age (Key Stages 3 and 4, 12–16 years) (Hutt & Donlan, 1987). Concern was also raised about the variable criteria for admission to language units, the nature and extent of integration, the use of manual signing, and staffing ratios. However, at this point little was known about the provision for children who did not attend language units. In 2000, a study was carried out to investigate policy and practice at local authority, health trust, and school levels concerning the current provision for children with SSLD (Dockrell et al., 2006; Lindsay et al., 2005a, 2005b). The views of 97 local authorities and 129 speech and language therapy (SLT) services in England and Wales were collected. The study mapped in detail

the provision made by local authority and SLT services. The local authority survey identified the range of educational provision, while the survey of SLT services explored the types of support offered by SLTs to educational provision specifically for children with SSLD.

The local authority survey confirmed that support for children with SSLD was not simply provided in language units. At all key stages the majority of local authorities provided support in mainstream schools; 98.9% of local authorities reported this style of provision at Key Stage 2. Language units and other specialized language resources located in mainstream schools were more common at reception and Key Stage 1 (90.7%) and Key Stage 2 (84.2%); however, fewer than one-third of local authorities made this provision at Key Stage 3 or 4. Nevertheless, this was a major development since 1987, when language units had almost exclusively been provided at Key Stage 1. In the primary-school years, the number of specialist placements available varied across the local authorities; about half provided only one language unit or integrated resource, others provided two and up to five or more. However, children with SSLD were also routinely placed in other specialist integrated resources (i.e., those designated for children with mild-to-moderate learning difficulties). Relatively few local authorities had special language schools (~8%), while approximately two-thirds of the local authorities placed children with SSLD in special schools for children with mild-to-moderate learning difficulties and almost half used other specialist schools. Local authorities also increasingly used placements provided by other authorities or the voluntary sector from nursery to Key Stage 3/4.

SLT services reported a similar range of provision. Four out of five provided services to children with SSLD in mainstream schools up to Key Stage 2. Support for students in secondary school was reduced but was still provided by over half of the services. However, fewer than 10% of SLT services made provision to mainstream schools post-16. Support to specialist language resources was highest at Reception and Key Stage 1 (83.7%), lower at Key Stage 2 (72.9%), and dropped considerably to 25.6% and 3.9% at Key Stage 3/4 and post-16, respectively.

The data from SLT services and local authorities provide evidence for a complex pattern of provision. Local authorities had developed specialist integrated resources for children with SSLD, and SLT services were supporting children in these placements. On the other hand, local authorities were using, and SLTs were supporting, a range of other special schools and specialized integrated resources for children with other developmental disorders (e.g., moderate learning difficulties). Furthermore, support for children with SSLD in mainstream was the most common type of provision across both local authority and SLT services.

The study also confirmed earlier findings regarding variability in language unit entry criteria, including the severity of language problem, nature of language problem, primary speech and language problem, level of cognitive or nonverbal skills, and requirement for there to be a discrepancy between language and nonverbal ability. There was lack of consistency across local authorities about placement decisions and about who would quality for entry into a specialized service.

The survey highlighted the diversity of educational placements that were designated to meet the needs of children with SSLD, but it was not designed to provide a detailed picture of the children who were placed in the services, their level of needs, and the ways in which teaching was specialized to the meet the children's needs.

PLACEMENTS, LEVEL OF NEED, APPROACHES TO TEACHING, AND ACADEMIC ATTAINMENTS

Examining need in two local authorities

To address some of these issues, we draw on data collected from a cohort of children based in two local authorities over a ten-year longitudinal study covering primary and secondary education.

We identified children at the beginning of Key Stage 2 (Year 3, age 8). To ensure that the range of provision was not constrained by geographical and local policy decisions, children were identified in two local authorities, one urban and one rural.

Our study was designed to test the following hypotheses:

1. Severe language difficulties are likely to persist irrespective of the children's educational placement.

2. The demands of the Key Stage 2 curriculum are likely to highlight the extent of children's language learning needs.

3. Staff members in both specialist and mainstream institutions will be aware of individual students' language learning needs.

Children's placement in schools is determined by a range of factors, including preferences of the family and the child, availability of schools, the severity and extent of a child's language and non-language difficulties, and local authority directives. In contrast to studies examining the efficacy of specific interventions (see, e.g., Ebbels, van der Lely, & Dockrell, 2007), these educational and personal dimensions prevent random allocation to schools, and the numbers of participants prevent an analysis at the level of the school. However, all the parents interviewed in this study were happy with the choice of secondary school for their child and felt that in Year 7 the schools were meeting the children's needs (Dockrell & Lindsay, 2007). Comparisons across variables such as severity of language difficulty and nonverbal ability provided the opportunity for an initial investigation of the different settings and the identification of the pedagogic practices to which the pupils were exposed.

We identified children through special educational needs coordinators, speech and language therapists, and educational psychologists. This allowed a broader approach than defining the sample by focusing on provision types alone. We excluded any child who was reported to have an additional difficulty that might question the specific nature of the language problem. A total of 59 children remained in the sample, and this represented 0.75% of the Year 3 population across the local authorities. This was a more representative sample of the population than children drawn from integrated resources alone. Participants were assessed on a range of language and literacy tasks (see Dockrell et al., 2007).

There was no difference between the local authorities on any language, literacy, or cognitive measure at any point in the study. At first assessment (age 8), participants had statistically significantly higher scores on the nonverbal measure than scores on all measures of language (Mean Z score TROG = –1.5; Bus Story = –1.6) and literacy scores (Mean Z score Reading Accuracy = –1.1; Reading Comprehension = –1.3; Spelling = –1.5); all differences represented large effect sizes (Dockrell et al., 2007).

At age 8, children were variously placed across different types of educational provision: 40 children (68%) were in mainstream schools with additional support, 9 (15%) were in special schools for children with language difficulties, and 10 (17%) were in integrated resources. Figure 9.1 illustrates the movement of pupils over time between different types of provision

in the urban authority (hatched bar) and the rural authority (dotted bar). As Figure 9.1 shows, over the following 8 years a total of 46% of pupils moved between different types of provision, with 14% moving more than once. Movements occurred between all types of provision at each point. Between Year 9 (14 years) and Year 11 (16 years) pupils moved from mainstream to a specialist language resource, from a general integrated resource to mainstream, from a special language school to mainstream, and from schools for children with moderate learning difficulties to both mainstream and a specialist language resource. Children in the urban authority moved significantly more often than did those in the rural authority, $t(53) = -2.1$, $p = .04$. Thus, our first analysis suggested that it was characteristics of the local authority rather than pupils' needs that were influencing current placements.

To examine this further, we considered the extent to which children's placements indicated level of need as assessed by standardized assessments. A sample of all Year 3 children who met the criteria for SSLD in two national special language schools were included to extend the number of children in specialist provision, providing a total sample of 69.

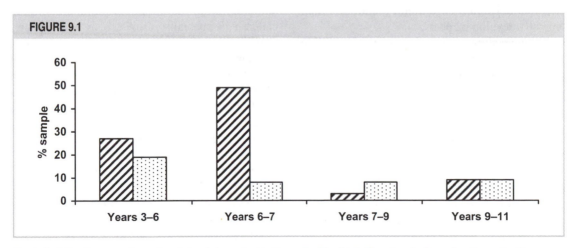

FIGURE 9.1

Graph depicting the percentage of participants in rural education authorities (dotted bars) and urban education authorities (striped bars) that moved placement across the different assessment phases of the study.

Are pupils in specialist provision those with the greatest level of need?

We tested the hypothesis that children in different forms of provision were experiencing different levels of educational need. At each point in time comparisons were made across forms of provision in relation to nonverbal ability, receptive and expressive language, reading decoding, reading comprehension, and spelling. Additionally, we examined the children's production of written text in Year 6 (age 11) and Year 9/10 (age 14–15).

The first question we considered was whether children in specialist provision (integrated resources and special schools) had higher levels of need than those in mainstream schools on measures of language and literacy across three phases of the project: Year 3, Year 6, and Year 9/10. No measures differentiated the children in Year 3. In Year 6, both groups were performing significantly below average on measures of language and literacy, but the only measure that differentiated the two populations was expressive language; the performance of pupils in specialist provision was significantly lower than that of pupils in mainstream schools. By the end of Key Stage 3, young people in specialist placement were performing significantly worse on measures of nonverbal ability, expressive language, reading comprehension, and writing. Pupils in mainstream settings were also demonstrating significant levels of deficit in language and literacy relative to their typically developing peers.

Grouping all specialist provision together might fail to discriminate the pupils' needs in terms of either the severity of the pupil's difficulties or the specificity of their language needs. By Year 6 (age 11), sufficient numbers of children had moved to other specialist provision to allow a more detailed analysis by comparisons across these different cohorts of children.

The first analysis examined intensity of support in mainstream, integrated resources, and special schools. Analyses by intensity of provision revealed no significant differences on any measure in Year 6. A similar analysis of placements in Year 11 (age 15–16) revealed significant group differences for expressive language and reading

comprehension. Pupils in integrated resources and mainstream settings performed significantly better than pupils in special schools on measures of expressive language. For reading comprehension, pupils in mainstream performed significantly better than those in integrated resources and special schools, while those in integrated resources and special schools did not differ significantly. Again scores for all groups were significantly below age expectations.

We next examined the differences between children in mainstream schools, those in specialist language resources and language schools, and those in nonspecific integrated resources and special schools designed for children with other developmental difficulties. In Year 6 the only measure that differentiated the three groups was nonverbal ability: children in nonspecific integrated resources and special schools had significantly lower scores than did the other two cohorts, who were performing within the average range. By the end of Key Stage 3, differences between the cohorts were evident for both nonverbal ability and expressive language, but these were only significant between the mainstream and nonspecific special provision groups. Young people in specialist language provision did not differ significantly from either those in mainstream or those in nonspecific specialist services.

These analyses suggest that while all children have significant language learning challenges, children in specialist provision as a group are more impaired on a minority of assessments. Although these differences are statistically significant, their clinical or educational significance has not been established. Note also that since many pupils move between types of provision, the data cannot inform on long-term prognoses nor speak to the efficacy of the different settings.

Is educational placement an indicator of support provided?

Children's needs in Year 6 were met in three ways: individual and group sessions outside the classroom or in-class support. Many children received combinations of these approaches. All children in special schools received all modes of support, whereas this was the case for only 50% of the children in integrated resources and mainstream schools. We also considered the professionals involved across settings and organization. In all but one case pupils who were in special schools were receiving support from a combination of professionals, including speech and language therapists, individually, in groups, and within classrooms. Moreover, for pupils in integrated resources, individual work was provided either by a combination of professionals (including an SLT) or by SLT alone. In contrast, both group work and in-class support were characterized by greater variation in the staff involved.

The pattern of support for children in mainstream settings was much more varied. Of the children, 75% received individual support; of these, 45% received support from education support staff alone, 32% from SLTs, and 22% from a combination of professionals. For both group and individual work, the majority of children received their support in class (group work = 85%; individual = 91%). Children in specialist provision were therefore receiving higher levels of support and a greater range of professional involvement.

In Year 6 the ways in which staff worked with the children was explored in greater detail. We surveyed both teachers and SENCOs but discuss only teacher data, as the response rate was higher ($N = 66$) and their responses revealed a greater awareness of what was happening in the classrooms for these pupils. Extra support was provided for all the pupils in special schools and integrated resources and for 74% of the children in mainstream settings, both within the class and by withdrawal. Teachers reported differentiation of the curriculum for all pupils in special schools and integrated resources and 84% of pupils in mainstream classrooms. This was complemented by the use of different teaching strategies for children in mainstream settings (73%), integrated resources (90%), and special schools (69%).

In Year 7 data were collected from both teachers and SENCOs. Extra support was typically implemented in all or almost all settings (mainstream = 96%; integrated resources = 100%; special schools = 94%) both within the class and by withdrawal. The data revealed a pattern similar to those collected in Year 6. Teachers reported differentiating the curriculum for all pupils in special schools, 75% of pupils in integrated resources, and 84% of pupils in mainstream classrooms. This was complemented by the use of different teaching strategies for all children in integrated resources and special schools and 91% of the mainstream children. Teachers in mainstream provision were more likely to report setting easier work (71%) than teachers in integrated resources (50%) or special schools (31%). The latter result is unsurprising, given the range of pupil abilities across the settings. Setting different objectives for the pupils was also frequently reported (mainstream, 71%; integrated resources, 88%; special schools, 81%), as was the use of specialist materials (mainstream = 38%; integrated resources = 67%; special schools = 88%). However, there was no difference in the reported use of specialist programs (mainstream = 52%; integrated resources = 50%; special schools = 69%).

A number of differences are therefore evident across the settings with respect to their systems to address the children's educational needs. These differences reflect general approaches to learning and instruction; objective data examining specific aspects of pedagogy were not collected. An important question remains as to whether these differences are reflected in pupil outcomes.

Educational achievement at school leaving

Attainments at the end of compulsory secondary schooling (Year 11, age 16) across the placements were examined from individual data provided by the Department for Education and Skills (Department for Children, Schools and Families) for pupils' General Certificate of Secondary Education (GCSE) results. In the United Kingdom, pupils take the GCSE examinations in a range of subjects. They are graded A*–G, the target level being Level 2 (A*–C). Pupils took an average of seven formal qualifications (range 0–14), with a mean of 5 GCSEs and with a smaller but sizable proportion taking the lower-level qualifications. Pupils passed an average of 5 GCSEs, with the majority of pupils achieving their qualifications at

Level 1 (D–G). Nonetheless, 12.5% of the pupils achieved 5 GCSEs at Level 2. These levels of achievement differ significantly from mainstream pupils in the respective local authorities but are significantly better than those of pupils with other special educational needs (Dockrell et al., 2007).

Pupils' performance differed according to their educational placement (special or mainstream). Young people in special schools were more likely to take entry-level qualifications and achieved fewer GCSE passes overall. There was a trend for pupils in other specialist provision to achieve lower results; however, there were no statistically significant differences in the average number of points achieved, which is a grade-related rather than qualification-related criterion. Pupils in mainstream placements recorded the highest number of GCSE points ($M = 178$, $SD = 172$, range 0–816), but this did not differ significantly from either those in specialist language placements ($M = 170$, $SD = 99$, range 10–390) or those in nonspecific specialist provision in Year 11 ($M = 89$, $SD = 55$, range 46–204). Mean scores are significantly different from the average GCSE points achieved by pupils attending mainstream schools (348 points in 2005). Interestingly, every child in the specialist language placements had achieved some GCSE points by the age of 16, but three pupils in mainstream settings had not achieved any points to date. Further examination of the GCSE data with larger samples and appropriate controls and conceptual analysis might help to further understand these patterns.

Summary

Children presented similar patterns of language and cognitive needs across the different types of provision. These needs were characterized by marked difficulties with language and literacy. Differences between settings on these measures were small and were evident only for measures of expressive language, reading comprehension, and nonverbal ability. The needs of the children were typically met by an emphasis on curriculum differentiation and changing objectives to include children in the curriculum at both primary and secondary school. Analysis of academic attainment at GCSE based on grade-related criteria revealed no statistically significant differences between the settings.

Meeting the educational needs of children with SSLD

Children with SSLD require support, at different points in their development, either directly or indirectly, from speech and language therapists. It is less clear whether there is a special pedagogy for these children. Distinctive group characteristics do not necessarily mean that different approaches to teaching are required or are differentially effective. As in other areas of special need, there is little by way of reliable and valid data to support the view that children with SSLD require distinct kinds of teaching or educational programs (Lewis & Norwich, 2005). Indeed, the evidence from therapy studies questions the specific nature of the children's language needs. Children with below-average nonverbal IQ may benefit as much from therapy as do children with average nonverbal abilities (Cole et al., 1992).

There are however, critical features that are applicable to all learners, although different emphasis on the particular features will be required for different children and at different time points (Anderson, 1990; Brown, 1988). These principles can be applied to optimize learning, but these must be both conceptualized and operationalized in relation to the individual child's learning and developmental needs and to the setting in which the teaching and learning are to take place (Lewis & Norwich, 2005). The underlying tenet is that those learning more slowly need more time to learn and more deliberate planning to ensure progress (Reason, 1998). Lewis and Norwich have formalized a taxonomy of pedagogic strategies that are relevant to supporting the educational needs of children with SSLD. The underpinning notion in this taxonomy is intensification. In addition, the strategies identified concern the process of learning rather than where learning takes place. These strategies are premised on an understanding of the cognitive demands of the task, ways to intensify instruction, and criterion-referenced tools for monitoring progress. The importance of the nature rather than the mere amount of resources is also stressed by a recent Office of Her Majesty's Chief Inspector report (2006) which concludes that:

> The provision of additional resources to pupils—such as support from teaching assistants—did not ensure good quality intervention or adequate progress by pupils. There was a misconception that provision of additional resources was the key requirement for individual pupils, whereas . . . key factors for good progress were: the involvement of a specialist teacher; good assessment; work tailored to challenge pupils sufficiently; and commitment from school leaders to ensure good progress for all pupils. (p. 2)

Table 9.1 provides indicative guidelines of strategies that support effective learning and ways in which they can be intensified to support learners who are struggling with the curriculum. Examination of the research literature provides experimental evidence demonstrating the relevance of a number of these high-intensity strategies for children with SSLD.

Thus, there is evidence that modification of instructional approaches can support learning for a range of pupils with different learning needs. There is increasing evidence that children with SSLD will benefit from learning environments that are sensitive to these pedagogic approaches.

These teaching approaches have been highlighted by local authorities judged to be providing good practice for children with SSLD (Lindsay & Dockrell, 2005). SENCOs in good-practice local authorities reported breaking tasks into small steps always or often (89% of the time and at least sometimes 100% of the time). Verbal repetition by the adult was also very common (81.2% and 99.2%, respectively), although the nature of this verbal input was not examined (see Radford, Ireson, & Mahon, 2006).

The way forward

Research, policy, and practice evaluations indicate that it is not *where* but *how* support occurs that is crucial. The first step (Tier 1) in addressing the needs of children with SSLD should be the provision of an appropriate learning environment, typically driven by an understanding of the principles of learning and the cognitive prerequisites of the task to be learnt. In these contexts support will typically involve integrating language learning and subject learning (Wellington & Wellington, 2002). There is no evidence from the current data to suggest that the children should experience a qualitatively different curriculum in the first instance. Establishing that appropriate opportunities exist for a child to learn and that the strategies are in place to support this learning is an empirical question. Appropriate methodologies are required to achieve this objective.

Where the teaching and learning contexts meet these criteria and children have had access to such learning environments on a regular basis but difficulties still persist, a second tier of intervention needs to be considered. Interventions need to be strongly associated with the target skill, based on solid evidence, and matched to the educational context (Gillam & Gillam, 2006). As Justice (2006) argues, interventions at this stage need to be systematic, explicit, and intense. They also need to be monitored using the appropriate criterion referenced measures (Dockrell & Law, 2007). This supplemental support will typically be provided in small groups or one-to-one settings. Key principles that optimize achievement for those with literacy difficulties have been identified and have been shown to apply to children with speech and language problems (Gillon, 2000).

Treatment nonresponders following second-tier interventions create particular challenges; more research is required to determine how many children are nonresponsive to traditional forms of interventions, and why this might be so. Suggestions have been made that these pupils should be provided with more intensive intervention, possibly by short-term pull-out intervention (Fuchs, Mock, Morgan, & Young, 2003; Vaughn & Fuchs, 2003; Vaughn, Linan-Thompson, & Hickman, 2003). Alternatively, placement may be offered in settings where staff knowledge and expertise can meet the specific needs at a specific point in time and responses to the more specialist interventions can be monitored.

TABLE 9.1

Effective pedagogic strategies for children with SSLD

| Examples of pedagogic strategies | Continua of strategies for perceived attainment levels | | Experimental evidence demonstrating relevance for children with SSLD |
	High intensity	Low intensity	
Provide opportunities for transfer	Explicit and teacher-led	Autonomous—teacher-led	Teaching grammar to school-aged children (Ebbels, 2007)
Provide examples to learn concepts	Many and varied, but maximal difference on single criterion stressed	Few examples provided	Children benefited from frequent and widely spaced presentations for verb learning (Riches, Tomasello, & Conti-Ramsden, 2005)
Provision of practice to achieve mastery	Extensive and varied	Little	Children performed significantly better in a morpheme acquisition task in an imitation condition than a simple exposure condition (Connell & Addison Stone, 1992)
Provision of task-linked feedback	Immediate, frequent, explicit, focused, and extrinsic	Deferred moving to self-evaluation	Facilitating the correction of reading miscues during the oral reading of children with SLI (Kouri, Selle, & Riley, 2006)
Checking for preparedness of the next stage of learning	Explicit and frequent teacher monitoring emphasized	Fleeting (by teacher) self-monitoring stressed	
Shape task structure	Small discrete steps, short-term objectives emphasized	Larger steps, longer-term goals emphasized	

After Lewis & Norwich (2005).

The introduction of tiered interventions requires that specialists work in a collaborative format to establish the intervention in the mainstream classroom (Kovaleski, 2002). This ensures treatment fidelity and overcomes ad hoc solutions to children's difficulties (Flugum & Reschly, 1994). This stepwise system means that interventions are evaluated at each stage. "Response to Intervention" measures can provide both data on effective interventions for children with language learning problems and a rationale for providing more specialist services or support. An intervention-oriented service delivery is thereby constructed (Reschly & Ysseldyke, 2002).

With the Response to Intervention approach there is general agreement that classroom instruction must be adequate in the first instance and that interventions should occur regardless of student category; however, there is less agreement about whether Tier 2 interventions should be generic or specialized and at what point treatment resistors should be identified. The model also has potential implications for collaboration between professionals. Thus, greater "value-added" may be provided by involvement of SLTs in early phases of education. In the later phases of compulsory education, literacy experts and subject specialists may provide greater "value-added" for pupils.

There are a number of strengths of this approach for children with SSLD. First, it addresses the range of additional problems experienced by children with SSLD, and their needs are targeted directly. It is based on children's language learning needs in the educational setting and thereby circumvents some of the problems with diagnosis. The decision about support is based on the child's progress and is therefore less susceptible to the vagaries of different service models. It also has the potential for providing clinicians with a method of allocating limited resources, and it is not limited by the child's placement.

By corollary, there are a number of significant challenges. The success of the approach is premised on educational staff and therapists working together, and there are well-documented difficulties with this. Monitoring change depends on the design of appropriate criterion-based measures to evaluate change and requires reliable and valid indicators of language skills beyond the age of 5. It is not clear that such measures exist. Implementing Tier 1 levels of teaching is dependent on a skilled workforce, and there is a well-documented gap in teachers' knowledge and understanding of the different kinds of special needs (Scruggs & Mastropeiri, 1996), and SSLD in particular (Dockrell & Lindsay, 2001). Given the level of responsibility placed on teaching assistants for many pupils, their lack of training is a major concern for successful undertaking of a pedagogic role (Blatchford, Russell, Bassett, Brown, & Martin, 2004; Riggs & Mueller, 2001).

There are also challenges in evaluating research to introduce evidence-based practice at Tiers 2 and 3 (Fey, 2006; Gillam & Gillam, 2006).

CONCLUSIONS

This chapter has explored the challenges of meeting the educational needs of children with SSLD. The current analysis suggests that the key dimension for raising the achievements of the children is *how* teaching occurs, rather than *where* teaching occurs. A number of implications follow from this analysis. A basic prerequisite is the provision of sufficiently intensive and monitored support. This requires teachers who are trained and sensitive to the needs of diverse learners and are experienced and knowledgeable in implementing appropriate pedagogical modifications. Moreover, some teaching adaptations may require reduced pupil/teacher ratios and specialist training. Support provided depends on the identification of pupil's individual needs, and addressing these needs should be complemented by working with SLTs and using interventions that are effective and linked to the children's educational priorities. Both education staff and SLTs will require an expertise in ensuring the fidelity of interventions and appropriate monitoring techniques.

This chapter has focused solely on the academic dimensions of a pupil's schooling. The extent to which such conclusions hold for areas of social and emotional development, behavioral challenges, independence, and self-esteem are yet to be evaluated.

ACKNOWLEDGMENTS

We would like to thank the organizations that have funded the research reported in this chapter: Gatsby Foundation, Economic Social Research Council, Nuffield Foundation, and the

Department for Education and Skills/Department for Children, Schools, and Families. The project would have been impossible without the time and commitment of the professionals, parents, and pupils involved. Special thanks to the steering group and Professor Klaus Wedell for continued support and guidance.

NOTE

1 In the United Kingdom, the term "moderate learning difficulty" refers to children who have attainments below expected levels in most areas of the curriculum and have greater difficulty than peers in acquiring basic literacy and numeracy skills and in understanding concepts. They may also have associated speech-language delay.

REFERENCES

Anderson, J. R. (1990). *The adaptive character of thought.* Hove, UK: Lawrence Erlbaum Associates.

Aram, D. M., Morris, R., & Hall, N. E. (1993). Clinical and research congruence in identifying children with specific language impairment. *Journal of Speech and Hearing Research, 36,* 580–591.

Archibald, L. M., & Gathercole, S. E. (2006). Prevalence of SLI in language resource units. *Journal of Research in Special Educational Needs, 6*(1), 3–10.

Beitchman, J. H., Wilson, B., Brownlie, E. B., Inglis, A., & Lancee, W. (1996). Long-term consistency in speech/language profiles: II. Behavioral, emotional, and social outcomes. *Journal of the American Academy of Child and Adolescent Psychiatry, 35,* 815–825.

Bishop, D. V. M., & Clarkson, B. (2003). Written language as a window into residual language deficits: A study of children with persistent and residual speech and language impairments. *Cortex, 39,* 215–237.

Blatchford, P., Russell, A., Bassett, P., Brown, P., &

Martin, C. (2004). *The effects and role of teaching assistants in English primary schools (Years 4 to 6) 2000–2003. Results from the Class size and Pupil-Adult Ratios (CSPAR) Project, Research Report 605.* London: Department for Education and Skills.

Botting, N. (2005). Non-verbal cognitive development and language impairment. *Journal of Child Psychology and Psychiatry, 46*(3), 317–326.

Brown, A. L. (1988). Motivation to learn and understand: On taking charge of one's own learning. *Cognition and Instruction, 5,* 311–321.

Catts, H. W., Fey, M. E., Tomblin, J. B., & Zhang, X. (2002). A longitudinal investigation of reading outcomes in children with language impairments. *Journal of Speech, Language, and Hearing Research, 45,* 1142–1157.

Cigman, R. (2007). *Included or excluded? The challenge of the mainstream for some SEN children* (pp. 15–22). London: Routledge.

Cole, K. N., Dale, P. S., & Mills, P. E. (1992). Stability of the intelligence quotient–language quotient relationship: Is discrepancy modeling based on a myth? *American Journal of Mental Retardation, 97,* 131–143.

Connell, P., & Addison Stone, C. (1992). Morpheme learning of children with specific language impairment under controlled instructional conditions. *Journal of Speech and Hearing Research, 35,* 844–852.

Conti-Ramsden, G., & Botting, N. (1999). Classification of children with specific language impairment. *Journal of Speech, Language, and Hearing Research, 42,* 1195–1204.

Conti-Ramsden, G., Crutchley, A. C., & Botting, N. (1997). The extent to which psychometric tests differentiate subgroups of children with specific language impairment. *Journal of Speech and Hearing Research, 4,* 765–777.

Cowan, R., Donlan, C., Newton, E. J., & Lloyd, D. (2005). Number skills and knowledge in children with specific language impairment. *Journal of Educational Psychology, 97,* 732–744.

Department for Education and Skills. (2005). *Statistics of education: Schools in England* (National Statistics First release No. SFR 24/2005). London: Author.

Dockrell, J. E., George, R., Lindsay, G. A., & Roux, J. (1997). Professionals' understanding of specific language impairments: Implications for assessment and identification. *Educational Psychology in Practice, 13,* 27–35.

Dockrell, J. E., & Law, J. (2007). Measuring and understanding patterns of change in intervention studies with children: Implications for evidence based practice. *Evidence Based Communication, Assessment and Intervention, 1*, 86–97.

Dockrell, J. E., & Lindsay, G. A. (2001). Children with specific speech and language difficulties: The teachers' perspective. *Oxford Review of Education, 27*(3), 369–394.

Dockrell, J. E., & Lindsay, G. (2007). Identifying the educational and social needs of children with specific speech and language difficulties on entry to secondary school. *Educational and Child Psychology, 24*, 100–114.

Dockrell, J. E., Lindsay, G. A., Connelly, V., & Mackie, C. (2007). Profiling the written language difficulties of children with language and communication problems, *Exceptional Children, 73*, 147–164.

Dockrell, J. E, Lindsay, G., Letchford, B., & Mackie, C. (2006). Educational provision for children with specific speech and language difficulties: Perspectives of speech and language therapist managers. *International Journal of Language and Communication Disorders, 41*, 423–440.

Dunsmuir, S., Clifford, V., & Took, S. (2006). Collaboration between educational psychologists and speech and language therapists: Barriers and opportunities. *Educational Psychology in Practice, 22*, 125–140.

Dyson, A., Farrell, P., Polat, F., Hutcheson, G., & Gallannaugh, F. (2004). *Inclusion and pupil achievement* (Research Report RR578). London: Department for Education and Skills.

Ebbels, S. (2007). Teaching grammar to school aged children with specific language impairment using Shape Coding. *Child Language, Teaching, and Therapy, 23*, 67–93.

Ebbels, S., van der Lely, H., & Dockrell, J. E. (2007). Intervention for verb argument structure in children with persistent SLI: A randomized control trial. *Journal of Speech, Language, and Hearing Research, 50*, 1330–1349.

Fey, M. (2006). Commentary on "Making evidence-based decisions about child language intervention in schools" by Gillam & Gillam. *Language, Speech, and Hearing Services in Schools, 37*, 316–319.

Flugum, K. R., & Reschly, D. J. (1994). Prereferral interventions: Quality indices and outcomes. *Journal of School Psychology, 32*, 1–14.

Fuchs, D., Mock, D., Morgan, P., & Young, C. (2003). Responsiveness-to-intervention: Definitions, evidence, and implications for the learning disabilities construct. *Learning Disabilities: Research and Practice, 18*(3), 157–171.

Fujiki, M., Brinton, B., & Clarke, D. (2002). Emotion regulation in children with specific language impairment. *Language, Speech, and Hearing Services in Schools, 33*, 102–111.

Gillam, S. L., & Gillam, R. (2006). Making evidence-based decisions about child language intervention in schools. *Language, Speech, and Hearing Services in Schools, 37*, 304–315.

Gillon, G. (2000). The efficacy of phonological awareness intervention for children with spoken language. *Language, Speech, and Hearing Services in Schools, 31*, 126–141.

Hill, E. (2004). Non-specific nature of specific language impairment: A review of the literature with regard to concomitant motor impairments. *International Journal of Language and Communication Disorders, 36*, 149–171.

House of Commons Education and Skills Committee. (2006). *Special Educational. Needs. Third Report of Session 2005–06*. London: The Stationery Office

Hutt, G. J., & Donlan, C. (1987). *Adequate provision? A survey of language units*. London: ICAN.

Justice, L. (2006). Evidence-based practice, response to intervention and the prevention of reading difficulties. *Language, Speech, and Hearing Services in Schools, 37*, 284–295.

Kamhi, A. (1998). Trying to make sense of developmental language disorders. *Language, Speech, and Hearing Services in Schools, 29*, 35–44.

Kouri, T., Selle, C., & Riley, S. (2006). Comparison of meaning and graphophonemic feedback strategies for guided reading instruction with language delays. *American Journal of Speech-Language Pathology, 15*, 236–246.

Kovaleski, J. F. (2002). Best practices in operating prereferral intervention teams. In A. Thomas & J. Grimes (Eds.), *Best practices in school psychology* (Vol. 4, pp. 645–656). Washington, DC: National Association of School Psychologists.

Lahey, M. (1990). Who shall be called language disordered? Some reflections and one perspective. *Journal of Speech Hearing Research, 55*, 612–620.

Law, J., Boyle, J., Harris, F., Harkness, A., & Nye, C. (2000). The prevalence and the natural history of primary speech and language delay: Findings from a systematic review of the literature. *International Journal of Language and Communication Disorders, 35*(2), 165–188.

Leonard, L. B. (1997). *Children with specific language impairment*. Cambridge, MA: MIT Press.

Lewis, B., & Freebairn, L. (1992). Residential effects of pre-school phonology disorder in grade school, adolescence and adulthood. *Journal of Speech and Hearing Research, 35,* 819–831.

Lewis, A., & Norwich, B. (Eds.). (2005). *Special teaching for special children? Pedagogies for inclusion.* Maidenhead, UK: Open University.

Lindsay, G. (2003). Inclusive education: A critical perspective. *British Journal of Special Education, 30,* 3–12.

Lindsay, G. (2007). Educational psychology and the effectiveness of inclusive education/mainstreaming. *British Journal of Educational Psychology, 77,* 1–24.

Lindsay, G., & Dockrell, J. E. (2005). *Educational provision for children with specific speech and language difficulties: The identification of good practice. Report to the Nuffield Foundation.* Coventry, UK: CEDAR, University of Warwick.

Lindsay, G., Dockrell, J. E. Mackie, C., & Letchford, B. (2005a). Local Educational Authorities' approaches to provision for children with specific speech and language difficulties in England and Wales. *European Journal of Special Needs Education, 20,* 329–345.

Lindsay, G., Dockrell, J. E., Mackie, C., & Letchford, B. (2005b). The roles of specialist provision for children with specific speech and language difficulties in England and Wales: A model for inclusion. *Journal of Research in Special Educational Needs, 5,* 88–96.

Lindsay, G., Dockrell, J., & Strand, S. (2007). The behaviour of children with specific speech and language difficulties: Follow-up age 8–12 years. *British Journal of Educational Psychology, 77,* 811–828.

Mroz, M. (2006). Providing training in speech and language for education professionals: Challenges, support and the view from the ground. *Child Language Teaching and Therapy, 22,* 155–176.

Nation, K., Clarke, P., Marshall, C., & Durand, M. (2004). Hidden language impairments in children. *Journal of Speech, Language, and Hearing Research, 47,* 1411–1423.

Norbury, C. F. (2004). Factors supporting idiom comprehension in children with communication disorders. *Journal of Speech, Language, and Hearing Research, 47,* 1179–1193.

Office of Her Majesty's Chief Inspector. (2006). *The annual report of Her Majesty's Chief Inspector of Schools 2004/5.* London: Ofsted.

Palikara, O., Lindsay, G., Cullen, M.-A., & Dockrell, J. E. (2007). Working together? The practice of educational psychologists and speech and language therapists with children with specific speech and language difficulties. *Educational and Child Psychology, 24,* 77–88.

Radford, J., Ireson, J., & Mahon, M. (2006). Triadic dialogue in oral communication tasks: What are the implications for language learning? *Language and Education, 20,* 191–210.

Rapin, I., & Allen, D. A. (1987). Developmental dyspraxia and autism in preschool children: Characteristics and subtypes. In J. Martin, P. Fletcher, P. Grunwell, & D. Hall (Eds.), *Proceedings at the First International Symposium on Specific Speech and Language Disorders in Children* (pp. 20–35). London: Afasic.

Reason, R. (1998). Effective academic interventions in the United Kingdom: Does the "specific" in specific learning difficulties (disabilities) now make a difference to the way we teach? *Educational and Child Psychology, 15,* 71–83.

Reschly, D. J., & Ysseldyke, J. E. (2002). Paradigm shift: The past is not the future. In A. Thomas & J. Grimes (Eds.), *Best practices in school psychology* (Vol. 4, pp. 3–20). Washington, DC: National Association of School Psychologists.

Riches, N., Tomasello, M., & Conti-Ramsden, G. (2005). Verb learning in children with SLI. *Journal of Speech, Language, and Hearing Research, 48,* 1397–1411.

Riggs, C. G., & Mueller, P. H. (2001). Employment and utilization of paraeducators in inclusive settings. *Journal of Special Education, 35,* 54–62.

Rustemier, S. (2002). *Social and educational justice: The human rights framework for inclusion.* Bristol, UK: Centre for Studies on Inclusive Education.

Scruggs, T., & Mastropeiri, M. (1996). Teacher perceptions of mainstreaming and inclusion. *Exceptional Children, 63*(1), 59–74.

Sebba, J., & Sachdev, D. (1997). *What works in inclusive education?* London: Barnardos.

Stothard, S. E., Snowling, M., Bishop, D. V. M., Chipchase, B. B., & Kaplan, C. A. (1998). Language-impaired preschoolers: A follow-up into adolescence. *Journal of Speech, Language, and Hearing Research, 41,* 407–418.

Tomblin, J. B., Records, N. L., Buckwalter, P., Zhang, X., Smith, E., & O'Brien, M. (1997). The prevalence of specific language impairment in kindergarten children. *Journal of Speech, Language, and Hearing Research, 40,* 1245–1260.

Tomblin, B., & Zhang, X. (2006). The dimensionality of language ability in school age children. *Journal of Speech, Language, and Hearing Research, 49,* 1193–1208.

Tomlinson, J. (1997). Inclusive learning: The report of the Committee of Inquiry into post school education of those with learning difficulties and/or disabilities in England 1996. *European Journal of Special Educational Needs, 12,* 184–196.

Van Weerdenburg, M., Verhoeven, L., & Van Balkom, H. (2006). Towards a typology of specific language impairment. *Child: Care, Health and Development, 32*(4), 504–505.

Vaughn, S., & Fuchs, L. S. (2003). Redefining learning disabilities as inadequate response to instruction: The promise and potential problems. *Learning Disabilities Research & Practice, 18,* 137–146.

Vaughn, S., Linan-Thompson, S., & Hickman, P. (2003). Response to instruction as a means of identifying students with reading/learning disabilities. *Exceptional Children, 69*(4), 391–409.

Walsh, R. (2005). Meaning and purpose: A conceptual model for speech pathology terminology, *Advances in Speech-Language Pathology, 7,* 65–76.

Wedell, K. (2005). Dilemmas in the quest for inclusion. *British Journal of Special Education, 32,* 3–11.

Wellington, W., & Wellington, J. (2002). Children with communication difficulties in mainstream science classrooms. *School Science Review, 83,* 81–92.

Young, A. R., Beitchman, J. H., Johnson, C., Douglas, L., Atkinson, L., Escobar, M., & Wilson, B. (2002). Young adult academic outcomes in a longitudinal sample of early identified language impaired and control children *Journal of Child Psychology and Psychiatry, 43*(5), 635–645.

Zigmond, N. (2003). Where should students with disabilities receive special education services? Is one place better than another? *Journal of Special Education, 37*(3), 193–199.

10

Improving grammatical skill in children with specific language impairment

Susan Ebbels

INTRODUCTION

School-aged children with specific language impairment (SLI) have difficulties with many areas of language, including particular areas of grammar: verb morphology, syntax, and selection of verb arguments. In terms of verb morphology, they omit the past tense *–ed*, as in "yesterday I walk_ home" (Rice, Wexler, & Cleave, 1995; van der Lely & Ullman, 2001), the third-person singular *–s*, as in "he like_ chocolate" (Leonard et al., 2003), and the verb *be*, as in "I drawing a

picture" (Leonard et al., 2003). In terms of syntax, they have difficulties comprehending some syntactic structures such as passives (e.g., *the fish is eaten by the man*—Bishop, 1979; van der Lely, 1996) and datives (e.g., *give the pig the dog*—van der Lely & Harris, 1990). They also have difficulties producing questions (Leonard, 1995; van der Lely & Battell, 2003), in particular object wh-questions, making errors such as "what did they drank?" and "who Mrs. Brown see?" (van der Lely & Battell, 2003). In terms of production of argument structure, they omit obligatory verb arguments; for example, "the woman is placing on the saucepan" (Ebbels, 2005; Thordardottir

& Weismer, 2002), and use fewer optional arguments (Ingham, Fletcher, Schelletter, & Sinka, 1998; King, 2000). In addition, they use fewer verb alternations, for example, *the girl is opening the door* versus *the door is opening* (Schelletter, Sinka, Fletcher, & Ingham, 1998; Thordardottir & Weismer, 2002), and are more likely to link arguments to incorrect syntactic positions with change-of-state verbs, like *fill*, producing errors such as "the lady is filling the sweets into the jar" (Ebbels, Dockrell, & van der Lely, 2007a).

Relatively few published intervention studies including school-aged children with SLI (i.e., over 5 years of age) exist. Some have targeted specific areas of morphology (some of which have not otherwise been noted as areas of difficulty)—for example, use of the verbs *be* and *do* (Leonard, 1975; Mulac & Tomlinson, 1977; Weismer & Branch, 1989), past-tense morphology (Ebbels, 2007), and pronouns (e.g., *they* and *he*—Courtwright & Courtwright, 1976; Weismer & Branch, 1989). Others have targeted formation and/or comprehension of particular syntactic structures—for example, active and passive sentences (Bishop, Adams, & Rosen, 2006; Ebbels & van der Lely, 2001), the dative construction (Ebbels, 2007), questions (e.g., Ebbels, 2007; Ebbels & van der Lely, 2001; Wilcox & Leonard, 1978), and reversible sentences involving prepositions such as *under/over, above/below* (Bishop et al., 2006). Finally, a handful have focused on argument structure (Bryan, 1997; Ebbels, van der Lely, & Dockrell, 2007b; Spooner, 2002). Other intervention studies have had more general or broader targets, often aiming to improve language on a range of standardized tests (e.g., Tallal et al., 1996) or focusing on the method of intervention while covering a wide range of targets (e.g., Camarata, Nelson, & Camarata, 1994; Fey, Cleave, & Long, 1997; Fey, Cleave, Long, & Hughes, 1993; Friedman & Friedman, 1980).

The majority of published intervention studies have indicated that intervention is generally successful, regardless of the targets or methods used. However, a few important exceptions exist: these are often the studies with more rigorous designs, where the success of an intervention is harder to prove. Thus, it is important that more studies with

these types of designs are carried out in order to establish which interventions are most effective.

IMPORTANT FACTORS IN INTERVENTION STUDIES

The ultimate goal of intervention research is to establish which method is the most effective for which areas of language, for which children (in terms of age, severity, and pervasiveness of language difficulties), using which method of delivery. The effectiveness of an intervention is also indicated by whether positive effects are maintained after intervention ceases, whether they generalize to similar linguistic targets, and whether intervention increases the spontaneous use and comprehension of language targets in a range of settings.

In order to establish effectiveness, studies require adequate experimental control. Preferably, children should be assigned randomly to treated and untreated groups. Such a study is often called a *randomized control trial* (RCT). If the treated group make greater progress, this must be because of the treatment. However, it is often difficult to set up an RCT in SLI research. First, there may be practical constraints that prevent assignment from being entirely random. This is a problem, as it means that the groups may differ from one another in ways other than receiving—or not receiving—the treatment. Second, the assessment of the children should be "blind"—that is, it should be conducted by someone who does not know which children have been treated, so that any bias is removed. Failure to achieve either of the above means that confounding variables may be present in the experiment and may be the cause of the improvement in the treated group.

An alternative (but less satisfactory) approach is to use a single group of children and to treat some items or a particular language skill and to use other items or another language skill as untreated controls. This has the merit that no children go untreated but raises other problems. If the design uses treated and untreated items, these should be randomly assigned. In the same way that random assignment ensures that groups of children are similar, this ensures that groups of items are of similar difficulty. If the design uses an untreated skill, there is the challenge of deciding what that skill should be. In both designs, there is the potential that generalization may occur from the treated to the untreated items/ skill. Though clinically desirable, this outcome is, unfortunately, open to the alternative explanation that other factors—such as maturation, other external input, or familiarity with the test items or situation—are responsible for the changes seen during the treatment period. Generalization may be rendered unlikely in designs that compare different language skills by selecting a control skill that is distant from the treated one. Unfortunately, this makes it harder to judge whether the control skill is of a level of difficulty similar to the treated skill. If it is more difficult or developmentally more advanced, an improvement in the treated skill might still be due to maturation, with the control remaining unchanged. A possible solution to this problem is to extend the design to include a period of treatment of the control. Improvement in both areas only at the time when treatment is offered then increases confidence that the results are a direct consequence of the treatment offered.

Group studies are usually seen as preferable to individual case studies because their results can be generalized to other similar children. However, case studies are particularly valuable in the early stages of research, as they can indicate that a particular therapy has potential and deserves further investigation. To be informative, they need to achieve a reasonable level of experimental control. Case studies have particular difficulty controlling for factors such as maturation, other external input, or familiarity with the test items or situation. One way of controlling for these is to have "multiple baselines." In this case, more than one language area or target is tested preintervention. Then, only one area receives intervention, but all are retested. If progress occurs only in the area receiving intervention, other external factors are unlikely to have accounted for this change. The next area can then be targeted. If this also improves, there is stronger evidence that the

intervention itself is causing the change. However, these designs suffer from the same difficulty encountered by group studies where untreated items or language skills are used as controls. If the "control" target improves when it is not targeted, this could be due either to generalization of effects from the intervention (i.e., the intervention is effective) or to other factors external to the intervention (i.e., the intervention is not effective). Again, control targets need to be distant from the intervention targets so that intervention effects do not generalize to them.

Some intervention studies do not use untreated groups of children or targets but, instead, compare two different interventions to see which is more effective. If one of these interventions has already been "tested" in a previous study involving experimental control and has been shown to be effective, the results would determine if the untested intervention is less, more, or equally effective relative to the tested method. However, if neither has been studied previously in a controlled trial, it is impossible to know whether any progress with either or both interventions is due to the intervention itself or to other factors.

In studies without experimental control, the effects of maturation can be controlled for to a certain extent by using standardized measures. If children improve on standard scores, this is usually taken to mean that their progress is greater than would normally be expected for children of the same ages on that test. However, the use of standard scores cannot avoid the influence of other external factors, such as school or parental input or familiarity with the test items or situation. Unless a control group is used, one also cannot know whether improvements are due to practice in doing the test.

In this chapter, I aim to summarize the evidence base regarding intervention for grammatical difficulties for school-aged children (over 5 years of age) with language impairments. I have grouped the studies by the method of intervention, but where other factors, such as targets, diagnosis and age, maintenance and generalization of progress, and method of delivery were reported, these are detailed with each study and also summarized at the end of the chapter. Appendices 10A–10F show summaries of the key features of all the studies discussed, this time grouped by target into tables and sorted within each table according to the likely reliability of the evidence based on the level of experimental control used.

INTERVENTION METHODS

Three main methods of improving grammar in school-aged children with language impairments have been studied: grammar facilitation, acoustically modified speech, and metalinguistic methods.

Grammar facilitation methods

Grammar facilitation methods are the mostly widely investigated in intervention research studies. These methods aim to make target forms more frequent, which is hypothesized to help children identify grammatical rules and give them practice producing forms they tend to omit. The most common grammar facilitation approaches are imitation, modeling, or focused stimulation and recasting.

Imitation

Imitation approaches usually involve the adult providing a nonverbal stimulus (e.g., a picture) and a target form; the child then imitates this and receives reinforcement for correct productions. The adult model and reinforcements are gradually reduced until the child produces the target in response to the nonverbal stimulus only.

A randomized control trial showed that this type of intervention (using the Monterey language program) was effective at improving production of syntax in 24 children aged 5;5–6;10 (Matheny & Panagos, 1978). Another RCT (with nine children aged 4;4–6;3) showed this program plus a home carryover phase (8 × 10 min over 2 weeks conducted by parents) to be effective at improving the production of yes/no questions in the clinic setting (0–100% correct; Mulac & Tomlinson, 1977). However, progress only generalized to other settings for those children who also received

"extended transfer" training: additional sessions with the clinician and parent at outdoor locations and with the parent at home, where the target form was elicited in the context of conversation and stories.

Modeling/focused stimulation with or without evoked production

In modeling and focused stimulation approaches the child is not required to respond, merely to listen to examples of the target structure. Modeling approaches direct the child's attention to the stimuli but do not give any explicit guidance on which particular features to attend to—for example, "listen to *how* I'm asking questions" (Weismer & Branch, 1989). Focused stimulation, in contrast, does not direct the child's attention to the model in any way. Evoked production in response to a picture or situational stimulus may follow the modeling or focused stimulation period. The child does not imitate the precise words used in the model but produces a novel utterance that uses the same rule. Feedback is usually given regarding the correctness of the child's production. The degree of modeling is gradually reduced as the child begins to use the new rule productively.

One study showed that modeling without evoked production was effective in teaching auxiliary *is* and auxiliary inversion to three children with expressive SLI (aged 5;5–6;11), but the addition of evoked production led to a more stable learning pattern (Weismer & Branch, 1989). However, neither method was successful in teaching *"he"* to a fourth child (aged 5;6) who had both expressive and receptive language difficulties.

A study of eight children (aged 5–9 years) found that modeling with evoked production increased the ability of an experimental group to produce *is* and *don't,* whereas a delayed therapy group made no progress (Leonard, 1975). Another study involving 24 children (aged 3;8–8;2) showed that modeling with evoked production increased accuracy of production of wh-questions (Wilcox & Leonard, 1978). A delayed therapy group made no progress until they, too, received therapy. Use of *does* and *is* inversion generalized to other wh- constructions requiring inversion, and participants trained on *where* showed greater use of untrained *wh*-words than those trained on *who* and *what*.

Courtwright and Courtwright (1976) compared the effectiveness of modeling versus imitation methods for teaching eight children (aged 5–10 years) the correct use of *they* in subject position (as opposed to *them*). The children in both groups improved on their initial performance, but those in the modeling group showed greater progress.

Recasting

Recasting methods are designed to be nonintrusive conversational approaches to language teaching. The adult does not initiate the teaching directly, but manipulates play activities to increase the chances of the child using certain targeted grammatical forms. If the child fails to use the target form or makes an error, the adult immediately follows his or her utterance with a modified version that includes the target form (a "recast"). For example, if a child says "teddy fall down," the adult may follow this with "yes, teddy *fell* down." The theory behind this approach is that the child is more likely to be interested in what the adult is saying if it links semantically to the situation and the child's own prior utterance. The immediate contrast between the two forms should also focus the child's attention on the features of the utterances that differ. In addition, the child does not need to parse the adult's meaning and thus should have more processing resources available for analyzing the target form in the recast.

Three studies compared the effectiveness of recasting with imitation at increasing production of a range of morphosyntactic structures in children with SLI (Camarata & Nelson, 1992; Camarata et al., 1994; Nelson, Camarata, Welsh, Butkovsky, & Camarata, 1996). These found that targets treated with either type of intervention improved more than did untreated targets, but recasting was more effective than imitation in promoting *spontaneous* use of target forms. In contrast, imitation led to faster *elicited* production of the target in children aged 4;0–6;10 (Camarata et al., 1994). However, there was evidence of a Target type × Child × Intervention method interaction. Camarata and Nelson (1992) found that children with SLI (aged 4;9–5;11) acquired

the passive construction faster with recasting, whereas they acquired the gerund faster with imitation. Individual variation was revealed in Camarata et al. (1994) when 3 of the 21 participants acquired targets only with imitation and 3 only with recasting.

Modeling/focused stimulation plus recasting

Some intervention studies have used a combination of the methods discussed above. In particular, modeling with evoked production, together with recasting, has been shown to be effective for generalization of newly learned grammatical rules to spontaneous discourse in four children aged 4;6–9;2 with SLI (Culatta & Horn, 1982). Progress on the first grammatical rule targeted for each child was also maintained during intervention on the second rule (3.5–8 weeks). This method was also effective at increasing grammatical accuracy and range in children aged 3;0–5;11 (Tyler, Lewis, Haskill, & Tolbert, 2002) and 30 children aged 3;8–5;10 (Fey et al., 1993, 1997).

The studies by Fey and colleagues investigated the role of parents in the delivery of intervention. Their first study (Fey et al., 1993) revealed a significant effect of intervention, whether delivered by parent or clinician. This contrasted with the children who received no intervention and made very little progress. The children in the clinician group received both individual and group intervention (groups of 4–6 children), whereas those in the parent group had no direct therapy with the clinician. Instead, the clinician trained the parents to use modeling and recasting. The children in the clinician group made more reliable progress than did those in the parent group. However, the reason for this is unclear as the interventions differed in content and setting as well as administrator. The primary method used in both groups was modeling and recasting, but the children in the clinician group also carried out imitation drills and participated in groups. Thus, it could be the clinician, the imitation drills, or the group work that was responsible for the more reliable progress in the former group. The parent gains were bimodally distributed; therefore it seems that some child–parent pairs were more successful than others.

However, the authors were unable to establish what variable accounted for this.

The second study (Fey et al., 1997) provided an additional five months' intervention to half of the children in the original study. Again, these children made significant progress, whereas the dismissed group did not. However, this latter group also did not show a decrease in scores, indicating that they maintained the effects of the original intervention, even if they did not continue to improve. Pre- and posttests in both studies analyzed use of grammar in conversation between the child and the parent at the clinic. Therefore, these studies provide information on generalization to spontaneous language and also to different settings for the parent interaction group and to different interlocutors for children in clinician group.

General approaches

Several studies compare general intervention approaches involving a mixture of techniques. However, only one included language-impaired children over 5 years of age with nonverbal IQs in the normal range (Friedman & Friedman, 1980). This study compared two broad intervention approaches with children (aged 3;2–5;9) taught in groups of four. The first was a conversational approach (but included imitation, focused stimulation, elicitation, and recasting); the second, a more structured approach, involved imitation, modeling, reinforcement, and generalization. No main effect of treatment was found; both groups showed equal and significant gains. However, the lower functioning children (in terms of both language and nonverbal IQ) benefited more from the structured approach and the higher functioning children more from the interactive approach. This study therefore highlights the need to consider the relationship between the success of intervention methods and the characteristics of the children involved.

Summary of grammar facilitation approaches

Several studies, including some randomized control trials, have investigated the effectiveness of grammar facilitation methods. These generally indicate that these methods are effective for improving expressive morphology and syntax in preschool and early school-aged children with expressive language delays and disorders. Studies comparing the different methods indicate that modeling is best accompanied by evoked production, and recasting tends to lead to faster generalization to spontaneous speech than does imitation. However, different children and targets appear to respond best to different approaches. Further studies are now needed to establish which child and target characteristics affect responsiveness to different treatment methods.

Acoustically modified speech (including Fast ForWord)

Intervention studies using acoustically modified speech have focused mainly on the processing of sounds and comprehension of spoken language rather than expressive language. They are based on the theory that children with SLI have difficulty processing rapid or brief stimuli (Tallal, Stark, & Mellits, 1985) and aim to improve this underlying deficit by training the auditory system using acoustically modified speech. The children's general language abilities are hypothesized to improve as a direct consequence of their improved temporal processing abilities. Tallal et al. (1996) tested this hypothesis in two studies. In the first, seven children (mean age: 7 years) carried out speech and language listening exercises and listened to children's stories, both recorded with acoustically modified speech for approximately 100 hours over four weeks. The authors reported that the children's language comprehension improved significantly, approaching or exceeding normal limits for their age, whereas they had initially scored 1–3 years below their chronological age. Unfortunately, there were no untreated or differently treated control groups and a very small number of participants. Thus we cannot be certain that the reported improvements are the result of the intervention. In addition, all data are given in age equivalents instead of standard scores, and hence we do not know how the pretherapy scores compared with the expected range for their age; these may also have been within normal limits. The results are therefore difficult to interpret and may be misleading.

Tallal et al.'s (1996) second study explicitly investigated the effect of modified speech by comparing the language gains in two groups of children (aged 5–10 years), carrying out the same tasks as in Study 1, either with or without modified speech (again, no untreated control groups were included). Both groups made significant progress, but the group trained with modified speech made significantly more progress than the other group. The authors also stated that progress was "substantially maintained" six weeks later, although test performance at follow-up was not reported.

Further studies (Tallal, 2000; Tallal, Merzenich, Miller, & Jenkins, 1998) involved over 500 children aged 4–14 years who scored at least 1 standard deviation below the mean on one or more standardized language tests. This was the only criterion for inclusion in the study, and the children had a wide range of diagnoses. The authors reported that approximately 90% of children who "complied with the study protocol" showed significantly improved performance (at least 1 *SD* change from pretraining to posttraining) on standardized speech, language, and processing measures, regardless of diagnosis. However, no control data were provided with which to compare progress. Also, they do not clarify what proportion of the 500 children originally included failed to "comply with the study protocol." The graphs showing the change from pre- to posttherapy only show 171 participants, leaving 329 children unaccounted for. Without further information about these children, it is difficult to give any meaningful interpretation to the results.

Independent case study investigations of language progress following Fast ForWord intervention (Friel-Patti, DesBarres, & Thibodeau, 2001; Gillam, Crofford, Gale, & Hoffman, 2001; Loeb, Stoke, & Fey, 2001) all confirmed that the majority of children make some progress with some areas of language, although the changes were less dramatic than in Tallal et al.'s (1996) original study, and the children with the most severe language impairments appeared to benefit the least (Friel-Patti et al., 2001; Gillam et al., 2001). These studies address some of the concerns regarding the use of age-equivalent scores and the lack of data regarding maintenance of gains in the original studies. Friel-Patti et al. (2001) found that while age-equivalent scores improved, these changes were not clinically significant (i.e., did not exceed the standard error of measurement of the tests). Loeb et al. (2001) found that only half the gains were maintained three months after the intervention was completed. They also found that improvements on standardized tests did not generalize to spontaneous speech—that is, changes in comprehension did not generalize to expressive language.

The core hypothesis of the Fast ForWord program (that language progress results from improved auditory processing) is also brought into question by two of these studies: Loeb et al. (2001) found that those children who made no progress in auditory processing still progressed in grammar, while Gillam et al. (2001) found very similar changes in language performance for children using a different set of computer programs focused on language, but without modified speech. They suggested that the changes in performance could be due to improved attention, listening, and response rates (engendered by both computer programs), rather than to improved auditory processing.

An independent randomized control trial (Cohen et al., 2005) compared the progress of children with receptive and expressive SLI (aged 6–10 years) using Fast ForWord with those using other computer-based language programs and a no-treatment control group. All three groups made significant gains in language scores, but there was no additional benefit seen for either group using computer-based intervention. The authors therefore concluded that Fast ForWord (and the other computer games) provided no additional benefit to the children over and above the benefit gained from their current therapy and educational support. Similarly, Bishop et al. (2006) also found no difference between children (aged 8–13 years) trained either with or without modified speech and untrained children who received only their "standard" therapy package.

In summary, the original studies using the Fast ForWord approach had several weaknesses, and independent case studies have questioned their findings. Recent randomized control trials indicate that Fast ForWord and similar programs with acoustically modified speech provide no additional benefit over standard therapy and educational support.

Metalinguistic approaches

Metalinguistic approaches provide explicit teaching of language, often in the context of specific visual cues. An early paper (Lea, 1965) indicated that color-coding the parts of speech (using the "Color Pattern Scheme") could help children with "receptive aphasia" to produce written language despite extremely limited comprehension and expressive spoken language. Kaldor, Robinson, and Tanner (2001) described use of colored shapes ("Spotlights on Language Communication System") to aid language development in children with SLI, some of whom had characteristics associated with the autistic spectrum. Unfortunately the evidence for both the Color Pattern Scheme and Spotlights is anecdotal, and no studies have been published regarding their efficacy. A study with secondary-aged children (aged 9;0–12;1) targeted the use of subordinating conjunctions (Hirschman, 2000). However, although the children were described as having SLI, they did not meet standard diagnostic criteria, as their average *verbal* IQ was over 100; therefore this study is not discussed further. The effects of two metalinguistic approaches (Colourful Semantics and Shape Coding) that have been studied in children with SLI are discussed below.

Colourful Semantics

The Colourful Semantics system (Bryan, 1997) color codes thematic roles in sentences in order to help children identify thematic roles and create a variety of argument structures. Several case studies have been carried out using this or similar methods (Bryan, 1997; Guendouzi, 2003; Spooner, 2002), but unfortunately none include experimental controls. Hence it is difficult to know how much of the progress is directly related to the intervention. Bryan's (1997) original study of a child aged 5;10 showed that after three months of intervention, his age-equivalent

score on a simple test of expressive language had increased by 12–18 months, the majority of his sentences contained the correct argument structure, and he used more verbs. She also reported that progress generalized to spontaneous language during "news time." Spooner (2002) found that one child (aged 6;3) used more argument and adjunct phrases after five months of intervention using this method. Another child (aged 9;9) seemed to benefit less, but both children improved their use of conjunctions, verb morphology, and pronouns and in their ability to retrieve known words. This progress was also evident on formal language tests.

Guendouzi (2003) considered changes in expressive language in the spontaneous speech of two children. They received therapy that required them to "build up sentences using color-coded word cards to represent the various semantic clausal roles." Therefore, although Bryan's (1997) study is not mentioned and very few details are given of the content and delivery of the therapy, this study appears to use a method similar to Colourful Semantics. One participant (aged 7;0) made some progress, while the other (aged 6;10) did not. Guendouzi analyzed the children's language in detail and concluded that the method was not suited to the younger child, who appeared to have word-finding difficulties rather than a syntactic impairment.

Shape Coding

The Shape Coding system (Ebbels, 2007) uses a combination of shapes, colors, and arrows to indicate phrases, parts of speech, and morphology, respectively. It was originally conceived as a combination of the "Color Pattern Scheme" and "Colourful Semantics" systems, but it has since been developed so it can also show complex sentence structures and verb morphology. Each shape is linked to a question word, color, and symbol (Writing with Symbols, 2000: Widget Software, 2008). Examples of Shape Coding for one active and one passive sentence are shown in Figure 10.1. The efficacy of this system has been investigated for teaching verb argument structure, expression, and comprehension of passives and

FIGURE 10.1

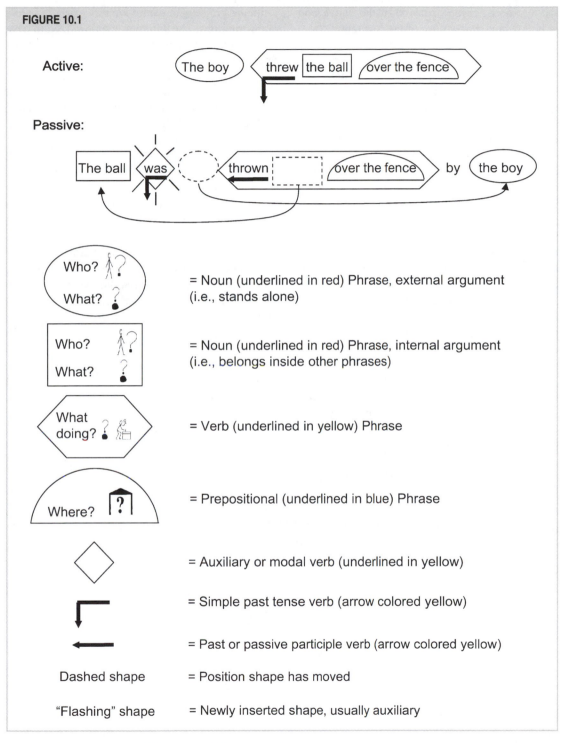

Example (plus key) of Shape Coded active and passive sentences.

wh-questions, comprehension of the dative construction, and written use of the past tense.

A randomized control trial (Ebbels et al., 2007a) with 27 secondary-aged pupils (aged 11;0–16;1) targeted verb argument structure. This study compared therapy using the Shape Coding system with therapy focusing on verb semantic representations and a control therapy (focused on inferencing, which was not predicted to have any effect on verb argument structure). Both the Shape Coding and verb semantic methods were based on detailed hypotheses regarding the underlying reasons for the participants' difficulties with verb argument structure, and both groups made significant progress, particularly in linking arguments to the correct syntactic positions (i.e., reducing errors such as "she is filling the water into the glass"). Progress generalized to control verbs and was maintained three months after intervention ceased. The Shape Coding group also used more optional arguments after therapy. The control group showed no progress in verb argument structure.

Ebbels and van der Lely (2001) investigated the efficacy of the Shape Coding system for improving expression and comprehension of passives and wh-questions using four case studies (aged 11–14 years) in a multiple baseline design. Three of the four participants showed significant progress (which was maintained 10 weeks later) in both their comprehension and their production of passives. Only two had difficulties comprehending wh-questions pretherapy, and both showed significant progress in this area (which was also maintained at follow-up). All four children showed short-term progress with the production of wh-questions, but only one child maintained this at a significant level by follow-up. The three participants who responded best participated in a follow-up study (Ebbels, 2007) targeting comprehension of the dative construction (e.g., *the boy is giving the girl the rabbit*) and "wh-" comparative questions (e.g., *what is bigger than a cat?* vs. *what is a cat bigger than?*). All three received intervention on datives, but, due to a change of therapist, only two received intervention for wh-comparatives. Two of the three participants showed sig-

nificant progress in their comprehension of dative constructions. The third was hypothesized to have additional short-term memory difficulties, which made progress on this area more difficult, due to the need to remember the order of three key nouns. However, this participant made significant progress in comprehension of "wh-" comparative questions, as did the other participant who was taught this structure.

The Shape Coding studies discussed above all involved individual therapy sessions. However, a study on the use of the past tense in writing (Ebbels, 2007) involved group teaching. A class of nine pupils (aged 11–13 years) were taught using the Shape Coding system during English lessons. Six used the past tense more after the class sessions, but two more made progress only when they received additional intervention in a pair. Possible explanations are either that they merely needed more intervention time, or that they needed a more individualized approach, which could be provided for a pair, but not in a group of nine. Unfortunately, no control group was included in this study; its findings should therefore be treated with caution.

Summary of metalinguistic approaches
Studies of metalinguistic approaches indicate that they can be effective for school-aged children with language impairments. However, only a limited number of areas of language have been studied in controlled experiments. Therefore, further work is necessary to establish for which children and targets these approaches are most effective.

FACTORS INFLUENCING INTERVENTION SUCCESS

Targets of intervention
Grammar facilitation methods have focused on the production of a wide range of morphological and syntactic targets, and some (e.g., Culatta & Horn, 1982; Mulac & Tomlinson, 1977) have focused on generalization of grammatical tar-

gets to spontaneous speech. However, none has considered language comprehension. Studies using acoustically modified speech have (with the exception of Bishop et al., 2006) focused on general language abilities, not specific morphological or syntactic targets. Positive effects of modified speech have been reported in some studies, particularly for comprehension, although it is unclear whether these effects were due to the modified speech itself. However, two randomized control trials failed to find any difference in progress made by those receiving intervention with or without modified speech, and these two groups did not differ from controls who only received standard intervention. Studies of metalinguistic methods have mainly focused on specific areas of grammar. However, some studies have measured the effects of these methods on general expressive language (Guendouzi, 2003; Spooner, 2002).

In general, all published studies show positive results for both grammar facilitation and metalinguistic methods, but further research is needed for both methods. The efficacy of metalinguistic methods has been studied only in a limited number of areas of grammar, and no data are currently available on the efficacy of grammar facilitation methods on comprehension. The data on acoustically modified speech are more mixed, with several studies indicating that this method may not provide additional benefits over "standard" therapy provision.

Diagnosis and age

Studies of grammar facilitation methods have focused only on expressive language and included many children whose comprehension is age-appropriate. In contrast, the participants in studies of acoustically modified speech and metalinguistic methods have usually had both comprehension and expressive language difficulties. However, this could be a function of age, as those children whose language difficulties persist are often those who have more pervasive difficulties (Bishop & Edmundson, 1987). The majority of grammar facilitation studies have been carried out with children under the age of 7, often with preschool-

ers, although a few studies using these methods include children aged between 7 and 10 years (e.g., Courtwright & Courtwright, 1976; Culatta & Horn, 1982; Leonard, 1975; Wilcox & Leonard, 1978). Studies using acoustically modified speech mainly involve children in the primary years (5–10 years), although some (e.g., Tallal et al., 1998) include children up to the age of 14 years. Studies of the metalinguistic method of Colourful Semantics have involved children aged 5–9 years, and those of the Shape Coding method have involved secondary-aged children (aged 11–16 years).

The differing age ranges used in studies of the different methods make the efficacy of these methods difficult to compare. It is possible that different methods are more appropriate and more effective for children at different ages and for different language profiles. Thus, it may be that grammar facilitation methods work best with younger, less impaired children, some of whom may only have a language delay. On the other hand, metalinguistic methods may work better with school-aged children with more pervasive and persistent language impairments. Further studies comparing methods within particular age groups and levels of impairment are now required.

Maintenance of progress

Very few studies have considered whether progress made immediately after intervention was maintained at the same level after a period without intervention, or indeed whether the participants continued to improve. Fey et al.'s (1997) grammar facilitation study included children who had participated in their 1993 study but did not have any additional intervention. This group showed no change after the additional period, showing that their initial progress was maintained but they did not continue to make progress after intervention ceased. In terms of acoustically modified speech methods, Tallal et al. (1996) claimed that progress was maintained six weeks after intervention ceased, but they did not provide any evidence for this. However, Loeb et al. (2001) found that 61% of the language gains made were maintained after three months.

One metalinguistic study (Ebbels et al., 2007b) reported no difference in measures taken immediately after intervention and three months later—that is, progress was maintained but did not continue to improve. Of the four case studies reported in Ebbels and van der Lely (2001), two participants maintained progress made in comprehension and production of passives and comprehension of wh-questions up to 30 weeks after intervention ceased; however, they did not maintain their progress in the production of wh-questions. One participant made some progress in comprehension of passives immediately post-therapy, but his scores continued to rise in the 20 weeks after the therapy on passives ceased. His progress on the production of passives was less dramatic and not maintained at follow-up, but he did maintain progress in the production of some types of wh-questions. The fourth participant made limited progress and did not maintain this progress after intervention ceased.

In summary, we have indications for all therapy methods that progress can be maintained but does not usually continue after intervention has ceased. However, more evidence needs to be gathered in this area, particularly regarding the relationship between the degree of progress and maintenance of that progress and whether it is easier to maintain progress for some targets than for others.

Generalization of progress

Several studies of grammar facilitation methods have found that progress generalized from specific items to other related items (Wilcox & Leonard, 1978), to spontaneous speech (e.g., Camarata & Nelson, 1992; Camarata et al., 1994; Culatta & Horn, 1982; Friedman & Friedman, 1980), and even to phonological skills (Matheny & Panagos, 1978; Tyler et al., 2002). Studies using modified speech found effects on general language comprehension tests (Gillam et al., 2001; Tallal, 2000; Tallal et al., 1996, 1998) but not on spontaneous speech (Friel-Patti et al., 2001; Loeb et al., 2001). Studies of metalinguistic methods found intervention on verb argument structure generalized to other verbs (Ebbels et al., 2007b) and to general language tests and sponta-

neous speech (Bryan, 1997; Guendouzi, 2003; Spooner, 2002).

Very few studies have considered whether progress generalized beyond the setting where the intervention took place. Fey et al. (1993, 1997) took language samples in the clinic during play between the children and their parent. For the group who had intervention at home, the testing and intervention settings differed, but the adult remained constant. For those who had the clinic intervention, the setting remained constant, but the adult differed. Both groups made progress, and therefore we can conclude that progress generalized across settings for one group and across interlocutors for the other group. Mulac and Tomlinson (1977) took language samples both in the clinic and at home and found that all children improved in the clinic setting, but only those who had also had intervention at home improved at home. Thus, it seems that progress was limited to the settings where intervention had taken place. Loeb et al. (2001) found very little generalization of Fast ForWord training to other settings, as measured by teacher and parent questionnaires. No studies were found where both setting and interlocutor differed between testing and intervention. Thus, data is required to show the extent to which grammar intervention generalizes away from the intervention setting and the adult who delivered the intervention.

Methods of delivery

The overwhelming majority of studies aiming to improve children's grammatical abilities involve one-to-one delivery of intervention by a clinician or (for the modified speech studies) by a computer. There are, however, a few exceptions. A few studies have delivered intervention—at least partly—in groups (for past tense, see Ebbels, 2007; see also Fey et al., 1993, 1997; Friedman & Friedman, 1980). Ebbels (2007) found that most pupils made progress in the group, but two made little progress until given additional therapy as a pair. Fey et al. (1993, 1997) contrasted two therapy packages—one delivered directly by a clinician (individually and in groups) and one via parents. The children in the clinician group made more reliable progress than did those in the parent group. However, the reason for this is unclear, as the interventions differed in content as well as administrator. Mulac and Tomlinson (1977) gave parents exercises to do with their children in addition to one-to-one clinician-directed intervention. This led to improved generalization of new skills to the home setting.

No studies were found in which grammatical therapy proved to be effective when delivered by teachers or assistants, despite the fact that it is becoming increasingly common in the United Kingdom for therapy to be delivered in groups by assistants. However, this method of delivery can be effective for teaching reading and vocabulary to primary-school children if assistants are given a high level of training, supervision, and support (Snowling & Hulme, chapter 11, this volume). Studies are therefore urgently required to establish whether such methods can be effective for improving children's grammatical difficulties and, if so, what level of training, supervision, and support are required.

FUTURE RESEARCH IMPLICATIONS

Many areas of grammar have been targeted in intervention studies, but many gaps remain. In particular, grammar facilitation methods have focused only on expressive language, primarily with younger children. In contrast, metalinguistic methods have focused on both comprehension and production skills, but only a few aspects of language have been investigated and mostly with older children. Thus, both of these methods should be investigated further with different age groups, targeting both comprehension and production of language.

The few studies that measured maintenance of progress indicate that it is usually maintained. However, Ebbels and van der Lely (2001) demonstrated that maintenance of new skills can vary between children and between language targets within the same child. Therefore, studies

that investigate this variability systematically are required. Few studies have investigated whether progress made during treatment generalized to spontaneous speech, to broader language abilities, or to related linguistic targets. Furthermore, no study was found that included measures of progress in spontaneous speech—or, indeed, comprehension—taken in settings *and* with interlocutors that differed from those of the intervention. Mulac and Tomlinson (1977) indicated that for effects to generalize to different settings, specific generalization work needs to occur in those settings. Therefore, it cannot be assumed that therapy gains will generalize outside the therapeutic setting. This is obviously an area that needs to be addressed with some urgency to establish how wide-ranging the effects of therapy are.

Most studies have investigated the effectiveness of one-to-one clinician-led therapy. A few measured the effectiveness of therapy delivered by a clinician in a group or by the child's parent. No published studies were found that investigated the effectiveness of grammatical intervention delivered by assistants—probably the method of delivery most commonly used in the United Kingdom. However, when addressing this gap in the literature, we need to proceed with care. As argued by Pring (2004) and Robey and Schulz (1998), trials of different methods of delivery need to use intervention methods that have already been proven to be efficacious (preferably in randomized control trials) with the same type of children (in terms of age and diagnosis) and targets. If any of these variables is altered in addition to the method of delivery and the trial is unsuccessful, it will be impossible to know whether it was the method of delivery or the actual intervention itself that was at fault.

CLINICAL IMPLICATIONS

The intervention research base needs further development before clinicians can make reliable judgments regarding the appropriateness of different intervention approaches and methods of delivery for individual children and particular grammatical targets. However, it is important for clinicians to make informed decisions using the best evidence provided by research. I would suggest that clinicians who wish to target the grammatical difficulties of a school-aged child should first establish which areas of grammar are causing difficulties. They should then decide which areas they wish to treat and in which order. These decisions should be based on factors such as functional importance (e.g., the impact of the grammatical deficit on access to the curriculum and friendships), the order in which syntactic forms are acquired in typical development, and a plan of how to proceed from one target to another, as one target may require prior learning of another.

Having decided on the linguistic targets, they should then consider whether any particular method of intervention delivery has been shown to be effective (preferably in a study including experimental control) for that target and for children of a similar age and diagnosis to the child they wish to treat. The studies discussed in this chapter are shown in tables grouped by language target in the Appendices to aid clinicians in this process. The studies are ordered in terms of the level of experimental control provided and hence their reliability.

If no published study matches the particular combination of child and target factors clinicians are presented with, they might be wise to base their therapy on the study that provides the closest fit. In cases where the combinations of variables differ from those in published studies or where the closest study includes no experimental controls, they could consider carrying out a controlled study, either a single case or group study, which could then be published to fill the gap in the literature.

The final step is to choose the method of delivery. The research evidence is primarily based on one-to-one delivery of therapy by a clinician. For a variety of reasons, clinicians may not be able or wish to offer this method of delivery, but they should be aware that a change in the method of delivery may affect the effectiveness of the intervention. In this case, it would of great value to the speech and language therapy community as a whole if they could base their therapy on research that involves children and targets most similar to those they wish to treat and if they could carry out a study evaluating their chosen method of delivery, which would have the potential to fill a large and important gap in the literature.

SUMMARY

The speech and language therapy profession urgently needs more studies of intervention that can be used to inform clinical decisions regarding the best methods of interventions for particular children and their language needs. Due to the small number of studies involving school-aged children, clinicians will inevitably have to base their decisions on a best-fit approach. However, this means that clinicians are constantly carrying out many potential research studies as part of their clinical practice. Thus, it is important that clinicians are given the time and the support necessary to carry out and publish such studies. The result would be a broader evidence base, which would benefit both clinicians and the children we treat.

ACKNOWLEDGMENTS

I would like to thank Tim Pring and Courtenay Norbury for their helpful comments on earlier versions of this chapter.

REFERENCES

Bishop, D. V. M. (1979). Comprehension in developmental language disorders. *Developmental Medicine and Child Neurology, 21*, 225–238.

Bishop, D. V. M., Adams, C. V., & Rosen, S. (2006). Resistance of grammatical impairment to computerized comprehension training in children with specific and non-specific language impairments. *International Journal of Language & Communication Disorders, 41,* 19–40.

Bishop, D. V. M., & Edmundson, A. (1987). Language-impaired 4-year-olds: Distinguishing transient from persistent impairment. *Journal of Speech and Hearing Disorders, 52,* 156–173.

Bryan, A. (1997), Colourful semantics. In S. Chiat, J. Law, & J. Marshall (Eds.), *Language disorders in children and adults: Psycholinguistic approaches to therapy.* London: Whurr.

Camarata, S. M., & Nelson, K. E. (1992). Treatment efficiency as a function of target selection in the remediation of child language disorders. *Clinical Linguistics & Phonetics, 6,* 167–178,

Camarata, S. M., Nelson, K. E., & Camarata, M. N. (1994). Comparison of conversational-recasting and imitative procedures for training grammatical structures in children with specific language impairment. *Journal of Speech and Hearing Research, 37,* 1414–1423.

Cohen, W., Hodson, A., O'Hare, A., Boyle, J., Durrani, T., McCartney, E., et al. (2005). Effects of computer-based intervention using acoustically modified speech (Fast ForWord Language) in severe mixed receptive-expressive language impairment: Outcomes from a randomized control trial. *Journal of Speech, Language, and Hearing Research, 48,* 715–729.

Courtwright, J. A., & Courtwright, I. C. (1976). Imitative modelling as a theoretical base for instructing language-disordered children. *Journal of Speech and Hearing Research, 19,* 651–654.

Culatta, B., & Horn, D. (1982). A program for achieving generalization of grammatical rules to spontaneous discourse. *Journal of Speech and Hearing Disorders, 47,* 174–180.

Ebbels, S. H. (2005). *Argument structure in specific language impairment: From theory to therapy.* Unpublished doctoral thesis, University College London, London.

Ebbels, S. H. (2007). Teaching grammar to school-aged children with specific language impairment using Shape Coding. *Child Language Teaching and Therapy, 23,* 67–93.

Ebbels, S. H., Dockrell, J. E., & van der Lely, H. K. J. (2007a). *Production of change-of-state verbs: A comparison of children with specific language*

impairments and typically developing children. Manuscript submitted for publication.

Ebbels, S. H., & van der Lely, H. (2001). Meta-syntactic therapy using visual coding for children with severe persistent SLI. *International Journal of Language & Communication Disorders, 36,* 345–350.

Ebbels, S. H., van der Lely, H. K. J., & Dockrell, J. E. (2007b). Intervention for verb argument structure in children with persistent SLI: A randomized control trial. *Journal of Speech, Language, and Hearing Research, 50,* 1330–1349.

Fey, M. E., Cleave, P. L., & Long, S. H. (1997). Two models of grammar facilitation in children with language impairments: Phase 2. *Journal of Speech, Language, and Hearing Research, 40,* 5–19.

Fey, M. E., Cleave, P., Long, S. H., & Hughes, D. L. (1993). Two approaches to the facilitation of grammar in children with language impairment: An experimental evaluation. *Journal of Speech and Hearing Research, 36,* 141–157.

Friedman, P., & Friedman, K. (1980). Accounting for individual differences when comparing the effectiveness of remedial language teaching methods. *Applied Psycholinguistics, 1,* 151–170.

Friel-Patti, S., DesBarres, K., & Thibodeau, L. (2001). Case studies of children using Fast ForWord. *American Journal of Speech-Language Pathology, 10,* 203–215.

Gillam, R. B., Crofford, J. A., Gale, M. A., & Hoffman, L. M. (2001). Language change following computer-assisted language instruction with Fast ForWord or Laureate Learning Systems software. *American Journal of Speech-Language Pathology, 10,* 231–247.

Guendouzi, J. (2003). "SLI," a generic category of language impairment that emerges from specific differences: A case study of two individual linguistic profiles. *Clinical Linguistics & Phonetics, 17,* 135–152.

Hirschman, M. (2000). Language repair via metalinguistic means. *International Journal of Language & Communication Disorders, 35,* 251–268.

Ingham, R., Fletcher, P., Schelletter, C., & Sinka, I. (1998). Resultative VPs and specific language impairment. *Language Acquisition, 7,* 87–111.

Kaldor, C., Robinson, P., & Tanner, J. (2001). Turning on the spotlight. *Speech and Language Therapy in Practice* (Summer), 10–13.

King, G. (2000). Verb complementation in language impaired school age children. In M. Aldridge

(Ed.), *Child language* (pp. 84–91), Cleveden, UK: Multilingual Matters.

Lea, J. (1965). A language system for children suffering from receptive aphasia. *Speech Pathology and Therapy, 8*, 58–68.

Leonard, L. B. (1975). Developmental considerations in the management of language disabled children. *Journal of Learning Disabilities, 8*, 44–49.

Leonard, L. B. (1995). Functional categories in the grammars of children with specific language impairment. *Journal of Speech and Hearing Research, 38*, 1270–1283.

Leonard, L. B., Deevy, P., Miller, C., Charest, M., Kurtz, R., & Rauf, L. (2003). The use of grammatical morphemes reflecting aspect and modality by children with specific language impairment. *Journal of Child Language, 30*, 769–795.

Loeb, D. F., Stoke, C., & Fey, M. E. (2001). Language changes associated with Fast ForWord Language: Evidence from case studies. *American Journal of Speech-Language Pathology, 10*, 216–230.

Matheny, N., & Panagos, J. M. (1978). Comparing the effects of articulation and syntax programs on syntax and articulation improvement. *Language, Speech, and Hearing Services in Schools, 9*, 50–56.

Mulac, A., & Tomlinson, C. N. (1977). Generalization of an operant remediation program for syntax with language delayed children. *Journal of Communication Disorders, 10*, 231–243.

Nelson, K. E., Camarata, S. M., Welsh, J., Butkovsky, L., & Camarata, M. (1996). Effects of imitative and conversational recasting treatment on the acquisition of grammar in children with specific language impairment and younger language-normal children. *Journal of Speech and Hearing Research, 39*, 850–859.

Pring, T. (2004). Ask a silly question: Two decades of troublesome trials. *International Journal of Language & Communication Disorders, 39*, 285–302.

Rice, M. L., Wexler, K., & Cleave, P. L. (1995). Specific language impairment as a period of extended optional infinitive. *Journal of Speech and Hearing Research, 38*, 850–863.

Robey, R. R., & Schultz, M. C. (1998). A model for conducting clinical-outcome research: An adaptation of the standard protocol for use in aphasiology. *Aphasiology, 12*, 787–810.

Schelletter, C., Sinka, I., Fletcher, P., & Ingham, R. (1998), English speaking SLI children's use of locative/contact and causative alternation. In M. Garman, C. Letts, B. Richards, C. Schelletter, & S. Edwards (Eds.), *Issues in normal and disordered child language: From phonology to narrative. The New Bulmershe Papers* (pp. 106–117). Reading, UK: University of Reading.

Spooner, L. (2002). Addressing expressive language disorder in children who also have severe receptive language disorder: A psycholinguistic approach. *Child Language Teaching and Therapy, 18*, 289–313.

Tallal, P. (2000), Experimental studies of language learning impairments: From research to remediation. In D. V. M. Bishop & L. Leonard (Eds.), *Speech and language impairments in children: Causes, characteristics, intervention and outcome* (pp. 131–155), Hove, UK: Psychology Press.

Tallal, P., Merzenich, M. M., Miller, S., & Jenkins, W. (1998). Language learning impairments: Integrating basic science, technology, and remediation. *Experimental Brain Research, 123*, 210–219.

Tallal, P., Miller, S. L., Bedi, G., Byma, G., Wang, X. Q., Nagarajan, S. S., et al. (1996). Language comprehension in language-learning impaired children improved with acoustically modified speech. *Science, 271*, 81–84.

Tallal, P., Stark, R. E., & Mellits, D. (1985). The relationship between auditory temporal analysis and receptive language development: Evidence from studies of developmental language disorder. *Neuropsychologia, 23*, 527–534.

Thordardottir, E. T., & Weismer, S. E. (2002). Verb argument structure weakness in specific language impairment in relation to age and utterance length. *Clinical Linguistics & Phonetics, 16*, 233–250.

Tyler, A., Lewis, K. E., Haskill, A., & Tolbert, L. C. (2002). Efficacy and cross-domain effects of a morphosyntax and a phonology intervention. *Language Speech and Hearing Services in Schools, 33*, 52–66.

van der Lely, H. K. J. (1996). Specifically language impaired and normally developing children: Verbal passive vs adjectival passive sentence interpretation. *Lingua, 98*, 243–272.

van der Lely, H. K. J., & Battell, J. (2003). Wh-movement in children with grammatical SLI: A test of the RDDR hypothesis. *Language, 79*, 153–181.

van der Lely, H. K. J., & Harris, M. (1990). Comprehension of reversible sentences in specifically language-impaired children. *Journal of Speech and Hearing Disorders, 55*, 101–117.

van der Lely, H. K. J., & Ullman, M. T. (2001). Past tense morphology in specifically language impaired and normally developing children. *Language and Cognitive Processes, 16,* 177–217.

Weismer, S. E., & Branch, J. M. (1989). Modeling versus modeling plus evoked production training: A comparison of 2 language intervention methods. *Journal of Speech and Hearing Disorders, 54,* 269–281.

Widget Software (2008). Writing with Symbols (2000) [Computer software]. Cambridge, UK: Widgit Software.

Wilcox, J. M., & Leonard, L. B. (1978). Experimental acquisition of Wh-questions in language-disordered children. *Journal of Speech and Hearing Research, 21,* 220–239.

Appendix 10A: Studies targeting improvement in general receptive and expressive language

Study	Age (yrs)	Diagnosis	Intervention method	Method of delivery	Controls? y/n	Controls? Group	Total hrs. therapy with SLT / computer program	Results	Progress maintained?	Progress generalized?
Cohen et al., 2005	6–10	SLI (receptive & expressive)	acoustically modified speech: Fast ForWord vs. other computer programs	computer (1:1)	y	RCT: 2 therapy groups + control group	6–60 hrs. (FFW), 2–82 (other programs)	therapy groups improved no more than control group	N/A	N/A
Gillam et al., 2001	6;11–7;6	language impairment	acoustically modified speech: Fast ForWord vs. other computer programs	computer (1:1)	n	4 children, 2 randomly assigned to each type of therapy, including standard scores	33 hrs.	all children made some progress	not tested	to spontaneous speech and general language tests for 1 FFW child and 2 on other programs
Tallal et al., 1998; Tallal, 2000	4–14	wide range of diagnoses	acoustically modified speech: Fast ForWord	computer (1:1)	n	pre- vs. posttest, standard scores	50–67 hrs.	children who "complied with the study protocol" (only 35%?) improved significantly	not measured	to general language tests

Study	Age (yrs)	Diagnosis	Intervention method	Method of delivery	Controls? y/n	Group	Total hrs. therapy with SLT / computer program	Results	Progress maintained?	Progress generalized?
Loeb et al., 2001	5;6–8;1	SLI	acoustically modified speech: Fast ForWord	computer (1:1)	n	pre- vs. posttest, including standard scores	30–50 sessions (hrs. unclear, but probably 50–84 hrs.)	3/4 children completed program; made gains on some standardized tests	after 3 months, 61% of gains maintained	to some general language tests; little change in spontaneous speech, few differences reported by parents and teachers
Friel-Patti et al., 2001	5;10–9;2	language learning disabled (2 also ADHD)	acoustically modified speech: Fast ForWord	computer (1:1)	n	pre- vs. posttest, including standard scores	26–53 hrs.	3/5 children improved	not measured	to some general language tests for 3/5 children; not to spontaneous speech

Appendix 10B: Studies targeting improvements in general receptive language only

Study	Age (yrs)	Diagnosis	Intervention method	Method of delivery	Controls? y/n	Group	Total hrs. therapy with SLT / computer program	Results	Progress maintained?	Progress generalized?
Tallal et al., 1996 (Study 2)	5;2–10;0	language learning impaired (receptive and expressive)	acoustically modified speech: Fast ForWord vs. unmodified speech	computer (1:1)	n	2 therapy groups (not randomly assigned), no untreated control group, not standard scores	88–116 hrs.	both groups improved comprehension, more with modified than unmodified speech	not measured	to general language tests
Tallal et al., 1996 (Study 1)	5;9–9;1	language learning impaired (receptive and expressive)	acoustically modified speech: Fast ForWord	computer (1:1)	n	pre- vs. posttest, not standard scores	88–116 hrs.	language comprehension improved significantly	not measured	to general language tests

Appendix 10C: Studies targeting improvements in general expressive language only

Study	Age (yrs)	Diagnosis	Intervention method	Method of delivery	Controls? y/n	Controls? Group	Total hrs. therapy with SLT / computer program	Results	Progress maintained?	Progress generalized?
Matheny & Panagos, 1978	5;5–6;10	articulatory and syntactic problems	grammar facilitation imitation vs. articulation therapy	direct (1:1)	y	RCT: 2 therapy groups + control group	unspecified over 5 months	both groups made significant progress in both syntax and articulation; control group made no progress	not measured	to general language test
Guendouzi, 2003	7;0 & 6;10	SLI	metalinguistic: similar to Colourful Semantics	not stated, direct (1:1) implied	n	2 case studies pre- vs. posttest, no standard scores	not stated	one child made progress, one did not	not measured	to spontaneous speech

Appendix 10D: Studies targeting improvements in a wide range of expressive morphological and syntactic targets

Study	Age (yrs)	Diagnosis	Intervention method	Method of delivery	Controls? y/n	Controls? Group	Total hrs. therapy with SLT	Results	Progress maintained?	Progress generalized?
Fey et al., 1993 (Wave 1)	3;8–5;10	marked delays in grammar development	grammar facilitation: modeling /focused stimulation + recasting (+ imitation for Group 1)	Group 1: direct (1:1) + group (4–6 children); Group 2: indirect through parent groups and individual parent sessions	y	RCT: 2 therapy groups + control group	Group 1: 60 hrs. (children), Group 2: 56 hrs. (parents)	both therapy groups improved more than controls; more reliable progress in Group 1	not measured	to spontaneous speech
Fey et al., 1997 (Wave 2)	not stated 4;1?–6;3?	marked delays in grammar development	grammar facilitation: modeling /focused stimulation + recasting (+ imitation for Group 1)	as above	y	RCT: 2 therapy groups + controls (5 previously in Group 1 and 5 in Group 2)	Group 1: 60 hrs. (children, in addition to 60 in first study), Group 2: 15 hrs. (parents-in addition to 56 in first study)	both therapy groups improved more than controls	dismissed control group showed no change; therefore progress maintained for 5 months	to spontaneous speech
Nelson et al., 1996	4;7–6;7	SLI, < 1.25 SD on MLU and sent rep tests	grammar facilitation: imitation vs. recasting	direct (1:1)	y	individual targets assigned to 2 therapy methods vs. no therapy	Mean of 18.1 sessions (length not stated)	treated targets better than untreated targets; targets produced quicker and generalized more with recasting	not measured	to spontaneous speech at home

Appendix 10D: Studies targeting improvements in a wide range of expressive morphological and syntactic targets (continued)

Study	Age (yrs)	Diagnosis	Intervention method	Method of delivery	Controls? y/n	Controls? Group	Total hrs. therapy with SLT	Results	Progress maintained?	Progress generalized?
Culatta & Horn, 1982	4;6– 9;2	language disordered, primarily expressive only	grammar facilitation: modeling/focused stimulation + recasting	direct (1:1)	y	4 case studies: multiple baseline	14.25–20.25 hrs.	90% accuracy reached on trained targets, little progress on second target during baseline period	yes: for at least 3.5 weeks	to spontaneous speech
Camarata et al., 1994	4;0– 6;10	SLI, primarily expressive	grammar facilitation: recasting vs. imitation	direct (1:1)	n	2 targets per child randomly assigned to 2 therapy methods	20 hrs.	success of methods varied between children; imitation led to quicker elicited production	not measured	to spontaneous speech, quicker with recasting than imitation
Camarata & Nelson, 1992	4;9– 5;11	SLI	grammar facilitation: recasting vs. imitation	direct (1:1)	n	2 or 4 targets per child randomly assigned to 2 therapy methods	16–32 hrs.	success of methods varied between targets	not measured	to spontaneous speech, quicker with recasting than imitation
Friedman & Friedman, 1980	3;2– 5;9	severe language problems, especially expressive; comprehension also delayed	grammar facilitation: conversational vs. more structured	direct group work (4 children)	n	2 therapy groups (not randomly assigned), no control group	384 hrs.	both groups improved equally; lower functioning children showed more progress with more structured approach	not measured	to spontaneous speech

Appendix 10E: Studies targeting specific expressive language targets

Specific targets	Study	Age (yrs)	Diagnosis	Intervention method	Method of delivery	Controls? y/n	Controls? Group	Total hrs. therapy with SLT	Results	Progress maintained?	Progress generalized?
expressive argument structure	Ebbels et al., 2007a	11;0–16;1	SLI (receptive and expressive)	metalinguistic: Shape Coding vs. verb semantics	direct (1:1)	y	RCT: 2 therapy groups + control group	4.5 hrs.	both therapy groups improved more than controls	after 3 months	to control verbs
yes/no question formation	Mulac & Tomlinson, 1977	4;4–6;3	failed on the generalization of "is" interrogative	grammar facilitation: imitation (+ transfer program for Group 1)	direct (1:1) + parents given tasks to do, but no mention of training parents	y	RCT: 2 grammar therapy groups + control group (articulation therapy)	2.8 hrs. + for Group 1–1.92 hrs. transfer program	both grammar therapy groups improved in the clinic situation	20–26 days after end of therapy	to other settings only if extended transfer training given (Group 1 only)
wh-question formation	Wilcox & Leonard, 1978	3;8–8;2	language disordered	grammar facilitation: modeling + evoked production	direct (1:1)	y	therapy vs. delayed treatment group, RCT except for 3 children	not stated	therapy group improved more than controls	not measured	"does" and "is" inversion generalized to other wh-questions
finite morphemes	Tyler et al., 2002	3;0–5;11	language and phonological impairment (all expressive, some also receptive)	grammar facilitation: focused stimulation (including recasts and expansions) vs. elicited production	direct (1:1) + group	y	2 grammar therapy groups + control group (not randomly assigned)	15 hrs.	grammar groups improved more than control group (phonology training)	not measured	to spontaneous speech; also to phonological skills

Appendix 10E: Studies targeting specific expressive language targets (*continued*)

Specific targets	Study	Age (yrs)	Diagnosis	Intervention method	Method of delivery	Controls y/n	Controls Group	Total hrs. therapy with SLT	Results	Progress maintained?	Progress generalized?
"is," "don't"	Leonard, 1975	5–9	no use of "is" or "don't"	grammar facilitation: modeling	direct (1:1)	y	therapy vs. delayed treatment group (not randomly assigned)	1.25 hrs.	therapy group improved more than controls	not measured	not measured
wh-question and passive formation	Ebbels & van der Lely, 2001	11–14	SLI (receptive and expressive)	metalinguistic: Shape Coding	direct (1:1)	y	4 case studies: multiple baseline	10 hrs. on passives, 20 hrs. on *w*-questions	3/4 children showed significant progress with passives, all progressed with wh-questions	after 30 weeks: passives for 2 children, wh-questions for 1 child	not measured
"they"	Courtwright & Courtwright, 1976	5–10	disordered in use of "they" (used "them" instead)	grammar facilitation: modeling vs. imitation	direct (1:1)	n	2 therapy groups (not randomly assigned)	1 hr.	modeling group improved more than imitation group	not measured	to spontaneous speech
use and inversion of aux. "is" (3 children), use of "he" (1 child)	Weismer & Branch, 1989	5;5–6;11	expressive language delay (one also had phonological and comprehension difficulties)	grammar facilitation: modeling versus modeling + evoked production	direct (1:1)	n	4 case studies: alternating treatments, not multiple baseline	4.67–7.5 hrs.	both approaches effective for "is" (children with expressive language delay), no progress with "he" for child with additional difficulties	not measured	not measured

Target area	Study	Age	Diagnosis	Approach		n	Measure	Dosage	Outcome	Generalisation	Generalised to
expressive language, especially argument structure	Spooner, 2002	6;3 & 9;9	expressive and receptive language disorder, + word finding	metalinguistic: Colourful Semantics	direct (1:1)	n	pre-vs. posttest, including some standard scores	approx 22 hrs.	one child progressed in argument structure; both children improved other areas of expressive language	not measured	to general language tests
expressive argument structure	Bryan, 1997	5;10	expressive language disorder	metalinguistic: Colourful Semantics	direct (1:1)	n	pre-vs. posttest, not standard scores	approx 22 hrs.	most sentences contained correct argument structure	not measured	to a general language test and spontaneous speech in class
past tense morphology	Ebbels, 2007	11–13	SLI	metalinguistic: Shape Coding	direct group + (for 2 children) 1:2	n	pre-vs. posttest, not standard scores	approx 16 hrs. (+ approx 4 hrs. for 2 children)	6 children improved with group therapy, 2 improved only after additional paired therapy	not measured	to spontaneous writing

Appendix 10F: Studies targeting specific receptive language targets

Specific targets	Study	Age (yrs)	Diagnosis	Intervention method	Method of delivery	Controls y/n	Group	Total hrs. therapy with SLT / computer program	Results	Progress maintained?	Progress generalized?
reversible sentences (passives, comparatives and sentences including prepositions)	Bishop et al., 2006	8–13	receptive language impairment	acoustically modified vs. unmodified speech	computer (1:1)	y	RCT: 2 therapy groups + control group	1.5–7.25 hrs.	no differences between groups	N/A	N/A
comprehension of passives and wh-questions	Ebbels & van der Lely, 2001	11–14	SLI (receptive and expressive)	metalinguistic: Shape Coding	direct (1:1)	y	4 case studies, multiple baseline	10 hrs. on passives, 20 hrs. on wh-questions	3/4 children progressed with passives, 2/2 progressed with wh-questions	at 30 weeks	not measured
comprehension of dative and wh-comparative questions	Ebbels, 2007	11–14	SLI (receptive and expressive)	metalinguistic: Shape Coding	direct (1:1)	y	3 case studies, multiple baseline	10 hrs. on each structure	2/3 children progressed with dative, 2/2 progressed with wh-comparative questions	not measured	not measured

11

Reading intervention for children with language learning difficulties

Margaret J. Snowling and Charles Hulme

It is now widely recognized that oral language skills provide the critical foundation for literacy development and, therefore, that children with spoken language difficulties are at risk of literacy problems (Catts & Kamhi, 2005). Moreover, since literacy skills are required in order to access the curriculum and most frequently are the means by which children are asked to demonstrate their knowledge, educational underachievement is a common scenario for children with a history of speech and language difficulties (Nathan, Stackhouse, Goulandris, & Snowling, 2004a; Snowling, Adams, Bishop, & Stothard, 2001). This chapter begins by outlining a model within which to conceptualize the relationship between reading and language impairments before turning to a review of effective interventions. We then discuss the issue of children who fail to respond to demonstrably effective interventions and pro-

vide preliminary evidence that language-based interventions may be useful for supporting their literacy development. This evidence suggests that language-based interventions at the foundations of literacy development should be helpful, and two such interventions are discussed. The chapter closes with a summary of what we still need to know about reading intervention.

THE RELATIONSHIP BETWEEN READING AND LANGUAGE IMPAIRMENTS

The developmental nature of reading and language impairments makes understanding their interrelationships complex. Studies of typically developing children suggest that different components of reading build on different oral language abilities (Muter, Hulme, Snowling, & Stevenson, 2004); phonological skills predict decoding abilities, whereas language skills beyond phonology are predictors of reading comprehension (Cain, Oakhill, & Bryant, 2004). Against this backdrop, studies of children with specific reading disorders show that clear dissociations are possible. Dyslexia is a neurodevelopmental disorder characterized by poor reading and spelling that is out of line with general cognitive ability. Dyslexia primarily affects the acquisition of word-level decoding skills in reading and can be traced to a deficit in phonological skills (Ramus et al., 2003; Snowling, 2000). In contrast to dyslexia, poor comprehenders can decode well but have difficulty in understanding what they are reading. Such specific reading comprehension difficulties are associated with weaknesses in vocabulary and with grammatical and inferencing skills (Nation, chapter 3, this volume).

However, prospective studies of children at high risk of reading difficulties paint a much more complex picture. Among children with speech and language impairments identified before reading instruction begins, the risk of reading difficulty is associated with poor language rather than poor phonology, at least as evidenced by poor speech output (Bishop & Adams, 1990; Catts, 1993; Nathan, Stackhouse, Goulandris, & Snowling, 2004b; Raitano, Pennington, Tunick, & Boada, 2004). There are, however, some exceptions. First, if speech difficulties persist up until the time the child has to learn to read, then problems with the acquisition of phoneme awareness and reading-related skills are common (Bird, Bishop, & Freeman; 1995; Nathan et al., 2004b) and there is a strong relationship between aberrant speech and spelling processes (Stackhouse & Snowling, 1992). Second, the demands of reading change with time, and satisfactory literacy development cannot be assumed for children who make a good start in learning to read. Thus, Stothard, Snowling, Bishop, Chipchase, and Kaplan (1998) found that during the school years there was a relative decline in the reading standard scores of children with a history of preschool specific language impairment. Specifically, the incidence of

reading difficulties defined by problems in word-level decoding skills (dyslexia) had risen from 6% at the age of 8 years (Bishop & Adams, 1990) to 24% at the age of 15 years. In a similar vein, Snowling, Muter, and Carroll (2007) reported that children from families with a history of dyslexia who showed normal literacy development at 8 years went on to experience problems of reading fluency and of spelling in early adolescence (12–13 years).

Together, these findings highlight that learning to read is a developmental process involving the interaction of different language skills, and different language skills may be important for learning to read at different times. From this perspective, how well a child reads will depend on the balance of oral language skills that he or she brings to the task of learning to read (or spell). Furthermore, once literacy development has begun, reciprocal interactions between oral and written language skills complicate the picture. It has been argued, for example, that learning to read in an alphabetic system fine-tunes the child's phonological skills—in particular, his or her phoneme awareness (Castles & Coltheart, 2004; Morais & Kolinsky, 2005). Similarly, reading development has an impact on vocabulary size, and children who read less may show declines in vocabulary growth over time (Stanovich, 1986; Stothard et al., 1998).

On the basis of findings such as these, Bishop and Snowling (2004) proposed a two-dimensional model of the relationship between reading and language impairments (Figure 11.1). According to this model, phonological deficits carry the risk of decoding difficulty, while broader oral language deficits are risk factors for reading comprehension problems. Children with different reading profiles fall within different quadrants of the model. Thus, in its classic form, dyslexia is situated in the bottom right quadrant, because it is associated with good oral language skills but specific phonological deficits (Snowling & Hulme, 1989). In sharp contrast, poor comprehenders fall into the upper left quadrant, because they typically have good phonological skills but poor nonphonological language skills. However, since language and reading skills both reflect developmental processes, the positioning of individual children is

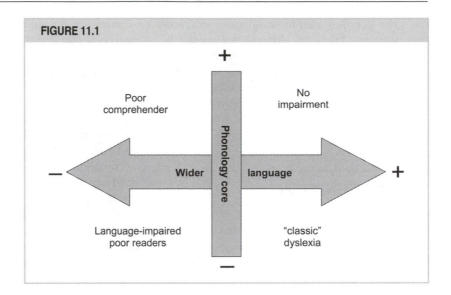

FIGURE 11.1

Two-dimensional model of the risk of reading difficulties (after Bishop & Snowling, 2004).

not necessarily static (although there does appear to be considerable continuity over time; Nation & Snowling, 2004). Factors that might be expected to modify literacy outcomes will include severity of underlying language impairments (e.g., Griffiths & Snowling, 2002), general cognitive resources (Stothard et al., 1998), the presence of comorbid difficulties (e.g., in attention control; Torgesen, 2000), and, of course, experiential factors. Such a view is compatible with the hypothesis that developmental disorders, such as dyslexia, are brought about by the action of multiple genes, some with general and others with specific effects, acting in interaction through different environments (Rutter, 2005).

ASSESSMENT OF READING AND LANGUAGE SKILLS

The view of the relationship between reading and language skills outlined above carries with it implications for assessment and intervention. Literacy assessment for children with language delays and difficulties, as for all children, should ideally include assessments of single-word reading, decoding (nonword reading) and prose reading skills, as well as spelling and writing abilities (Goulandris, 2006). But more is needed to uncover the individual vulnerabilities as well as the cognitive strengths that may provide compensatory resources. For children who have specific decoding difficulties, it is usual to include in-depth assessment of phonological skills (phonological awareness, phonological memory, and rapid naming skills). In addition, the inclusion of tests of receptive and expressive vocabulary is recommended, at the least to monitor growth in vocabulary size and, more generally, to check on the integrity of wider language abilities. For children with specific reading comprehension difficulties, a comprehensive language assessment is desirable, and this should include tests of listening comprehension, vocabulary, grammar, and inferential skills (Snowling & Stackhouse, 2006).

But should such assessment be the starting point for intervention? This is a more difficult question. While it is obvious at a gross level that assessment will dictate how intervention should proceed—after all, there is absolutely no point in training reading accuracy in a poor comprehender—we do not yet know how detailed a language assessment has to be in order to set up an effective intervention program. Arguably, although the science of reading is mature, the science of reading intervention is much less advanced, and one of the important questions that intervention studies need to address is "who benefits most from which type of intervention?"

READING INTERVENTION

During the past 20 years, there have been two important influences on the teaching of reading and spelling to children with difficulties. The first is Reading Recovery, associated with Marie Clay in New Zealand, and the second is phonological awareness training, associated with Isabelle Liberman in the United States, Lynette Bradley and Peter Bryant in the United Kingdom, and Ingvar Lundberg in Sweden. Such approaches have been found to be successful in helping failing readers, and the important ingredients of these can be seen in contemporary approaches to intervention. In a now classic study in the United Kingdom, Hatcher, Hulme, and Ellis (1994) compared three forms of intervention for 7-year-old poor readers: phonological awareness training (P), reading instruction (R), and combined training in reading and phonological awareness (R+P), each delivered by trained teachers. The most effective intervention was the R+P integrated program, which incorporated training in phonological awareness and letter knowledge. In addition, metacognitive work made explicit the links between these skills in the context of writing. Crucially, sessions also included reading from carefully selected books, of appropriate difficulty for each individual child. This work has formed the basis of a series of intervention studies conducted by our group at the University of York.

The Reading with Phonology program

The Reading with Phonology program (R+P; Hatcher, 2006) begins with an assessment of a child's reading and spelling strategies, in order to provide a picture of his or her strengths and weaknesses in tackling words that are difficult to read or write. The assessment battery includes a test of print concepts (after Clay, 1985), an early word recognition test comprising words frequently encountered in early reading books, and a test of letter knowledge. A key element is the *"running record"* in which the child is required to read a section of a book independently and without support from the teacher (this can be as few as 20 words or a passage of between 100 and 200 words, depending on level of proficiency). While the child is reading, the teacher records the child's reading behaviors (such as errors, self-corrections, sounding out, losing the line). The record yields a reading accuracy score that is used to determine whether the text is at an easy (>94% correct), instructional (90–94% correct), or difficult (<90% correct) level for the child, and the record can be analyzed to determine whether the child is using appropriate reading strategies. The child is also asked to write "a short story" (this might be just a sentence) and then to read it aloud and to write his or her name and some key words. These writing samples provide information about the child's level of written language, spelling, and handwriting skills and are analyzed to assess how well the child can segment sounds for spelling. More formally, the child receives a comprehensive test of phonological awareness—Sound Linkage (Hatcher, 2000)—which taps awareness of different sound units (syllables, rimes, phonemes). Performance on the test is used to determine the point at which training in phonological skills should begin and to monitor progress during the intervention.

The main elements of the Reading with Phonology teaching approach are:

- training in letter knowledge
- teaching concepts of print
- training to manipulate the sounds of words, particularly phoneme awareness
- applying letter and sound knowledge to word reading and writing (phonics)
- reading text at an easy level (for reinforcement, practice, and confidence)

- reading text at an instructional level (to practice decoding words in context, with teacher support)

- writing a simple story (could be just one word or one sentence, with support).

The findings from the assessment are used to plan the first lesson, which follows a set format and is delivered within an agreed time frame. Subsequently the content of the lesson is titrated to take account of the pace at which the child is learning. Lessons are individual and last for 30 minutes, usually twice a week. Progression within the program follows Clay's (1985) procedure of consolidating children's reading strengths with material that can be read with more than 94% accuracy. A second objective is working to overcome confusions and learning new skills with text that can be read with 90–94% accuracy. The running record is also used to identify the set of skills to be taught at the next level. A key skill that teachers need to develop is how to choose books at the appropriate level. In the United Kingdom, a database of books that have been graded for difficulty is available on the Internet; however, this frequently requires updating because books go out of print.

Modifications of the Reading with Phonology program

The success of the R+P program when delivered individually to children with reading delay was a spur to future development. Initially, in the hope that it might be possible to circumvent reading difficulties in "at-risk" groups, we adapted the approach for delivery by mainstream teachers to whole classes of children in 20 schools (Hatcher, Hulme, & Snowling, 2004). Schools were divided into four groups, and within each group the teaching was somewhat different. Teachers from all groups were taught to deliver the reading component of the program and encourage phonic analysis of the text. However, in three out of four groups the teaching was supplemented by work on oral phonological awareness. This was delivered either at the level of the phoneme, the rime, or using both rimes and phonemes.

In this mainstream approach, it is important to emphasize that children at risk of literacy problems were taught alongside their peers in whole classes over the first two years of school (5 terms in all)—that is, the whole group received what we would consider "quality first" teaching. Diary records indicated that typically the children received the phonological aspects of the work in the classroom and read to the teacher individually, but there was considerable variation in the intensity of the approach across the 20 schools involved. The findings for the majority of children in these classes who were learning to read normally was that they did not show any additional benefits of the phonological training. Importantly, however, the approach was helpful for children at risk of reading difficulties on school entry. For "at-risk" children, supplementing the reading curriculum with phoneme awareness training during the first five terms of school slowed the decline in reading attainment (relative to their peers) that was seen in at-risk children who did not receive such training.

The findings of this study were enlightening. They showed clearly that R+P is a helpful approach for children entering school with poorly developed oral language and phonological skills; however, its effects were small. It seemed clear to us that, in order to be effective, it would be necessary to move to a more individualized approach—teaching literacy skills to at-risk children alongside their mainstream peers did not enable them to keep up. Furthermore, although in the original R+P approach phonological awareness training followed a sequence of large to small units, in this study we had shown that training at the phoneme level is most effective. Accordingly, we have focused on phoneme level training in subsequent work on reading intervention.

Delivering intervention on an individual basis is a costly process, and our next step was to consider whether we could modify the R+P approach for delivery by trained teaching assistants. Hatcher et al. (2006a) piloted such a program in which the reading elements of the approach were taught on a one-to-one basis and small group work was directed to training in phoneme awareness, letter knowledge, and linkage activities. The program was delivered by trained teaching assistants on a daily basis (for 12 weeks) and was compared with the UK Early Literacy Support program of teaching. The training and support of teaching assistants is regarded as fundamental to the success of reading intervention, and—importantly in our view—the teaching assistants were supported fortnightly in tutorials throughout the intervention. At the end, the findings were pleasing: both programs were effective for groups of 6-year-old children whose reading was developing slowly in their second year in school. Indeed, they were effective in moving their reading skills from the low average to the average range for their age.

We were now left with the crucial question of whether such an approach could be effective for children with more significant difficulties in learning to read. To address this issue, we conducted a randomized controlled trial, targeting 5–6 year-old children selected for being in roughly the bottom 8% of the population for reading development (Hatcher et al., 2006b). The children who participated were allocated at random to receive the intervention either for a 20-week period (20-week intervention group) or for a 10-week period (10-week intervention group; these children acted as a "waiting-list" control group for the first 10 weeks and then received the teaching during Weeks 10–20). (At the beginning of the study, the 10-week intervention group were marginally better at reading than the 20-week group; this difference was unexpected, given that allocation to group had been random. Baseline differences were controlled statistically in all analyses.)

The results of the study were very encouraging (see Figure 11.2). After 10 weeks of daily intervention, the children in the 20-week intervention group had made gains of nearly 4 standard score points on a test of single-word reading ability, which was significantly more than controls in the "waiting list" group, who made negligible gains. During the subsequent 10 weeks, when both groups received the intervention, the 10-week intervention group began to catch up with the 20-week group, once they were given the intervention.

But would this approach prove to be effective in schools once the research team retreated from

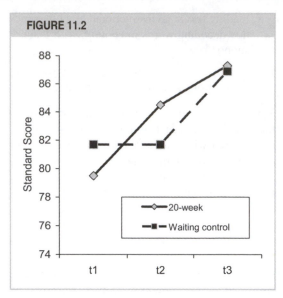

FIGURE 11.2

Progress of Year 1 children at three time points in response to reading intervention using *Reading with Phonology* (Hatcher et al., 2006b)

the scene? This is an important question that the local authority in which we worked was keen to address. In the year following the completion of our research, 50 teaching assistants and one teacher from 38 primary schools undertook a four-day training program delivered by members of the local authority in six venues across the county (coordinated by Glynnis Smith, Consultant in Inclusion). Following training, the "trainees" delivered the R+P program to 142 children, the majority being children in Year 1.

Children received an average of 38 sessions in a 10-week period, and the teaching assistants tested the children before and after they carried out the intervention. On average, children made over 7 months' progress in reading during the 10-week period (Gibbs & Smith, 2006). Although it is impossible to be certain that the gains were due to the program and not a more general effect of the special attention they received, we are encouraged that the findings of this field trial replicate those of the research trials. In short, we think the results are educationally very significant and underline the efficacy (as well as cost-effectiveness) of R+P as an early intervention for children with literacy difficulties at the end of the first year in school.

Notwithstanding the above, we need to signal a note of caution. Although we have consistently found that the average gain in reading skills as a result of the R+P intervention is good, it is important to stress that some children remained very poor readers (in the study by Hatcher et al., 2006b, 28% of the 20-week and 21% of the 10-week intervention group had standard scores below 80 at the end of the intervention). Such children clearly require ongoing support if their literacy skills are to be brought to within the average range. Moreover, children varied in their responsiveness to the teaching they received, and a small number could be defined as treatment "nonresponders." These children were typically those with more severe phonological impairments, poor vocabulary skills, and of lower socioeconomic status.

Intervention for treatment nonresponders

The finding of a poor response to intervention by socially disadvantaged children with relatively poor receptive vocabulary and poor phoneme awareness prompted us to look at these children in greater detail. By the time of this second phase of our study, the children were aged 7;7 years, and approximately 22 months had elapsed since they had received the R+P program. In the interim, the majority of these children had not received any specific literacy support, though it is difficult to validate this report because formal records were not available.

The assessment battery was exploratory and included a broad sweep of cognitive and linguistic measures. In addition to reading and spelling tasks, we included three phoneme awareness tests (segmenting, blending, and deletion), and a test of letter knowledge. We assessed language skills using tests of expressive grammar and vocabulary (as assessed by word definitions), and phonological skills using a test of nonword repetition. We also assessed more general cognitive resources using speed of processing tests from the Wechsler Intelligence Scale for Children (WISC–III; Wechsler, 1992) and tests of sustained and divided attention.

As might be expected, we found considerable heterogeneity in the children's profile. However, on average, these children showed very poor language (vocabulary and grammar) and very poor phoneme awareness for their age. In contrast, their speed of processing skills was broadly within the normal range, but with a tendency to have problems in attention control. It may have been appropriate simply to have provided these children with a further course of R+P, perhaps delivered more intensively on an individual basis. Indeed, such an approach has been reported to be effective (Torgesen, 2005) but, again, not for all children (Whiteley, Smith, & Connors, 2007). Instead, we felt it appropriate to design and pilot an intervention that would take account of the fact that these children had significant oral language impairments. If it is the case, as has been hypothesized, that oral language—and particularly vocabulary development—is the pacemaker of phonological awareness (Carroll, Snowling, Hulme, & Stevenson, 2003; Walley, 1993) then boosting children's vocabulary and other oral language skills should benefit the development of their metalinguistic awareness.

Accordingly, Duff et al. (2008) developed an integrated program of reading, phonological awareness, and vocabulary training, named Reading with Vocabulary Intervention (REVI). REVI was designed as a 9-week program for delivery on a one-to-one basis by teaching assistants to children with poor reading in the context of poor oral language and incorporates the basic elements of the R+P program (Hatcher et al., 2006b). To take into account the attentional problems of the children and the likely benefits of distributed practice, daily instruction was divided into two 15-minute sessions.

The first session began with 5 minutes of reading, first from an "easy" book and then from a book at the instructional level. This reading book was used as a springboard for a subsequent five minutes of vocabulary instruction. Following the practice of Beck, McKeown, and Kucan (2002), a word or a general concept from the instructional book was rephrased using a more "sophisticated" (or two-tier) word—for example, *watch* was rephrased as *observe*; *make,* as *construct.* The teaching assistant first contextualized the word, showing how it related to the book, explained its meaning, and gave the child examples of the word in other contexts. The child's role was to repeat the target word several times to assist in securing a phonological representation and to engage with the word's meaning by generating examples of its use in different contexts. This procedure derives from the assumption that the simple vocabulary in the texts that poor readers are able to read is too limited to boost vocabulary development, and hence sophisticated words have to be taught to such children in a rich and multicontextual manner (Beck, Perfetti, & McKeown, 1982; Beck et al., 2002).

The last 5 minutes of the session were spent on a narrative writing task. The children used a sequence of pictures as prompts from which to tell a story. Following some oral work on the quality of the language, the teaching assistant encouraged the child to write down a small part of the story.

The second session each day involved a modification of the R+P program (above). The first three minutes were spent revising the target vocabulary taught in the earlier session. This was followed by 5 minutes of phonological awareness training involving segmenting, blending, and deletion of initial, medial, and final phonemes. Three minutes were then dedicated to the teaching of sight words through multisensory activities. After this, the teaching assistant introduced the child to a new book at the instructional level of reading, using this time to discuss concepts about print. The child also had an opportunity to link his or her emerging phonological and sight word skills to reading when reading the book with the teaching assistant and then alone (3 minutes). The session finished with revision and reinforcement of the day's target vocabulary and sight words (1 minute). Every fifth day of the intervention was designated as a consolidation day.

A group of 12 children defined as "treatment nonresponders" received the intervention. At the time of its delivery, the children were aged 8 years, and their reading skills fell roughly within the bottom 7% of the population. In the absence of a control group, it was important that we had been able to monitor the progress of these children over a baseline period, during which time they made no statistically significant gains in the reading, phonological awareness, or oral language abilities that we measured. In contrast, by the end of the intervention they had made significant gains in word reading, letter–sound knowledge, phoneme segmentation, and expressive grammar. In addition, by the end of the intervention, the children were significantly better at defining words that they had been taught than those they had not. Figure 11.3 shows a comparison of the mean progress made per week on each measure during the intervention and control periods, indicating the size of the gains in terms of effect sizes. It can be seen that children failed to make any significant progress on the measures during the baseline control period, in contrast to the demonstrable progress made during the intervention period. We revisited the children some six months after the intervention ceased to monitor maintenance of gains. Gains made in phoneme awareness and in vocabulary were maintained, and reading raw score increased significantly in the maintenance period.

A proposed metric by which to evaluate and compare the efficacy of interventions is the number of standard score points in reading gained per hour (McGuiness, McGuiness, & McGuiness, 1996). During the initial period of intervention (Hatcher et al., 2006b) the present group had gained, on average, a negligible 0.02 standard score points per hour of intervention. In contrast, these same children gained a mean of 0.13 standard score points per hour of the REVI program. This is a statistically significant but slow rate of progress, and it is important to point out that the reading skills of the majority of the children remained below average by the end of the intervention.

Early intervention at the foundation of literacy skills

Together, the findings of the reading intervention studies described above are salutary. It is quite clear that interventions can be effective, but at the same time a growing body of evidence indicates that there is always a visible minority of children who fail to respond (Fuchs & Fuchs, 2002).

FIGURE 11.3

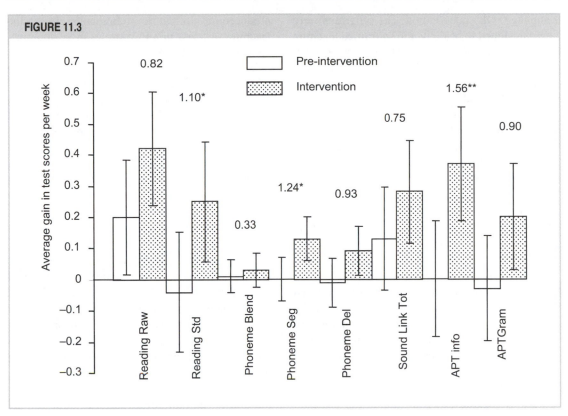

Response of treatment "nonresponders" to a language-based form of reading intervention (REVI) (Duff et al., 2008). The white bars are the average gains in raw score made on each measure per week during the pretreatment phase; the gray bars show the average corresponding gains made during the treatment period (with 95% within-subject confidence intervals). Effect sizes are placed above the bars; asterisks indicate statistically significant differences following a paired-samples *t* test.

Although the evidence base is thin, clinical experience suggests that these nonresponders include a high proportion of children with oral language difficulties who come to school ill-prepared to develop literacy. Such children arguably should be given intervention as soon as they enter school. Logically, there are two different ways to support their language needs with a view to safeguarding their literacy development. The first is what might be called the direct approach—that is, to provide these children with intervention that targets the development of preliteracy and literacy skills. The second is an indirect approach. This approach takes as its starting point the finding that oral language is the pacemaker of phoneme awareness and is a better predictor of reading development in

children from high-risk groups than phonological awareness. Within this view, children who enter school with poor speech and language should receive training in oral language skills—particularly vocabulary—because this will foster the development of metalinguistic skills, including phoneme awareness. The latter approach should also be more helpful than the former for the development of reading comprehension.

Based on this theoretical rationale, Bowyer-Crane et al. (2008) compared two different intervention programs designed to promote foundation literacy skills in children during their first school year: a Phonology with Reading (P+R) intervention (so named to highlight the fact that the program was designed for nonreaders) and an Oral

Language (OL) intervention. The programs were again designed to be delivered by trained teaching assistants on a daily basis, alternating between individual and small group ($n = 4$) sessions, as in our previous work. They were similar in structure to each other and ran over two 10-week periods, separated by the summer vacation of the first year. Within each 10-week period, there was an induction week, followed by three 3-week blocks, consisting of 2 weeks of new teaching and a week of consolidation.

The P+R program was a downward adaptation of the successful R+P program and had three main components: letter–sound knowledge, phonological awareness, and reading books at the instructional level. Direct teaching in sight word recognition was also included, in order to build up children's reading vocabulary. Children were trained in letter–sound knowledge using the Jolly Phonics program (Lloyd, 1998), and letter–sound knowledge was reinforced through reading, writing, and phonological awareness activities at the phoneme level. The phoneme-level training focused on blending and segmenting exercises in line with guidelines provided by the National Reading Panel (2000) report. For those children not yet able to pronounce specific phonemes, work on articulatory awareness and phoneme production was included in the individual sessions.

Children engaged with books on a regular basis and were encouraged to link letter–sound knowledge and phoneme awareness in the context of listening to storybooks. In each individual teaching session the child read two books to the teaching assistant, who took a running record. In the case of children who could not yet read at all, the "cut-up" story activity was substituted (Clay, 1985; Hatcher et al., 2006b).

The oral language (OL) program targeted listening comprehension, vocabulary knowledge, expressive language, inferencing, and question-generation skills. Activities to encourage independent speaking, good listening skills, and narrative skills were adapted from a variety of sources that, we felt, incorporated good practice (e.g., Rhodes, 2001). In addition, one of the teaching principles embodied in the program was the use of modeling by the teaching assistants. Thus, when a child produced an immature grammatical form, the teaching assistant would model a more appropriate version of the sentence.

Vocabulary was selected for teaching using two criteria: that it was age-appropriate and instructional, and that it was related to one of the selected topics. The vocabulary to be taught included a selection of nouns, verbs, comparatives, and spatial terms, and all words were taught using methods that encouraged children to use them in different contexts (Beck et al., 2002). A special emphasis was placed on question words: as well as answering questions, children were encouraged to seek information by generating their own questions.

Teaching assistants from 20 schools took part in this research, and each taught in both arms of the intervention. They received four days of training before the intervention began (two days on each arm) and one day midway through. In addition, each teaching assistant attended a group tutorial fortnightly and was observed teaching once. These occasions provided opportunities for the research team to provide feedback on teaching and to monitor the treatment fidelity of the program.

The design of the research was a randomized controlled trial. We began by screening some 900 children from 23 schools on a test of expressive vocabulary. On the basis of this screening, we identified the 10 children with the lowest vocabulary scores in each of 20 schools for further assessment of phonological, language, and literacy skills. We then chose, from these 10 children, the 8 with the lowest verbal composite scores to take part in the intervention. Within each school, 4 of these children were randomly allocated to the P+R and 4 to the OL program. Members of the research team were blind to the allocation and remained so until after the postintervention testing was complete.

The two interventions had differential effects, but both were successful in promoting some of the fundamental language skills that underpin reading. As expected given our previous work, we found that the P+R program had statistically significant effects on letter knowledge, spelling, phoneme awareness, and prose reading accuracy at the end of the intervention, and we found associated gains in decoding skill, as measured by nonword reading, after a 5-month maintenance period. It is important to remember that these effects were over and above any such gains made by the OL group, who were also receiving special attention. Perhaps for this reason, the effect on early word reading was only marginally significant: each of the children, including those in the OL group, was receiving "quality first" literacy teaching in the classroom, which may have diluted the apparent effects of our intervention. The oral language program, by contrast, had selective effects on the acquisition of specific vocabulary and on expressive grammar.

To summarize, the children who received the P+R program made better progress in basic reading skills and phoneme awareness, whereas the children who received the OL program made better progress in vocabulary and grammatical skills. The effects obtained were moderate to large in size, and most were maintained at follow-up 5 months after the intervention ceased. For present purposes, a key question is to what extent these interventions promoted literacy skills. As already noted, the P+R program appeared to promote decoding skills, which are, of course, fundamental to the development of proficient reading skills. However, neither program had a specific effect on the development of word recognition or reading comprehension. How should these findings be interpreted? In the absence of an untreated control group, the data are inherently ambiguous. It might be that both groups had benefited significantly, but for different reasons: perhaps direct instruction in sight word reading had benefited the P+R group, whereas work on oral language had boosted the children's ability to consolidate links between the printed and the spoken forms of words?

To clarify this issue, we compared the performance of the intervention groups on single-word reading to that of a large sample of 564 of their peers. We used a standard score below 85 for reading as a cut-off for being "at risk" of literacy problems. Overall, 46.5% of the children in the intervention sample remained at risk of reading difficulties, compared to 17.6% in the peer group. However, a larger percentage of the OL group

(68.1%) than of the P+R group (50%) remained at risk, and 7.1% of children in the P+R group now had above-average reading scores (greater than 115), while none of the OL children had scores in this range. It seemed, therefore, that the P+R program had a stronger effect on literacy development than did the OL program. However, these findings do not rule out the possibility of "sleeper" effects that may have positive effects on the children's progress at a later stage. Moreover, we think that the gains in oral language skills observed for the OL group will be beneficial more generally in terms of their participation in school.

TAKING STOCK OF THE EVIDENCE

Children who enter school with poor speech and language skills are at high risk of educational failure, not least because they have literacy difficulties. In this group, word-level decoding skills are an issue for many, and problems with reading comprehension are widespread. To date, only a limited amount of research has specifically addressed how best to intervene to promote these children's literacy skills and so stem the downward spiral of educational underachievement that ensues. Our own program of intervention research has had many positive outcomes: we now know with some certainty how we can intervene early to promote reading skills in children who are failing. We also know how to train and support teaching assistants effectively and how much they benefit in professional terms. However, we have also learned a hard lesson from this research, which is that children with oral language impairments appear to be the least easy to help—a finding echoed by Hindson et al. (2005), who reported that children from families with a history of dyslexia respond less well to early intervention than do peers who do not carry this risk. As yet, we still do not know precisely why these children are "resistant" to treatment. Perhaps some are on a slow developmental trajectory and not yet "ready" (in terms of the development of their phonological system) for learning to read? Perhaps others have more specific phonological difficulties and, in particular, difficulties consolidating new knowledge acquired through phonological learning processes? For still others, comorbid difficulties—for example, in attention control—are likely obstacles to learning. In many ways, then, we are left with as many questions as answers. However, it seems to us that a productive way forward, building on the success of our early intervention programs, would be to proceed to implement a version of our Oral Language intervention to be delivered in preschool to children with language delay, and for these children then to receive, at school entry, training in phonology and reading skills.

What general implications do our findings have for choosing intervention strategies? Inevitably, decisions about the management of children's reading and language difficulties are shaped by the current educational climate. The current climate is one of inclusion, where the aim is to educate children with language-based learning difficulties together with their peers in mainstream classrooms. Although this is a laudable aim, many professionals who work with these children are concerned that their needs are best met by intensive individualized programs of intervention, and these cannot easily be delivered in a mainstream setting. In an ideal case, a child's language difficulty and hence likely reading impairment will be identified early, and appropriate support will be given in the classroom. If such arrangements are insufficient to ensure normal progress, then a staged process of management needs to begin. We would argue that targeted support delivered to small groups of children by a trained teaching assistant is a good second-stage approach, and we have preliminary evidence that for children who do not respond well to such treatments one-to-one teaching can be helpful. However, we would also like to make the point that most of the research we have conducted has involved short-term interventions. Such interventions are also one of the mainstays of today's education system. However, such short-term interventions may neither be sufficiently intensive nor last long enough to meet the needs of many children. We believe that we need to move to intervention studies that last for longer and in which teaching continues until

children reach some specified level of competence (as in the approach originally pioneered in studies of Reading Recovery—e.g., Clay, 1985). Realistically, however, it may be that a minority of children require ongoing support for years rather than weeks. For such children, the aims of intervention may not be to eliminate their reading and language difficulties but, rather, to ameliorate these difficulties and support them, so that they can better access other areas of the curriculum.

ACKNOWLEDGMENTS

The first author wishes to acknowledge the support of a British Academy Research Fellowship during the preparation of this chapter. The intervention research was supported by the Nuffield Foundation, Economic and Social Research Council, and North Yorkshire County Council. Thanks go to many collaborators and, specifically, to Claudine Crane, Fiona Duff, Elizabeth Fieldsend, Julia Carroll, and Peter Hatcher.

REFERENCES

Beck, I. L., McKeown, M. G., & Kucan, L. (2002). *Bringing words to life: Robust vocabulary instruction.* New York: Guildford Press.

Beck, I., Perfetti, C., & McKeown, M. (1982). The effects of long-term vocabulary instruction on lexical access and reading comprehension. *Journal of Educational Psychology, 74,* 506–521.

Bird, J., Bishop, D. V. M., & Freeman, N. H. (1995). Phonological awareness and literacy development in children with expressive phonological impairments. *Journal of Speech and Hearing Research, 38,* 446–462.

Bishop, D. V. M., & Adams, C. (1990). A prospective study of the relationship between specific language impairment, phonological disorders and reading retardation. *Journal of Child Psychology and Psychiatry, 31,* 1027–1050.

Bishop, D. V. M., & Snowling, M. J. (2004). Developmental dyslexia and specific language impairment: Same or different? *Psychological Bulletin, 130*, 858–888.

Bowyer-Crane, C., Snowling, M. J., Duff, F., Fieldsend, E., Carroll, J., Miles, J., et al. (2008). Improving early language and literacy skills: Differential effects of an oral language versus a phonology with reading intervention. *Journal of Child Psychology and Psychiatry, 49*(4), 422–432.

Cain, K., Oakhill, J., & Bryant, P. E. (2004). Children's reading comprehension ability: Concurrent prediction by working memory, verbal ability, and component skills. *Journal of Educational Psychology, 96*, 31–42.

Carroll, J., Snowling, M. J., Hulme, C., & Stevenson, J. (2003). The development of phonological awareness in pre-school children. *Developmental Psychology, 39*, 913–923.

Castles, A., & Coltheart, M. (2004). Is there a causal link from phonological awareness to success in learning to read? *Cognition, 91*, 77–111.

Catts, H. W. (1993). The relationship between speech-language and reading disabilities. *Journal of Speech and Hearing Research, 36*, 948–958.

Catts, H. W., & Kamhi, A. G. (Eds.). (2005). *Language and reading disabilities* (2nd ed.). Boston, MA: Pearson.

Clay, M. (1985). *The early detection of reading difficulties* (3rd ed.). Tadworth, UK: Heinemann.

Duff, F., Fieldsend, E., Bowyer-Crane, C., Hulme, C., Smith, G., Gibbs, S., & Snowling, M. (2008). *Reading with Vocabulary Intervention: Evaluation of an instruction for treatment non-responders.* Revision under review.

Fuchs, L. S., & Fuchs, D. (2002). Curriculum-based measurement: Describing competence, enhancing outcomes, evaluating treatment effects, and identifying treatment nonresponders. *Peabody Journal of Education, 77*, 64–84.

Gibbs, S., & Smith, G. (2006). *Report on a field trial of reading intervention to the Director of Education, North Yorkshire County Council.* Retrieved April 5, 2008, from http://www.york.ac.uk/res/crl/research.html

Goulandris, N. (2006). Assessing reading and spelling skills. In M. J. Snowling & J. Stackhouse (Eds.), *Dyslexia, speech and language: A practitioner's handbook* (2nd ed., pp. 98–127). London: Whurr.

Griffiths, Y. M., & Snowling, M. J. (2002). Predictors of exception word and nonword reading in dyslexic children: The severity hypothesis. *Journal of Educational Psychology, 94*(1), 34–43.

Hatcher, P. (2000). *Sound linkage* (2nd ed.). London: Whurr.

Hatcher, P. (2006). Phonological awareness and reading intervention. In M. J. Snowling & J. Stackhouse (Eds.), *Dyslexia, speech and language: A Practitioner's handbook* (2nd ed., pp. 167–197). London: Whurr.

Hatcher, P. J., Goetz, K., Snowling, M. J., Hulme, C., Gibbs, S., & Smith, G. (2006a). Evidence for the effectiveness of the Early Literacy Support Programme. *British Journal of Educational Psychology, 73*, 351–367.

Hatcher, P., Hulme, C., & Ellis, A. W. (1994). Ameliorating early reading failure by integrating the teaching of reading and phonological skills: The phonological linkage hypothesis. *Child Development, 65*, 41–57.

Hatcher, P. J., Hulme, C., Miles, J. N. V., Carroll, J. M., Hatcher, J., Gibbs, S., et al. (2006b). Efficacy of small group reading intervention for beginning readers with reading-delay: A randomized controlled trial. *Journal of Child Psychology & Psychiatry, 47*, 820–827.

Hatcher, P. J., Hulme, C., & Snowling, M. J. (2004). Explicit phoneme training combined with phonic reading instruction helps young children at risk of reading failure. *Journal of Child Psychology & Psychiatry, 45*, 338–358.

Hindson, B., Byrne, B., Fielding-Barnsley, R., Newman, C., Hine, D. W., & Shankweiler, D. (2005). Assessment and early instruction of preschool children at risk for reading disability. *Journal of Educational Psychology, 97*, 687–704.

Lloyd, S. (1998). *The phonics handbook: A handbook for teaching reading, writing and spelling* (3rd ed.). Chigwell, UK: Jolly Learning.

McGuiness, C., McGuiness, D., & McGuiness, G. (1996). Phono-graphix: A new method for remediating reading difficulties. *Annals of Dyslexia, 46*, 73–96.

Morais, J., & Kolinsky, R. (2005). Literacy and cognitive change. In M. J. Snowling & C. Hulme (Eds.), *The science of reading: A handbook* (pp. 188–204). Oxford: Blackwell.

Muter, V., Hulme, C., Snowling, M. J., & Stevenson, J. (2004). Phonemes, rimes, vocabulary, and grammatical skills as foundations of early reading development: Evidence from a longitudinal study. *Developmental Psychology, 40*, 665–681.

Nathan, L., Stackhouse, J., Goulandris, N., & Snowling, M. J. (2004a). Educational consequences of developmental speech disorder: Key Stage 1 National Curriculum Assessment results in English and Mathematics. *British Journal of Educational Psychology, 74*, 173–186.

Nathan, E., Stackhouse, J., Goulandris, N., & Snowling, M. J. (2004b). The development of early literacy skills among children with speech difficulties: A test of the "critical age hypothesis." *Journal of Speech, Language, and Hearing Research, 47*, 377–391.

Nation, K., & Snowling, M. J. (2004). Beyond phonological skills: Broader language skills contribute to the development of reading. *Journal of Research in Reading, 27*, 342–356.

National Reading Panel (2000). *Report of the National Reading Panel: Reports of the subgroups.* Washington, DC: National Institute of Child Health and Human Development Clearing House.

Raitano, N. A., Pennington, B. F., Tunick, R. A., & Boada, R. (2004). Pre-literacy skills of subgroups of children with phonological disorder. *Journal of Child Psychology & Psychiatry, 45*, 821–835.

Ramus, F., Rosen, S., Dakin, S. C., Day, B. L., Castellote, J. M., White, S., et al. (2003). Theories of developmental dyslexia: Insights from a multiple case study of dyslexic adults. *Brain, 126*, 1–25.

Rhodes, A. (2001). *Rhodes to language.* Northumberland, UK: STASS.

Rutter, M. (2005). *Genes and behavior.* Oxford, UK: Blackwell.

Snowling, M. J. (2000). *Dyslexia.* Oxford, UK: Blackwell.

Snowling, M. J., Adams, J. W., Bishop, D. V. M., & Stothard, S. E. (2001). Educational attainments of school leavers with a preschool history of speech-language impairments. *International Journal of Language & Communication Disorders, 36*(2), 173–183.

Snowling, M. J., & Hulme, C. (1989). A longitudinal case study of developmental phonological dyslexia. *Cognitive Neuropsychology, 6*, 379–403.

Snowling, M. J., Muter, V., & Carroll, J. M. (2007). Children at family risk of dyslexia: A follow-up in adolescence. *Journal of Child Psychology & Psychiatry, 48*, 609–618

Snowling, M. J., & Stackhouse, J. (Eds.). (2006). *Dyslexia, speech & language: A practitioner's handbook* (2nd ed.). London: Whurr.

Stackhouse, J., & Snowling, M. J. (1992). Barriers to literacy development in two cases of developmental verbal dyspraxia. *Cognitive Neuropsychology, 9*, 273–299.

Stanovich, K. E. (1986). Matthew effects in reading: Some consequences of individual differences in the acquisition of literacy. *Reading Research Quarterly, 21*, 360–364.

Stothard, S. E., Snowling, M. J., Bishop, D. V. M., Chipchase, B., & Kaplan, C. (1998). Language impaired pre-schoolers: A follow-up in adolescence. *Journal of Speech, Language, and Hearing Research, 41*, 407–418.

Torgesen, J. K. (2000). Individual differences in response to early interventions in reading: The lingering problem of treatment registers. *Learning Disabilities Research & Practice, 15*, 55–64.

Torgesen, J. K. (2005). Recent discoveries on remedial interventions for children with dyslexia. In M. J. Snowling & C. Hulme (Eds.), *The science of reading: A handbook* (pp. 521–537). Oxford, UK: Blackwell.

Walley, A. (1993). The role of vocabulary development in children's spoken word recognition and segmentation ability. *Developmental Review, 13*, 286–350.

Wechsler, D. (1992). *Wechsler Intelligence Scale for Children* (3rd ed.). New York: The Psychological Corporation.

Whiteley, H. E., Smith, D., & Connors, L. (2007). Young children at risk of literacy difficulties: Factors predicting recovery from risk following phonologically-based intervention. *Journal of Research in Reading, 30*, 249–269.

12

Intervention for children with pragmatic language impairments

Catherine Adams

INTRODUCTION

Many children who have communication delays or impairments show difficulty in the domain of pragmatics—the understanding of how language is used in social contexts. When pragmatics as a linguistic discipline was first applied to child language disorder, the focus was on identifiable speech acts of children (Meline & Brackin, 1987) and the formal pragmatic devices observed in developing expressive language. Since that time, greater understanding of the relationship between cognitive, social, and language development, as well as increased interdisciplinary practice and research, has resulted in a much broader view of

the scope of pragmatics. In addition, the nature of and overlap between developmental psychopathological conditions and language impairment have become clearer. A more contemporary approach to pragmatics in child language disorder focuses therefore on the notion of "social communication," which encompasses both the formal aspects of pragmatics, social inferencing and verbal social interactions.

Communication interventions have struggled to keep up with this broadening of the conceptualization of pragmatics in child communication disorders into complex cognitive domains. This challenge has been compounded by the recognition that children across the spectrum of pervasive developmental disorders (i.e., autism and Asperger's syndrome) have significant need for communication interventions that target pragmatic skills. Increasing understanding of the nature of such conditions has led to greater numbers of children being identified (Rutter, 2005). Conti-Ramsden, Simkin, and Botting (2006) found that children with a history of specific language impairment (SLI) were more likely to present with features of autistic spectrum disorder at some stage in their development, albeit possibly in a subtle form. The relationship between SLI and autism spectrum conditions is therefore considered to be much closer than was previously thought (Bishop & Norbury, 2002). Increasing numbers of children with communication needs in pragmatics and social domains are therefore presenting for intervention to speech and language therapy services.

In this chapter, current diagnostic issues surrounding pragmatics and language disorders are briefly reviewed, and the current state of pragmatics intervention is outlined, along with some limitations. The principal purpose of this chapter is to present a framework for social communication intervention aimed at children who have pragmatic language impairments (PLI), providing an explicit route from assessment to intervention planning for these children, a description of intervention activities contained in the intervention program, and an outline of a randomized control trial of intervention we are currently undertaking. The evidence base for pragmatics intervention and related social communication interventions is summarized, and indications of appropriate future research strategies for intervention are presented.

Bishop (2000) describes pragmatic language impairment (PLI) as a condition that is intermediate between autism and language disorder. There is now reasonable consensus that children who have PLI possess some of the characteristics seen in children with SLI, such as grammatical and word-finding difficulties, and that some children with PLI have additional mild social difficulties similar to those seen in high-functioning children with autism spectrum disorders (ASD) or Asperger's syndrome, and some of them have language and social and pragmatic deficits (Adams, 2001; Bishop & Adams, 1989). PLI, therefore, is most commonly considered to be present in those children who do not exhibit significant symptomatology in all three aspects of the autism triad but who have a distinct difficulty with social communication. These children are likely to dominate conversations and are relatively unskilled in their ability to handle topic and information requirements in discourse, but they may show semantic and word-finding difficulties seen in children with SLI, and some may show some of the social interaction deficits and problems of social cognition seen in high-functioning ASD and Asperger's syndrome. Children with PLI are also thought to show problems with inference, nonliteral comprehension, and social skills (these features are examined with reference to theoretical bases for intervention below). In reality, there is little hard evidence for disproportionate difficulty with any of these characteristics in children with PLI (Bishop, Chan, Adams, Hartley, & Weir, 2000; Botting & Adams, 2005), and these language features are also seen in children with SLI (Norbury, 2005). In PLI, it seems that unusual language behaviors stand out because of these children's relative grammatical and phonological competence. Another possibility is that relatively mild expressions of the rigidity of thinking impact on language functioning in the form of difficulty in generating relevant ideas (Turner, 1999). Unfortunately it is not currently possible to tease these factors apart, but research continues to address the source of pragmatic difficulties.

Thus within the population of children who have PLI, there is a considerable variety of clinical pictures. Two brief descriptions of cases that fall into this category are shown in Table 12.1. Child 1 had a diagnosis of receptive language difficulty, and Child 2 had a diagnosis of Asperger's syndrome, but both would be considered to have characteristics of PLI, demonstrating that the term PLI functions as a descriptor. Important details contained in the case descriptions are, however, not reflected in their original diagnostic labels. For instance, no one had ever suspected that Child 2 had a word-finding difficulty, since he was very talkative and the diagnostic label implies that his language is normal. From a therapeutic viewpoint, the cases are remarkable for what they have in common in terms of social and language needs.

TABLE 12.1

Two children who have pragmatic language impairments with different clinical diagnoses

Child 1	Child 2
History of receptive language disorder	History of language delay followed by rapid development
Relatively passive in classroom	Finds it hard to keep up with classroom activity
Marked discourse problems	Verbose—tends to dominate conversations
Disorganized narratives (oral and written)	Formulaic narratives
Vocabulary limited for age	Significant word-finding difficulty
Produces tangential or irrelevant responses	Produces tangential or irrelevant responses
Interprets idiomatic language literally	Interprets idiomatic language literally
Low scores on inference tasks	Low scores on inference tasks
Changes topic frequently	Changes topic frequently
Shows anxiety in new situations	Shows anxiety in new situations
Is socially somewhat naive	Is socially somewhat naive
Finds it difficult to make friends	Finds it difficult to make friends

Current intervention for pragmatics

Diagnostic debates about PLI have been reported extensively in the literature (Bishop, 2000; Boucher, 1998) but have not served to elucidate appropriate interventions. Developing treatments has been left to resourceful practitioners. There is a clear need for theoretical frameworks on which to base intervention. An integrated approach is required—one that addresses the diversity of social, pragmatic, and language difficulties of a broad range of children with PLI—and this will be termed a social communication approach. This is preferred to pragmatics intervention since children with PLI present with more than solely pragmatic difficulties; however, reference will also be made to therapies that have focused on pragmatics as a principal component.

Key texts that have influenced current intervention practice in the United Kingdom have always given recognition to the three major developmental social, cognitive, and linguistic influences on pragmatics (Brinton & Fujiki, 1999; McTear & Conti-Ramsden, 1992; Prutting & Kirchner, 1987). However, there is no substantial validated framework for pragmatics intervention. Practitioners tend to view pragmatics as a broad-based set of behaviors, encompassing inference and social participation rather than simply the more formal linguistic devices seen in conversational exchanges and narratives. So the scope of clinical pragmatics is immediately broader than that of the traditional narrow view of pragmatics; this is one key to where an intervention framework might emerge. Practitioners have also been resourceful in the development of intervention programs (Firth & Venkatesh, 1999; Rinaldi, 2001), which are widely used and which draw on a typology of pragmatic behaviors rather than a theoretical framework. Some resources focus on encouragement of the formal linguistic aspects of pragmatic instruction, such as use of register and speech acts, and this, while valuable, has restricted application for some of the more able children with PLI. Practitioners, being aware of these limitations, have employed techniques and strategies used with related groups (e.g., Social Stories: Gray, 1998). There is, nevertheless, some consensus that therapy is resource- rather than principle-driven due to the research vacuum, and that there is little or no existing guidance to support these decisions. The main challenges that remain in pragmatics intervention therefore are:

- lack of a consistent theoretical framework to support intervention choices
- lack of a method of linking assessment findings to intervention priorities
- absence of evidence to support effectiveness
- lack of understanding of what it is about intervention which prompts change
- indications as to which children will benefit from which approach
- evidence to help establish best long-term provision for these children as they move through the school years.

How can theoretical research assist in supporting intervention choices?

Speech and language practitioners, being a dynamic and inventive group, have simply got on with the job of creating therapies that address specific pragmatic problems in the absence of intervention frameworks. To take the example of inference, practitioners talk about "assessing inference," "not being very good at inference," "doing inferences" in therapy. There is an implicit assumption that (a) we all understand what inferences are and (b) it is possible to improve the ability to make inferences during therapy. In reality, inferences are very difficult to identify and subtype, and we have no idea whether inference improves with therapy. By examining these assumptions, there is potential to explore the problems that an absence of theoretical framework brings.

Inferencing is about filling in unstated infor- mation in discourse. A theoretical framework to support inference therapies should inform prac- titioners that there are several types of infer- ence, with some inferences created from world knowledge applied to the interaction (elabora- tive inferences); others created from information provided earlier in the discourse (bridging infer- ences) and inferences created from word mean- ings. As humans we are constantly creating a running elaborated script of events from physical, contextual, and linguistic evidence. This helps us to create a rich representation of the context and people's behavior in that context and contributes to the redundancy of language. There are there- fore many different levels of representation and knowledge—only some of which are linguisti- cally represented—that are involved in inferential ability and are very difficult to constrain system- atically in assessment or intervention. Secondly, relatively little precise information exists regard- ing the emergence of types of inferential abil- ity, except that elaborative inferences appear to emerge before other types (Hudson & Slackman, 1990) and there are age norms in clinical use. A way forward may be to pay more attention to the type of inference and the types of cognitive and language representations we present children with in intervention and to work more systemati- cally on building up subskills of language com- prehension and memory.

Social skills training and social communication deficits

An intervention framework should also specify methods of intervention that have firm grounding in learning theories and effectiveness research. This statement needs justification, and in order to do this, the evidence status of one type of inter- vention currently used with children who have social communication difficulties or autism spec- trum disorders (ASD) will be explored. Social skills training is now the intervention norm in educational settings in the United Kingdom for children with such conditions and is frequently supported by the speech and language therapist within a consultancy model. Social skills train- ing methods arose within a behaviorist model (Thiemann & Goldstein, 2004) with a rationale based on modeling and reinforcement of the performance of specific social communicative acts, such as "greetings" and "looking at the speaker." The literature on social skills training is extensive. Numerous small-scale studies or single-case studies report "improvements" in social skills (De Boo & Prins, 2007; Kapp-Simon, McGuire, Long, & Simon, 2005).

Despite the profusion of reports, large-scale group studies of social skills training for children with ASD or social communication deficits are relatively lacking. In a recent review of 79 treatment studies of social skills training for children who have ASD, Matson, Matson, and Rivet (2007) point out the lack of robust methodologies, very small treatment effects, and the mixed quality of research design. In a further meta-analytical study, synthesis of data from a large number of single-case studies shows that social skills interventions have been minimally effective for children with ASD (Bellini, Peters, Benner, & Hopf, 2007). Comparisons of different training strategies are rare, training is provided in packages rather than being individualized, and often the nature of the social skills training is poorly specified. The evidence to show that social skills are generalized beyond the therapeutic setting or what impact they have on real-world understanding is relatively weak (Sanosti & Powell-Smith, 2006). Moreover, a lack of robust assessment measures and a profusion of subjective rating scales of limited validation have added to the confusion over the efficacy of such approaches. For example, Chung et al. (2007) studied the effects of social skills training that targeted social communication skills, over a period of 12 weeks, for four children with ASD aged 6–7 years. Using a rating scale and behavioral observation as outcome measures, they claim that the results suggest that the social skills training was effective in improving social communication skills. The difficulty of making such claims with no control condition and such small samples is clearly evident and reflects the chosen research approaches common within educational settings. Whereas the level of interest in social skills training research is laudable, there is clearly a need for coordination of large-scale studies to provide clear guidelines for practice.

Alarmingly, social skills training is being increasingly rolled out with inappropriate assumptions made about the effectiveness of this training for many groups of children. The merit of social skills training as a blanket approach to remediation of social communication disorders in children may, therefore, be especially suspect. The rationale of social skills training as promoting "performance" of communicative acts is far removed from the development within the child of an understanding of, and reflection upon, the complex rules of language and social interaction. What many social skills training programs tend to ignore is that, without adequate language comprehension and metalinguistic ability, it is likely to be difficult for children with PLI, or related conditions in which language is relatively weak, to understand, recall, and generalize gains made in training. Rather than training superficial social performance, we should approach social communication intervention via the establishment of adequate underpinning of skills such as language comprehension. Given the popularity of social skills training among speech and language therapists, there are very few studies that investigate social skills and language impairment. In an interesting small-scale study of children from a mainstream primary school in the United Kingdom, Godfrey, Pring, and Gascoigne (2005) showed that children with language problems made less progress than typically developing children in a social skills training program aimed at improving conversational skills. This suggests that when children have complex communication needs across language and social domains, training them to perform communicative acts will not, in isolation, be an effective intervention strategy, and a more comprehensive framework will be required to support therapy planning.

CURRENT PERSPECTIVES ON SPEECH AND LANGUAGE INTERVENTIONS FOR PLI

Relatively little research has focused on the effectiveness or efficacy of current management for children with PLI (Law, Garrett, & Nye, 2003). Studies that have considered intervention for a broad range of children's pragmatic difficulties (Bedrosian & Willis, 1987; Camarata & Nelson, 1992) have generally found positive progress, but the methodologies of these studies preclude them from being accepted as strong scientific evidence. Single-case studies have provided valuable information regarding progress with individualized therapy for children with PLI (Adams, 2001; Olswang, Coggins, & Timler, 2001; Timler, Olswang, & Coggins, 2005).

All of this research indicates that the communication skills of children with PLI and associated conditions probably benefit from speech and language therapy and indicate that specific improvements in pragmatic skills, which directly impinge upon the child's quality of communication, might be possible. Adams, Lloyd, Aldred, and Baxendale (2006) carried out an exploratory study of a series of interventions for PLI. Six children with PLI, aged between 6 and 11 years, participated in an intensive intervention aimed at social interaction and pragmatic skills only. The aim of this study was to generate a signal of change in communication behavior—that is, to ensure that there was a measurable amount of change in an observable behavior, which could be reliably demonstrated in most subjects and which could be scaled up to a larger study. The measurable outcomes chosen in this study were a combination of language subtests from the Clinical Evaluation of Language Fundamentals (CELF; Semel, Wiig, & Secord, 2004) and the Assessment of Comprehension and Expression (6–11) (ACE; Adams, Cooke, Crutchley, Hesketh, & Reeves, 2001) and the conversational coding measure employed in Adams (2001) and Bishop et al. (2000). Language measures tended to show strong change associated with intervention—thus generating a strong signal that these measures could be essential in a future randomized controlled trial. Figure 12.1 shows the profile of ACE and CELF subtest percentiles at pre- and postintervention for one subject in the study; the figure shows a clear upward trend for all language subtest percentiles, which is statistically significant.

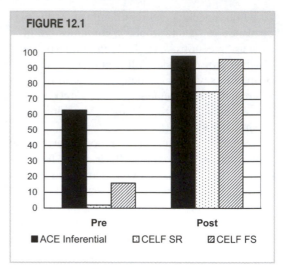

FIGURE 12.1

Mean pre- and posttherapy percentile ranks achieved on standardized tests by Child 3 (Adams et al., 2006).

However, Adams et al. (2006) also raised some of the measurement difficulties inherent in this heterogeneous group. Within even such a small group, some children presented with significant, measurable language impairments (see Figure 12.1), whereas other children, who still have clear pragmatic difficulties in everyday discourse and who emerge as communication-impaired on measures such as Bishop's Children's Communication Checklist–2 (Bishop, 2003), function at ceiling on language tests and may present a verbose and even precocious profile of structural language abilities. How can we accurately measure change in these children that is associated with intervention? Adams et al. (2006) achieved this by comparing conversational coding indices derived from semistructured interactions between adult and child (see Figure 12.2). Despite the small changes that are evident from visual inspection of Figure 12.2, these were in excess of calculated variation rates (Adams & Lloyd, 2005) and were therefore considered to be clinically significant.

Nevertheless the difficulty of measurement remains an issue for pragmatic behaviors. Outcomes based on standardized tests are subject to practice factors, though this can be offset to

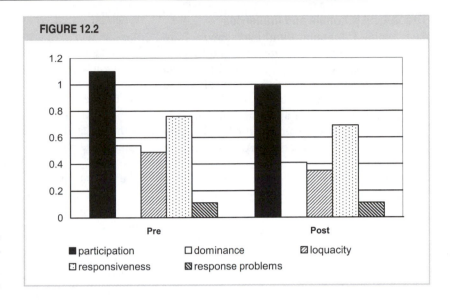

FIGURE 12.2

Mean pre- and posttherapy conversational behavior index scores for Child 1 (Adams et al., 2006).

some extent by the presence of a control condition. Outcomes based on detailed coding of pragmatic behaviors raise issues of reliability and stability that are only partly resolved and need to be repeated in new trials. Coding conversation behaviors is immensely labor-intensive and impractical at a clinical level, but new methods are being addressed to translate coding procedures into validated rating scales.

THE SOCIAL COMMUNICATION INTERVENTION PROJECT

The preliminary work of Adams et al. (2006; Adams, Baxendale, Lloyd, & Aldred, 2005) provided a sufficiently clear signal that interventions for children with PLI were worthy of further exploration. A revised framework of social communication intervention was therefore developed to support a randomized controlled trial of intervention. The framework consists of an assessment protocol, a procedure for mapping assessment to individualized intervention, a set of planning forms, and a large resource of therapeutic activities. The program is suitable for children aged

between 6 and 11 years, though some younger able children will be able to access the content of the program and some older children may also benefit from more challenging activities. The intervention activities are set out in a standard format with purpose, targets, and evaluation strategies in addition to strategies for accessing the appropriate level of input or making demands that will achieve optimal learning for that child. The program incorporates:

- a rationale based on developmental social, pragmatic, and psycholinguistic trajectories
- a set of language, pragmatic, and social assessments that enable mapping to intervention priorities
- a procedure for decision making providing a principled route from a set of assessments to intervention goals
- the detailed goals and activities of the intervention.

The program therefore contains elements that will be easily recognizable to practitioners. It should be noted that the framework and associated manual of intervention have not yet been subject to validation procedures and remain experimental at this stage.

Theoretical rationale and influences

The Social Communication Intervention Project (SCIP) development team has interdisciplinary experience across language impairment and autism interventions. We were further influenced by contemporary work on collaborative education practices, child-centered approaches to language delay (Tannock & Girolametto, 1992), and early childhood autism interventions (Aldred, Green, & Adams, 2004).

In the framework, social communication is seen as the integration of three main components that interact in development:

1. social interaction and social understanding: development of social interaction and empathy; development of shared and mutual knowledge;

2. language pragmatics: development of formal, pragmatic devices;

3. language processing: development of formal language-specific syntactic, semantic, and phonological processing.

It is important to emphasize that, although these three aspects have been separated in the framework, for many communicative tasks it is impossible to differentiate between social, cognitive, and linguistic ingredients of competence, as all three must function as a coordinated whole. It follows that communication interventions should therefore aim to promote a synergistic competence in which all aspects of development are combined to support pragmatics.

The framework includes two important assumptions: first, *social cognitive development is a primary factor* in the satisfactory development of pragmatic skills. This implies that for children whose social development has been adversely affected, there are potential constraints on what changes can be achieved in pragmatics interventions. This indicates that the intervention framework must make provision for compensatory, adaptive interventions as well as impairment-based treatments. Second, *language ability contributes to social communication competence* primarily in terms of comprehension competence but pervades all social communication tasks, including those of narrative organization. The implication is that language therapies will influence pragmatic ability and broader social communication. Given that children with PLI have difficulties to varying degrees across social cognitive and language domains, the framework must make provision for both and attempt to match the child's needs to appropriate choices of intervention.

The key components of intervention in SCIP

The content of the SCIP has been derived from expertise in both speech and language therapy and from cognitive-behavioral approaches used in child psychiatry. This combination of knowledge across disciplines *and* a specialist approach to the underlying language disorders is one of the key features of the program. The three main components of the program (see Figure 12.3) are now described, with a brief rationale for each.

Intervention Component 1: Social interaction and social understanding

The first component of SCIP, "Social interaction and social understanding," aims to develop awareness, understanding, observation, and insight into the meaning of social cues and the relationships to children's reciprocal interactions. Developing understanding is the beginning of a process facilitated through adult scaffolding. These skills are initially be coached in a one-to-one situation where good examples are illustrated and sabotage—games in which "rules" are flouted—is used to elicit understanding and insight into problem-solving strategies. This part of the program also focuses on friendship skills as one of the most pertinent social situations for primary-school-age children (Bauminger, 2002; Fujiki, Brinton, Hart, & Fitzgerald, 1999) and on the inferring of emotions, known to be a prevalent need in PLI and SLI populations (Spackman, Fujiki, & Brinton, 2006).

Each component is divided for practical reasons into several aspects of development that have theoretical or developmental coherence within that domain and are known to be typical areas of need for children with PLI.

FIGURE 12.3

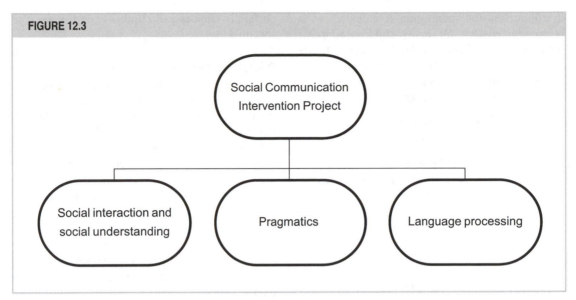

Principal components of the Social Communication Intervention Project.

The subcomponents of "Social interaction and social understanding" are:

- "Understanding social context"
- "Understanding emotions"
- "Developing and understanding flexibility"
- "Understanding social cues"
- "Understanding nonstated social information"
- "Understanding friendships."

Intervention Component 2: Pragmatics

Children with PLI tend to be poor at matching style to context and at providing adequate information for listeners. In this component, intervention focuses on direct work on the formal aspects of pragmatics at a reflective or metapragmatic level, explicitly talking about rules and conventions and putting these into practice, learning the effective language forms for different personal intentions, ways of manipulating language forms in context to convey changes of meaning, and the rules of conversational exchanges.

The "Pragmatics" component is divided into six subcomponents:

- "Interlocutor skills and clarifications"
- "Understanding information requirements"
- "Turn-taking conventions"
- "Topic management conventions"
- "Conversational mechanics"
- "Matching style to context."

Intervention Component 3: Language processing

"Language processing" refers to the understanding and production of linguistic forms, including grammatical and semantic competence. Research has confirmed the presence of persistent characteristics of SLI in children with PLI (Adams, 2001; Botting & Conti-Ramsden, 1999; Norbury, 2005). The underlying rationale is that work on linguistic competence supports the understanding and expression of social conventions but also, crucially, supports the development of complex verbal understanding through which complex social meanings are conveyed. In this component, particular attention is paid to high-level features of language organization, such as the construction of narratives and the relationships among word meanings. The development of self-help strategies in comprehension monitoring is included, as it is recognized that for many children adaptive interventions are important for their personal self-esteem and long-term maintenance of gains.

The "Language processing" component is divided into six subcomponents:

- "Word-finding and semantics"
- "Narrative construction"
- "Expansion of vocabulary"
- "Expansion of understanding of idiomatic language"
- "Comprehension of text and complex sentences"
- "Comprehension monitoring."

Mapping assessment to intervention

Sound interventions are built upon comprehensive assessment data. The next step in SCIP entails the use of a set of well-validated instruments and checklists to plan intervention. In this mapping exercise an individual child's assessment profile is transferred to a set of priorities for intervention using a clearly defined procedure. In large-scale research studies of complex interventions, this is an essential process in order to control the route through the program and ensure stability of clinical judgments. The mapping process will be of value in broader practice as a principled method of decision making and prioritization, but it requires validation in research first.

The SCIP intervention framework then specifies a route from the child's assessment profile to a set of linked therapy choices. In the experimental version of the intervention manual assessment results are compared to criteria that trigger intervention. It should be noted carefully that there are limitations to this procedure at the present time. Generally, trigger criteria for nonstandardized test assessments are based solely on clinical expertise, though it is anticipated that validation via feedback from case studies over time will improve this position. Secondly, it is possible that some children's assessment profile will trigger every single component and aspect of intervention and that this simply cannot be practically achieved. Therefore, prioritization criteria based

on family choices and clinical expertise are also specified.

Prioritizing intervention goals

Having identified intervention needs from the mapping process, goals of therapy are selected in SCIP according to prioritization guidelines. For some children there may be only a few, or there may be many aspects within the three domains that are highlighted. The practitioner may prioritize some aspects of intervention based on individual clinical need. In order to do this, a clinical decision-making process needs to be carried out. A principled decision-making process similar to the procedures employed in McCartney et al. (2004) is used in SCIP and reflects common clinical expert practice. Decisions are based on the following:

- What aspects of intervention would have maximum impact on the child's well-being and ability to function in a social group?
- What aspects of communication and social behavior have parents and teachers identified as priorities for their children (Knott, Dunlop, & Mackay, 2006)?
- What aspects of intervention would promote the most immediate change in communication function?
- What aspects of intervention would best address current language functioning?

Goals of intervention and activities

Having chosen intervention goals, therapy then proceeds via a series of activities and contextualization actions linked to those goals in the manual. In the example provided in Figure 12.4, the child's assessment profile and prioritization of needs has suggested that work within the "Pragmatics" unit, "Understanding information requirements" subcomponent, should be targeted in the child's intervention program.

In the program, each subcomponent contains several goals, aimed at building up the behaviors and skills identified by assessment. For example, if the Pragmatics subcomponent, Understanding Information Requirements has been identified as

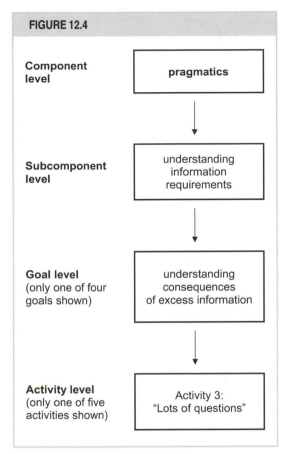

FIGURE 12.4

Component level	**pragmatics**

| Subcomponent level | understanding information requirements |

| Goal level (only one of four goals shown) | understanding consequences of excess information |

| Activity level (only one of five activities shown) | Activity 3: "Lots of questions" |

Subcomponents of Pragmatics in SCIP, showing one goal within Understanding Information Requirements and the route to activities aimed toward achieving that goal.

a priority after assessment mapping, then the first three goals for that subcomponent are:

1. understanding sequencing and information shown in pictures;
2. missing out part of verbal sequences verbal only;
3. understanding the consequences of excess information.

Goal 3, in turn, has five associated activities: for example, an activity in this goal is aimed at showing the child what happens when speakers ask too many questions and engaging them in games in which they listen and ask too many questions in a sabotage procedure. The complete activity is shown in Exhibit 12.1.

Contextualization action

Interventions that are delivered in a one-to-one therapist/child setting have the benefit of allowing intensive practice of targeted social understanding, language, and pragmatic skills. However, the limitation of any clinic-based intervention is that gains made and even understood by the child in one context may not be remembered or actioned in other contexts. SCIP therefore has as a central feature a series of contextualization actions associated with all components and subcomponents. This values the important role of people in the child's life with whom he/she will interact frequently and naturally. Support for child–familiar adult interactions and the adaptation of the environment with learning supports has a significant and long-term impact on that child's development (Rubin & Laurent, 2004). The overarching contextualization action is therefore the adaptation of communication complexity and style by those working around the child. This is the first action that is instigated outside intervention sessions and is achieved through informal training and advice. Interestingly, teachers and parents are often unaware that, say, language comprehension may need to be simplified and supported for a child who is verbose and appears linguistically precocious. Once it is established that the language performance belies actual comprehension, the scene is set to match input to ability more appropriately. Other contextualization activities are related to each subcomponent in turn. Some may involve bringing what is discussed in therapy into the classroom; others, bringing into therapy what happens outside, or linking activities directly to curriculum or small group work in the classroom.

A RANDOMIZED CONTROLLED TRIAL OF SOCIAL COMMUNICATION INTERVENTION

Having formulated a framework for intervention, we are now in a position to test rigorously whether the intervention is effective. There is a tension in evidence-based practice between

EXHIBIT 12.1: Example of an activity in SCIP

Unit: pragmatic
Subcomponent: understanding information requirements
Goal: understanding the consequences of excess information
Activity: "Lots of questions"

- *Purpose*

  To demonstrate the consequences of asking too many questions in social situations

- *Materials*

  Conversation situation cards with topics

  Toy figures or puppets who come along to ask lots of questions

  Detective figure or picture

- *Procedure*

  Start up a conversation using the situation cards; after a few turns, start to ask lots of questions about the topic, without allowing the child to answer them.

  Stop and talk about what happened, and how this made the child feel.

  Repeat, asking the child to role-reverse or speak through the puppet.

  Talk about what happened: too many questions, not interesting, didn't understand what you were asking, etc.

  Repeat using the detective figure and another figure. We're going to pretend that we saw someone stealing a bike, and the detective is going to ask us all questions. Vary the number of questions that the policeman asks, and ask the child to identify whether the policeman is asking too many questions and whether the questions he asked were useful and relevant. Reflect on this: did he ask you questions that you knew the answer to? Did he ask you things you couldn't possibly know? How many questions?

  Role-reversal: allow the child to be the detective—asking too many questions, or just enough.

  Draw up some summary rules about asking questions and put these in the Homebook.

- *Success Criteria*

  The child will demonstrate awareness of an appropriate questioning style.

  Move to Activity 4 in this goal.

- *Input guidance*

  Observe the child's responses, and if he or she is unsuccessful or is finding the task too easy, react in one of the following ways:

Ways to make the activity easier:	*Ways to increase complexity:*
Use shorter conversations/fewer questions	Use greater number of questions
Ask a series of questions to demonstrate an interrogative style and say this is what you need to watch out for	Relate this to information needs at a more abstract level
Allow the child to watch you using good and poor questioning styles	Introduce someone else into the activity
	Move to next activity

scientific requirements of the evidence, the realistic practicalities of acquiring such evidence, and the need to produce evidence that can be translated into real treatments that families and educators want. Accepted levels of strength of evidence consistently rate the randomized controlled trial (RCT) as the strongest type of evidence (Sackett et al., 1996). A well-conducted RCT should have the advantage of control over bias (through random allocation to condition) and chance (principally through size) and should meet accepted standards, such as blinding of assessors to group status. RCTs of clinical interventions in pediatric speech-language therapy are relatively rare and often have methodological weaknesses that lessen their impact on policy or cause them to be discarded.

Based on their previous work, Adams and her colleagues have developed a research protocol for the SCIP, a randomized controlled trial of intervention for children with pragmatic language impairments that is in progress at the time of publication. In this trial, 99 children meeting a broad definition of PLI and aged between 6 and 11 years, who attended mainstream primary schools in North West England or Scotland, participated in either an intervention based on SCIP as outlined above or a control condition in which children continue to receive their usual speech and language intervention. Children were randomly assigned to groups and completed assessments at the start of therapy, immediately after therapy, or six months later, with an equivalent schedule of assessment for control children. Children received 20 sessions of individually tailored intervention mapped from their Time 1 assessment profiles and delivered by a specialist speech and language therapist or a trained assistant practitioner. The challenges of moving from case-based exploration of interventions for children with PLI to a full randomized controlled trial are:

1. *Stability and validity of pragmatic measures and their use as outcome measures*: Parent report instruments (of pragmatic functioning) such as the CCC–2 (Children's Communication Checklist–2; Bishop, 2003) are prone to reliability problems, and in this RCT they were supplemented by an observational measure (ALICC: Analysis of Language Impaired Children's Conversation; Bishop et al., 2000).

2. *The heterogeneous nature of PLI*: This remains an outstanding problem for many trials in speech and language therapy across patient populations. The SCIP RCT addresses this in part by an analysis of possible moderating variables that may explain intervention results based on case characteristics.

3. *How best to incorporate families' and children's perspectives and values of the intervention*: Given the complexity of these children and their intervention needs, a crucial variable in change may lie *outside* the content of the annualized intervention. The extent to which families and schools were offered an opportunity to engage in the intervention and the extent to which this provision is taken up was recorded using interviews and questionnaires.

4. *Controlling variables in a complex intervention*: The most commonly reported fault of speech and language therapy trials tends to be a lack of detail of the intervention given and lack of control over how it was interpreted by research therapists. The credibility of RCTs relies on their qualities of validity (control over the delivery and nature of the intervention), reliability (outcomes could be repeated in another context), and generalizability (the study group is representative of the broad clinical population). Woolf (2001) asked if complex interventions can ever meet these characteristics of an RCT. Specifically, problems abound in speech-language therapy concerning the precision of intervention delivery, who delivers it, and whether there are unmeasured variables that affect outcomes. One way to circumvent this is to produce a manual of intervention with clear assessment and intervention pathways, such as in the SCIP study outlined above. Woolf suggests that rather than abandoning RCTs for complex interventions, we should

modify them by measuring treatment fidelity, which is an external measurement of the extent to which the experimental intervention is being delivered as specified in the mineralization process.

Mediators and moderators of social communication intervention

Whereas it is essential that effectiveness of a pragmatics intervention should be able to be demonstrated using robust methodology, such findings can have limited generalization because it is not known what moderating factors within the children or which mediating factors within the intervention prompted the change. Treatment moderators "specify for whom or under what conditions the treatment worked" (Kraemer, Wilson, Fairburn, & Agras, 2002). In intervention studies of children with PLI, moderators might be social cognitive skills, other nonverbal abilities possessed by the child, or language capacity on entering therapy, such as grammatical comprehension. It might, for instance, be predicted that children with better insight into others' minds and motivations might understand the process of learning about social rules and social understanding more easily than those who do not. Similarly, children with relative strength in verbal comprehension might find it easier to access the intervention than children with limited comprehension of language. By identifying and assessing moderating factors in social communication intervention studies, we might be able to better direct interventions at individuals who will benefit the most and adapt therapies for those who cannot access them so easily.

Treatment mediators are the possible mechanisms of change through which a treatment achieves its effects (Kraemer et al., 2002). The value of establishing mediators is to narrow down the key elements of an intervention to the essential content, thus enhancing the *efficiency* of an intervention for its recipients. Applied to studies of intervention for children with PLI, it is important to establish a causal link between elements of the intervention and outcomes. Establishing causality is far more difficult, however, than establishing an association, and it demands a large quantity of data for statistical analysis. One potential mediator in a pragmatics intervention might be the level of skill (perhaps in terms of finely tuned input) of the therapist; others might be the frequency of the intervention or the strategies used to contextualize language gains in the classroom. In reality, establishing causality of a mediator requires a series of RCTs, in which the mediator is systematically varied. Neither of these is easy to achieve in studies of intervention for children with PLI, because of limitations of funding, of accessibility to children, and, therefore, of statistical power.

CONCLUSION

In this chapter, a framework for social communication intervention, which has potential to be accessed by children with pragmatic language impairments and their families and schools, has been presented. The framework has emerged from a synthesis of evidence regarding social, pragmatic, and linguistic competence in these children. Consideration has also been given to the way in which this intervention might be evaluated in an evidence-based practice context and to the current limitations of raising evidence for socially complex interventions. Further challenges remain in the shape of children's and families' attitudes and values of the intervention, which undoubtedly influence outcome. If speech and language practitioners can implement theoretically motivated interventions for children with PLI and subject these to the highest-level of methodological scrutiny, then there is potential to influence policy and broader clinical and educational practice.

REFERENCES

Adams, C. (2001). Clinical diagnostic studies of children with semantic-pragmatic language disorder. *International Journal of Language & Communication Disorders, 36*, 289–306.

Adams, C., Baxendale, J., Lloyd, J., & Aldred, C. (2005). Pragmatic language impairment: Case studies of social and pragmatic language therapy. *Child Language Teaching and Therapy*, *21*, 227–250.

Adams, C., Cooke, R., Crutchley, A., Hesketh, A., & Reeves, D. (2001). *Assessment of Comprehension and Expression 6–11*. Windsor, UK: NFER-Nelson.

Adams, C., & Lloyd, J. (2005). Elicited and spontaneous communicative functions and stability of conversational measures with children who have pragmatic language impairments. *International Journal of Language & Communication Disorders, 40*, 333–348.

Adams, C., Lloyd, J., Aldred, C., & Baxendale, J. (2006). Exploring the effects of communication intervention for developmental pragmatic language impairments: A signal-generation study. *International Journal of Language & Communication Disorders, 41*, 41–66.

Aldred, C., Green, J., & Adams, C. (2004). A new social communication intervention for children with autism: Pilot randomised controlled treatment study suggesting effectiveness. *Journal of Child Psychology and Psychiatry*, *45*, 1420–1430.

Bauminger, N. (2002). The facilitation of social-emotional understanding and social interaction in high-functioning children with autism. *Journal of Autism and Developmental Disorders*, *32*, 283–398.

Bedrosian, J. L., & Willis, T. L. (1987). Effects of treatment on the topic performance of a school age child. *Language, Speech, and Hearing Services in Schools*, *18*, 158–167.

Bellini, S., Peters, J. K., Benner, L., & Hopf, A. (2007). A meta-analysis of school-based social skills interventions for children with autism spectrum disorders. *Remedial and Special Education*, *28*, 153–162.

Bishop, D. V. M. (2000). Pragmatic language impairment: A correlate of SLI, a distinct subgroup, or part of the autistic continuum? In D. V. M. Bishop & L. Leonard (Eds.), *Speech and language impairments in children: Causes, characteristics, intervention and outcome* (pp. 99–113). Hove, UK: Psychology Press.

Bishop, D. V. M. (2003). *The Children's Communication Checklist* (Version 2). London: Harcourt Press.

Bishop, D. V. M., & Adams, C. (1989). Conversational characteristics of children with semantic-pragmatic disorder. II: What features lead to a judgement of inappropriacy? *British Journal of Disorders of Communication*, *24*, 241–263.

Bishop, D. V. M., Chan, J., Adams, C., Hartley, J., & Weir, F. (2000). Conversational responsiveness in specific language impairment: Evidence of disproportionate pragmatic difficulties in a subset of children. *Development and Psychopathology*, *12*, 177–199.

Bishop, D. V. M., & Norbury, C. F. (2002). Exploring the borderlands of autistic disorder and specific language impairment: A study using standardised diagnostic instruments. *Journal of Child Psychology and Psychiatry*, *43*, 917–929.

Botting, N., & Adams, C. (2005). Inferential and semantic abilities in children with communication disorders. *International Journal of Language & Communication Disorders*, *40*, 49–66.

Botting, N., & Conti-Ramsden, G. (1999). Pragmatic language impairment without autism: The children in question. *Autism*, *3*, 371–396.

Boucher, J. (1998). SPD as a distinct diagnostic entity: Logical considerations and directions for future research. *International Journal of Language & Communication Disorders*, *33*, 71–108

Brinton, B., & Fujiki, M. (1999). Social interactional behaviours of children with specific language impairment. *Topics in Language Disorders*, *19*, 49–69.

Camarata, S. M., & Nelson, K. E. (1992). Treatment efficiency as a function of target selection in the remediation of child language disorders. *Clinical Linguistics & Phonetics*, *6*, 167–178.

Chung, K. M., Reavis, S., Mosconi, M., Drewry, J., Matthews, T., & Tasse, M. J. (2007). Peer-mediated social skills training program for young children with high-functioning autism. *Research in Developmental Disabilities*, *28*, 423–436.

Conti-Ramsden, G., Simkin, Z., & Botting, N. (2006). The prevalence of autism spectrum conditions in adolescents with a history of specific language impairment. *Journal of Child Psychology and Psychiatry*, *47*, 621–628.

De Boo, G. M., & Prins, P. J. (2007). Social incompetence in children with ADHD: Possible moderators and mediators in social skills training. *Clinical Psychology Review*, *27*, 78–97.

Firth, C., & Venkatesh, K. (1999). *Semantic-pragmatic language disorder*. Bicester, UK: Winslow.

Fujiki, M., Brinton, B., Hart, C. H., & Fitzgerald, A. H. (1999). Peer acceptance and friendship in children with specific language impairment. *Topics in Language Disorders*, *19*, 34–48.

Gray, C. A. (1998). Social stories and comic strip conversations with students with Asperger syndrome and high-functioning autism. In E. Schopler & G. Mesibov (Eds.), *Asperger syndrome or high-functioning autism?* New York: Plenum Press.

Godfrey, J., Pring, T., & Gascoigne, M. (2005). Developing conversational skills in mainstream schools: An evaluation of group therapy. *Child Language Teaching and Therapy, 21,* 251–262.

Hudson, J. A., & Slackman, E. A. (1990). Children's use of scripts in inferential text processing. *Discourse Processes, 13,* 375–385.

Kapp-Simon, K. A., McGuire, D. E., Long, B. C., & Simon, D. J. (2005). Addressing quality of life issues in adolescents: Social skills interventions. *Cleft Palate–Craniofacial Journal, 42,* 45–50.

Knott, F., Dunlop, A. W., & Mackay, T. (2006). Living with ASD: How do children and their parents assess their difficulties with social interaction and understanding? *Autism, 10,* 609–617.

Kraemer, H. C., Wilson, G. T., Fairburn, C. G., & Agras, S. W. (2002). Mediators and moderators of treatment effects in randomized clinical trials. *Archives of General Psychiatry, 59,* 877–883.

Law, J., Garrett, Z., & Nye, C. (2003). *Speech and language therapy interventions for children with primary speech and language delay or disorder. The Cochrane Library, Issue 3.* Oxford, UK: Update Software.

Matson, J. L., Matson, M. L., & Rivet, T. T. (2007). Social-skills treatments for children with autism spectrum disorders: An overview. *Behaviour Modification, 31,* 682–707.

McCartney, E., Boyle, J., Bannatyne, S., Jessiman, E., Campbell, C., et al. (2004). Becoming a manual occupation? The construction of a therapy manual for use with language impaired children in mainstream primary schools. *International Journal of Language & Communication Disorders, 39,* 135–148.

McTear, M., & Conti-Ramsden, G. (1992). *Pragmatic disability in children.* London: Whurr.

Meline, T. J., & Brackin, S. R. (1987). Language-impaired children's awareness of inadequate messages. *Journal of Speech and Hearing Disorders, 52,* 263–270.

Norbury, C. F. (2005). The relationship between theory of mind and metaphor: Evidence from children with language impairment and autism spectrum disorders. *British Journal of Developmental Psychology, 23,* 383–399.

Olswang, L. B., Coggins, T. E., & Timler, G. R. (2001). Outcome measures for school-age children with social communication problems. *Topics in Language Disorders, 21,* 50–73.

Prutting, C. A., & Kirchner, D. M. (1987). A clinical appraisal of the pragmatic aspects of language. *Journal of Speech and Hearing Disorders, 52,* 105–109.

Rinaldi, W. (2001). *Social Use of Language Programme (SULP)* (Revised). Windsor, UK: NFER-Nelson.

Rubin, E., & Laurent, A. C. (2004). Implementing a curriculum-based assessment to prioritize learning objectives in Asperger syndrome and high-functioning autism. *Topics in Language Disorders, 24,* 298–315.

Rutter, M. (2005). Incidence of autism spectrum disorders: Changes over time and their meaning. *Acta Paediatrica, 94,* 2–15.

Sackett, D. L., Rosenberg, W. M. C., Muir Gray, J. A., Haynes, R. B., & Richardson, W. S. (1996). Evidence based medicine: What it is and what it isn't. *British Medical Journal, 312,* 71–72.

Sanosti, F., & Powell-Smith, K. A. (2006). Using social stories to improve the social behaviour of children with Asperger syndrome. *Journal of Positive Behaviour Interventions, 8,* 43–57.

Semel, E., Wiig, E., & Secord, W. (2004). *Clinical evaluation of language fundamentals* (4th ed.). Hove, UK: Harcourt.

Spackman, M. P., Fujiki, M., & Brinton, B. (2006). Understanding emotions in context: The effects of language impairment on children's ability to infer emotions. *International Journal of Language & Communication Disorders, 41,* 173–188.

Tannock, R., & Girolametto, L. (1992). Re-assessing parent-focused language intervention programs. In: F. Warren & J. Reichle (Eds.), *Causes and effects in communication and language intervention.* Baltimore: Paul H. Brookes.

Thiemann, K. S., & Goldstein, H. (2004). Effects of peer training and written text cueing on social communication of school-age children with pervasive developmental disorder. *Journal of Speech, Hearing, and Language Research, 47,* 126–144.

Timler, G. R., Olswang, L. B., & Coggins, T. E. (2005). "Do I know what I need to do?" A social communication intervention for children with complex clinical profiles. *Language, Speech, and Hearing Services in Schools, 36,* 73–85.

Turner, M. (1999). Repetitive behaviour in autism: A review of psychological research. *Journal of Child Psychology and Psychiatry, 40,* 839–849.

Woolf, N. (2001). Randomised trials of socially complex interventions: Promise or peril? *Journal of Health Services Research Policy, 6,* 123–126.

13

Diagnostic concepts
and risk processes

Michael Rutter

DIAGNOSTIC CONCEPTS

The traditional concept of the diagnosis of specific language impairment (SLI) was that it was a specific diagnostic category involving a pure language problem. The presumption was that it was both separate from normal variations in the timing of language acquisition and separate from other developmental and psychopathological disorders. Current official classification systems such as DSM–IV (American Psychiatric Association, 2000) and ICD–10 (World Health Organization, 1996) use the terminology of the overarching concept of developmental disorder. The implication of that term is that SLI is thought to be crucially different from acquired disorders

of language. Both classification systems go on to make categorical distinctions among several supposedly different types of SLI.

SLI and normal variations

The first issue that needs to be addressed concerns the differentiation between SLI and normal variation. There are four key findings that are relevant to the differentiation between SLI and normal variation. First, all epidemiological studies have shown huge individual variation in the age at which children first speak, regardless of how "first speaking" is conceptualized and measured. In essence, this marked individual variation is directly comparable with the huge variations seen for all other developmental milestones, such as the eruption of primary and secondary dentition, walking independently, and reaching puberty. The second key finding is that of markedly later talkers at the age of 2 to 3 years, about half appear to have caught up by age 5 years (Dale, Price, Bishop, & Plomin, 2003; Rescorla, 2005). Third, of those late talkers who have caught up by age 5 years, most continue to show normal language performance, but, on the other hand, minor subtle deficits may be evident in some (Stothard, Snowling, Bishop, Chipchase, & Kaplan, 1998). Fourth, in the children with SLI that involves receptive difficulties, which persists into the school years, follow-up studies have shown that continuing language and/or literacy problems—often associated with social difficulties—are frequently still evident in adolescence and adult life (Clegg, Hollis, Mawhood, & Rutter, 2005; Horwitz et al., 2003).

Three key conclusions are indicated. First, persistent SLI is clearly *not* just a normal variation. This conclusion derives from the consistent evidence that impairment persists for such a long time beyond the normal age of language acquisition and that it involves a wide range of functioning. If SLI were simply an extreme of normal variation, meaning a maturational lag and not any kind of disorder, it would be expected that the age at which children with persistent SLI master language would be on a normally distributed curve, albeit at one end of this curve. However, that is not at all what is found: the age of acquiring language is way beyond a normal curve. It is very unlikely that this extreme derives from the lack of adequate teaching of language in an otherwise normal child, because, ordinarily, language is not learned through the process of direct teaching.

Second, most of the late talkers who do catch up by age 5 or thereabouts do truly represent a normal variation in that there are few, if any, serious sequelae. In short, although SLI is not simply a normal variation, there are many cases of late acquisition in language that do represent normal variation. Third, there is probably no entirely sharp categorical distinction between SLI and normal variation: in other words, a proportion of those who catch up might have a milder variety of SLI. This is suggested by the minor sequelae found in some instances and by the very wide variation in the overall severity of SLI.

Can SLI and normal variation be differentiated before speech begins?

This is a very crucially important clinical issue because, of course, many children are brought to a clinic by their parents just because speech has not begun. Depending on local circumstances, the referral may be to a pediatrician, or to a child psychiatrist, or to a speech-language pathologist or therapist—or the concern may be expressed only at primary care level to the family doctor or to the practice's associated health visitor or nurse. It would be most unhelpful if the answer given—because, say, the child was not using single words by the age of 2 years or was not using phrase speech by, say, 30 months—were that many children are late in talking and most grow out of it and develop perfectly normally. That would be statistically correct, but a "wait-and-see" policy would be clinically irresponsible if it meant overlooking children whose problems warranted more substantial investigation (see Baird, chapter 1, this volume). It may be concluded that, to some extent, SLI and normal variation can be differentiated before speech begins, but we need to recognize that research findings on key features are limited or lacking and the differentiation is probabilistic and subject to substantial error.

Nevertheless, a broad-based clinical assessment (Bishop & Norbury, 2008; Rutter, 1985) can serve to differentiate normal variation from a range of disorders that require more detailed attention. Of course, such disorders are by no means confined to SLI: they would include, for example, deafness, autism spectrum disorders, and severe intellectual disability (ID)—to mention but three patterns that need to be considered. A disorder, rather than normal variation, is more likely if the child's babble is impaired in quantity or abnormal in quality; if there is limited use of babble for social communication; if an understanding of language is limited; if there is little attention to other people's talk; if there is little communicative use of gesture; if there is poorly developed pretend play; if there is a positive family history of definite language problems; if socioemotional functioning is impaired; and/or if there are problems in motor control as indexed by marked drooling, problems in chewing, and/or problems in blowing. If none of these show abnormalities, the probability—but not certainty—is that there may be nothing more than a normal variation in language acquisition. If, on the other hand, any or all of these indicators show problems, some form of disorder (not necessarily SLI) would need to be considered and further investigation would ordinarily be indicated.

Some children are not referred because of a delay in the first use of words but, rather, because language development seems to be proceeding so slowly that there is a concern. Accordingly, the next question is whether SLI and normal variation can be differentiated by the severity of language impairment after speech begins in the preschool years. The basic answer is that the severity of language impairment provides a rather poor guide to the differentiation. Nevertheless, although the degree to which overall language development is impaired is a poor guide, there are indications of the likelihood that language problems will persist according to the type of functions that are affected (see Bishop & Norbury, 2008). Other things being equal, persisting problems are least likely if difficulties are confined to phonological errors in speech; conversely, they are most likely if there is impairment in receptive language. It follows that the need is for a broad-based clinical assessment and not just the use of psychometric tests.

The utility of quantitative measures

It is necessary to go on to ask whether the weak predictive value provided by the overall level of language impairment in the preschool years means that quantitative measures (i.e., standardized tests) of speech, language, and associated functions are unhelpful and not indicated. Clearly, that would be a completely unwarranted inference. It is crucially important to obtain systematic measures of the child's skills, weaknesses, and differences from normally expected patterns—because they play a vital role in diagnosis, prognosis, and the planning and evaluation of treatment.

SLI and general intellectual disability

The next question is whether the notion that SLI involves a specific language disability that is not just part of a more general intellectual disability (ID) is valid. Up to a point, that is a valid differ-entiation. Although few systematic comparisons have been made, it is obvious that SLI is very different from severe ID in numerous ways. To begin with, severe ID is usually associated with gross brain pathology, is frequently due to specific pathogenic genetic abnormalities, and is associated with a markedly reduced fecundity and also markedly reduced life expectancy, none of which applies to SLI. The implication is that it would not be sensible or useful to diagnose SLI in the presence of a severe ID.

The main problem, however, with requiring that SLI should only be diagnosed if there is a significant discrepancy between IQ and language level is that this does not work at all well in practice. It will be appreciated that the discrepancy approach is being applied within the normal range of IQ variation, and that is quite different from severe ID. We have to conclude that, however it is handled statistically, the IQ–language discrepancy approach is not useful. This is partly a question of the wide confidence interval that applies to any tests of either IQ or language in young children. That is, the particular level used in any discrepancy calculation will be much influenced by which particular test is employed. However, it is not just a measurement issue. There are also conceptual and empirical problems.

Thus, twin studies show that children in monozygotic pairs may be discordant for SLI defined in discrepancy terms, but concordant for cognitive impairments that include—but are not confined to—language (Bishop, North, & Donlan, 1995). Third, follow-up studies of children with severe and persistent SLI have tended to show an emerging—albeit usually slight—impairment in nonverbal skills that is evident at the time a child reaches adolescence (Botting, 2005; Clegg et al., 2005; Stothard et al., 1998). Both the genetic liability and the clinical course indicate that SLI must be viewed as extending beyond a pure language disorder.

On the other hand, it is important to recognize that this does not necessarily mean that mild ID and SLI are basically the same thing. That is because the starting point for both the genetic and the follow-up studies is a child identified as having a clear-cut SLI. The findings might look rather different if, instead, the starting point were either children with mild ID or children in the general population. To that extent, the IQ–language discrepancy approach may reflect a valid notion, even though discrepancy measurement does not provide a method that works in practice.

Two rather separate issues need to be considered with respect to the possible overlap between mild ID and SLI. First, some cases of mild ID are due directly to genetic disorders such as Down syndrome, Williams syndrome, or Prader–Willi syndrome—none of which appears to play a significant role in SLI. It would seem prudent to exclude from SLI children with mild ID that is due to these (or other) genetic conditions. On the other hand, the great majority of cases of ID probably represent the bottom end of the normal distribution (Einfeld & Emerson, 2008). The question, then, is whether SLI in a child with, say, a nonverbal IQ of 105 is fundamentally different (with respect to either etiology or response to interventions) from one with a nonverbal IQ of 55 or 60. For example, are the susceptibility genes in the first instance different from those in the second instance? The only honest answer is that we do not know.

The second issue is whether, if for practical reasons there is to be (what would have to be an arbitrary decision) any kind of nonverbal IQ cut-off, this should be set at 85 or 70 or some other point? Fey, Long, and Cleave (1994) in a small-scale study examined the utility of an 85 cut-off in relation to the response to intervention. No statistically significant differences were found, but there were only 8 individuals with an IQ between 70 and 84, meaning that the statistical power was too low to test for a difference. No comparison was made with a cut-off of 70. Once again, it is necessary to conclude that the evidence on which to make an empirically based decision is simply not available. There is no substantial body of evidence supporting any particular cut-off, but, equally, it remains unknown how far SLI in the absence of ID differs from that in its presence. The answer may depend on whether the interest is in etiology or intervention or prognosis. As the evidence now stands, it would seem that it is probably best to exclude from SLI cases with severe ID (defined as an IQ of 50 or below) plus those with a known directly genetic condition. An IQ in the 70 to 84 range should probably *not* give rise to exclusion, but possibly a cut-off excluding individuals with a nonverbal IQ below 70 might be reasonable.

Validity of subcategories of speech/language disorders

If the question is considered in relation to the subcategories as defined in the currently prevailing DSM–IV and ICD–10 classifications, the answer has to be that the differentiations among the subcategories are not valid because there is so much overlap among the different types of language disability. On the other hand, in a way the answer has also to be "yes," because it is clinically useful, and validated by empirical research findings, to differentiate among different varieties of language disability (Bishop & Norbury, 2008). Thus, for example, there are important differences among speech sound problems, prosodic abnormalities, expressive language impairment, receptive language impairment, and pragmatic problems. The conclusion is that these should be measured systematically but that it is better to deal with them dimensionally in pattern terms rather than assume sharp categorical distinctions as if they represented entirely different disorders.

Differentiation among neurodevelopmental disorders

The next diagnostic issue is whether or not SLI is meaningfully different from other neurodevelopmental disorders (such as dyslexia, autism, and ADHD). The research findings indicate a host of important differences. Clearly, it is both clinically useful and scientifically valid to differentiate among those disorders. On the other hand, the evidence also indicates a substantial degree of overlap and some shared features (Bishop & Rutter, 2008). For example, this is evident in the fact that all of these disorders exhibit a substantial male preponderance, and all begin in early life. It is necessary to conclude that it may be important for research to examine the basis of commonalities among these disorders, as well as the differences among them.

Does SLI differ from acquired language disorders?

SLI has been conceptualized as a neurodevelopmental disorder, and, hence, it is necessary to question whether it differs from acquired language disorders (implied by the developmental concept). In fact, children who have unilateral brain lesions in early childhood do not typically have specific language difficulties (Bates & Roe, 2001; Vargha-Khadem, Isaacs, van der Werf, Robb, & Wilson, 1992). Aphasic-type symptoms after brain lesions are not seen unless the damage occurs in middle childhood or later. Furthermore, brain imaging findings with respect to SLI do *not* indicate a focal unilateral lesion. It is also relevant that numerous studies have shown that various speech/language problems change in their neural underpinning during the early years. For example, up to the age of about 6 months babies all over the world are able to make the same phonological discriminations, but from the second half of the first year onwards their phonological discriminations are restricted to those present in the language of upbringing. In other words, initially language input is not relevant, whereas in the second half of the first year it becomes relevant (Kuhl et al., 1997; Werker & Vouloumanos, 2001). This is the basis for the fact that people from Japan have great difficulty with the "r"/"l" differentiation—because it is not present in the Japanese language. In the same way, clinically it has been known for a long time that severely deaf children make normal sounds up to about the middle of the first year, but thereafter their vocalizations have the characteristic of distortion. It is also pertinent that, as judged by imaging findings, the neural basis of second-language acquisition seems to differ from that of first-language acquisition (Kim, Relkin, Lee, & Hirsch, 1997). In summary, the differentiation between SLI and acquired language disorders is valid, but the pattern of similarities and differences is not entirely straightforward.

Diagnostic category or psychopathological dimension?

At first sight it might be thought that empirical data should be able to provide an answer to the categorical or dimensional issue, but that would constitute a misunderstanding of what is involved. To begin with, many conditions are both. Thus, severe ID is best viewed as a biological category, because its causes are quite different from the causes of individual variations in IQ within the normal range (Einfeld & Emerson, 2008); nevertheless, both in terms of educational achievement and social functioning, it functions best as a dimension. In other words, variations within the normal range and the disability ranges have broadly similar effects (Einfeld & Emerson, 2008). The second point is that the same applies to most multifactorial medical conditions, such as coronary artery disease, hypertension, and asthma—if they are severe in degree, they obviously constitute a disease category. Thus, coronary artery disease may lead to a heart attack involving coronary artery obstruction and the death of heart muscle, and it may also lead to death. Similarly, hypertension may go on to a "malignant" phase in which there is severe kidney damage and all sorts of other complications. In both of these cases, it would be absurd not to treat the condition as a category. On the other hand, at an earlier point in the disease progression it works best to consider the features dimensionally. Thus, heart physicians and respiratory physicians may—and do—make categorical disease diagnoses, but they also, in their routine clinical practice, measure functioning in dimensional fashion.

CONCEPTS OF RISK AND OF CAUSATION

There is good evidence of strong genetic influences on the liability for SLI, but the findings also indicate that—possibly with uncommon exceptions—SLI is *not* due to a single gene operating in deterministic fashion (Bishop & Norbury, 2008; Newbury & Monaco, chapter 6, this volume). Rather, it is a multifactorial disorder. This means that it is likely to arise as a result of the combined effect of multiple genes (each of which may have only a small effect) and multiple environmental factors (each of which probably has only a small effect). Again, the same applies across the whole of medicine (Hernandez & Blazer, 2006; Rutter, 2006). In no way is this peculiar to SLI. In addition, however, it is necessary to appreciate that genetic influences may operate through their effect on environmental susceptibility, rather than on a biological pathway to SLI as such (see Rutter, 2008). Moreover, the genetic effects may vary according to different SLI features, and the nongenetic effects may involve random developmental perturbations and not just specific risk environments. Biological development works in a probabilistic, and not deterministic, fashion.

Issues in the study of risk

The first, and most basic, question that needs to be asked with respect to risk is whether the associations between postulated risk factors and SLI are truly causal (Rutter, 2007; Rutter, Pickles, Murray, & Eaves, 2001). It is important to appreciate that there are many different reasons why a statistically significant association may *not* reflect causation. Thus, for example, it might arise because of "social selection"—meaning that the individuals who experience the risk factor are systematically different from those who do not. The association therefore represents the origin of the risk factor and not its environmentally mediated effect on the outcome—in this case SLI. The need is for some form of natural experiment to test the causal inference. This has very rarely been done, and hence our understanding of the causal pathways involved in SLI is quite limited.

The second issue is whether the same risk factors apply to all aspects of language development—that is, for example, do the risk factors associated with severe impairments in receptive language apply equally to problems in speech sound production? It is not known with any certainty whether or not this is the case, but almost certainly there is likely to be some variation according to which aspect of language is being considered. A somewhat related issue is whether the same set of risk factors operates in all cases of SLI. Probably it does not. It is more likely that the risk will vary from individual to individual. That is what is implied in the notion of a multifactorial disorder. It is a commonplace to find that there is more than one causal route to the same particular

outcome (Rutter, 1997). Finally, we need to ask whether there is any causal influence that is *necessary* for SLI to occur, even if it is not *sufficient* on its own. Once again, we do not know the answer. It might apply to some aspect of genetic liability, but that is uncertain—that is, it could turn out to be the case that there are no cases of SLI that are purely environmental in origin. It is probable that the genetic influence will vary from individual to individual, but it is conceivable, though not yet shown, that some degree of genetic susceptibility is always required. It is necessary to go on to consider whether the risk factors for SLI operate categorically or dimensionally. Almost certainly, most will operate dimensionally, because that is what has been found with multifactorial medical disorders such as coronary artery disease or asthma. In other words, it is necessary to consider not just whether someone has had some particular risk factor, but how severely, and for what duration of time, the risk experience has occurred.

The understanding provided by brain imaging and molecular genetics

It may well be felt that all this seems very uncertain and most unsatisfactory. Many people are likely to hope that the availability of structural and functional brain imaging and of the identification of specific susceptibility genes (as found through molecular genetic technologies) may allow a much better understanding of the nature of the causal pathways. It is indeed likely that they will be very helpful in the search for an understanding of the basic pathophysiology of SLI, but, on their own, they will not provide answers on causes—for two rather different reasons. First, the finding of an imaging difference between SLI and other groups is just a correlation. It could constitute an index of a neural cause of SLI, but it also could be the consequence of impaired language functioning (i.e., a reverse causation), or it could reflect a positive compensatory neural response. Various experimental strategies can help in differentiating between these alternatives, but, on their own, brain imaging findings cannot safely be interpreted as measuring a causal neural effect on language development. The second concern is that the imaging findings ordinarily indicate *where* the brain is active in relation to a specific task, but they do not show the *nature* of the neural functioning that is going on during the undertaking of that task and the cognitive and affective processing that is involved. Spectroscopy and other new imaging developments do rather more, but even they are limited in what they can show. Much the same applies to molecular genetics. The findings, too, are correlational: on their own, they do not indicate what the gene is affecting. Of course, the findings provide a strong indication that the gene is involved in some way in the causal pathways, but what they do not show is exactly what is involved. Thus, for example, the gene may be concerned with responsivity to the environment rather than with SLI as such. That is the implication of the growing body of evidence on the importance of gene–environment interactions (Hernandez & Blazer, 2006; Mackay & Anholt, 2007; Rutter, 2006; Rutter et al., 2006). Knowing where in the genome a particular susceptibility gene exists indicates where the action lies, but other research strategies are needed to show what the gene does. It opens the way to a much better understanding of the neural underpinning of SLI, but the actual identification of the neural processes involves a much broader range of biological research strategies.

While it is necessary that we recognize and accept the limitations in what genetics and brain imaging on their own can tell us now, it is equally necessary that researchers and practitioners alike appreciate the immense potential of both technologies to foster the elucidation of the brain processes that underlie SLI and underlie successful compensatory strategies. Thus, identification of susceptibility genes for SLI needs to be followed by biological studies to determine what the genes "do" in terms of their effects on problems, and then by different types of research designed to determine the causal mechanisms involved in the pathways leading from the proteins to the clinical syndrome of SLI (see Rutter, 2006). In some instances, these pathways are likely to involve gene–environment interactions, necessitating research to examine the processes involved in the coaction of genes and environment. None of that is likely to happen quickly,

but the research can and will be done; the results will in time provide an understanding of how brain processes are involved in the workings of the mind—in this case, with respect to SLI. That knowledge is highly likely to change the ways in which both preventive and therapeutic interventions are conceptualized and undertaken. Similarly, brain imaging, by identifying the areas of the brain involved in task performance, can determine when they differ between individuals with SLI and typically developing individuals (see, e.g., Frith, 2003; Frith & Frith, 2008), and thereby point to the ways in which brain processes develop awry in SLI and to the brain systems involved in circumventing and overcoming the impairments associated with SLI. Once more, of course, the success of these quests depends on integrating imaging research both with other biological studies and with environmental investigations. Ultimately, it is likely that the findings should and will influence practice.

CLINICAL IMPLICATIONS OF RISK CONCEPTS

Given that so much of the evidence indicates that many risk factors operate dimensionally, it is necessary to ask what the clinician should say is the diagnosis when presented with a child with SLI. As far as the family is concerned, the true situation (insofar as that is known) should be explained—indicating the features of the pattern that are most important in the case of this particular child. Fortunately, in the United Kingdom most services do not operate in a "tick-box" diagnostic fashion. For services that work on the basis of the needs of each individual child, the same discriminating formulation should be more useful than a single diagnostic label. On the other hand, some services unfortunately *do* have a tick-box approach, and for them it is reasonable to use the label that provides an entry ticket, provided that it is consistent with the overall formulation and provided that the service is likely to meet the child's needs.

It is necessary to go on to ask, in similar fashion, whether dimensional risk concepts affect treatment decisions. *Whether* to provide treatment obviously requires a categorical answer. On the other hand, this should be based on the level of impairment as much as on the diagnosis as such. More importantly, the *nature* of the treatment offered should be influenced by the particular pattern of affected language features. The assessment of that pattern will usually require dimensional assessments.

A further question is whether treatment should be provided only when the SLI involves significant functional impairment. There is little justification for an intensive intervention if "spontaneous recovery" is extremely likely. On the other hand, treatment could be justified if it were shown that its provision "speeded up" the process of recovery. Moreover, even if spontaneous recovery is to be expected, parents may want—and would benefit from—guidance on how they should respond to their late-talking child. Third, if there were evidence that preventive intervention of a risk factor reduced the likelihood of impairment, this might be worthwhile. The parallel would be the use of statins in preventing coronary artery disease. Up to now, however, the applicability of such effective treatments for SLI has not been shown. Similarly, we need to ask whether dimensional concepts should affect treatment planning. Most crucially, they suggest the need to shift from a focus on treating some overall entity of SLI to a focus on the various different facets of SLI. For example, what is needed to aid pragmatic skills is not likely to be the same as what is needed to alleviate speech sound problems.

Needs in relation to the development of better methods of intervention

It is all too apparent that there is very limited knowledge on which treatments are most effective for which problems; even more, we lack evidence on which aspects of the intervention mediate the efficacy (Ebbels, chapter 10, this volume). There is a need for a greater use of randomized controlled trials (RCTs) as well as observational designs. There are several reasons why RCTs are strongly favored as the best way of testing the efficacy of any kind of intervention, but perhaps their greatest strength is that they ensure that both measured and unmeasured "confounders" are randomly distributed between experimental and control groups (Academy of Medical Sciences, 2007). The term "confounders" simply refers to variables other than the one being studied that influence outcome. The key point is that, as a result of both practitioner choice and family choice, individuals who do and do not receive the intervention tend to be systematically different. The consequence is that the benefits associated with treatment may have nothing to do with treatment but have everything to do with the kinds of individuals who receive treatment. The importance of "unmeasured" confounders is that usually we do not know enough about the predictors in order to decide what to measure and what to take account of in the statistical analysis. With respect to SLI, there is the additional consideration that language skills tend to improve with increasing age, leaving open the question of whether the gains over time derive from the treatment or of increasing age (and the experiential gains that that will bring). Cahan and Cohen (1989) provide a nice example of how that question may be tackled—using the question of duration of schooling as the example.

One further key point is that people often think of studies of effectiveness as just asking whether some specified form of intervention "works" in the sense of bringing about the desired gains—in language or whatever other outcome is being studied. But, as Weersing and Weisz (2002) pointed out, that is to take much too narrow a view of the question. We need to know *why* and *how* an intervention works if we are to devise better methods in the future. Intervention studies can and should constitute a hypothesis-testing enterprise. Thus if, for example, we suppose that SLI is due to an auditory processing deficit, we need to determine whether auditory training improves language functioning. Note that it is *not* enough to show that such a training program is associated with language gains, or even that such gains are greater than with some other program with a different focus. The point is that an intervention might lead to gains in auditory processing *and* in language, but still without the gains in the one *mediating* or accounting for the gains in the other. It could be that the intervention leads to some individuals improving their processing and others gaining language, but, within the intervention group, the degree to which processing improves bears no relationship to whether or not language improves. On the face of it, that sounds complicated, but in fact it is not. All that it requires is a quantified measure of the postulated features supposed to mediate treatment efficacy. In planning and undertaking such trials, there needs to be a comparison between alternative forms of intervention, and not just a comparison with doing nothing. Moreover, there needs to be a focus on the specifics of different language outcomes and the use of designs that carry the potential of identifying which features mediate the benefits. We have a long way to go before that is achieved, but the benefits of achieving that goal could transform practice.

In that connection, two further points need to be made. First, if RCTs involve a "no-treatment" comparison group, there is the danger that any apparent advantage of the intervention being studied will be a consequence of the negative effect of individuals being denied treatment (see Molling, Lockner, Sauls, & Eisenberg, 1962). The solution lies in ensuring that either the control condition involves an equal intensity of some form of support or the control group is able to receive the active treatment after the trial is complete, or some combination of the two. If the RCT involves comparison with an established treatment of known efficacy, a no-treatment comparison would be both unethical and unnecessary. Regrettably, that is not the situation in the case of interventions with SLI. Conversely, if the RCT involves a comparison among active treatments, one of which is focused on a mechanism not thought to be relevant for SLI (as in the case of Gillam et al., 2008), that provides an effective way of testing claims that some particular treatment claimed to have specificity is effective. In this example, the RCT showed that such claims with respect to auditory processing were *not* justified. On the other hand, the lack of difference among the different forms of intervention could be a consequence of all being equally effective or equally ineffective. The two possibilities have radically different

practice implications, but in the absence of some form of "placebo" comparisons they cannot be differentiated, and claims that the RCT provides a lead on what treatments "work" are completely unjustified.

The second point is that when some treatment involves strong commercial considerations (i.e., there is a profit to be made if it is shown to be effective), special caution is needed (see Bishop, 2007, in press; Rack, Snowling, Hulme, & Gibbs, 2007). In these circumstances, independent replication by researchers who have no vested interest in the result is essential, and departures from RCT (and other scientific) requirements are particularly worrying.

Practitioners need rigorous studies evaluating intervention efficacy and should not be afraid of negative findings. The history of medicine includes many examples of treatments shown to be ineffective despite the strong beliefs of their advocates. The treatment of peptic ulcer by means of milk diets and removal of part of the stomach (absolutely routine in the 1950s) is a particularly well-known example. In that instance, further research went on to show which treatment approaches *were* effective. We need to have the same confidence that this can be achieved with SLI, with respect to either the demonstrated efficacy of some of the current methods or their replacement with different, better interventions. Science and practice need to move ahead in an iterative fashion, hand in hand, with each benefiting the other (see Rutter, 1999).

CONCLUSIONS

It is appropriate to conclude by asking whether our understanding of the nature and causes of SLI, and our interventions, is improving. The answer to both questions is a clear-cut "yes," as earlier chapters in this volume have demonstrated. But, as is the way of science, the answers to a first set of questions often point to the need to address a further set of issues. A lot is known about these new issues and how they might be tackled. The volume serves to summarize the state of play on these, but also it outlines the important challenges that remain.

REFERENCES

Academy of Medical Sciences (2007). *Identifying the causes of disease: How should we decide what to believe and when to take action?* London: Author.

American Psychiatric Association (2000). *Diagnostic and statistical manual of mental disorders* (4th ed., text revision). Washington, DC: Author.

Bates, E., & Roe, K. (2001). Language development in children with unilateral brain injury. In C. A. Nelson & M. Luciana (Eds.), *Handbook of developmental cognitive neuroscience* (pp. 281–307). Cambridge, MA: MIT Press.

Bishop, D. V. M. (2007). Curing dyslexia and attention-deficit hyperactivity disorder by training motor co-ordination: Miracle or myth? *Journal of Paediatrics and Child Health, 43*, 653–655.

Bishop, D. V. M. (in press). Evaluating behavioural interventions for learning disabilities. *Journal of Paediatrics and Child Health.*

Bishop, D. V. M., & Norbury, C. F. (2008). Speech and language disorders. In M. Rutter et al. (Eds.), *Rutter's child and adolescent psychiatry* (5th ed.). Oxford, UK: Blackwell.

Bishop, D. V. M., North, T., & Donlan, C. (1995). Genetic basis of specific language impairment: Evidence from a twin study. *Developmental Medicine & Child Neurology, 37*, 56–71.

Bishop, D. V. M., & Rutter, M. (2008). Neurodevelopmental disorders. In M. Rutter et al. (Eds.), *Rutter's child and adolescent psychiatry* (5th ed.). Oxford, UK: Blackwell.

Botting, N. (2005). Non-verbal cognitive development and language impairment. *Journal of Child Psychology and Psychiatry, 46*, 317–326.

Cahan, S., & Cohen, N. (1989). Age versus schooling effects on intelligence development. *Child Development, 60*, 1239–1249.

Clegg, J., Hollis, C., Mawhood, L., & Rutter, M. (2005). Developmental language disorder—a follow-up in later adult life: Cognitive, language, and psychosocial outcomes. *Journal of Child Psychology and Psychiatry, 46*, 128–149.

Dale, P. S., Price, T. S., Bishop, D. V. M., & Plomin, R. (2003). Outcomes of early language delay: 1. Predicting persistent and transient delay at 3 and 4 years. *Journal of Speech, Language, and Hearing Research, 46*, 544–560.

Einfeld, S., & Emerson, E. (2008). Intellectual disability. In M. Rutter et al. (Eds.), *Rutter's child and adolescent psychiatry* (5th ed.). Oxford, UK: Blackwell.

Fey, M. E., Long, S. H., & Cleave, P. L. (1994). Reconsideration of IQ criteria in the definition of specific language impairment. In R. Watkins & M. Rice (Eds.), *Specific language impairments in children* (pp. 161–178). Baltimore: Paul H. Brookes.

Frith, C. (2003). What do imaging studies tell us about the neural basis of autism? In G. Bock & J. Goode (Eds.), *Autism: Neural basis and treatment possibilities* (pp. 149–176). Chichester, UK: Wiley.

Frith, C., & Frith, U. (2008). What can we learn from structural and functional brain imaging? In M. Rutter et al. (Eds.), *Rutter's child and adolescent psychiatry* (5th ed.). Oxford, UK: Blackwell.

Gillam, R. B., Loeb, D. F., Hoffman, L. M., Bohman, T., Champlin, C. A., Thibodeau, L., et al. (2008). The efficacy of Fast ForWord language intervention in school-age children with language impairment: A randomized controlled trial. *Journal of Speech, Language, and Hearing Research, 51*, 97–119.

Hernandez, L. M., & Blazer, D. G. (Eds.) (2006). *Genes, behaviour, and the social environment: Moving beyond the nature–nurture debate.* Washington, DC: National Academies Press.

Horwitz, S. M., Irwin, J. R., Briggs-Gowan, M. J., Bosson Heenan, J. M., Mendoza, J., & Carter, A. S. (2003). Language delay in a community cohort of young children. *Journal of the American Academy of Child & Adolescent Psychiatry, 42*, 932–940.

Kim, K. H. S., Relkin, N. R., Lee, K.-M., & Hirsch, J. (1997). Distinct cortical areas associated with native and second languages. *Nature, 388*, 171–174.

Kuhl, P. K., Andruski, J. E., Chistovich, I. A., Chistovich, L. A., Kozhevnikova, E. V., Ryskina, V. L., et al. (1997). Cross-language analysis of phonetic units in language addressed to infants. *Science, 277*, 684–686.

Mackay, T. F. C., & Anholt, R. R. H. (2007). Ain't misbehavin'? Genotype–environment interactions and the genetics of behavior. *Trends in Genetics, 23*, 311–314.

Molling, P., Lockner, A., Sauls, R. J., & Eisenberg, L. (1962). Committed delinquent boys: The impact of perphenazine and of placebo. *Archives of General Psychiatry, 7*, 70–76.

Rack, J. P., Snowling, M. J., Hulme, C., & Gibbs, S. (2007). No evidence that an exercise-based treatment programme (DDAT) has specific benefits for children with reading difficulties. *Dyslexia, 13*, 97–104.

Rescorla, L. (2005). Age 13 language and reading outcomes in late-talking toddlers. *Journal of Speech, Language, and Hearing Research, 48*, 459–472.

Rutter, M. (1985). Infantile autism. In D. Shaffer, A. Erhardt, & L. Greenhill (Eds.), *A clinician's guide to child psychiatry* (pp. 41–68). New York: Free Press.

Rutter, M. (1997). Comorbidity: Concepts, claims and choices. *Criminal Behaviour and Mental Health, 7*, 265–286.

Rutter, M. (1999). The Emanuel Miller memorial lecture 1998. Autism: Two-way interplay between research and clinical work. *Journal of Child Psychology and Psychiatry, 40*, 169–188.

Rutter, M. (2006). *Genes and behaviour: Nature–nurture interplay explained.* Oxford, UK: Blackwell.

Rutter, M. (2007). Proceeding from observed correlations to causal inference: The use of natural experiments. *Perspectives on Psychological Science, 2*, 377–395.

Rutter, M. (Ed.) (2008). *Genetic effects on environ-mental vulnerability to disease.* Chichester, UK: Wiley.

Rutter, M., Moffitt, T. E., & Caspi, A. (2006). Gene–environment interplay and psychopathology: Multiple varieties but real effects. *Journal of Child Psychology and Psychiatry, 47*, 226–261.

Rutter, M., Pickles, A., Murray, R., & Eaves, L. (2001). Testing hypotheses on specific environmental causal effects on behavior. *Psychological Bulletin, 127*, 291–324.

Stothard, S. E., Snowling, M. J., Bishop, D. V. M., Chipchase, B. B., & Kaplan, C. A. (1998). Language-impaired preschoolers: A follow-up into adolescence. *Journal of Speech, Language, and Hearing Research, 41*, 407–418.

Vargha-Khadem, F., Isaacs, E., van der Werf, S., Robb, S., & Wilson, J. (1992). Development of intelligence and memory in children with hemiplegic cerebral palsy: The deleterious consequences of early seizures. *Brain, 115*, 315–329.

Weersing, V. R., & Weisz, J. R. (2002). Mechanisms of action in youth psychotherapy. *Journal of Child Psychology and Psychiatry, 43*, 3–29.

Werker, J., & Vouloumanos, A. (2001). Speech and language processing in infancy: A neurocognitive approach. In: C. A. Nelson & M. Luciana (Eds.), *Handbook of developmental cognitive neuroscience* (pp. 269–280). Cambridge, MA: MIT Press.

World Health Organization (1996). *The ICD–10 classification of mental and behavioural disorders in children and adolescents.* Cambridge, UK: Cambridge University Press.

Author index

Subject index